365 Selected Paprika Recipes

(365 Selected Paprika Recipes - Volume 1)

Angela Duncan

Copyright: Published in the United States by Angela Duncan/ © ANGELA DUNCAN

Published on December, 07 2020

All rights reserved. No part of this publication may be reproduced, stored in retrieval system, copied in any form or by any means, electronic, mechanical, photocopying, recording or otherwise transmitted without written permission from the publisher. Please do not participate in or encourage piracy of this material in any way. You must not circulate this book in any format. ANGELA DUNCAN does not control or direct users' actions and is not responsible for the information or content shared, harm and/or actions of the book readers.

In accordance with the U.S. Copyright Act of 1976, the scanning, uploading and electronic sharing of any part of this book without the permission of the publisher constitute unlawful piracy and theft of the author's intellectual property. If you would like to use material from the book (other than just simply for reviewing the book), prior permission must be obtained by contacting the author at author@slushierecipes.com

Thank you for your support of the author's rights.

Content

365 AWESOME PAPRIKA RECIPES 9

1. Roasted Cauliflower Salad 9
2. Steak Roll Ups With Salsa Casera, Manchego And Pepitas 9
3. "4 Fresh Chiles And A Ghost" Chili 10
4. "Chuck" Full Of Flavor Chili 11
5. "DLQ" (delish, Low Cal And Quick)Spinach Stuffed Mushrooms 12
6. A SHRIMP AND QUINOA PAELLA ... 12
7. A Cream Cauliflower And Red Pepper Duet 13
8. Ahi Tuna With Angel Hair Pasta 14
9. Almond Bean Spread With A Hint Of Spain 14
10. Ansel Adams's Eggs Poached In Beer 15
11. Artichoke & Parmesan Burgers With Lime Mayonnaise & Roasted Red Peppers 15
12. Asha Gomez's Smoky Hazelnut Chocolate Cookies 16
13. Auntie Sui's Potato Salad 16
14. Avocado Hummus 17
15. BEER CAN CHICKEN TACOS 17
16. Bacon Jam 18
17. Bacon Wrapped Brown Sugar Pork Loin . 19
18. Beef Strogonoff 19
19. Beef Tips & Gravy 20
20. Beer Oyster Mushrooms Tacos With Mango Slaw 21
21. Bengali Shrimp Masala 21
22. Best Boston Baked Beans 22
23. Best Ever Turkey Chili 22
24. Birthday Paella 23
25. Blackened Fish Tacos With Piña Colada Salsa 24
26. Body And Soul 24
27. Bone Marrow On Toast Beer Beef & Veal Shank Soup (as An Afterthought) 25
28. Braised Basque Short Ribs 26
29. Braised Chicken Thighs With Tomato And Honey 26
30. Braised Tuna And Chickpeas 27
31. Bratball Sub 27
32. Broiled Spicy Steak With Garlic Chips On Gorgonzola Crostini 27
33. Bryant Terry's Mustard Green Harissa 28
34. Buffalo Cauliflower Tots With Blue Cheese Dipping Sauce 29
35. Buffalo Style Quinoa Chili 30
36. Bunny's Broiled Egg Sandwiches 30
37. Buttermilk Fried Chicken 30
38. Cajun Spiced Stuffed Golden Peppers 31
39. Caldo Gallego (Galician Broth) 32
40. Caldo Verde (Portuguese Soup With Cauliflower) 32
41. Carrot And Ginger Butternut Squash Soup 33
42. Cauliflower Miso Soup 33
43. Cauliflower Paprikash 34
44. Cauliflower Fritters With Smoked Salmon, Prosciutto Herbed Dressing. 35
45. Cevapcici With Lime Mayo Dip 35
46. Chef Ken's Indian Cauliflower Steaks With Tomato Sauce 36
47. Cherry Pie Beef Ribs 36
48. Chiccoli Shirataki 37
49. Chick Pea Hummus 37
50. Chicken Chorizo Meatballs 38
51. Chicken Flautas 38
52. Chicken Mustard Croquettes 39
53. Chicken Nuggets With Warm Kimchi Bacon Ranch Dip 40
54. Chicken That Fancies Itself Spanish With Lemons, Onions & Olives 41
55. Chickpea Chili 42
56. Chickpea, Tomato, And Roasted Red Pepper Skillet Breakfast 43
57. Chili Con Nikki (with Brisket, Coffee & Chocolate) 43
58. Chili Stuffed Bell Peppers With Melted Cheese 44
59. Chipotle And Duck Confit Deviled Eggs With Microgreens 45
60. Chorizo And Black Beans, "Meanwhile" Style 45
61. Chorizo Style Seitan Tacos 47
62. Coconut Crusted Chicken Lettuce Wraps With Mango Lime Salsa 48
63. Coffee Baked Sweet Potatoes With Chili Spice, Crème Fraîche, Lime & Cilantro 48
64. Cold Busting Coconut Chicken Curry Soup

65. Copycat Vegan Sloppy Joes 49
66. Corn Salad With Tomatoes, Avocado, Quinoa And Feta 50
67. Corn Sundal 51
68. Corn, Bacon, And Clam Stew 51
69. Courgette Shakshuka 51
70. Cowboy Chow 52
71. Cracked Crab With Three Sauces 52
72. Cracking Bacon And Egg Breakfast Tortilla Cups 54
73. Creamy Dijon Sweet Potato Salad 54
74. Creamy Garlic Zoodles With Bursting Cherry Tomatoes 54
75. Creamy Mac N' Cheese 55
76. Crispy (Fried) Chickpeas 56
77. Croatian Bean Soup / Stew (Fažol I Testo) 56
78. Crunchy Tortilla Tostada With Tuna 57
79. Crème De Radish Pancetta Soup 57
80. Cucumber Appetizers 58
81. Cucumber Rounds With Savory Cores 58
82. Curried Chickpea Sandwich 58
83. Dad's Chorizo And Egg Breakfast Tacos . 59
84. Dark Chocolate Chili 60
85. Deep Fried Green Beans 60
86. Dev Aiolied Eggs 61
87. Deviled Egg Potato Salad 61
88. Deviled Eggs 62
89. Devilish Hogwart Eggs 62
90. Devils On Horseback In A Pool Of Blood 63
91. Double Sweet Corn And Lobster Chowder 63
92. Drunken Chicken Paprika 64
93. Dukkah 64
94. Easiest And Yummiest Burger Ever! 65
95. Eat Your Greens! Rainbow Chard With A Maple Vinegar Drizzle 65
96. Egg Tartines With Romesco And Greens 66
97. Eggnog Chicken & Waffles 67
98. Eggplant Chips With Honey 67
99. Eggplant And Cabbage Pitas 68
100. Eleanor's Vinegarette 68
101. Everyday Chicken Curry 69
102. Everything Bagel Spiced Nuts 69
103. Fake Snow Day Baked Beans 70
104. Farro With Eggs And Mushrooms 70
105. Fattet Hummus (Mid Eastern Savory Chickpea Bread Pudding) 71
106. Faux Bouillabaisse 72
107. Fennel & Green Garbanzo Polo 72
108. Feta Stuffed Grilled Poblano Peppers In A Sesame Peanut Sauce 73
109. Fish "Meatballs" In Spicy Red Pepper Sauce 74
110. Flatiron Chicken 74
111. Floribbean Shrimp And Grits 75
112. Foolproof Rolled Sandwiches Party Tray With Tomato Dip & Deviled Eggs 76
113. French Bread Eggs Benedict With Asparagus 77
114. Fresh Corn Salsa 77
115. Fresh Stuffed Red Pepper Shells With Pearl Couscous, Forbidden Rice, Kamut Or Red Quinoa 78
116. Friday Night Garlicky Roast Chicken And Potatoes 78
117. Fried Stuffed Zucchini Blossoms 79
118. Fried Shrimp Cakes Tortillitas De Camarones 79
119. Gandule Rice (Arroz Con Gandules) 80
120. Ganoush Is The New Guacamole 80
121. Garlic Brad Sticks With Garlic Infused Olive Oil 81
122. Gazpacho With Peaches And Jalapen?o ... 82
123. Gipsy Lunch 82
124. Gluten Free Pot Pie With Brown Rice Crust 83
125. Goat Cheese Croquettes 83
126. Golden Onion Dip 84
127. Gourmet Orange Cashew "Chicken" 84
128. Grandma's Hungarian Pork Stew (a/k/a "Sertesporkolt") 85
129. Greek Style Chickpea Soup 85
130. Green Hot Chili Peppers In My Backyard BBQ 86
131. Grilled Beef Fajitas 86
132. Grilled Butterfly Chicken With A Paprika And Herb Dry Rub 87
133. Grilled Lamb Chops & Garlic Scapes With Romesco Sauce 88
134. Grilled Pork Tenderloin With Roasted Red Pepper Sauce 89

135. Grilled Summer Squash With Charred Chickpeas, Raisins + Garlic Yogurt Sauce 89
136. Gumbo Z'Herbes II 90
137. Hash Browns, Spinach, And Froached Egg Stack 91
138. Hearty Spicy Kale And Pork Soup With White Beans 91
139. Herbed Soft Scramble 92
140. Honey Roasted Chicken With Garlic, Lavender, And Roasted Vegetables 92
141. Hot Chicken Recipe And Jalapeño Bacon Cheddar Waffle 93
142. Hummus With Sesame Seeds (no Tahini) 94
143. Hungarian Pork Paprikash 95
144. Hungarian Stuffed Reds With Red Quinoa 96
145. Instant Pot Uzbek Plov 96
146. Jalapeño Cream Cheese Dip 97
147. Juicy Vegan Meatballs And Gravy 97
148. Julie's Almost Famous Stuffed Fish 98
149. Jägerschnitzel (Pork Schnitzel With Red Wine Mushroom Sauce) 99
150. Kadu Ki Subzi 100
151. Kale Salad With Blood Oranges, Almonds And Cured Black Olive Dressing 100
152. Kale Salad With Spiced Chickpeas & Herbed Yogurt Dressing 101
153. Kentucky Derby Mini Hot Browns In Grana Padano Frico "Hats" 102
154. Lamb Burgers With Double Paprika Feta Spread, Cherry Peppers, And Kale 102
155. Lamb Stuffed Pattypans 103
156. Lecso (Hungarian Summertime Stew) 104
157. Lemon Cranberry Quinoa Salad 104
158. Lemon Scented Linguine With Scallops, Cauliflower And Lemon 105
159. Lentil Arugula Range Salad 106
160. Linguini With Corn, Potatoes, Shrimp And Herbs 106
161. Littleneck Clams With Sherry, Garlic And Smoked Paprika 107
162. MB's Infamous Pea Salad 107
163. Madeira Braised Oxtail Montaditos 108
164. Magic Mushrooms With Egg Noodles And Ricotta 109
165. Magical Pomegranate Molasses Chickpeas 110

166. Mamere's Tourtier 110
167. Maple Sweet Potato Cakes With Curried Greek Yogurt 111
168. Mediterranean Roasted Chickpea And Spinach Salad 111
169. Mel's Bean Pie 112
170. Michael Ruhlman's Rosemary Brined, Buttermilk Fried Chicken 113
171. Mini Frybreads With Smoked Paprika Aioli 114
172. Minted Beans And Ham 114
173. Mom's Potato Salad With A Twist (of Lemon) 115
174. Monterey Jack & Macaroni With Spinach And Roasted Tomato 115
175. Moroccan Carrot Salad By Way Of Israel 116
176. Moroccan Chickpea Pockets 117
177. Moroccan Onion Flatbread 117
178. Muscovado Baked Beans 118
179. Mushroom Goulash 119
180. Mushroom Stroganoff 119
181. My Favorite Fried Egg On Toast 120
182. My Favorite Vegan Mac And Cheese 120
183. My Oh So Buttery, Crispy & Moist Ritz Cracker Brined Chicken 121
184. NW Applewood Smoked Pork & Sauce 122
185. New Orleans Style Barramundi Fish Cakes With Creole Remoulade 123
186. No Tato Salad 124
187. North African Grilled Chicken Salad 125
188. North African Lamb Stew (Boktoff) 125
189. OMFGoulash! 126
190. Okinawan Taco Rice Bowls 127
191. One Pot Pasta Bolognese Style 128
192. Onion And Red Pepper Confit 128
193. Orzo With Butter & Parmesan A La Chicken Fritz 129
194. Oven "Fried" Chicken With Paprika & Tarragon 130
195. Paella 130
196. Paella Manantiales Calientes 131
197. Paella, Paella, Paella! 131
198. Paprika Roast Chicken 132
199. Paprika Scented Manchego Chorizo Puffs 133
200. Passover Brisket, Inspired By Libbie Miller

201. Passover Puffs 134
202. Patas Bravas With Smoked Paprika Tomato Sauce 134
203. Patatas Bravas 135
204. Peekytoe Crab Dip 136
205. Pimento Cheese Biscuits 136
206. Piri Piri Chicken Meatballs With Crispy Potatoes 137
207. Pollo Asado 138
208. Poor Man's Paella 138
209. Pork Loin And Butternut Squash With Fresh Herbs And Cider 139
210. Porotos Granads With Polenta Dumplings 140
211. Portobello Mushroom Tacos 140
212. Pot Sticker Hash Browns With Greens And Cheese 141
213. Prawn And Coriander Crostini 141
214. Preserved And Fresh Lemon Hummus 142
215. Pucker Up Lemon Sumac Chicken With Lemon Herb Board Sauce 142
216. Pulled Pork Baps With Apple Slaw And Tangy BBQ Sauce 143
217. Pulled Pork Sandwiches With Stone Fruit Salsa 144
218. Pulled Pork With Chile Barbecue Sauce . 146
219. Pumpkin & Butternut Squash Soup 147
220. Pureed Mustard Greens (Sarson Da Saag) 147
221. Purple Cauliflower Soup 148
222. Quick Chicken Paprika 148
223. Quick Curry | Gluten Free Vegan Yellow Curry 149
224. Red Cabbage Slaw With Honey Lime Cumin Vinaigrette 150
225. Red Chile Chicken And Hominy Soup ... 150
226. Red Pepper Chicken Paprika 151
227. Reuben Cheese (and A Beet Reuben) 151
228. Rice And Ground Beef Stuffed Bell Peppers And Onions 152
229. Rich Taco Meat 153
230. Roast Cauliflower + Avocado Salad With Spiced Yoghurt 153
231. Roasted Butternut Squash Queso 154
232. Roasted Butternut And Red Quinoa Salad With Spicy Lime Vinaigrette 155
233. Roasted Canela Cilantro Chicken 155
234. Roasted Carrots With Cauliflower Couscous 156
235. Roasted Cauliflower With Paprika And Greek Yoghurt Dip 156
236. Roasted Cauliflower With Za'atar And Lemons 157
237. Roasted Cauliflower, Fennel And Farro Pilaf 158
238. Roasted Corn, Poblano, And Bacon Salad With Maple Lime Vinaigrette 158
239. Roasted Cornish Game Hens 159
240. Roasted Dates & Honey Wings 159
241. Roasted Delicata Squash Stuffed With Autumn Farro 160
242. Roasted Eggplant With Cilantro Almond Salsa 160
243. Roasted Grape And Butternut Squash Salad With Kale And Parmesan 161
244. Roasted Pumpkin Seed Hummus With Gluten Free Rosemary Focaccia 162
245. Roasted Red Pepper Hummus 162
246. Roasted Red Pepper And Pomegranate Patatas Bravas 162
247. Roasted Romesco Sauce 163
248. Roasted Spiced Carrots With Pistachios .. 164
249. Roasted Stuffed Onion Gratin 164
250. Roasted Sweet Potato Mac N' Cheese 165
251. Roasted Tomato Eggplant Melts 165
252. Roasted Tomato And Carrot Soup 165
253. Rudy's BBQ Copycat Baby Back Ribs 166
254. Rustic Muddy Duck Paella 166
255. Saffron And Paprika Rice With Smoked Andouille Sausage 168
256. Salmon Cakes 168
257. Sausage Stuffed Mushrooms 168
258. Savory Lentil And Bok Choi Soup 169
259. Savoury Sausage And Butternut Squash Crepes 169
260. Seafood Paella 170
261. Semi Sweet Potato Mash With Spiced Caramelized Onions 171
262. Shakshuka 172
263. Shakshuka Spicy Israeli Tomato Stew 172
264. Shakshuka Focaccia 173
265. Sheet Pan Chicken And Cauliflower Bake 173

266. Sherried Potatoes Au Gratin 174
267. Short Rib & Pumpkin Chili 175
268. Short Ribs Braised In Red Wine And Vanilla 176
269. Shrimp Cooked In Smoked Sausage And Roasted Red Bell Pepper Jam Sauce 177
270. Shrimp Tacos With Corn Salsa 178
271. Shrimp And "grits" With Kahlua Bacon Jam 178
272. Shrimp And Grits By Way Of Spain 179
273. Shrimp, Avocado & Orange Salad 179
274. Simple Company Posole 180
275. Simple Turkish Eggs 180
276. Simple, Perfect Poached Eggs 181
277. Slightly Exotic Skillet Broccoli And Cauliflower 181
278. Slow Cooker Stout Beef Stew 182
279. Slow Roasted Lemon Chicken 183
280. Smoked Cauliflower Soup 183
281. Smokin' Chicken Noodle 184
282. Smoky Black Bean Burgers On Potato Buns 184
283. Smoky Chipotle Aioli 185
284. Smoky Delicata Bites 185
285. Smoky Gazpacho 186
286. Smoky Harvest Tomato Soup With Mozzarella Crostini 186
287. Smoky Pickled Asparagus 187
288. Smoky Seafood Fideos 188
289. Smoky Shitake Cranberry Cauliflower Galette With Marmalade Mustard Mascarpone 188
290. Smoky Tempeh & Hummus Sandwiches 189
291. Smoky And Sweet Roasted Pumpkin Soup 190
292. Smoky And Sweet Roasted Red Pepper With Tuna 190
293. Smoky, Spicy Roasted Corn Soup 191
294. Snap Crackle Pop!! Bombay Bhel Puri 192
295. Sopa De Ajo (Garlic Soup) 192
296. Southwest Sweet Potato Salad 193
297. Spaghetti 'in' Meat Balls 193
298. Spanish Chicken 194
299. Spanish Paella 194
300. Spanish Inspired Ragout With Butternut Squash, Chorizo, And Chickpeas 195
301. Spiced Potato Cakes 196
302. Spicy BBQ Chicken Quesadillas 196
303. Spicy Cannellini Beans 197
304. Spicy Corn & Scallop Chowder 197
305. Spicy Egg Curry 198
306. Spicy Indian Lentil Dal 199
307. Spicy Masala Rubbed Tofu Pitas With Mint Cumin Yoghurt Sauce 199
308. Spicy Moroccan Chickpea Soup 200
309. Spicy Pork Ragout With Cannellini And Orange 201
310. Spicy Spanish Garlic Shrimp Gambas Al Pil Pil 202
311. Spicy Tomato, Spinach & Egg Galette ... 202
312. Spicy, No Cook Beer Cheese Recipe 203
313. Split Pea Soup For A Winter's Day 204
314. Spring Vegetable And Red Pesto Tart 204
315. Strawberry Red Pepper Ice Cream 205
316. Stuffed Chicken 205
317. Stuffed Eight Ball Squash With Roasted Red Pepper Sauce 206
318. Stuffed Celery With Cream Cheese 207
319. Stuffing It Up Baby Artichoke 207
320. Sumac Chickpea Salad 208
321. Summer Cooler 208
322. Sun Dried Tomato Chorizo Garlic Shrimp 209
323. Sweet Chili Chicken Wings 209
324. Sweet Corn Tacos 210
325. Sweet Onion & Corn Quinoa Fritters With Fresh Corn & Basil Salad 210
326. Sweet Potato Gratin With Smoked Paprika And Cayenne 211
327. Sweet Potato And Cilantro Quesadilla With Fried Egg And Cumin Oil 212
328. Sweet And Smoky Beet Burgers 212
329. Taco Rice Or Takoraisu, Tex Mex Japanese Fusion 213
330. Tandoori Chicken Kebabs 213
331. Tandoori Coconut Chicken 214
332. Tangy Creamy Buttermilk Cucumbers ... 215
333. Thanksgiving Sauerkraut 215
334. That Bacon Roast Chicken 215
335. The Best Buddha Bowl | Chickpea Scramble Breakfast Bowl 216
336. Tilapia With Smoked Paprika Butter And Broccoli In Foil Packets 217
337. Tilapia With Black Cherry And Avocado. 217

338. Tofu Kebabs 218
339. Togarashi Grilled Cauliflower With Grilled Spring Onions And Plums. 218
340. Tomato Cheddar Biscuits 219
341. Tomato Soup With Paprika 219
342. Uncle Arje's Shakshuka (Eggs Poached In Tomato Sauce) 220
343. Vegan Beetloaf 221
344. Vegan Cashew Caesar Salad 221
345. Vegan Makhani (aka Butter Chicken Without The Butter Or Chicken) 222
346. Vegan And Gluten Free Étouffée 223
347. Vegan Butternut Squash Stew With Garbanzo Beans 224
348. Vegetabel Paella 224
349. Vegetarian Brazilian Bean Stew 225
350. Vegetarian Chopped "Liver" 225
351. Vegetarian Festivus 226
352. Veggie Chilli Cottage Pie 227
353. Warm Butternut Squash And Chicken Salad 227
354. Weeknight Enchiladas Verde 228
355. White & Navy Bean Salad With Watermelon Radishes And Lemon Tahini Dressing 229
356. White Bean And Barley Turkey Chili 230
357. Whole Roasted Cauliflower 230
358. Yellow Saffron Rice With Feta, Stewed Dates, And Pine Nuts 231
359. ZESTY GUACAMOLE WITH SPICED PITA CHIPS 232
360. Bacon And Egg Potato Salad 232
361. Beetroot And Oatmeal Baked Vegan Patties 233
362. Fresh Tomato And Summer Squash Soup 233
363. Shrimp Pimentón 234
364. Smoky Turkey Empanadas 234
365. "Eggs In Pipérade" Pizza With Crispy Prosciutto 235

INDEX 237

CONCLUSION 243

365 Awesome Paprika Recipes

***

1. Roasted Cauliflower Salad

Serving: Makes about 4 servings | Prep: | Cook: | Ready in:

Ingredients

- For the roasted cauliflower
- 1 nice size head cauliflower, broken into 1 to 2 inch florets
- 5 to 6 tablespoons extra virgin olive oil
- Salt and pepper
- Dressing (make while the cauliflower is roasting) and putting it all together
- 1/2 cup mayo
- 1 large garlic clove finely minced or put through a garlic press
- 1/2 teaspoon sweet Hungarian paprika
- 1/2 teaspoon Dijon mustard
- 1 teaspoon anchovy paste
- 2 tablespoons extra virgin olive oil
- 1/4 cup chopped parsley
- The roasted cauliflower

Direction

- For the roasted cauliflower
- Spread the cauliflower florets on a large rimmed baking sheet, drizzle with the olive oil and season with a little salt and pepper.
- Toss around and then roast in a pre-heated 425F oven for 25 to 30 minutes, stirring around at the 15 minute mark. You want the cauliflower to be a little browned on the edges.
- Dressing (make while the cauliflower is roasting) and putting it all together
- Place the mayo, garlic, paprika, Dijon mustard and anchovy paste in the bowl of a mini food processor and start processing. Slowly drizzle in the 2 tablespoons of olive oil with the machine still running.
- Place the warm roasted cauliflower in a bowl, toss with the dressing and stir in the chopped parsley. Serve warm or at room temperature.

2. Steak Roll Ups With Salsa Casera, Manchego And Pepitas

Serving: Serves 2 | Prep: | Cook: | Ready in:

Ingredients

- 1 pound Flank Steak
- 2 tablespoons Olive Oil
- Juice and Zest of One Lime
- 1 tablespoon Of Minced Garlic
- 1 teaspoon Chili Powder
- 2 teaspoons Paprika
- 1/4 cup HERDEZ® Salsa Casera
- 2/3 cup Shredded Manchego Cheese
- 3 tablespoons Pepitas (Pumpkin Seeds)
- Salt and Pepper
- Twine for Securing the Roll

Direction

- Remove flank steak from package and trim off any excess fat. You want to leave the marbling within the meat, but remove thick pieces of fat around the edges and any excess connective tissue. Transfer to a shallow dish that fits the whole piece of meat and season both sides liberally with salt and pepper.
- In a bowl, combine olive oil, lime juice and zest, garlic, chili powder and paprika. Pour over the steak allowing it to coat both sides.
- Refrigerate and allow to marinate for at least two hours or up to eight.

- Remove steak from the fridge when it's done marinating and allow to come to room temp. This would be a good time to preheat your grill. I like to heat one burner on medium-high and one on low just in case it starts getting too crispy.
- Using paper towels, soak up any excess marinade so the steak isn't too moist. Transfer to a cutting board.
- Start by spreading the HERDEZ® Salsa Casera all over the side of the steak facing up. On top of that, sprinkle on the manchego cheese followed by the pumpkin seeds. Lightly press the ingredients into the meat and get ready to roll.
- Cut 3 6-inch pieces of twine and have that ready beside you.
- Starting at the bottom of the flank steak, roll it up tightly, making sure the grain of the meat is running horizontally. When you get to the end, secure the roll with the cut pieces of twine and trim off any excess.
- Salt and pepper the outside of the roll one last time to your liking.
- Grill on the medium-high side of your grill about 5 minutes per side, until the internal temperature reaches 135 degrees Fahrenheit. Keep an eye on it and move it to the cooler side of the grill if necessary.
- Remove from the grill and allow to rest for at least 5 minutes before slicing into 4 rounds.
- Serve alongside a big salad and cilantro-lime rice. Enjoy!

3. "4 Fresh Chiles And A Ghost" Chili

Serving: Serves 10-12 | Prep: | Cook: | Ready in:

Ingredients

- 4 cloves of garlic, finely chopped
- 2 small onions, chopped
- 4 thick slices of bacon, - preferably smoked - chopped (optional but strongly recommended)
- 3 poblano peppers, chopped
- 4 jalapenos peppers, chopped
- 4 serrano peppers, chopped
- 1 habanero peppers, chopped
- 1 dried ghost chile, chopped (optional)
- 3 tablespoons chili powder (medium hot or hot)
- 2 tablespoons cumin
- 1 tablespoon paprika
- 1 pound ground beef
- 1 pound ground pork (optional: you may also make this recipe with 2 pounds of ground beef only)
- 1 can (14oz) black beans, washed and rinsed
- 1 can (14oz) kidney beans, washed and rinsed
- 1 large can (28oz) of tomato sauce or diced tomatoes (for a chunkier chili)
- 1 can of beer (optional, highly recommended)
- salt and pepper
- sour cream, for garnish (optional)
- shredded monterey or cheddar cheese, for garnish (optional)
- cilantro, chopped, for garnish
- 1 tablespoon masa harina

Direction

- In a large pan (I use a Dutch oven), cook the bacon until it becomes crisp, stirring. You do not have to add any vegetable oil or butter, because the bacon will release a lot of grease. However, if (for whatever reason) you decide NOT to use bacon, you need to melt 2 tbsps. of butter.
- Add all the chopped vegetables and the spices: the garlic, the onions, all the peppers, the chili powder, the cumin, the paprika and stir so that everything gets coated in the fat of the bacon (or the butter). Add a couple pinches of salt and pepper: don't worry at this stage, you can always add salt and pepper also at a later stage in the process.
- Let the vegetables and the spices cook for about 10 minutes, until the vegetables and chilis are softer, stirring every now and then.

Then stir in the meat, small batches at a time. You need to break the meat up with a wooden spoon, so that there are no large patches. It is a tedious process, but it will go relatively quickly. Cook the beef and the pork, stirring it, for another 10-15 minutes after that you have added it all, so that it is all broken up and it is not pink anymore.

- Add the beer, if you are using it, and let it reduce (5 minutes), while stirring. Add the tomato sauce and the beans, and stir. If you think the concoction is too dry, add some water, one table spoon at the time. Lower the heat so that the chili is simmering, and cook for 2-2 1/2 hours, stirring occasionally.
- Half an hour before the end, add the masa harina, and stir the chili so as to make sure it dissolves. This will thicken the chili. You may omit this step if you like you chili very soupy.
- To serve, transfer chili to bowls and garnish with cilantro, sour cream and the cheddar, if you want. Or you can serve it on rice, or on tortilla chips. Whatever you do, remember one thing: the chili con carne will get better (and hotter) the next day, and the day after next...and so on. So you should plan to cook it at least one day in advance.
- A word of caution about the chiles I use in this recipe: remember that by taking out the seeds and the veins of the chiles, you are reducing their heat by 70%... it is up to you: if you want your chili to be VERY hot, leave the veins and the seeds. If not, you can take them all out or do a mix of both. And be PARTICULARLY careful when handling habaneros and the optional ghost chile: you really need to protect your hands, or else you WILL regret it.

4. "Chuck" Full Of Flavor Chili

Serving: Serves 8-10 | Prep: | Cook: | Ready in:

Ingredients

- 2 tablespoons canola oil, divided
- 3 pounds ground chuck (if possible pick out a chuck roast and have the butcher grind it for you)
- 1 and 1/2 medium yellow onions, chopped
- 3-4 garlic cloves, minced
- 1 tablespoon dried oregano
- 2 teaspoons paprika, or 1 teaspoon paprika and 1 teaspoon smoked paprika
- 1 tablespoon cumin powder
- 3 and 1/2 to 4 tablespoons chili powder
- 1 and 1/2 to 2 teaspoons Kosher salt
- 1 teaspoon cayenne pepper
- 1-14 ounces can crushed tomatoes
- 1-14 ounces can whole tomatoes with juice, or diced tomatoes with juice
- 1-15 ounces can red kidney beans, drained (if you like a lot of beans, add a can of cannelini beans, drained)

Direction

- In a Dutch oven or large pot heat 1 tablespoon of the canola oil.
- Saute the ground chuck, breaking it up, until brown and no trace of pink.
- Remove the browned chuck to a colander and drain off all the fat. Set aside.
- Add the remaining tablespoon of canola oil to the pot, and cook the onions and garlic until translucent.
- Return the ground chuck to the onion and garlic mixture.
- Season with the oregano, paprika, cumin, chili powder, salt and cayenne pepper. Stir to combine and cook for several minutes on medium heat.
- Add the tomatoes. Stir to combine.
- Cover with lid, reduce heat to low, and cook slowly for an hour.
- Add the beans, and continue to cook, covered on low for an additional 20 minutes.
- Taste to adjust seasonings.
- It's even better the next day when the flavors have had a chance to meld.

5. "DLQ" (delish, Low Cal And Quick) Spinach Stuffed Mushrooms

Serving: Serves 3 | Prep: | Cook: | Ready in:

Ingredients

- 1 10 oz package of white button mushrooms
- 1 10 oz package of frozen chopped spinach, thawed
- 1 tablespoon olive oil
- 2 cloves of chopped fresh garlic
- 1/4 cup chopped red onion
- 1/4 cup dry white wine
- 1 large egg
- 1 teaspoon lemon juice
- 1/4 teaspoon ground black pepper
- 1/2 teaspoon chicken bouillion powder
- 3 tablespoons parmesan cheese
- 1/3 cup seasoned whole wheat breadcrumbs
- 1 teaspoon paprika

Direction

- Preheat oven to 350 degrees. Spray the bottom of a 9"x13" glass roasting pan with an olive oil spray.
- In a large sauce pan, sauté garlic in olive oil till fragrant; add onions, cover and cook till soft. Discard garlic.
- Clean mushrooms and remove stems. Place the mushroom caps in the glass pan. Chop mushroom stems and add to the hot oil.
- Add white wine and cover. Cook over medium heat till mushrooms soften. Remove lid, increase heat and cook off liquid till mushrooms are barely wet. Remove from heat.
- Squeeze the water out of the spinach and place the drained spinach in a large bowl.
- Mix in the egg, lemon juice, black pepper, chicken bouillon powder, parmesan cheese and breadcrumbs. Add the mushroom mixture and stir to thoroughly incorporate into the spinach.
- Spoon the mixture into each mushroom cap, piling about 2 inches above the top of the mushroom in a cone shape. Dust lightly with paprika. Spritz all over lightly with an olive oil spray. Bake at 350 for 30 minutes or until the tops start to brown.

6. A SHRIMP AND QUINOA PAELLA

Serving: Serves 4-6 people | Prep: | Cook: | Ready in:

Ingredients

- SHRIMP AND QUINOA PAELLA
- 1 pound shrimp, peeled and deveined, thawed if frozen
- 1/2 teaspoon paprika, divided
- 1 lemon, halved
- 4 tablespoons olive oil, divided
- 1/2 medium onion
- 1 clove garlic
- 2 anchovies, packed in oil
- 2 tablespoons tomato paste
- 1 cup quinoa, rinsed
- 2 cups chicken stock, or vegetable stock, or water
- 1/2 bunch chard, greens only, chopped
- 1/8 teaspoon ground saffron or a pinch of saffron threads
- 1/2 cup frozen peas, thawed
- 1/2 cup frozen corn, thawed
- salt
- pepper
- 1 handful parsley, chooped for garnish
- Swiss Chard Stalk Salsa
- 1 tablespoon olive oil
- 1/2 a medium onion
- 1 clove garlic
- 1/2 bunch swiss chard stalks, chopped
- 1 tablespoon lemon, zested and halved
- 1 tablespoon yogurt
- 1 handful parsley, chopped
- salt
- pepper

Direction

- SHRIMP AND QUINOA PAELLA
- In a medium sized bowl season shrimp with salt and pepper, 1/4 teaspoon paprika and the juice of half a lemon. Toss to coat well and set aside for 10-30 minutes if you have time otherwise cook right away.
- Heat 2 tablespoons olive oil in a large pan over medium/high heat. Add shrimp and cook for 2-3 minutes on each side. Do in batches if necessary. Transfer shrimp to a plate and set aside.
- Turn the heat down to medium and add remaining 2 tablespoons of olive oil. Add onion and cook until onion softens. About 6 minutes.
- Add garlic and anchovies. Stir and break down the anchovies. Melting them into the onion and garlic. About 1 minute.
- Add the tomato paste and stir into the onion, garlic, anchovy mix. Cook until fragrant. About 2-4 minutes.
- Add quinoa and stir into the sofrito (the tomato paste mixture). Toast the quinoa for 2 minutes.
- Add the chard, stock or water, remaining 1/4 teaspoon paprika, and saffron. Stir to incorporate and the heat up and bring to a quick boil. Cover and lower heat. Simmer for 10 minutes.
- Remove lid. Stir in the green peas and corn and warm through. About 5 minutes. Season with salt and pepper according to taste. Add the shrimp back to the pan and warm through if necessary. Garnish with parsley and squeeze the other lemon half over the whole thing. Serve with Swiss Chard Stalk Salsa if desirable. Enjoy.
- Swiss Chard Stalk Salsa
- Heat the olive oil in a small pan over medium heat. Add onion with a small pinch of salt cook until onion softens. About 6 minutes. Add Swiss chard stalks, garlic and lemon zest. Saute until stalks soften a little and become fragrant. About 6-8 minutes.
- Remove from heat and allow to cool for a few minutes. Transfer to serving bowl and stir in yogurt, parsley and squeeze in juice from half a lemon. Season with salt and pepper to taste. Add more yogurt or lemon juice as desired. Serve alongside Shrimp And Quinoa Paella.

7. A Cream Cauliflower And Red Pepper Duet

Serving: Serves 4 | Prep: | Cook: | Ready in:

Ingredients

- olive oil
- 1 teaspoon Hungarian sweet or hot paprika
- 1 clove garlic, peeled and chopped
- 1 sweet onion, chopped
- 1 sage leaf
- 1 ounce fresh lemon zest
- florets from 1 cauliflower head
- 2-3 ounces sliced fresh sweet red peppers
- kosher salt to taste
- fresh milled black pepper to taste
- 1 shot dry vermouth
- 1 shot vodka
- 1 pound small heirloom tomatoes
- 2 ounces fresh lemon juice
- 1 ounce capote capers
- 2 ounces black olives, pitted
- 1/2 cup cauliflower puree
- 1/2 cup roasted red pepper puree, skinless
- 3 tablespoons flat leaf parsley
- splash of cream
- creme fraiche or sour cream, optional garnish

Direction

- In a heated sauté pan, add the paprika. Next stir in some oil. Add the chopped garlic, onion, sage leaf, and lemon zest.
- Add the cauliflower florets and fresh red peppers to the pan, stirring. Season with salt and pepper.

- Add the vermouth and vodka. Next add the tomatoes and lemon juice. When the tomatoes are cooked, remove their skins. Add the capers, black olives, cauliflower and pepper puree. Simmer.
- Before serving add a splash of cream, but do not boil. Garnish with fresh herbs. Serve this as a soup with crusty bread or as sauce over cauliflower noodles, egg noodles or rice. Optional: garnish with crème fraiche or sour cream.

8. Ahi Tuna With Angel Hair Pasta

Serving: Serves 4 | Prep: | Cook: | Ready in:

Ingredients

- Ingredients for the Pasta
- 1 pound angel hair pasta
- 1 small shallot, diced
- 1 zucchini, chopped
- 1/2 cup red bell pepper, thinly sliced
- 1/2 cup mini-roma tomatoes, cut in half (or cherry tomatoes)
- 3 tablespoons champagne vinegar
- 1/4 cup olive oil, divided
- 1/4 cup reserved pasta water
- Fresh cilantro
- Ingredients for Tuna
- 1 tablespoon spanish paprika
- 2 teaspoons ground coriander
- 1 teaspoon dried oregano
- 1 teaspoon chili powder
- 1 1/2 teaspoons ground mustard
- Olive oil for searing
- 4 (4 oz) fillets of ahi tuna

Direction

- Cook the pasta by following the package less 2 minutes and set aside in a bowl. You can add a little water or olive oil while it sits. Reserve 1 cup of pasta water.
- Take a large sauté pan over medium heat and add in 1 tablespoon olive oil. Add in shallot and cook for 2 minutes. Next add in zucchini and bell pepper. Let sauté for 4 minutes. Turn heat off and add in tomatoes and champagne vinegar. Let sit until tuna is ready.
- In a small bowl combine paprika, coriander, oregano, chili powder and ground mustard. Move to a plate and coat each tuna on both sides. Set aside.
- Heat your indoor grill pan over medium-high heat. Once hot add in olive oil to coat the bottom of the pan. Add tuna and sear for 2-3 minutes (depending on the thickness). Flip over and turn off heat and let the fish heat through.
- Take the pan with the vegetables and turn to medium heat. Once hot add in pasta, 2 tablespoons olive oil and using thongs to combine ingredients. Add in cilantro and if you need more liquid add some pasta water 1 tablespoon at a time. Taste for any additional seasonings.
- On a board, slice tuna.
- To serve add pasta to the bottom of the plate and divide the tuna pieces to 4 plates.

9. Almond Bean Spread With A Hint Of Spain

Serving: Serves 4-6 | Prep: | Cook: | Ready in:

Ingredients

- 1 cup dried Arikara beans (or substitute white kidney beans)
- 4 sprigs thyme
- 3 1/2 cups water
- 1-2 leeks (depending on their size)
- 4 tablespoons olive oil
- 1/2 cup whole almonds
- 2 teaspoons sherry vinegar
- salt to taste
- smoked paprika

Direction

- Rinse the Arikara beans and cook them, covered, on very low heat with about 3 1/2 cups of water, the thyme sprigs and a pinch of water until very soft, about four hours. Add more water during the cooking process if necessary and when the beans are done, add more salt to taste.
- Remove the root and green stem from the leek, slice lengthwise, and wash thoroughly. Cut into 1/2 inch slices. Heat a large skillet over medium low heat, add the olive oil, and saute the leeks for about 10 minutes, until they are very soft, but avoid browning them. Add the cooked beans and their cooking liquid and simmer with the leeks to meld the flavors and reduce the broth. The final mixture should have about a half cup of syrupy liquid remaining.
- Meanwhile, toast the almonds in a dry skillet until fragrant. Transfer them to a food processor and pulverize into a fine meal. Add the leeks and beans and process for several minutes until smooth. Add the sherry vinegar and pulse. Taste and add more salt if necessary.
- Transfer to a bowl and dust with smoked paprika. Serve with fresh vegetables or crusty bread.

10. Ansel Adams's Eggs Poached In Beer

Serving: Serves 1 | Prep: | Cook: |Ready in:

Ingredients

- 1/4 cup (2 ounces) butter
- mixed spices
- dash sherry
- 1 bottle dark malt liquor or strong ale (ordinary beer is not strong enough)
- 1/4 teaspoon salt
- 2 eggs
- 2 pieces toast
- dash paprika

Direction

- Melt butter in microwave oven, but do not allow to brown. Add a dash of mixed spices and sherry.
- In a small bowl, microwave malt or ale with 1/4 teaspoon salt just to the boiling point. Carefully slide eggs into this hot liquid, cover with paper plate or glass bowl (to retain thermal heat), and cook as desired in microwave. (See note below on microwave cooking.)
- While eggs are cooking in microwave, make 2 pieces of toast. Spread part of the butter-spice mix over the toast.
- Serve eggs on the toast, and pour over the rest of the butter-spice mix. Add a dash of paprika.
- Note on microwave cooking: I like my eggs poached soft. I find that 1 egg in the hot ale or malt takes about 1 minute to cook, 2 eggs about 2 minutes, etc., all the way up to 8 eggs about 8 minutes. When working with as many as 8 eggs, the bowl should be moved around every 2 to 3 minutes.

11. Artichoke & Parmesan Burgers With Lime Mayonnaise & Roasted Red Peppers

Serving: Serves 4 | Prep: | Cook: |Ready in:

Ingredients

- for the burgers
- 1 large red pepper
- 1 pound good quality lean ground beef
- 2 tablespoons bacon bits
- 4 artichoke hearts (use the canned variety), finely chopped
- 1 large clove garlic, minced
- 1 tablespoon mayonnaise
- 1 tablespoon freshly squeezed lemon juice

- zest of 1 lemon
- 1/8 teaspoon paprika
- 1/4 cup grated parmesan cheese
- 1/4 teaspoon salt
- 1/4 teaspoon pepper
- 4 ciabatta buns
- for the lime mayonnaise
- 4 tablespoons mayonnaise
- zest of 1 lime
- 1 1/2 tablespoons freshly squeezed lime juice
- freshly ground black pepper to taste

Direction

- Wash the red pepper, cut it into quarters, clean out seeds and set aside
- Place the ground beef in a large mixing bowl, add the bacon bits and chopped artichoke hearts; set aside
- In a small bowl mix together the garlic, 1 tbsp. mayonnaise, lemon juice and zest, paprika, parmesan cheese, salt and pepper, and blend together well
- Add the cheese mixture to the ground beef mixture and mix together well with your hands; divide into 4 equal parts and shape into hamburger patties; set aside
- In a small bowl make the lime mayonnaise by combining the 4 tbsp. mayonnaise, lime zest, lime juice and black pepper; refrigerate until needed
- Heat grill to medium-high heat and cook hamburger patties and red pepper quarters for 5 minutes on each side; transfer to a plate
- Cut roasted red pepper quarters into thin slices
- Cut buns in half and top with hamburgers, a good dollop of lime mayonnaise and red pepper slices; serve and enjoy!

12. Asha Gomez's Smoky Hazelnut Chocolate Cookies

Serving: Makes 10 cookies | Prep: | Cook: | Ready in:

Ingredients

- 1 cup unbleached all-purpose flour
- 1/2 cup white granulated sugar
- 2 teaspoons smoked sweet paprika, divided
- 2 large eggs
- 1 cup (8 ounces) Nutella, at room temperature
- 1/4 cup (2 ounces) hazelnuts, roasted, skinned, and chopped (see Editor's Notes)
- Cooking spray
- 1 tablespoon confectioners' sugar, for dusting

Direction

- Heat the oven to 350°F.
- In a medium bowl, using your hands, mix together the flour, sugar, 1½ teaspoons of the smoked paprika, and eggs to form a crumbly dough. Mix in the Nutella and hazelnuts and work to form a smooth dough, no more than 2 minutes.
- Spray a cookie sheet with cooking spray and set aside.
- Separate the dough into 10 equal parts, using your palms to roll them into round balls. Place the balls on the cookie sheet, 1 inch apart. Bake for 6 to 8 minutes, or until the cookies are flat discs, crisp around the edges. Remove the cookies from the oven; dust with the remaining smoked paprika and confectioners' sugar. Eat them immediately or after they have cooled down.

13. Auntie Sui's Potato Salad

Serving: Serves 2-4 | Prep: | Cook: | Ready in:

Ingredients

- 1 pound waxy potatoes, e.g. Yukon Gold
- 3 large hard-boiled eggs, shelled & coarse chopped
- 1 can mandarin oranges, drained
- 1 cup diced sweet apples
- 1/2 cup mayonnaise, plus more if needed

- Salt, Pepper
- Paprika, optional

Direction

- Peel potatoes and cut into large 1 inch-ish dice. Gently boil in salted water until just tender, but still somewhat firm. Drain well and transfer to large bowl.
- Add mayo and toss to coat the potatoes. Add more mayo, 1Tb increments, if the mixture looks too dry. You don't want the potatoes swimming in mayo, but you also do not want it dry.
- Add eggs and apples, gently combine with the potatoes.
- Check the seasoning and add salt, in 1/2 tsp increments. Because the potato salad will be chilled and served cold, you will need to salt it to your preference and then add a little bit more. The salad should taste just slightly overseasoned while it's still warm. Add pepper, ~1/2 tsp or to taste.
- Gently fold in orange segments. Optional: Sprinkle the top of the potato salad with some sweet paprika. This is more of a decorative touch.
- Cover the bowl and chill the salad for at least 2 hours before serving.

14. Avocado Hummus

Serving: Serves 6 | Prep: | Cook: |Ready in:

Ingredients

- 1 Big, Beautiful, Ripe Avocado, peeled & pitted
- 3-2/3 cups Yotam & Sami's Basic Hummus Recipe (https://food52.com/recipes...)
- 2 teaspoons Ground Cumin
- 1/4 teaspoon Ground Cayenne Pepper
- Smoked Paprika for garnish
- Fresh Parsley or Cilantro for garnish

Direction

- Start with Yotam Ottolenghi & Sami Tamimi's Basic Hummus Recipe
- Add Avocado, Cumin and Cayenne in the food processor and blend until smooth - 5 minutes.
- Serve in your favorite bowl, garnished with smoked paprika and parsley or cilantro, and a side of freshly toasted naan strips.

15. BEER CAN CHICKEN TACOS

Serving: Makes 8-10 tacos | Prep: | Cook: |Ready in:

Ingredients

- beer can chicken
- 1 whole chicken
- 1 can of your favourite beer
- 1 teaspoon paprika
- 1 teaspoon dried oregano
- 1 teaspoon mustard powder
- 1 teaspoon brown sugar
- 1 teaspoon chill powder
- 1 teaspoon sea salt
- 1 teaspoon black pepper
- 1 tablespoon olive oil
- 1 cup barbecue sauce (i use sweet baby ray's)
- tacos (guacamole & pickled red onions)
- 2 ripe avocados
- 1 small red onion, finely chopped
- 1 garlic clove, minced
- 1 lime, zest & juice
- 1 tablespoon fresh cilantro, chopped
- Pinch salt & pepper (to taste)
- 1 roma tomato, chopped
- 1 large red onion, thinly sliced
- 1 teaspoon salt
- 1 teaspoon raw sugar
- 5 black pepper corns
- 2 cloves of garlic, smashed
- 1 cup apple cider vinegar

- 8-10 corn tortilla shells

Direction

- For the chicken: rub chicken with paprika, oregano, mustard powder, pepper, salt, chili powder and oil. Empty half of beer can into a glass and drink. Shove the half-filled beer can up the chicken carcass. With the bbq preheated to 400 degrees, place chicken on the grill. Cook for approximately 1 hour (or until chicken is fully cooked) and continuously base with bbq sauce. Let rest until cool enough to handle. Shred chicken and toss with remaining bbq sauce. Set aside until you are ready to assemble tacos.
- For the guacamole: in a mixing bowl add avocados, small red onion, garlic, lime juice, lime zest, pepper, salt and cilantro. Mash until smooth and creamy. Stir in tomatoes. Set aside until you are ready to assemble tacos.
- For the pickled onions: in a mason jar add large sliced red onions, sugar, salt, vinegar, garlic cloves and peppercorns. Seal lid tight and shake until all the flavours are blended.
- To assemble tacos begin with the corn tortilla. Top with pulled chicken, guacamole, pickled onions and cilantro. Garnish plate with a fresh lime.

16. Bacon Jam

Serving: Makes 1 1/2 cups | Prep: | Cook: | Ready in:

Ingredients

- 10 ounces bacon, maple-smoked and nitrate-free
- 1 heaping cup chopped onions (about 2 small onions)
- 1/2 teaspoon paprika
- 4 cloves garlic, pressed
- 3 tablespoons maple syrup
- 1 to 2 tablespoons dark brown sugar
- 1/4 cup apple cider vinegar
- 3/4 cup 3/4 cup beer (milk stout or malt beverage)
- Note: If using malt beverage cut the dark brown sugar down to 1 tablespoon

Direction

- Chop bacon into 1/2-inch strips.
- Heat a large, high-rimmed sauté pan over medium-high heat. Add bacon and cook until browned and just crisp. (The crisper the bacon, the more texture your jam will have.)
- Once bacon is browned, remove from pan and place on a paper towel-lined plate to drain excess fat. Set aside.
- Pour out the excess bacon grease into a disposable container, leaving about 1 tablespoon fat in the pan. This will look like a film of fat in the pan. Turn heat to medium-low and add onions. Sauté the onions until translucent.
- Add paprika and garlic to the onions and turn heat down to low. Stir a few times to evenly distribute garlic, then add the maple syrup. If using milk stout, add 2 tablespoons brown sugar; if using malt beverage, add 1 tablespoon brown sugar. Cook until the brown sugar has dissolved. When you pull a spoon along the bottom of the pan, the liquid should slowly move back into place.
- Add the vinegar and beer (milk stout or malt beverage). Turn to medium-high heat and bring the mixture to a boil. Reduce the heat and add bacon. Allow to simmer gently for 15 minutes, or until the liquid has started reducing. When you pull your spoon along the bottom of the pan, the line you drew should fill back in very slowly.
- Turn off heat and let sit for 10 to 20 minutes while you set up your blender (or food processor) with the blade attachment.
- Pour the bacon jam into your blender and pulse for 1 to 2 minutes, until the desired consistency is reached. (I prefer the consistency of chutney over that of jelly.)

- Refrigerate for 1 hour before eating to allow it to solidify, but sneak in a couple of spoonful if you like it warm.
- Store in your refrigerator in an airtight container for up to 1 month.

17. Bacon Wrapped Brown Sugar Pork Loin

Serving: Serves 3-4 | Prep: | Cook: | Ready in:

Ingredients

- Pork Loin
- 3 pounds bone-in pork loin roast
- 5-6 pieces of bacon
- 1/2 teaspoon chili powder
- 1/4 teaspoon hot Spanish paprika
- 1 teaspoon salt
- 1/4 teaspoon cumin
- 1/2 teaspoon cinnamon
- Brown Sugar Glaze
- 1/2 cup dark brown sugar
- 1 tablespoon flour
- 1 tablespoon apple cider vinegar
- 1/4 teaspoon mustard powder

Direction

- So let's line a roasting pan with aluminum foil and place your big hunk of pork on that sucker. Preheat your oven to 375F.
- In a small bowl, make your spice rub. Combine the salt, black pepper, paprika, cumin, cinnamon, and chili powder.
- And give that pork a good rub down.
- Then we'll wrap the whole thing in some bacon. P.S. - the technical term for wrapping something in fat (in this case, bacon) is "barding."
- Place the roast in the oven and roast for about 50-60 minutes.
- Meanwhile, in a small saucepan under medium heat, combine the ingredients for the glaze - the brown sugar, flour, cider vinegar, and mustard powder.
- Simmer until the sugar is dissolved.
- Drizzle glaze over top of pork roast and continue to roast for about 25-35 minutes longer, or until internal temperature has reached 160F.
- Let rest for about 10 minutes and then slice into 1 inch thick portions. Serve with your starch of choice and enjoy!

18. Beef Strogonoff

Serving: Serves 6 | Prep: 0hours5mins | Cook: 0hours35mins | Ready in:

Ingredients

- 3 pounds fillet steak
- 2 tablespoons flour
- 4 tablespoons sunflower oil
- 1 onion - medium size finely chopped
- 2 garlic cloves finely chopped
- 1/4 cup cognac - good quality
- 1 tablespoon Dijon mustard
- 1 tablespoon Worcestershire Sauce
- 1/2 cup tomato sauce
- 4 tablespoons ketchup
- 1 tablespoon Paprika
- 3/4 cup cream
- 2 teaspoons flour or corn starch
- 3/4 cup Button mushrooms, clean and finely sliced
- 1 pinch salt
- 1 tablespoon lemon juice freshly squeezed
- 1 pinch parsley finely chopped for garnish

Direction

- Cut the steak into slices 0.5in thick, then cut each slice across the grain into strips 0.5in wide. Dust with the flour to coat (for sealing meat).
- Divide the beef in 4 parts. In a wide pan over high heat, add 3 tablespoons of oil and quickly

seal the slices of beef. Remove each batch and continue until all the meat is cooked (the meat only needs a quick seal because it will be cooked in the sauce afterwards - otherwise it will become rubbery).

- When all the beef is sealed, add it back to the pan, add the chopped onions and garlic and stir well. Let cook for 3 minutes.
- Add the cognac to deglaze the pan, stirring very well the bottom of the pan and let cook over medium heat until the alcohol has evaporated.
- Add the Paprika, the Dijon mustard, the ketchup, the Worcestershire Sauce, mix well and cook 2 minutes.
- Add the tomato sauce and the ketchup, mix and cook for 12 minutes. Season with salt.
- In a sauté pan, over high heat add 1 tablespoon of oil and stir fry the clean and sliced button mushrooms until golden.
- In a bowl, add the flour or corn starch and add a little cream and whisk well so you don't get lumps. Add the remaining cream, whisking well. Add a ladle of hot Strogonoff sauce to the cream mixture and whisk.
- Pour the cream and starch mixture back in the pot, add the Button mushrooms and mix well. Simmer over low heat for 10 minutes to cook the starch and mix all the flavors, stirring from time to time. The sauce should thicken but be smooth, coating well the meat. Remove from the heat and add the lemon juice and check the seasoning.
- At this point you can put the Strogonoff aside until you are ready to serve. Serve hot in a terrine sprinkled with the parsley.
- It is usually served with cooked Basmati rice.

19. Beef Tips & Gravy

Serving: Serves 5-6 | Prep: | Cook: | Ready in:

Ingredients

- 1/4 cup canola oil
- 5 onions, roughly chopped
- 3 garlic cloves, sliced thinly
- 1 tablespoon dried marjoram
- 1 & 1/2 tablespoons tomato paste
- 3 tablespoons paprika
- 1 & 1/2 teaspoons cayenne pepper
- 1/2 cup white wine vinegar
- 1/2 cup red wine
- 6 cups chicken stock
- 2 bay leaves
- zest from 1 lemon
- 3 pounds sirloin, cut into chunks
- 1 tablespoon cornstarch
- 1 tablespoon cold water
- salt and pepper to taste

Direction

- Turn a crockpot on high setting.
- Heat the oil in a large skillet over medium high heat. Add the onions and cook until soft, about 25 minutes. Add garlic and marjoram and stir until fragrant and garlic softens, about 2-3 minutes. Add in the tomato paste and stir constantly for about 3 minutes. Add paprika and cayenne pepper and stir well. Remove from heat and let flavors meld together.
- Add the mixture to the heated crockpot and add vinegar. Stir well, cover, and let vinegar absorb into vegetables for about 2-3 minutes. Add in chicken stock, bay leaves, and lemon zest.
- Sprinkle sirloin chunks with salt and pepper. In same skillet for onions, add beef chunks (you can wipe the skillet if you want to, but I think it adds to the beef so I didn't). Brown chunks on all sides and then add to crockpot. Deglaze skillet with red wine, scraping the sacs from the pan. Add wine to crockpot as well. Stir mixture, cover, and let cook on high for at least 3 hours. The longer it sits, the more tender the meat will be.
- Uncover crockpot and carefully take out beef with a slotted spoon and transfer to bowl. Tent with aluminum foil. Pour crockpot liquid and onions into a large sauce pan and bring to a boil until reduced to about 5 cups, about 15

minutes. Let cool momentarily and blend with immersion blender until mixture is nice and smooth. Season with salt and pepper. If you want to thicken the liquid just a tad, mix 1 tablespoon cornstarch with 1 tablespoon cold water in a small bowl. Add to liquid and stir. Then add blended liquid, along with beef chunks, back into crockpot. Turn to low or warm setting. Let simmer for about 5-10 minutes and serve along with rice or egg noodles and some roasted vegetables.

20. Beer Oyster Mushrooms Tacos With Mango Slaw

Serving: Makes 10 tacos | Prep: | Cook: | Ready in:

Ingredients

- Beer-oyster mushrooms
- 500 grams Oyster mushrooms
- 1/4 cup Ale beer of your choice
- Splash Lime juice
- 1/2 teaspoon Smoked paprika
- 1 tablespoon Olive oil
- Salt
- Mango Slaw
- 2 Ripe mangoes cut into small cubes
- 1 cup White cabagge cut into thin strips
- 1 Medium red onion cut into thin strips
- 1 Jalapeño pepper sliced
- 3 tablespoons Lime juice
- 1 dash Olive oil
- Handful Cilantro

Direction

- Beer-oyster mushrooms
- Cut the mushrooms into strips. In a large skillet, heat one tablespoon of olive oil over medium-high heat.
- Cook the mushrooms until they are browned. It is important at this point not move or shake the pan because otherwise they will not brown.
- Then add salt, lime juice, paprika and the beer.
- Let the alcohol evaporate and check the salt. Reserve.
- Mango Slaw
- In a bowl put the cabbage, mango, onion and jalapeno pepper.
- Season with lime juice, a drizzle of olive oil and salt. I refrigerate covered by at least one hour.
- Serve the mushrooms and the slaw in a homemade corn tortilla with avocado and a pinch of sea salt.

21. Bengali Shrimp Masala

Serving: Serves 4-6 | Prep: 0hours0mins | Cook: 1hours0mins | Ready in:

Ingredients

- 1/2 teaspoon turmeric
- 2 pounds peeled, deveined shrimp (smaller is better here, don't go for the jumbo prawns)
- 1/2 pound cauliflower, chopped
- 1/2 cup ghee or vegetable oil
- 1 1/2 cups finely chopped onions
- 3 cloves garlic, finely chopped
- 1 teaspoon ground cumin
- 2 teaspoons ground coriander
- 1 1/2 teaspoons paprika
- 1/4 cup plain yogurt (full fat is best)
- 1 1/2 teaspoons salt
- 1/2 teaspoon red pepper flakes
- 1/4 cup heavy cream
- 10 ounces frozen peas
- Basmati rice, to serve

Direction

- Bring 1 quart of water to boil. Add turmeric, shrimp, and cauliflower; cook for 3-4 minutes, until shrimp are just done. Drain the shrimp and cauliflower while reserving the turmeric water, and set aside.

- Heat ghee in a large pan over high heat, and add onions. Fry onions until they turn golden brown and translucent, stirring constantly. Add garlic and cook for another minute.
- Reduce heat, add cumin, coriander and paprika. Stir together, then add half the reserved cooking liquid. Increase heat and boil uncovered for about 10 minutes.
- Add the remaining liquid and boil for another 20 minutes, until the sauce is thick.
- Add yogurt, salt, and red pepper flakes. Cook for another 2-3 minutes.
- Add shrimp and cauliflower back in, and cook until shrimp is heated through.
- Turn off heat, add peas and heavy cream, mix, and let rest for at least 15 minutes before you serve it over basmati rice.

22. Best Boston Baked Beans

Serving: Serves 6-8 | Prep: | Cook: | Ready in:

Ingredients

- 2 cups dried beans such as Ireland Creek Annie, if you can find them, or navy or anasazi beans
- 4 strips bacon
- 1 onion, diced
- 4 cloves garlic, minced
- 1 teaspoon ground cumin
- 1/2 teaspoon spicy smoked paprika
- 1 tablespoon brown sugar
- 1/4 cup ketchup
- 1 tablespoon mustard
- 1 tablespoon molasses
- 1/4 cup cider vinegar
- 4 cups water, heated

Direction

- Preheat the oven to 250 degrees. Cut the bacon into small strips (most easily done with scissors) and saute in a Dutch oven until the strips are fairly crispy. Reserve the bacon and drain off all but about 2 Tbsps. bacon fat. Add the chopped onion and saute until soft. Add the garlic, cumin, paprika, and brown sugar and saute for another couple of minutes. Meanwhile, mix together the ketchup, mustard, molasses, and vinegar. Pour this mixture into the pot. Rinse the mixing cup with some of the hot water and add this and the remaining water to the pot. Add the rinsed beans and bacon bits, mix and heat the contents of the pot to a simmer. Then cover the pot and transfer to the oven.
- Cook the beans in the oven for about 3 1/2 hours, stirring occasionally, until they are soft, but not falling apart. Add a little more water if they get too dry during the cooking process. Raise the heat to 400 degrees, remove the top, add salt if needed, and cook for another half hour until the sauce becomes thick and caramelized.

23. Best Ever Turkey Chili

Serving: Serves 4 | Prep: | Cook: | Ready in:

Ingredients

- Olive oil
- 2 tablespoons tomato paste
- 1 medium to large onion, chopped
- 5 cloves garlic, minced
- 1/2 red bell pepper, chopped
- 1 teaspoon chili powder
- 1/2 teaspoon hot paprika
- 1/2 teaspoon dried coriander
- 1/4 teaspoon oregano
- Dash of cinnamon
- 1 pound ground turkey breast
- 1 cup dark beer, such as Leffe Brown
- one 28-ounce can diced tomatoes
- one 15 1/2-ounce can kidney beans, drained
- 1/2 teaspoon hot sauce or chile paste
- Salt and pepper

- Sour cream, chopped chives, cilantro, and/or shredded cheese, for topping

Direction

- Heat a bit of olive oil in a large pot over medium heat. Add the tomato paste, onion, garlic, and red pepper, then cook, stirring occasionally, until softened. Add the chili powder, hot paprika, coriander, oregano, and cinnamon; stir and allow to cook until aromatic, 1 minute.
- Add the ground turkey and cook, breaking it up with a spoon, until lightly browned. Pour in the beer and allow to cool down slightly.
- Add the tomatoes, beans, and hot sauce or chili paste.
- Allow the chili to simmer, uncovered, until thickened, about 40 minutes. Season with salt and pepper to taste. Top with sour cream, chopped chives, cilantro, and/or shredded cheese.

24. Birthday Paella

Serving: Serves 6 | Prep: | Cook: |Ready in:

Ingredients

- 1 5 pound bag mussels
- 3 large, ripe tomatoes
- 10 blanched almonds, ideally Marcona
- 3 cloves garlic
- 1/4 cup Italian parsley, packed
- 1/3 cup plus 2 tablespoons olive oil
- 1 package dried chorizo, cut into 1/4 inch slices
- 1 pound shrimp, peeled
- 2 teaspoons sweet pimentón de la Vera (Spanish smoked paprika)
- Kosher salt
- Freshly ground black pepper
- 1 1/2 pounds chicken thighs, ideally boneless and skinless
- 1/4 teaspoon saffron threads
- 4 1/2 cups chicken stock
- 1/2 cup dry Sherry
- 2 cups Calrose or Bomba rice
- About 1 bottle beer (lager works well)
- 1 cup frozen peas

Direction

- Place the mussels in a bowl of very cold water and place the bowl in the fridge. Every 30-40 minutes or so, change the water (for a total of at least 2 water changes). Slice tomatoes in half, and grate each on a box grater over a bowl. Discard skins; set pulp aside. In a food processor or mortar, puree parsley, garlic and almonds with a tablespoon or two of water until smooth.
- Heat 1/2 tablespoon olive oil in a large pan over high heat. Add chorizo pieces to pan and cook until lightly browned. Remove with a slotted spoon and set aside. Season shrimp with salt and 1/2 teaspoon paprika. Sear the shrimp in the hot pan until golden brown and almost cooked through.
- With a slotted spoon, remove shrimp. Season chicken pieces with salt and pepper, add to same pan, and brown on one side until deep golden. Remove chicken from pan and set aside.
- Set 18-inch paella pan over two burners at high heat on the stove top, and heat 1/3 cup olive oil. Add tomato pulp and cook until darkened, about 5 minutes. Add 1 1/2 teaspoons paprika and 1/4 teaspoon saffron, and cook for about 1 minute. Add chicken pieces and sherry and cook until sherry is evaporated (you'll have liquid in the pan, but no longer be able to smell the sherry). Add chicken stock; bring to a boil.
- Stir garlic, almond and parsley puree into the pan. Sprinkle rice across the pan and stir until the grains are submerged, then don't stir again. Add red peppers. Cook on high heat for 10 minutes, rotating the pan on the two burners to distribute heat. Using a small spoon, test rice and stock and add salt as needed.

- Reduce heat to medium-low and continue cooking for 10 minutes. Test rice again. If the rice is drying out but still needs some more cooking time in order for it to tenderize, add some beer (or water or chicken stock) to the dry spots. The amount of beer needed will vary greatly depending on your rice, heat, etc., but we used about a bottle of beer.
- If the rice is still hard, turn the heat down to low and continue to cook the rice until all parts of the dish are tender. You might need to intermittently cover the pan with a big sheet of tin foil. I wish that I could give you more specific directions, but I think that this is one of those dishes that you have to watch and play with, at least until you're practiced with it. We found that our total cooking time for the rice was about 50 minutes, about 10 of which were covered.
- When all of the rice is tender but a little bit of extra liquid remains in the pan, scatter the mussels over the top, scatter the shrimp and peas around. Cover with tin foil and cook for about 5-7 more minutes, until the mussels are open.
- In this last little part, listen for a crackling sound to ensure the bottom is toasting but not burning. It might be necessary to increase the heat to medium-high, but again, listen and pay attention to the dish. Remove from heat, leave the foil cover in place, and let sit for 5 minutes.
- Use a metal spoon to scrape toasted rice from bottom of pan and serve.

25. Blackened Fish Tacos With Piña Colada Salsa

Serving: Makes 4 tacos | Prep: | Cook: | Ready in:

Ingredients

- 8 ounces White fish, such as tilapia
- 3 tablespoons Salt
- 1 tablespoon Ground black pepper
- 1 tablespoon Smoked paprika
- 1 teaspoon Cayenne pepper
- 1 cup Pineapple, small dice
- 2 tablespoons Cilantro, chopped
- 1 Lime

Direction

- Pat the fish fillets dry and let sit out while you prepare the spice rub.
- Combine the salt, pepper, paprika, and cayenne together in a small bowl. Heavily sprinkle over the fillets on all sides.
- Heat some oil in a skillet until smoking. Carefully lay the fish onto the oil. Cook on one side until deeply seared. Flip the fish over and do the same on the other side.
- Combine the pineapple, mango, onion, cilantro, and coconut in a bowl. Squeeze the juice of one lime over the salsa and toss to combine. Season with salt.
- Warm the tortillas and fill with pieces of fish and salsa. Garnish with lime wedges and cilantro leaves.

26. Body And Soul

Serving: Serves 2-4 | Prep: | Cook: | Ready in:

Ingredients

- The grains
- 1/3 cup brown teff grains
- 1 cup long grain brown rice
- 1 1/2 cups carrot juice
- 1 3/4 cups fish broth
- 1/2 cup finely grated carrot
- 1/2 inch ginger, peeled and grated
- 1 teaspoon Meyer lemon zest
- pinch of Maldon salt flakes
- The fish
- 2 tablespoons olive oil
- 1 pound filet of sole
- fresh milled pepper to taste
- pinch of Maldon salt flakes

- water just enough to cover the fish
- 1 Meyer lemon, thinly sliced
- 1 tablespoon chopped flat leaf parsley and sprigs of fresh dill
- 1 cup roast carrots and parsnips with garlic and onions (see other recipe)
- lemon wedges for garnish
- fresh dill for garnish
- sprinkle of sweet paprika, optional garnish

Direction

- The grains
- Heat the teff grains in a pan. Combine all the ingredients in a rice cooker or pan. Bring to a boil and let cook until tender, about 40 minutes.
- The fish
- In a shallow baking pan coat the bottom with olive oil. Season the fish with salt and pepper. Place the fish on top of the olive. Arrange the lemon slices, parsley, and dill on top. Pour water in the pan just enough to cover the top of the fish. On top of this arrange the roasted carrots and parsnips, with whatever other vegetables you have also roasted before (golden beets, yellow peppers, onions, garlic). If you don't have roasted carrots, then some plain cooked carrots and parsnips will do. They will contribute to the broth flavor.
- Bake in a 350 degree oven until the fish is cooked, about 20 minutes.
- Dish out the grains first. Serve the fish next to the grains. Top with the carrot and parsnips (with beets and peppers). Ladle the broth from the fish over everything. Serve with lemon wedges, fresh dill and a sprinkle of paprika.

27. Bone Marrow On Toast Beer Beef & Veal Shank Soup (as An Afterthought)

Serving: Serves 6-8 | Prep: | Cook: | Ready in:

Ingredients

- 3 pounds both beef and veal shank bones (make sure bones are big and have marrow inside w/ meat around)
- 3 bay leaves
- rustic bread toasted (sliced thin)
- 2 dark lager beers (I like San Miguel but any brand will do)
- 1/4 pound carrots (chopped small)
- 1/4 pound celery (chopped small)
- 1 red pepper (chopped small)
- 1 yellow pepper (chopped small)
- 1 Anaheim green pepper (optional) (chopped small)
- 1-2 large tomatoes – diced
- 2-3 cloves garlic (chopped or crushed)
- 1 large yellow onion (chopped)
- 1 1/2 pounds white rose (or any kind) potatoes (peeled and cut in lg. chunks)
- salt
- fresh ground pepper
- 1 teaspoon smoked paprika
- Himalayan sea salt

Direction

- Put beef and veal shanks in large stock pot and cover with beers and bay leaf. Bring beer to a boil and then boil over med-low heat for 1 ½ to 2 hours.
- Add water to fill pot ¾ full. Let cook a bit, then add chopped carrots, celery, peppers, tomatoes and garlic.
- Brown onion in olive oil (to fill bottom of sauté pan) until translucent. Add onion w/ olive oil to boiling pot.
- Continue to boil a few minutes and then add potatoes. Add the smoked paprika and salt and pepper to taste.
- Continue to cook until potatoes are tender, about an hour.
- Remove bones from soup; take off surrounding meat; put meat back in soup. Let cook on low.
- Remove marrow from bones, spread on toasted rustic bread. Sprinkle with a little

- Himalayan sea salt (or your favorite salt) and enjoy...
- When ready to eat soup, sprinkle w/ a little fresh chopped parsley, and add a little fresh squeezed lemon juice if desired.

28. Braised Basque Short Ribs

Serving: Serves 2 | Prep: | Cook: |Ready in:

Ingredients

- 1 tablespoon olive oil
- 1 pound beef short ribs (about 2 ribs--ask the butcher to cut in half)
- 1 medium yellow onion, diced
- 1 medium carrot, peeled and diced
- 1 small red bell pepper, finely diced
- 2 cloves garlic, minced
- ½ teaspoon smoked Paprika (pimenton)
- 3/4 cup Rioja (or other red wine)
- 1 cup beef stock
- ½ cup diced tomatoes
- ½ teaspoon kosher salt
- 1 bay leaf
- ¼ cup pitted Kalamata or Nicoise olives
- 1/4 cup fresh parsley leaves

Direction

- Position a rack in the center of oven and preheat to 300°F. Heat olive oil in a medium Dutch oven or heavy-bottomed saucepan over high heat. Brown short ribs on all sides, about 2 minutes per side. Remove to plate.
- Reduce heat to medium. Add onions and carrots. Sauté until tender, about 5 minutes. Add the peppers, garlic and paprika, and cook until fragrant, about 2 minutes. Stir in red wine, stock, tomatoes, salt, and bay leaf and return heat to high. Bring to simmer, cover, and bake in oven about 2 1/2 hours, until very tender, turning short ribs over halfway through cooking.
- Remove pot from oven and spoon off excess fat from surface. Carefully remove short ribs to plate. Discard bay leaf and bring sauce to a boil over high heat. Reduce until liquids thicken and reduce by one third, about 8 minutes. Off heat, stir in olives and taste for seasoning. Return short ribs to pot and heat through. To serve, divide the short ribs between two plates, ladle sauce over top, garnish with parsley, and serve with crusty French bread.

29. Braised Chicken Thighs With Tomato And Honey

Serving: Serves 4 | Prep: | Cook: |Ready in:

Ingredients

- 1 tablespoon olive oil
- 4 medium chicken thighs (bone-in, skin-on), about 2 pounds
- Kosher salt and freshly ground pepper
- 2 shallots
- 2 garlic cloves
- 1 (1-inch) piece peeled ginger
- 1 medium sweet potato
- 1/4 teaspoon turmeric
- 1/4 teaspoon paprika
- 1/4 teaspoon ground cinnamon
- 1 tablespoon honey
- 1 tablespoon tomato paste
- 1 cup chicken broth
- 2 tablespoons orange juice
- Torn mint leaves for garnish, optional

Direction

- Heat oil in a large heavy skillet over medium-high. Season chicken with salt and pepper and add to skillet. Brown chicken in hot oil, skin-side down, about 7 minutes. (Reserve skillet and fat in pan.)

- While chicken browns, finely chop shallot, garlic and ginger. Thinly slice sweet potatoes and set aside.
- Raise heat on reserved skillet to medium-high. Add chopped shallot, garlic, ginger, turmeric, paprika and cinnamon and cook, stirring, 1 minute. Add honey and tomato paste and cook, stirring, 1 minute. Stir in chicken broth and add chicken to pan, covered with sweet potato slices and chickpeas. Cover and simmer chicken until cooked through, 10 to 12 minutes. Before serving, stir in orange juice and scatter mint over servings.

30. Braised Tuna And Chickpeas

Serving: Serves 4 | Prep: | Cook: | Ready in:

Ingredients

- 3 tablespoons olive oil
- 1 garlice clove, minced
- 1 tablespoon paprika
- 1 19 oz can chickpeas
- 1 large or 2 small cans of tuna
- 1/2 teaspoon salt
- 1/2 teaspoon pepper
- 1 bayleaf
- 1 cup water
- 1/2 teaspoon dried oregano
- 1 teaspoon white vinegar
- 1 tablespoon parsley or chives (for garnish)

Direction

- In a large pan, heat 3 tbsps. olive oil over medium heat and sauté the garlic for 1-2 minutes.
- Add the tbsp. paprika to the oil, followed by tuna and chickpeas and cook for 3 minutes.
- Add the salt, pepper, water, and the bay leaf. Bring to a boil, then lower heat to med-low and let simmer for 15 minutes, or until all the water has evaporated. Stir occasionally.
- Add 1 tsp white vinegar and oregano, and sprinkle with parsley or chives before serving.

31. Bratball Sub

Serving: Serves 6-8 | Prep: | Cook: | Ready in:

Ingredients

- 2 pieces white bread torn into pieces
- .5 cups milk
- 2 pounds ground pork
- 1 pound ground veal
- 2 teaspoons sugar
- .5 tablespoons ground coriander
- .5 tablespoons ground sage
- .5 teaspoons smoked sweet paprika
- .5 teaspoons nutmeg
- .5 teaspoons mace
- 2 teaspoons salt
- .5 teaspoons pepper
- 1 whole egg, beaten

Direction

- Preheat oven to 400 degrees F
- Mix the milk and the torn up bread in a small bowl. Let soak.
- Hand mix together pork, veal, sugar, coriander, sage, paprika, nutmeg, mace, salt, and pepper. Mix in egg and bread.
- Shape into meatballs (approximately 24) and place on an ungreased sheet pan.
- Place into preheated oven for 20 minutes or until cooked through and light brown.
- Serve on a crusty sub roll with mustard and sauerkraut.

32. Broiled Spicy Steak With Garlic Chips On Gorgonzola Crostini

Serving: Serves 2 | Prep: | Cook: | Ready in:

Ingredients

- 5 tablespoons olive oil, divided
- 4 large cloves of garlic, peeled, smashed and chopped
- 2 steaks, either NY strips with good fat marbling or rib-eye steaks
- 2 tablespoons butter, room temperature
- 1 teaspoon chipotle pepper in adobo sauce, minced
- 4 sprigs cilantro, minced
- 2 slices bread sliced long enough to accomodate the steak
- 1/4 cup Gorgonzola blue cheese
- 1 tablespoon brown sugar
- 1/2 teaspoon coriander
- 1 teaspoon chipotle chili powder
- 1 teaspoon kosher coarse salt
- 1/2 teaspoon freshly ground pepper
- 1/2 teaspoon smoked paprika
- 1 teaspoon dried oregano
- 4 large garlic cloves, peeled and sliced
- pinch sugar

Direction

- Salt the steaks and marinate them in 3 Tablespoons of olive oil and 4 smashed and chopped garlic cloves while the steaks come to room temperature (about 1 hour).
- Make some compound butter by mashing together the butter, chipotle peppers and cilantro. Set aside.
- Prepare the spice rub by combining the brown sugar, coriander, ground chipotle pepper powder, salt, pepper, paprika and oregano together. When the steaks finish marinating, rub the spice mixture into both sides of the steaks, reserving 1/3 of the mixture to sprinkle on the cheese.
- Broil the steaks under the broiler for 6 minutes per side for medium rare with 1-inch thick steaks. While they're broiling, sauté the garlic chips in 2 Tablespoons of olive oil with a pinch of sugar sprinkled on the chips.
- When the steaks are done, remove from the oven. While they rest, broil the bread slices. Once both sides have toasted, put the gorgonzola cheese on the toast, sprinkle on the rest of the spice rub, and put back under the broiler until melted, about 1 minute. Remove from the oven.
- Now you're ready to assemble. Put the steak on the toast allowing the cheese to squeeze out a bit. Sprinkle the garlic chips on top and add a small scoop of compound butter.

33. Bryant Terry's Mustard Green Harissa

Serving: Makes about 1 cup | Prep: | Cook: | Ready in:

Ingredients

- 1 1/4 teaspoons coarse sea salt (divided)
- 1 cup packed chopped mustard greens
- 3 tablespoons extra-virgin olive oil
- 3 cloves garlic, minced
- 1/2 teaspoon coriander seeds
- 1/2 teaspoon cumin seeds
- 1 teaspoon smoked paprika
- 6 tablespoons chopped jalapeño chiles (seeds and ribs removed only if you want it less spicy)
- 1 teaspoon red pepper flakes
- 1/4 teaspoon cayenne pepper
- 1 tablespoon minced cilantro
- 1 tablespoon minced flat-leaf parsley
- 1 tablespoon freshly squeezed lemon juice
- 1 tablespoon red wine vinegar
- 2 teaspoons water

Direction

- Put about 4 cups of water in a medium saucepan and bring to a boil over high heat. Add 1 teaspoon of the salt, then add the mustard greens. Return to a boil and cook uncovered until the greens are wilted, about 2 minutes. Drain well.
- Warm the oil in a small skillet over low heat. Add the garlic and cook, stirring occasionally,

until the garlic starts to turn golden, about 5 minutes. Transfer to a small heatproof bowl and set aside to cool.
- In the same skillet, toast the coriander and cumin, shaking the pan occasionally, until fragrant. Let cool for a few minutes, then transfer to a mortar or spice grinder and grind into a fine powder.
- Transfer the powder to a blender (we found a mini-food processor works best). Add the jalapeños, paprika, red pepper flakes, cayenne, cilantro, parsley, lemon juice, vinegar, water, mustard greens, garlic oil, and the remaining 1/4 teaspoon salt. Puree until smooth.
- Taste and season with more salt if desired. Use immediately or store in a tightly sealed jar in the refrigerator for up to 1 week.

34. Buffalo Cauliflower Tots With Blue Cheese Dipping Sauce

Serving: Makes about 36 tots | Prep: | Cook: | Ready in:

Ingredients

- For the tots
- 1 pound cauliflower, cut into florets
- 1 1/2 cups mozzarella cheese, grated
- 2 eggs, lightly beaten
- 2 green onions, finely chopped
- 1 large garlic clove, minced
- 2-3 tablespoons vinegar-based hot sauce, like Frank's (depending on how hot you want it)
- 1/2 teaspoon smoked paprika
- 1/2 cup panko breadcrumbs
- 1 teaspoon sea salt
- 1/4 teaspoon freshly ground black pepper
- For the blue cheese dipping sauce
- 2 ounces blue cheese, crumbled
- 1/3 cup sour cream
- 2 tablespoons buttermilk
- 1 tablespoon lemon juice
- 1/2 teaspoon freshly ground black pepper
- Pinch sea salt

Direction

- To make the cauliflower tots, fill a large pot (that will fit a steamer basket) with about 2 inches of water and bring to a boil. Place a steamer basket in the bottom on the pan and steam the cauliflower florets until just barely tender, about 3-4 minutes. Spread the steamed cauliflower on a sheet pan and let cool to room temperature.
- Transfer 3/4 of the cauliflower to the bowl of a food processor. Pulse 8 to 10 times until the cauliflower is coarsely chopped, about the size of Israeli couscous. Transfer the chopped cauliflower to a large bowl. Add the remaining quarter of the cauliflower to the food processor and pulse 15 to 20 times until finely ground, almost bordering on being a paste, and add to the rest of the coarsely chopped cauliflower.
- Add the grated cheese, eggs, chopped green onion, garlic, hot sauce, smoked paprika, breadcrumbs, salt and pepper to the cauliflower and stir to combine. Let the mixture sit for 10-15 minutes (this will allow the breadcrumbs to soak up some of the moisture of the rest of the ingredients making it easier to mold into tots).
- While the buffalo cauliflower mixture is resting, preheat the oven to 400°F. Line a baking sheet with parchment and set aside.
- To form the tots, take a tablespoon of the buffalo cauliflower mixture and gently compress it in your hands, rolling it into an oval tot shape. Place the finished tot on your reserved parchment-lined baking sheet. Repeat with the remaining cauliflower.
- Bake the buffalo cauliflower tots until they are golden brown, flipping halfway through cooking, about 25-30 minutes total.
- While the buffalo cauliflower tots are baking, make the blue cheese dipping sauce. Combine all the dipping sauce ingredients in a medium bowl and whisk to combine. Set aside.
- Remove the buffalo cauliflower tots from the oven and let them sit to cool slightly, about 5

minutes. Pile on a platter and serve alongside the blue cheese dipping sauce.

35. Buffalo Style Quinoa Chili

Serving: Serves 2 to 4 | Prep: | Cook: |Ready in:

Ingredients

- 1 tablespoon olive oil
- 1 white onion, diced
- 3 stalks celery, diced
- one 8-ounce can tomato sauce
- one 14-ounce can diced tomatoes
- 1 cup vegetable broth
- 1 cup cooked black beans
- one 14-ounce can hominy
- 1 cup cooked quinoa
- 1/2 cup Frank's red hot sauce, or to taste
- 1 1/2 teaspoons smoked paprika
- 1 1/2 teaspoons cumin
- 1 teaspoon salt
- Freshly ground black pepper
- Blue cheese, for topping

Direction

- Heat the olive oil over medium in a saucepan and, once hot, add the diced onion and celery to the pan. Cook until soft, about 5 minutes.
- Stir in the diced tomatoes, tomato sauce, and vegetable broth. Bring to a boil then reduce to a simmer cook for 15 minutes. Add in black beans, hominy, quinoa, Frank's, smoked paprika, cumin, salt, and pepper. Continue to cook 15 more minutes, until the flavors have melded.
- To serve, ladle chili into broiler-safe bowls. Top with blue cheese and place under broiler until cheese melts, 3 to 5 minutes.

36. Bunny's Broiled Egg Sandwiches

Serving: Serves 4 - 6 | Prep: | Cook: |Ready in:

Ingredients

- 6 large eggs
- 8 ounces cream cheese, room temperature
- 6 slices good bread
- paprika
- salt

Direction

- Hard boil the eggs, and shell them as soon as you can safely handle them. Mash them together with the cream cheese. A potato masher works well.
- Heat the broiler in your oven. Spread the egg mix on the bread. (Crusts are optional, but I like the crunch when you leave them on.) Sprinkle with a little salt and paprika.
- Put the slices on a baking sheet under the broiler until browned on top. Quickly remove from the oven, cut each slice into four triangles, and serve warm.
- OPTIONS: Put 6 cloves of unpeeled garlic in the water with the eggs while they cook. Peel and add the garlic when you mash the egg and cream cheese.1/2 tsp Green Tabasco enhances the flavor, a hotter sauce or more perks it up! For the paprika, use smoked or hot. Just before serving, add dukkah, za'atar... just enough to enhance, not overwhelm. Bunny used white bread. I enjoy using bread with more body and nuts/seeds, etc.

37. Buttermilk Fried Chicken

Serving: Serves 4 | Prep: | Cook: |Ready in:

Ingredients

- For the spice mix:

- 1 teaspoon smoked paprika
- 1 teaspoon dried oregano
- 1 teaspoon dried thyme
- 1 teaspoon dried marjoram
- 1 teaspoon garlic powder
- 1/2 teaspoon freshly ground black pepper
- 2 teaspoons kosher salt
- 4 boneless, skinless chicken thighs (about 1 pound)
- For the flour and buttermilk dredges:
- 1 cup (140 grams) all-purpose flour
- 1 teaspoon cornstarch
- 1/2 teaspoon baking powder
- 1 cup (240 milliliters) buttermilk
- 1 egg
- 4 cups vegetable, canola, or peanut oil, for frying

Direction

- The day before you plan on frying the chicken, whisk together the paprika, oregano, thyme, marjoram, garlic powder, pepper, and salt to form the spice mix. Set aside 1 tablespoon of the spice mix, then sprinkle the rest all over the chicken thighs. Cover the chicken with plastic wrap and refrigerate overnight.
- To fry the chicken, mix together the flour, cornstarch, baking powder, and reserved spice mix in a pie plate or shallow dish.
- Mix together the buttermilk and egg in another pie plate or shallow dish.
- Set up a wire rack over a sheet tray. Fill a large, heavy skillet (I use my 12-inch cast-iron pan) with oil until 3/4-inch high. Set on high heat and bring to 360° F. Preheat the oven to 375° F.
- Dredge the chicken in the buttermilk mixture, then the flour mixture, then the buttermilk mixture again, and finally back into the flour.
- Fry the chicken for 4 to 5 minutes per side, until deep golden brown all over. If the chicken is not fully cooked (the internal temperature should read 165° F), place the chicken on the wire rack and bake for 8 to 10 minutes, or until just cooked through.

38. Cajun Spiced Stuffed Golden Peppers

Serving: Serves 6 | Prep: | Cook: | Ready in:

Ingredients

- 6 very large golden or orange bell peppers
- 1 lb/pkg of hot Italian sausage
- 1 cup cooked chicken, chopped
- 1 cup cooked shrimp (peeled, deveined, no tail--frozen)
- 1 onion chopped
- 2 stalks celery WITH the leaves, chopped
- Tops cut from the bell peppers, chopped
- 2 TBSP minced garlic
- 1 cup cooked spinach
- 1 1/2 cups cooked white rice
- 2 tsp cumin
- 2 tsp red pepper flakes
- 2 TBSP olive oil
- paprika to sprinkle on top
- salt n' pepper to taste

Direction

- PREHEAT oven to 400 degrees. Start a large pot to boil, add a TBSP salt. Cut the tops off the 6 bell peppers and set aside. Drop them 3 at a time into the boiling water for NO MORE THAN 4 minutes. Drain after blanching, run cold water over them, cut out the seeds and middle and toss away, then turn peppers upside down on a towel to dry.
- Add the olive oil to a large skillet and let it start heating. Cut the 5-6 sausages in the pack, into small pieces/slices, then toss in the skillet with the garlic, onion, chopped peppers, and celery, stir fry gently until nearly done, about 10 minutes, on medium heat.
- Add a half cup of warm water to the pan and add the rice--then fold it into the vegie-sausage mix. Add the chicken and the frozen (cooked) shrimp (I use 'small'), then sprinkle the red pepper flakes, Old Bay

Seasoning/Thatcher, and then the salt and pepper to taste. Cover and cook on low to let the rice and other items soak up the water and the flavors--about 5 minutes. Take off the heat and set aside.
- Spay a long glass baking dish with butter spray, then add a 1/4 inch of water. Salt the inside of each bell pepper, stuff with meat-vegie filling, sprinkle with paprika and place carefully into the baking dish. Bake on 400 for 30 minutes, then on 350 for 20 minutes. Peppers should be tender and the filling juicy. Good served with Herb-Roasted Onion-Stuffed Potatoes and Cumin-Spiced Butternut Stir-fry (see my Recipes here).

39. Caldo Gallego (Galician Broth)

Serving: Serves 8 | Prep: | Cook: | Ready in:

Ingredients

- 1 1/2 cups dried white beans
- 1 tablespoon salt
- 1 ham knuckle or 1 ham bone, or 1lb. pork bones
- 1 1/2 teaspoons paprika (preferably Spanish)
- 1/4 teaspoon pepper
- 1 pound potatoes, peeled and diced
- 1 bunch turnip greens, rinsed and coarsely chopped
- 2 spanish chorizos (6.5 oz total), cut into pieces

Direction

- Soak the beans overnight in cold water.
- Rinse beans then add them back to the pot with the pork.
- Cover with 8 1/2 cups of water and season them with the salt, pepper and paprika.
- Bring to a boil, then turn down heat and simmer 1 hour covered. (Skim off foam)
- Remove the pork bones from the broth and add the potatoes, turnips, and chorizo.
- If you like, pull the meat of the bones and add back to the pot.
- Return the pot to a simmer and cook for 30 more minutes.

40. Caldo Verde (Portuguese Soup With Cauliflower)

Serving: Serves 6 to 8 | Prep: 0hours0mins | Cook: 0hours0mins | Ready in:

Ingredients

- 2 pounds cauliflower florets (from 1 medium head)
- 1 teaspoon ground cumin, or to taste
- 1/2 tablespoon smoked paprika
- 2 pinches salt and pepper, plus more to taste
- 2 tablespoons olive oil, plus extra for roasting
- 1 Spanish onion, chopped
- 4 large garlic cloves, minced
- 1/2 teaspoon red pepper flakes
- 8 cups chicken stock
- 1/2 pound smoked turkey kielbasa, sliced (Wellshire Farms brand is particularly good)
- 1 bunch mustard greens, shredded
- 1/4 cup parsley, finely chopped
- 1/4 cup cilantro, finely chopped
- 1/2 lemon, juiced

Direction

- Preheat oven to 450 F. Toss cauliflower florets with cumin, smoked paprika, and liberal amounts of salt, pepper, and olive oil. Spread in a single layer in a roasting pan or baking dish and roast in the oven for 30 minutes.
- Remove florets and set aside. Deglaze the roasting pan with 1 cup of the chicken stock, stirring to scrape up browned bits. Mix in with the remaining stock.
- Sauté the onion in 2 tablespoons of olive oil over medium-medium high heat until tender and translucent and beginning to brown. Add garlic and pepper flakes and sauté until

fragrant, about 30 seconds. Add cauliflower and stock and bring to a boil, then reduce heat and simmer about an hour. Remove from heat and purée.

- Return the puréed soup to low heat. Add sausage and cook about 10 minutes. (You can brown the sausage beforehand if you like.) Add the mustard greens and parsley and simmer another 5 to 10 minutes until the greens soften a bit. Remove from heat. Stir in the cilantro and the lemon juice and season to taste with salt and pepper. Serve with a sprinkle of smoked paprika and a drizzle of olive oil.

41. Carrot And Ginger Butternut Squash Soup

Serving: Serves 6 | Prep: | Cook: |Ready in:

Ingredients

- 1 butternut squash
- 6 carrots
- 1/2 red onion, diced
- 1 tablespoon freshly grated ginger or ginger paste
- 4 cloves of garlic, sliced
- 1 tablespoon turmeric
- 1/2 tablespoon paprika (I used sweet paprika)
- 5 cups vegetable stock
- Kosher salt and ground black pepper to taste

Direction

- Pre-heat oven to 425° F.
- Carefully cut the skin off of the squash and chop it into 1-inch pieces.
- Cut the carrots into 1-inch pieces.
- Place the squash and carrots into a large bowl. Drizzle with 2 tablespoons of olive oil and hit the veggies with some kosher salt and ground black pepper.
- Sprinkle in the turmeric and the paprika.
- Cover and toss to evenly coat the veggies.

- Place the veggies onto a large baking tray, spaced out, and bake for approx. 30 minutes or until they are tender (test with a fork).
- Remove the veggies from the oven and set aside.
- In a large stock pot, heat 1 tablespoon of olive oil over moderate heat.
- Add the garlic and onions. Sauté until garlic is fragrant and onions are slightly translucent.
- Add the ginger, and sauté for another minute or so, stirring well.
- Finally, add the roasted vegetables to the stockpot.
- Add the vegetable stock, and bring to a simmer for approx. 5 minutes--just to let those flavors hang out for a bit!
- Now, time to puree. If you're using an immersion blender, go to town in the stockpot. If not, transfer some of the contents of the stockpot into a blender in batches, pureeing bit by bit until the soup has a smooth and silky texture. I always have a large bowl handy so I have somewhere to put the pureed soup.
- Serve it up! Optional: garnish with raw pepitas and/or plain Greek yogurt or sour cream.

42. Cauliflower Miso Soup

Serving: Serves 4-6 | Prep: | Cook: |Ready in:

Ingredients

- olive oil
- 8 garlic cloves, smashed
- 4 large shallots, peeled and quartered
- a few sprigs of sage
- 1/4 cup sherry vinegar, plus more for garnish
- 1 head cauliflower
- 3 carrots, roughly chopped
- a few dashes ground coriander
- a few dashes paprika
- 3 tablespoons white miso
- grapeseed oil
- scallions

Direction

- In a large stock pot add enough olive oil to coat the bottom of it. Warm it over medium heat and then add your smashed garlic cloves, quartered shallots and a sprig of sage. Sprinkle with a few pinches of salt. Allow to heat for 10-15 minutes, until everything is tender and browning. Remove the sprig of sage.
- Break up the head of cauliflower into small flowerettes and add to the pot with the carrots. Turn the heat up to high and add a few dashes of the coriander and paprika; stir. Once everything is sizzling, add 1/4 cup of the sherry vinegar, give it another few stirs and then add 6 cups cold water.
- Bring the pot to a boil and then turn it down a bit to let everything simmer for 30-45 minutes, or until the cauliflower is very tender.
- Turn off the heat and let cool a few minutes. Using an immersion blender (or working in small batches carefully with a standing blender), blend the soup continuously until very smooth and creamy. Add in three heaping tablespoons of white miso and blend well into the soup. It may take several minutes to reach the smoothest consistency. Heat the soup back up while you make the garnish.
- In a separate, small/shallow pan, add a 1/4" layer of grapeseed (or other high heat) oil and heat up. Add a sprig of sage and slivered scallions. Fry briefly until golden. Drain on a paper towel.
- Put soup in bowl, top with crispy sage and scallions, and drizzle with olive oil and a few drops sherry vinegar.

43. Cauliflower Paprikash

Serving: Serves 4 | Prep: 0hours15mins | Cook: 0hours45mins | Ready in:

Ingredients

- 1 head cauliflower
- 1/4 cup extra-virgin olive oil
- Kosher salt, to taste
- 1 large yellow onion, finely chopped
- 2 red bell peppers, finely chopped
- 5 cloves garlic, minced or Microplaned
- 1 tablespoon unsalted butter
- 1/4 cup paprika (mixed to taste; I did 3 tablespoons smoked, 1 tablespoon hot)
- Ground cayenne, to taste
- 3 tablespoons all-purpose flour
- 1 (15-ounce) can crushed tomatoes
- 2 cups water
- 3/4 cup whole-milk Greek yogurt, room-temperature
- Chopped, flat-leaf parsley, for garnish
- Buttered egg noodles, for serving

Direction

- Halve the cauliflower lengthwise (from flowery top to stem). Halve it again lengthwise. Trim any leaves from the bottom but leave the core intact. Add 3 tablespoons olive oil to a very wide, high-sided pan/pot. (This will be your one-stop shop for searing, then making the stew.) Set the pan over medium-high heat. Add the cauliflower quarters and brown on all sides (even the flowery tops!). We're just going for the color here — we don't need it to cook through. Transfer to a plate and sprinkle with salt. Leave the pan on the heat!
- Add another 1 tablespoon olive oil to the pan. Add the onion and bell pepper. Season with salt and stir. Sauté, stirring occasionally, for about 15 minutes, until the vegetables are soft and starting to caramelize. Add the garlic and stir. Cook for about 1 minute until fragrant. Add the butter. Let melt, then stir to incorporate. Add the paprika and cayenne and stir. Cook for a couple minutes to toast the spices. Add the flour and stir. Add the tomatoes and stir. Add the water and stir.
- Drop the heat to medium-low and nestle the cauliflower quarters in the paprikash sauce. Cover the pan. Simmer until the cauliflower is as tender as you like it. Season the sauce to

taste with salt. Just before serving, stir in the yogurt. Garnish with parsley. Serve with buttered egg noodles.

44. Cauliflower Fritters With Smoked Salmon, Prosciutto Herbed Dressing.

Serving: Makes six servings | Prep: | Cook: |Ready in:

Ingredients

- For the fritters
- 1/2 medium size steamed cauliflower head
- 1 lightly beaten large egg
- 1/2 cup flour
- 1/2 cup Parmesan cheese
- 1 cup chopped parsley
- 1 minced clove of garlic
- 1 teaspoon kosher salt
- 1 teaspoon pepper
- 1/2 teaspoon smoked paprika
- 3 tablespoons water
- 1 tablespoon Olive oil
- 3 slices of smoked salmon
- 3 slices of prosciutto.
- for the vinaigrette
- 1 tablespoon red wine vinager
- 3 tablespoons extra virgin olive oil
- 1 tablespoon Dijon mustard
- 1/2 teaspoon Kosher salt
- 1/2 teaspoon pepper
- 1 teaspoon herbs of Provence

Direction

- In a large bowl mash or cut cauliflower leaving it with a coarse texture small little pieces add flour, beaten egg, Parmesan cheese, parsley, scallions, salt, pepper, paprika to the cauliflower bowl and mix all together with a wooden spoon or with your hands better.
- Add the water little by little as you are mixing until batter will have a thick texture, it always work with 3 tbsp. of water which is 3/4 of a 1/4 cup. The point is having a thick batter which will allow to shape the fritters with your hands.
- On a skillet heat up one tbsp. of olive oil on a medium heat and add fritters. It will take about three minutes for each side, turn and cook for another three minutes. Following the amount of the ingredients on this recipe it will allow six fritters.
- In a small bowl add red wine vinegar, olive oil, Dijon, salt, pepper, herbs of Provence and whisk all together until emulsifies.
- Place fritters on a plate and top each differently, some with slices of smoked salmon and others with slices of prosciutto. It can be serve with a salad or steam vegetables (optional)
- Gently drizzle the vinaigrette over fritters just enough for each to get that herbed acid touch.

45. Cevapcici With Lime Mayo Dip

Serving: Serves 6 | Prep: | Cook: |Ready in:

Ingredients

- 1 pound lean ground beef
- 1 pound ground lamb
- 2 large cloves garlic, minced
- 1/4 cup onion, minced
- 2 tablespoons finely chopped fresh parsley
- 2 tablespoons finely chopped fresh basil leaves
- 2 teaspoons sweet paprika
- 1 teaspoon salt
- 1/2 teaspoon freshly ground black pepper
- 2 eggs, lightly beaten
- 1/2 cup mayonnaise
- 1/4 cup sour cream
- zest of 1 lime
- 3 tablespoons freshly squeezed lime juice
- 1 teaspoon sweet paprika
- Pinch black pepper

- 3 tablespoons olive oil

Direction

- In a large bowl mix together the first 10 ingredients with your hands until well combined
- With your hands shape meat mixture into long 1 inch thick rolls and cut into 3-inch long strips, making the cigar shaped cevapcici meatballs, set aside for a few minutes
- In a small bowl blend together mayonnaise, sour cream, lime zest and juice, paprika and pepper, then refrigerate until ready to serve as a dipping sauce for the cevapcici
- In a large frying pan heat olive oil on medium heat and cook meatballs, in batches, for about 10 minutes, turning often to brown evenly on all sides
- Serve with dipping sauce or with your favourite salad

46. Chef Ken's Indian Cauliflower Steaks With Tomato Sauce

Serving: Serves 3 | Prep: | Cook: | Ready in:

Ingredients

- 3 tablespoons olive oil, divided
- 1/2 large onion, 1/2" dice
- 1 teaspoon salt, divided
- 2 teaspoons fresh ginger, chopped or grated
- 1/2 tablespoon ground coriander
- 1/2 tablespoon ground cumin
- 1/2 tablespoon paprika (not smoked)
- 1 cinnamon stick
- 3 bay leaves
- 28 ounces can diced tomatoes
- 1 large cauliflower (3 lbs+)
- 1/2 teaspoon black sesame seeds, optional

Direction

- Preheat grill or grill pan on medium-high. (Alternatively, but you will lose the smoky flavor, preheat the oven to 400 degrees.)
- Meanwhile, heat 1 Tbsp. EVOO over medium-low heat in a medium pot. Add onion and garlic and sauté until translucent, about 5 minutes.
- Add 1/2 tsp salt, ginger, coriander, cumin, paprika, cinnamon and bay leaves to the pot. Stir to coat the onions and garlic. Then add the tomatoes with its juice. Simmer for 30 minutes (or more if you have the time, it will only improve).
- Cut 3 steaks from the cauliflower from the center of the head where the core is the thickest.
- Brush one side of each steak with 1 tsp EVOO and sprinkle with a pinch of salt. Grill oil-side down 2-4 minutes, depending on the heat of your grill. Brush the top of the steak with another 1 tsp EVOO while it's grilling. Turn over gently and grill the second side. (If roasting in the oven, brush both sides with remaining 2 Tbsp. EVOO and sprinkle with 1/2 tsp salt. Roast 15-20 minutes, turning halfway, until browned on both sides.)
- Remove and sprinkle with black sesame seeds, if using.
- To serve, spoon tomato sauce onto a platter or individual plate/bowl and top with the cauliflower steak (or vice versa).

47. Cherry Pie Beef Ribs

Serving: Serves 4 | Prep: | Cook: | Ready in:

Ingredients

- 2 pounds boneless country style beef ribs
- 1 tablespoon oil
- 20 ounces canned cherry pie filling
- 1 tablespoon Worcestershire sauce
- 2 tablespoons dijon mustard
- 1 tablespoon fresh minced ginger
- 1 tablespoon smoked paprika

- 12 ounces chopped red and yellow bell peppers
- 6 garlic cloves minced
- 1 teaspoon Beef Flavored Better Than Bouillon
- 1.5 cups water

Direction

- Start with heating a cast iron pan or other pan for browning meat over medium high heat with 1 Tbsp. oil (I use grape seed). Season two pounds of country style beef ribs with salt.
- Place the ribs in the heated pan and brown on all sides, giving it three or so minutes on each side. Once they're browned, place them in your pressure cooker (or slow cooker if you're Crock-Potting) along with 12 ounces quartered mini peppers, 1 Tbsp. minced fresh ginger, and 6 minced garlic.
- Next, in a small bowl, combine 20 ounces of cherry pie filling, 1 Tbsp. Worcestershire sauce, 2 Tbsp. Dijon mustard, 1 Tbsp. paprika, 1 tsp beef Better than Bouillon and 1½ cups water. Mix that together so it's incorporated then pour over the beef and veggies in your pressure cooker.
- If using an electric pressure cooker, cook on 'high' for 22 minutes. If using a Crock-Pot, cook on 'high' for 4 to 5 hours or 'low' for 6 to 8 hours.
- You'll know it's done because the beef will be fork tender and the sauce will be slightly thickened. Feel free to add some salt to the sauce if it needs extra seasoning. Serve the ribs with cherries, peppers and doused in sauce. Serve extra sauce for ladling on the side.

48. Chiccoli Shirataki

Serving: Serves 4-6 | Prep: | Cook: | Ready in:

Ingredients

- 2 Skinless Chicken Breasts - cut into small cubes
- 1/2 pound Broccoli Florets - steamed
- 1/2 Medium Sweet Onion - Diced (Vidalia if available)
- 4 Strips Thick Cut Turkey Bacon - Diced
- 2 tablespoons Minced Garlic
- 3 teaspoons Dried Oregano
- 2 teaspoons Red Pepper Flake
- 2 teaspoons Smoked Paprika
- 2 cups Pinot Grigio
- 1 pound Shirataki Spaghetti
- Olive Oil
- Salt, Pepper, Water

Direction

- Place chicken breasts in sealable container and add tablespoon garlic, teaspoon each of oregano, smoked paprika, black pepper and red pepper flake. Refrigerate at least one hour.
- Coat medium skillet lightly in olive oil and warm; add onion and garlic - slowly sweat onions; add turkey bacon and allow to cook fully and slowly. Bring to medium high heat and add vino. Allow to reduce.
- Prepare separate skillet the same and add chicken over high medium heat allowing to brown while cooking fully; add to other skillet.
- Briefly add broccoli florets to skillet vacated by chicken and allow to soak up the flavor; add to the other skillet.
- Rinse and drain shirataki noodles and add to skillet vacated by broccoli; cook 3-4 minutes. Salt and Pepper to taste and remove to half of serving platter; add contents of other skillet to other half and drizzle remaining flavour over shirataki. Sprinkle with parm/reg and parsley. Serve and enjoy.

49. Chick Pea Hummus

Serving: Serves 8 | Prep: | Cook: | Ready in:

Ingredients

- 2 cans chick peas, reserve the liquid from one can
- 1/3 cup lemon juice
- 1/3 cup sour cream
- 4 garlic cloves
- 1 1/2 teaspoons salt
- 1/2 teaspoon black pepper
- 1/2 teaspoon cumin
- 1 tablespoon olive oil
- 1/2 teaspoon paprika
- 1/2 teaspoon Mrs. Dash onion & herb
- 1/2 teaspoon Mrs. Dash garlic & herb
- 1/2 teaspoon Badia garlic & parsley

Direction

- Place the chick peas, reserved liquid, lemon juice, garlic, salt, pepper, and cumin in the blender and mix until creamy.
- Pour hummus into a medium bowl, and drizzle with olive oil, then sprinkle with paprika, and Mrs. Dash seasonings.
- Chill for an hour or two; serve with pita bread or tortilla chips.

50. Chicken Chorizo Meatballs

Serving: Makes about 3 dozen small meatballs | Prep: | Cook: | Ready in:

Ingredients

- 1 tablespoon olive oil or unsalted butter
- 1 medium sweet onion, finely diced
- 4 scallions, thinly sliced
- 3-4 garlic cloves, minced
- 1 large egg
- 1 pound ground chicken
- 10 ounces Mexican (soft) chorizo, removed from casing
- 1 cup finely crushed tortilla chips (preferably unsalted, but salted will work too)
- 1 teaspoon smoked paprika
- 1/2 teaspoon salt (if using unsalted chips, increase to 1 tsp)

Direction

- In a large skillet, heat oil or butter over medium heat. Add onion and cook, stirring frequently, for 8-10 minutes, or until the onions are soft and starting to turn golden. Add scallions and garlic and cook for another 30 seconds to a minute, or until the garlic is fragrant. Remove from the heat and let cool.
- In a large mixing bowl, beat egg thoroughly. Add the cooled onion mixture, ground chicken, chorizo, tortilla chips, smoked paprika, and salt. Mix until thoroughly combined. Cover the bowl with plastic wrap and refrigerate for 30 minutes to let the mixture firm up a bit.
- Preheat the oven to 325° F, and line a baking sheet with aluminum foil. Use lightly damp hands to shape the mixture into 1-inch meatballs. (You will likely need to wash off your hands and re-dampen them several times during the process.) Lay the meatballs out on the baking sheet. Bake for 30-35 minutes, or until the meatballs are cooked through.
- Remove the meatballs from the oven and transfer them to a paper towel-lined plate to drain (they'll start sticking to the foil as they cool, so work quickly). After a few seconds on the paper, transfer the meatballs to a serving platter. Serve warm, with toothpicks or cocktail forks for easy eating.

51. Chicken Flautas

Serving: Makes 6-8 servings | Prep: | Cook: | Ready in:

Ingredients

- Prep the Chicken:
- 3 tablespoons unsalted butter
- 1/4 cup organic unbleached flour
- 1 cup chicken stock (preferably homemade)
- 1 tablespoon chopped flat leaf parsley (or cilantro, if you prefer)
- 1 tablespoon fresh lemon juice

- 1 teaspoon grated onion
- Dash each of nutmeg and paprika
- fine sea salt and freshly ground pepper to taste
- 1 1/2 cups diced cooked chicken
- 12 flour tortillas
- Crème Fraîche or Sour Cream
- Avocado Sauce
- 2 ripe avocadoes (I prefer Hass)
- 1/2 teaspoon grated onion
- 1/2 cup sour cream or plain yogurt
- 1 teaspoon fresh lime juice
- 10 drops Tabasco sauce
- Pinch fine sea salt

Direction

- Prep the Chicken:
- Melt butter and blend in flour to make a light roux. (Be sure to cook the flour for a couple of minutes.) Add salt and stock. Cook, stirring until thick. Add parsley, lemon juice, onion, paprika, nutmeg and a dash of freshly ground pepper. Stir in chicken. Cool slightly.
- To Assemble Flautas, Place a heaping tablespoon of mixture on tortilla. Roll tightly, and fasten with a toothpick. Fry in deep hot fat for 1 or 2 minutes until tortilla is crisp and brown. Serve with a dollop of Crème Fraîche or sour cream and this sauce:
- Avocado Sauce
- Peel, seed and smash avocados. Add all the other ingredients. Mix until smooth. Spoon sauce over the cooked Flautas.
- Teacher's Tip: You could also make this dish with leftover Thanksgiving Turkey. No one would ever guess it was "leftovers."

52. Chicken Mustard Croquettes

Serving: Serves 4 | Prep: | Cook: |Ready in:

Ingredients

- Chicken Croquettes
- 1 pound chicken meat, raw, boneless and without skin
- 2 tablespoons chopped parsley
- 1 teaspoon grated fresh ginger
- 3 small shallots chopped finely
- 1 garlic clove
- 3 tablespoons Extra Virgin Olive Oil
- 2 teaspoons granulated Mustard
- 1 cup bread without the crust
- 1/4 cup whole milk
- salt
- pepper
- 1/2 cup bread crumbs
- 1 egg whole
- Vegetable oil for frying
- Honey Mustard Mayonnaise
- 3/4 cup mayonnaise
- 2 tablespoons wholegrain mustard
- 2 tablespoons honey, clear and runny
- 1/4 cup fresh cream
- salt
- pepper
- 1 pinch paprika

Direction

- For the Honey Mustard Mayonnaise: Whip the mustard with the honey and the mayonnaise. Add the cream and season with the paprika, salt and freshly grated pepper. Cover and chill.
- For the Chicken croquettes: Chop the shallots very finely. Peel the garlic, cut in half, remove the green inside, and chop very finely.
- In a sauté pan, add the olive oil and the onions and fry until translucid. Add the garlic, fry an extra 1 minute and remove from the heat. Let cool completely.
- Cut the inside of the bread (without the crust) in small pieces and measure 1 cup. Put in a bowl and add the milk. Mix with your hands until the milk is totally absorbed.
- Cut the chicken meat in small pieces making sure there are no bones. In a food processor pulse the chicken meat until is ground. Add the mustard, bread with milk, chopped parsley, cooled sautéed shallots and garlic,

and grated fresh ginger. Add some salt and freshly ground pepper. Pulse until combined. Check the seasoning. Chill for 30 minutes.
- Beat 1 whole egg in a bowl. Put the breadcrumbs in a plate. Make the croquettes taking some chicken mince and giving them a shape of a cylinder 1 1/2 inches long by 3/4 inches thick.
- Roll the croquettes in the egg and then in the bread crumbs. At this point you can chill them and wait until serving time, or freeze them in a tray and when frozen put them in a plastic bag.
- Heat the oil to medium temperature (the oil should be deep enough to come to half the height of the croquettes). Fry the croquettes slowly as you need to make sure the inside is well cooked. When golden on one side turn them over and continue frying until golden on the other side.
- Remove from the oil and put on kitchen paper towel to absorb excess oil.
- Serve with a green salad, mashed potatoes and the Honey Mustard Mayonnaise on the side.
- The croquettes can also be serve at room temperature for a picnic or made smaller (half the size) and served as finger food.

53. Chicken Nuggets With Warm Kimchi Bacon Ranch Dip

Serving: Serves 6-8 | Prep: | Cook: |Ready in:

Ingredients

- Fried Chicken Nuggets (Regular & Spicy)
- 1 tablespoon dijon mustard
- 1/4 cup pickle juice (or substitute: 1/4 c. vinegar, 1 tbsp. honey, 1 tbsp. Kosher salt, and 2 tsp. black pepper)
- 2 tablespoons extra virgin olive oil
- 2 pounds boneless chicken breasts, cut into 1 1/2-inch pieces
- 5 ounces Napa cabbage kimchi (for Spicy Nuggets)
- 1 cup rice flour (+ 1/2 cup for first coating)
- 1 tablespoon Kosher salt
- 1 tablespoon black pepper
- 1 cup rolled oats
- 1/4 cup onion powder
- 3 tablespoons garlic powder
- 1/2 tablespoon smoked paprika
- 1 tablespoon brown sugar
- 1 teaspoon gochugaru, Korean red pepper flakes (for Spicy Nuggets)
- 1/4 teaspoon ground cayenne pepper (for Spicy Nuggets)
- 3 eggs
- 1 cup vegetable oil
- Kimchi Bacon Ranch Dip
- 5 ounces napa cabbage kimchi (reserved from the Spicy Nuggets recipe, if they were priorly made)
- 4 strips of bacon, cooked & broken-up
- 1/2 cup sour cream
- 1/2 cup mayonnaise
- 2 tablespoons fresh chives, minced
- 1 teaspoon white vinegar
- 1 teaspoon runny honey or agave nectar
- 1/2 teaspoon onion powder
- 1/4 teaspoon mustard powder
- Kosher salt
- black pepper
- 1 pinch fresh dill or parsley, chopped (optional)

Direction

- Fried Chicken Nuggets (Regular & Spicy)
- In a small bowl, mix together the mustard, pickle juice, and extra virgin olive oil. Take your cut chicken pieces and place them in a resealable plastic storage bag. Pour the marinade on top, seal the bag, and massage the meat to fully coat the chicken pieces. Store in the refrigerator overnight, or for at least 6-hours. FOR SPICY NUGGETS: Drop the Napa cabbage kimchi into the resealable plastic storage bag with the chicken pieces, seal the bag, massage the meat together with the

kimchi. Store in the refrigerator overnight, or for at least 6 hours.
- Once the nuggets have marinated, take out a medium-sized bowl and drop in 1/2 cup of rice flour. Season it well with salt & pepper, and whisk it together. Transfer the nuggets to the bowl and coat them lightly. (For spicy nuggets, separate the kimchi from the chicken.)
- In a food processor, combine the rice flour mix, rolled oats, onion powder, garlic powder, smoked paprika, brown sugar, Kosher salt, and pepper. For spicy nuggets, add in the gochugaru and cayenne pepper as well!) Pulse until the mixture is very fine and combined. Transfer the oat-rice flour mixture into a bowl (or rimmed plate), and set aside.
- In another medium-size bowl, whisk together the eggs with a splash of water to create your egg wash, and set aside.
- Set up your dredging stations, and dredge in this order: rice flour-coated chicken > egg wash > seasoned oat-rice flour > clean plate. Remove a few pieces of chicken at a time from the flour, dip each into the egg wash, then the oat-rice flour, gently pressing the crumbs into the chicken, and set on a clean plate. Repeat steps with the remaining chicken pieces.
- In a large frying pan, heat the vegetable oil over medium-high heat for approximately 8-minutes. To test and see if the oil is hot enough, you can take a speck of leftover egged-breading and put it in the oil. If it sizzles / bubbles, it should be ready for frying.
- Carefully add the chicken nuggets to the pan in batches. Don't crowd them! Cook the nuggets on each side for about 3-4 minutes each or flipping as the edges look crisped up, using a spatula or chopsticks to flip them. Once the nuggets are cooked, transfer the chicken nuggets to a paper-towel-lined plate, or you can do as I do sometimes, and drop them to cool on a cooling rack with paper towels underneath.
- Season with a little salt on top while the nuggets are still hot, let them cool for a few minutes. Serve with Kimchi Bacon Ranch Dip!

- Kimchi Bacon Ranch Dip
- Lightly coat a small frying pan with olive oil, and set it over medium heat. Sauté the Napa cabbage kimchi for about 5-minutes, or until the kimchi is softened and the liquid reduced by at least half. Lower the heat, and mix in about a teaspoon of the sour cream to the sautéed kimchi, letting it continue to cook for about another minute. Turn the heat off, transfer the sautéed kimchi to a plate and let it cool for about 10-minutes.
- In a food processor, combine the kimchi, cooked bacon pieces, sour cream, mayonnaise, chives, onion powder, honey or agave nectar, vinegar (and chopped parsley and /or dill, if you decided to use them!) and season with salt and pepper. Blitz the mixture until it reaches a smooth texture, remembering to stop and taste frequently and adjusting seasonings however if you'd like them to be.
- Serve with your fresh-made chicken nuggets, or however you'd like it! Enjoy!

54. Chicken That Fancies Itself Spanish With Lemons, Onions & Olives

Serving: Serves 4-6 | Prep: | Cook: | Ready in:

Ingredients

- 1 whole chicken, about 4 pounds, cut into parts
- 1/2 cup plus 1 tablespoon flour
- 1/4 cup grated pecorino
- 3 teaspoons smoked paprika
- 1/4 cup olive oil
- Salt and freshly ground black pepper
- 3 medium lemons
- 2 large yellow onions, sliced
- 1 large fennel bulb, halved and sliced
- 12 whole garlic cloves, peeled
- 3/4 cup pitted green olives
- 1 pinch ground cinnamon

- 1 cup whole peeled tomatoes, crushed
- 1 cup white wine
- 1 bunch cilantro, roughly chopped

Direction

- Heat the oven to 425 degrees. Combine 1/2 cup of the flour, pecorino and 1 teaspoon of the smoked paprika in a large bowl. Heat the olive oil in a large, heavy pot (a big Dutch oven, perhaps?) over medium-high heat. Dry the chicken parts thoroughly with paper towels and sprinkle generously with salt and pepper on all sides. Dredge the chicken in the seasoned flour and then place in your pot in batches. Allow the chicken to thoroughly brown, about 5 minutes per side. Don't crowd the pan! Remove the chicken to a plate and repeat until all of your chicken pieces are golden and crispy-looking.
- Quarter the lemons, but zest one of them first; reserve the zest. (If your lemons have a thick pith, you'll want to zest all 3 and then juice them, discarding the pith; this will help you avoid a bitter sauce.) Add the onion, quartered lemons (or zest of 2 lemons and the juice of all 3), fennel, garlic, green olives, the remaining 2 teaspoons of smoked paprika, and cinnamon to the pot; cook until softened, golden, and overall mushy-looking, about 10 minutes. Taste for salt. Sprinkle the mixture with the remaining tablespoon of flour and stir over the heat for two minutes. Add the tomatoes and the wine and bring to a boil -- let bubble away for a minute or two. Add the lemon zest.
- Place the chicken pieces back into the pot, skin side up, along with any drippings from the plate. Poke the onion/fennel/garlic/olive mixture so it surrounds the chicken on all sides. Place in the oven, uncovered, and bake for 30 minutes, or until the chicken is cooked through.
- Garnish with cilantro. Serve warm. Delicious!

55. Chickpea Chili

Serving: Serves 4-6 (can be multiplied) | Prep: | Cook: | Ready in:

Ingredients

- 1 tablespoon canola oil
- 2 large sweet onions, diced
- 2 large cloves garlic, minced
- 1-2 jalapeño peppers, minced
- 1 medium eggplant, peeled and diced (discard big clumps of seeds)
- 4 cups cooked chick peas (see headnote)
- kosher salt
- chili powder (I like Penzey's Chili 3000)
- ground cumin
- ground ancho chiles
- 1 can fire-roasted tomatoes (I use Muir Glen)
- 1 bottle very dark beer
- 1/2 cup full-bodied red wine
- ground coriander
- dried oregano
- Dutch process cocoa powder
- Smoked paprika
- dark brown sugar
- fresh ground black pepper
- wedges of lime for serving
- sour cream and shredded cheddar cheese for serving if desired
- (optional) Tabasco sauce

Direction

- In a large Dutch oven, heat canola oil over medium heat. Add onions, garlic, and jalapeño pepper and a large pinch of kosher salt. Sauté, stirring frequently, until softened. Stir in eggplant, cover, and let eggplant cook with other vegetables for 10-15 minutes, stirring occasionally.
- Stir in 1 1/2 teaspoon cumin, 1 tablespoon of chili powder and 1/2 teaspoon of ground ancho chiles. Stir in chickpeas, making sure all surfaces are covered with spices. Turn heat to very low, cover pot, and let cook for 30 minutes, stirring occasionally.

- Pour in tomatoes, beer, wine, another teaspoon of cumin, 2 teaspoons of chili powder, a teaspoon of smoked paprika, a teaspoon of coriander, a tablespoon of cocoa powder, a teaspoon of kosher salt, 1/8-1/4 cup dark brown sugar and 1 teaspoon dried oregano. Bring chili to boil, then reduce heat and let simmer uncovered for another 1/2 hour.
- Turn heat off and let chili sit until about 1/2 hour before ready to serve. Taste it and adjust the seasoning to your taste. When ready to serve, raise heat gently to boil, then reduce heat and simmer chili for another 10-15 minutes. Taste and add salt, fresh ground black pepper, and other seasoning (more chili powder and /or cumin) to taste.
- Serve with a squeeze of lime. (I confess to liking sharp cheddar cheese and sour cream with my chili--it's your choice.) You can pass around some Tabasco sauce for more heat if you like.

56. Chickpea, Tomato, And Roasted Red Pepper Skillet Breakfast

Serving: Serves 2 | Prep: | Cook: | Ready in:

Ingredients

- 1.5 cups chickpeas, drained (1 can)
- 1 teaspoon paprika
- 2 tablespoons fresh thyme leaves
- 2 tomatoes, quartered
- 1/4 cup roasted red peppers
- 1/2 onion, diced
- 1 tablespoon olive oil
- 3 eggs
- 1/2 avocado
- 1/2 lemon, juiced
- 1 dash salt and pepper, to taste

Direction

- Get the grill in the oven nice and hot.
- In a small oven-proof skillet, saute chickpeas, onion, thyme and paprika in olive oil on the stove. Once the onions are soft, add the tomatoes and peppers for a minute, stirring into the spices and seasoning with salt, pepper, and lemon.
- Place under the grill in the oven for about 10 minutes, until tomatoes are getting brown edges.
- Remove and crack eggs over the dish. Bake for another 5 minutes, until the whites are cooked but the yolks are still soft.
- Serve with avocado and toast.

57. Chili Con Nikki (with Brisket, Coffee & Chocolate)

Serving: Serves 6-8 | Prep: | Cook: | Ready in:

Ingredients

- 3 pounds beef brisket, trimmed and sliced into 1 inch thick pieces
- 1 cup good coffee
- good pour of olive oil
- 2 teaspoons ground cumin
- 2 teaspoons smoked paprika
- 2 teaspoons dried oregano
- 1 teaspoon coriander seed
- 2 red onions, peeled and diced
- 3-4 fresh chiles (small green ones are good)
- 2-3 cinnamon sticks
- 4 gloves of garlic, crushed
- 1 28 oz can chopped tomatoes
- 2 tablespoons brown sugar
- 2-3 ounces dark chocolate
- 1 red pepper seeded and chopped
- 1 yellow pepper seeded and chopped
- 1 can beans (kidney, butter or pinto) drained
- sour cream
- chopped parsley or coriander

Direction

- Make coffee. Put oil in large casserole pot (with lid) and gently heat on low. Add cumin, paprika, oregano, coriander seed and onions. Fry for 10 minutes, until the onions soften. Seed and chop your fresh chiles and add to onions and spices.
- Add the meat and stir well to coat with onion and spices, and then add cinnamon sticks, garlic, salt and pepper, coffee, tomatoes, brown sugar and chocolate. Cover casserole dish with lid and simmer for about 3 1/2 hours, stirring occasionally.
- After a few hours break up the meat and pull it apart using a fork. Add the chopped peppers and beans. Leave to simmer for 30 minutes with the lid off until the meat is completely falling apart and delicious. If mixture gets too dry, add a little beef stock. If too runny, leave it to cook a bit longer until the liquid reduces.
- Ideally leave in fridge overnight, bring back to room temperature and heat through before serving. Sprinkle with fresh herbs and serve with rice, corn chips, corn bread and sour cream. Beer and Tequila optional!

58. Chili Stuffed Bell Peppers With Melted Cheese

Serving: Serves 8 | Prep: | Cook: | Ready in:

Ingredients

- Three Bean Chili
- 1 large onion
- 3 cloves garlic
- 2 tablespoons olive oil
- 1 pound ground beef
- 2 teaspoons paprika
- 2 teaspoons cumin
- 2 teaspoons cayenne pepper
- 2 tablespoons cocoa powder
- 4-6 tomatoes diced (or 2 cans diced tomatoes)
- 7 ounces tomato paste
- 1 bell pepper, chopped
- 14 ounces can black beans, drained and rinsed
- 14 ounces can red kidney beans, drained and rinsed
- 14 ounces can white beans, drained and rinsed
- 6 cups water
- 1/2 cup brewed coffee
- salt and pepper to taste
- cilantro as garnish (optional)
- Chili Stuffed Bell Peppers
- 8 red bell peppers
- 8 slices of white cheese

Direction

- Three Bean Chili
- Place a rather large pot on over medium heat and add in the olive oil. Next, add in onion and garlic and allow to brown, stirring occasionally. The chilli pepper next, remembering to stir so nothing burns. You can remove the chili pepper if you don't want it to be too spicy, or you can remove the seeds before you add it to the pot.
- Toss the beef in and allow it to brown, again stirring occasionally. Once the beef is browned and mixed with the onion, garlic and chilli add in the paprika, cumin, cayenne and cocoa powder and stir, allowing it to cook about a minute before adding in the tomatoes and paste. Mix well.
- Bring the pot to a boil, reduce to a simmer (just at or under medium heat) cover and allow to stew for at the very least an hour, but I'd let it cook a couple of hours, stirring occasionally to keep it from sticking and adding water as it cooks to keep it wet like a stew but not drowning like a soup. The longer it cooks or sits, the more the flavors meld and the better it tastes (second day chilli is always better!).
- Salt and pepper should be added about 10 minutes before you plan to eat, this will keep it from being too salty as the water evaporates.
- Chili Stuffed Bell Peppers
- Take a knife and insert it into the top of the pepper, cutting around the stem and remove

it. Wash out the little seeds and drain the water from the pepper as you prep the other peppers. Place the peppers on a baking sheet with the hole up.
- Spoon in the chilli until it reaches the top of the pepper, top with a cheese slice or shredded cheese. Rinse and repeat until all of your peppers are done. Bake in a preheated oven at 350F (180C) for about 20-30 minutes. Remove and allow to cool slightly before serving.

59. Chipotle And Duck Confit Deviled Eggs With Microgreens

Serving: Serves 8 (2 halves each) | Prep: | Cook: |Ready in:

Ingredients

- 8 eggs (boiled, cut in half, and yolks removed)
- 1/3 cup mayonnaise
- 2 tablespoons Hickory Farms chipotle ranch sauce
- Spice Lab's smoked chipotle sea salt (to taste)
- 1/2 teaspoon GOOD paprika
- 1 5oz D'Artagnan duck leg confit, shredded
- microgreens

Direction

- In a bowl, break the yolks up as fine as possible. Then mix in the chipotle ranch, mayonnaise, paprika, and sea salt to taste. Mix well until very smooth. Scoop out into a sandwich or piping bag for filling.
- Shred the meat from the duck leg and don't trim off any of the fat. It tastes great and helps the meat crisp. On medium high heat, warm the shreds through until just crispy and place on a plate to drain/cool.
- Lay out your egg halves and fill the cavities with the yolk filling followed by a few pieces of duck meat. Sprinkle some extra paprika or smoked chipotle sea salt over top if desired. I chose paprika.
- When you're serving them, add a few pieces of micro greens to each plate.

60. Chorizo And Black Beans, "Meanwhile" Style

Serving: Makes nearly 3 quarts | Prep: | Cook: |Ready in:

Ingredients

- 1 pound / 453 grams black beans
- 12 ounces / 340 grams / 3 medium Spanish-style chorizo
- 1 large onion
- 6 cloves of garlic
- Small bunch - 15-20 sprigs - cilantro
- Olive oil (or any neutral oil)
- 2 teaspoon ground cumin
- 1 teaspoon ground coriander
- ½ teaspoon ground allspice
- 1 teaspoon smoked paprika
- 2 stalks of celery
- Salt
- Black pepper
- 1 large bay leaf - or 2 small ones
- 1 14-ounce can diced tomatoes (preferably fire roasted, with green chilis)
- 2 tablespoons tomato paste
- 1 16-ounce can of kidney beans
- Zest of one orange
- Chipotles in adobo, to taste
- Juice of 2 limes
- Optional items for serving:
- Cheddar, grated, for garnishing
- Lime crema - 1 tablespoon lime juice per ½ cup sour cream with a pinch of salt
- Brown rice
- Tortilla chips for eating with, instead of a fork or spoon (kids love that)

Direction

- Put 5 ½ cups of water on to boil in a kettle or covered pot. Turn the slow cooker onto its "High" setting. NB: you'll be turning it down before the long cooking period begins.
- Meanwhile, cut the chorizo lengthwise and then crosswise into 1" chunks. Put them into a medium microwavable bowl or Pyrex pitcher with ½ cup water; cover tightly and microwave on high for 3 minutes. (I use my 2 cup Pyrex measure for this, putting the water in first.) When the cooking time is done, remove and leave the container covered. You'll be putting them back in. We're cooking them like this to render as much fat as we can before they go into the slow cooker for the day.
- Meanwhile, coarsely chop the onions and garlic and put them into a medium microwavable bowl or Pyrex-style 4-cup measure. Microwave for 3 ½ minutes. Softening them first in the microwave results in a better texture later (this tip, and to warm the spices with the aromatics, courtesy of Cook's Illustrated).
- Meanwhile, use a mortar and pestle to crush the oregano with the cumin, coriander, allspice and 8 - 10 grinds of black pepper. Cut the cilantro stems below the leaves into ⅛" pieces.
- When the onions are done, remove the cover, make a small well in the middle of the onions, add the cilantro stems, the crushed herbs and spices, and the smoked paprika, as well as a good glug (a tablespoon or so, but don't bother measuring) of olive oil. Cover tightly and microwave for another 3 minutes.
- Meanwhile, chop the celery into ½" chunks. Pick over the black beans to remove any shriveled ones and any dirt or stones. Put the beans and celery into the slow cooker.
- When the onions are done, remove them from the microwave and put the chorizo back in for another 2 minutes on high. Meanwhile, put the aromatics and herbs into the slow cooker, give everything a good stir and pour in 5 cups of boiling water.
- When the chorizo is done, pour off the liquid and discard the liquid, and add the chorizo to the slow cooker, along with a bay leaf and a good pinch of salt. Give it all a good stir, cover, TURN THE HEAT DOWN TO LOW, and let it cook for 8 - 9 hours.
- No less than 30 minutes before you plan to serve the chili (or sooner if you like, but not until the beans are quite tender), turn the slow cooker up to High. Drain the juice from the tomatoes into a medium microwavable bowl or pitcher and cook on maximum power for 4 minutes.
- Meanwhile, remove a cup or so of broth from the beans and stir the tomato paste into it. Pour it back into the slow cooker.
- Open and drain the kidney beans, and coarsely chop the cilantro leaves.
- Put the heated tomatoes and the cilantro leaves into the slow cooker; add the orange zest and give everything a good stir to incorporate fully.
- Microwave the kidney beans for 3 minutes -- do it in the same bowl or pitcher you used for the tomatoes -- and then add them to the slow cooker. Meanwhile, remove the bay leaves from the slow cooker.
- Stir in the chipotles in adobo, if using. Test for salt and pepper and correct as necessary. Add more chipotles to taste. (We serve the sauce -- Frontera brand which is available at Whole Foods Market here -- on the side to allow people to add individually to taste.)
- Once the cooker has been on "High" for 30 minutes, feel free to turn it back down to "Low" or "Warm" until you're ready to serve. Stir in the lime juice right before serving.
- Serve with grated cheddar, lime juice-spiked sour cream, pickled red onions and good tortilla chips. (We use the chips instead of forks and spoons.)
- Make ahead tips: The night - or up to 2 days before - you can prep and microwave the chorizo. . . Prep and microwave the aromatics and herbs. . . Chop the celery (stir it into and store it with the onions, if you've cooked them) . . . and pick over the beans and put them right in the slow cooker with the bay leaf. Be sure to heat the cooked chorizo for

about two minutes, and the onions for about 2 minutes. Feel free to reheat them together for 5 minutes, if that's more convenient. If you're serving lime cream, that can also be made in advance. Give it a good stir and test for salt right before serving. If you're serving cheese, you can grate it up to 3 or 4 days in advance. If serving rice, you can make that up to 4 days beforehand, or take some out of the freezer and warm it up, if you've got some already made.

- If you are prepping the chorizo ahead of time (cutting and microwaving), you can reserve the cooking liquid, chill it, remove and discard the fat that rises to the top, and use the liquid to replace part of the water to be added to the slow cooker. Heat it in the microwave to near boiling before adding to the pot.

61. Chorizo Style Seitan Tacos

Serving: Serves 4 | Prep: | Cook: | Ready in:

Ingredients

- For the Chorizo-style Seitan
- 2 cloves garlic, minced or finely grated
- 1 teaspoon tamari
- 1 1/2 tablespoons apple cider or red wine vinegar
- 2 tablespoons tomato paste
- 1/2 teaspoon dried oregano
- 1/2 teaspoon smoked paprika
- 1 teaspoon chili powder
- 1 teaspoon ground cumin
- 1/4 teaspoon ground cinnamon
- Crushed red pepper flakes
- 2-3 tablespoons water, to thin the marinade
- 8 ounces seitan, shredded, chopped or ground
- 2 teaspoons olive oil
- For the Tacos and Slaw:
- 4 cups shredded purple or green cabbage (or a mix)
- 3/4 cup packed, fresh chopped cilantro
- 1 tablespoon olive oil
- 1 tablespoon freshly squeezed lime juice
- drizzles of agave or maple syrup (optional)
- Salt and pepper to taste
- 8 6-inch soft flour or corn tortillas (use 100% corn for a gluten-free option)
- 2 cups cooked brown rice (optional)
- avocado wedges and thinly sliced radishes, for serving

Direction

- Whisk together the garlic, tamari, vinegar, tomato paste, oregano, smoked paprika, chili, cumin, cinnamon, and pepper flakes together with 2 tablespoons water. Add an extra tablespoon or so if this marinade is very thick. Place the chopped or ground seitan in a glass lock container and pour the marinade over it. Cover, shake to mix up the ingredients, and refrigerate for 8 hours, or overnight.
- To prepare the seitan, heat the olive oil in a medium-sized skillet over medium heat. Add the seitan and whatever marinade is in the container. Cook, stirring frequently, for 5-7 minutes, or until the seitan is warmed through and most of the marinade has been absorbed. Set the seitan aside.
- In a mixing bowl, toss together the cabbage, cilantro, olive oil, lime juice, and agave or maple syrup (if using). Season to taste with salt, pepper, and an additional drizzle of lime juice or oil, if needed.
- To prepare the tacos, you can toast your tortillas over an open gas burner set to very low flame for about 1 minute per side—this will give you a slightly browned, crispy texture. You can also preheat the oven to 350F before cooking the seitan, wrap all of the tortillas in foil, and allow them to warm up for 10-15 as you get everything else ready. To assemble, fill all of the tacos with even amounts of the seitan, brown rice, and cabbage slaw. Top with avocado wedges and sliced radishes. Serve.

62. Coconut Crusted Chicken Lettuce Wraps With Mango Lime Salsa

Serving: Serves 2 | Prep: | Cook: | Ready in:

Ingredients

- For the salsa
- 1 mango
- 1 lime, juiced
- 1/4 cup diced red bell pepper
- 1/4 cup chopped red onion
- 1/4 cup fresh cilantro, packed
- 1/2 jalapeño, deseeded
- For the chicken and to serve
- 1 pound chicken, breast or thighs
- 3 egg
- 1 1/4 cups shredded coconut, unsweetened
- 3/4 cup coconut flour
- 1/4 teaspoon paprika
- 1/4 teaspoon cumin
- Dash Salt
- Dash Freshly ground black pepper
- Coconut oil
- Butterhead lettuce leaves
- Shredded red cabbage

Direction

- Remove chicken from refrigerator to remove chill.
- Dice mango, bell pepper, and red onion. Mince cilantro and jalapeño. Add to a bowl with juice of one lime and mix to combine. Cover and refrigerate. Cut chicken into small pieces, keeping the size consistent. (You can do strips or "nuggets," like I used in this recipe.)
- Crack egg into a small dish and whisk. Add coconut flour to another flat, shallow dish, and add shredded coconut to a third dish. Season coconut flour with paprika, cumin, salt, and pepper. Mix to combine.
- Start by dipping chicken into coconut flour, followed by a dip in the beaten egg, and finally, into the shredded coconut. Place onto a dish until you have "breaded" all of the chicken.
- Heat a cast iron or stainless steel pan to medium-high heat and enough coconut oil to coat the pan.
- Add chicken to pan and cook for about 3 minutes per side, depending on how thick your pieces of chicken are. You may need to work in batches to not overcrowd the pan. Add more oil as needed.
- After removing the chicken, sprinkle with salt while it is still warm if desired.
- To assemble, distribute lettuce leaves, add chicken, top with salsa and shredded cabbage. Serve with lime wedge.

63. Coffee Baked Sweet Potatoes With Chili Spice, Crème Fraîche, Lime & Cilantro

Serving: Serves 2 as a main course, 4 as a side dish | Prep: | Cook: | Ready in:

Ingredients

- 1 pound coffee beans
- 2 jewel yams (sweet potatoes) of the same size
- 1/2 teaspoon sea salt
- 1/2 teaspoon smoked paprika
- 1/8 teaspoon ground cinnamon
- 1 pinch ground cayenne pepper
- 1 pinch brown sugar
- 4 tablespoons crème fraîche
- zest of 1 lime
- 1/2 cup fresh cilantro leaves

Direction

- Preheat the oven to 375 degrees Fahrenheit. Pour the coffee beans into a baking sheet. Prick the sweet potatoes all over with a fork and then nestle them into the coffee beans. Place the baking sheet into the oven and roast for 30 minutes, monitoring occasionally to make sure the beans are not smoking. If the oven is too hot the coffee beans will smoke and give off a burnt aroma to the sweet potatoes.

- After 30 minutes, turn the sweet potatoes over and stir the beans a bit. Turn the oven temperature down to 350 degrees Fahrenheit and continue baking the sweet potatoes until very tender and collapsed in their skins, about 30-45 minutes more. Test the sweet potatoes for doneness by piercing all the way through the flesh with a table knife. Set the sweet potatoes aside until just cool enough to handle. Once the coffee beans have cooled they can be discarded.
- Make the spice mixture. In a small bowl, stir together the sea salt, smoked paprika, ground cinnamon, cayenne, and brown sugar.
- Now prep the sweet potatoes as you would a baked Russet potato. Slice each potato in half lengthwise and use a fork to fluff the flesh. Sprinkle the spice mixture amongst the 4 sweet potato halves. Garnish each with a tablespoon of crème fraîche, a few pinches of lime zest, and some cilantro leaves. Serve warm potatoes immediately.

64. Cold Busting Coconut Chicken Curry Soup

Serving: Serves 8 | Prep: | Cook: | Ready in:

Ingredients

- 2 chicken breasts, cut into 1-inch cubes
- 2 sweet potatoes, peeled & diced
- 1 baker-sized potato, peeled and diced
- 1 can coconut milk
- 4 cups chicken broth
- 1 medium yellow onion, diced
- 1 cup water
- 2 cloves of garlic, finely diced
- 3 tablespoons curry powder
- 1 1/2 teaspoons paprika
- 1 teaspoon nutmeg, ground
- 1 dash red pepper flakes
- 1 pinch cayenne pepper (optional)
- salt & pepper, to taste
- 3 tablespoons olive oil
- 3 tablespoons cornstarch
- 2 green onions, for garnish
- your favorite rice, for serving

Direction

- In a large pot, heat olive oil over medium high. Add onion, garlic, curry, paprika, nutmeg, and other peppers (if using) and stir. Cook until onions become slightly transparent and just start to caramelize, then add chicken. Sauté for 5 to 7 minutes, stirring occasionally to cook evenly, until the chicken is almost fully cooked. (Begin cooking rice at this point if you intend to serve the soup over rice.)
- Add chicken broth and water. Bring to a gentle simmer and add both types of potatoes. Simmer uncovered until potatoes are fork tender, about 15 minutes.
- If you'd like your broth to be thicker, mix 3 tbsp. cornstarch with a few tablespoons of water and gently stir in to the soup. Simmer on high for an additional 5 minutes.
- Remove from heat and slowly stir in coconut milk. I like to go for the good, creamy stuff, but you can use light coconut milk if you choose. Add salt and pepper as desired. Serve over rice, if you choose, topped with green onions sliced on the bias (a.k.a. at an angle — this just makes them look prettier).

65. Copycat Vegan Sloppy Joes

Serving: Serves 6 | Prep: | Cook: | Ready in:

Ingredients

- 200 grams Swiss mushrooms, chopped in to small pieces

- 400 milliliters canned lentils, rinsed and drained
- 20 grams porcini mushrooms
- 1/3 cup boiling water
- 200 milliliters canned chopped tomatoes
- 2 bay leaves
- 2 cloves of garlic, crushed
- 1/2 teaspoon paprika
- 1 teaspoon dried oregano
- Tablespoon tamari or soy sauce
- 1 tablespoon olive oil
- 1 handful baby spinach, finely chopped
- 2 bullhorn peppers,
- 6 small burger buns

Direction

- Preheat oven to 200 degrees C. Slice the peppers in half and remove the core and seeds. Slice in to ribbons, drizzle with a little oil and place on a roasting tray. Roast for 25 minutes or until soft. Remove from the oven and set aside.
- Meanwhile, pour boiling water over the dried porcini mushrooms in a bowl and set aside for 10 minutes.
- In a small pan, heat the oil and add the garlic. Cook for thirty seconds before adding the bay leaves, paprika and oregano. Cook for another thirty seconds.
- Add the chopped mushrooms and stir to coat. Cook the mushrooms for 2 minutes until they are beginning to soften.
- Add the chopped tomatoes and strain the mushroom liquid from the porcini mushrooms in to the pot. Add the soy sauce.
- Chop the now hydrated porcini mushrooms and add them to the pot too.
- Add the lentils and stir through.
- Cook the mixture for around 20 minutes or until the liquid has cooked down and the mixture resembles a beef ragu.
- Take it off the heat and stir in the chopped spinach leaves.
- To assemble the sloppy joes, lightly toast the burger buns on a griddle. Lay a few pepper ribbons on the bun base and top with a good few spoonful of the ragu. Top with the bun top and serve.

66. Corn Salad With Tomatoes, Avocado, Quinoa And Feta

Serving: Serves 4 as a side, 2 as a main course | Prep: | Cook: | Ready in:

Ingredients

- 1 ear of corn
- 2 medium-sized tomatoes, diced
- 2 avocado, diced
- 100 grams feta, crumbled
- 1/2 teaspoon paprika
- 1 teaspoon dried thyme
- 1 pinch of espelette pepper (or other mild pepper)
- 2 tablespoons lemon juice

Direction

- Bring a large pot of water to boil. Remove and discard the green outer husk and silky threads from the corn. Cook the ear of corn for 5 minutes then cool in a cold water bath. Remove the corn kernels and reserve in a bowl.
- Rinse the quinoa under cold water. Put the quinoa and twice its volume in water in a pot and bring to boil. Reduce the heat and cook for 10 minutes with a lid. Let it stand for 5 minutes
- Make the dressing: mix the olive oil, lemon juice, pepper, cumin, paprika, thyme, salt and pepper
- Add the tomatoes, avocado, quinoa and corn. Stir well
- Top with the crumbled feta and serve

67. Corn Sundal

Serving: Makes ~ 2 cups | Prep: | Cook: | Ready in:

Ingredients

- 2 ears of corn on the cob
- 1/4 teaspoon turmeric
- 1/2 cup Finely diced shallots or the white part of scallions
- 1 tablespoon Canola oil
- 1 teaspoon mustard seeds
- 1/4 teaspoon asafetida
- 1/4 teaspoon Paprika
- 1 sprig curry leaves
- Salt to taste
- Juice of 1/2 a lemon
- 1-2 small green chillies cut into small pieces

Direction

- Boil the corn cobs in salted water adding turmeric to impart color.
- Remove from the water, allow to cool & remove the kernels off from the cob.
- Heat oil in a skillet and add the mustard seeds, when they sputter, add the shallots, green chiles, torn curry leaves and asafetida. Sauté till the shallots turn translucent.
- Add the boiled corn, paprika & any extra salt as required, stir to combine. Lower heat, cover and simmer for about 5-7 minutes to allow the flavors to combine.
- Transfer to a serving dish, drizzle with lemon juice & serve.

68. Corn, Bacon, And Clam Stew

Serving: Serves 4 | Prep: | Cook: | Ready in:

Ingredients

- 2 tablespoons Olive oil
- 1/2 pound thick-cut bacon, cut into lardons
- 1 tablespoon sweet smoked paprika
- 6 ears corn, shucked and cut from the cobs
- Salt, to taste
- 1/2 pound sungold yellow cherry tomatoes, halved
- half of one lemon
- 3 tablespoons bourbon
- 16 littleneck clams, scrubbed well
- 8 thick slices country bread, for serving
- small handful basil leaves, torn

Direction

- Place a large, deep heavy soup pot over medium heat. Add the oil and bacon, and cook until the fat is rendered and the lardons are browned. Stir in the paprika and cook for 30 seconds.
- Add the corn, season with salt, and stir, cooking for about 2 minutes. Stir in the tomatoes and cover. Cook until the tomatoes soften, about 5 minutes.
- Squeeze in the juice from the lemon and pour in the bourbon, stir, and turn off the heat. Add the clams with the mouth facing up. Turn on the heat to medium, cover the pot, and cook until the clams open, 5 to 10 minutes. Meanwhile, grill or toast the bread. Remove the pot from the heat, sprinkle with basil, and bring the bread and the pot -- and a trivet -- to the table for serving.

69. Courgette Shakshuka

Serving: Serves 4 | Prep: | Cook: | Ready in:

Ingredients

- 350 grams courgette/zucchini, spiralized or cut into thin strips
- 100 grams white onion, diced
- 50 grams red bell pepper, diced
- 3 pieces cloves garlic, minced
- 1/2 teaspoon paprika
- 1/2 teaspoon cumin seeds
- 400 grams diced tomatoes

- 250 milliliters water
- 2 pieces eggs
- 1 piece Salt to taste
- 1 piece Pepper to taste
- 30 olive oil

Direction

- Heat a tablespoon of olive oil in a pan.
- Sautee courgette/zucchini for 3-5 minutes over high heat. Set aside.
- Add a tablespoon of olive oil in the same pan. Sautee onions and bell pepper for 2 minutes.
- Add garlic, paprika and cumin seeds. Sautee for another minute.
- Add tomatoes and water. Simmer for 5 minutes.
- Add courgette/zucchini into the pan.
- Season with salt and pepper.
- With a spatula, form a dent for the eggs into the contents of the pan.
- Crack the eggs into the dent.
- Cover and simmer for 3-5 minutes.

70. Cowboy Chow

Serving: Serves 4 | Prep: | Cook: | Ready in:

Ingredients

- 1 pound 80/20 Ground Beef
- 1/2 Box of Medium Shell Pasta
- 1 Can of Campbell's Tomato Soup
- 2 teaspoons Garlic Powder
- 1 teaspoon Onion Powder
- 1 teaspoon Paprika
- 1 teaspoon Crushed Red Pepper
- Salt & Pepper to taste

Direction

- Bring 2-3 Cups of water to a boil in a large pot. Once the water is boiling, salt the water, and add your pasta shells. Cook 8-10 minutes, until al dente. Drain the pasta and return it to the pot you had cooked it in.
- While the water is boiling, begin to brown your ground beef. You'll want to use a decently large skillet over medium-high heat. I find with 80/20 that I never need to use oil to prevent sticking, as the fat content normally takes care of that. About half way through the process add the garlic powder, onion powder, paprika, crushed red pepper, salt and pepper. Continue until beef is completely cooked.
- Once the beef is completely cooked, add the can of tomato soup to the beef. Combine completely. Reduce heat to a simmer and let cook for an additional 2-3 minutes.
- Transfer the beef and tomato soup mixture to the pot with the pasta shells. Combine completely.
- Serve!

71. Cracked Crab With Three Sauces

Serving: Serves 6-8 | Prep: | Cook: | Ready in:

Ingredients

- Cracked Crab with Three Sauces
- 6 Dungeness crab, 2-2 ½ lbs each
- 1 recipe Sauce Verte (see below)
- 1 recipe Spicy Smoked Paprika Aioli (see below)
- 1 recipe Drawn Butter (see below)
- 2 lemons, cut into wedges
- Several pounds of ice
- Three Sauces - Sauce Verte, Drawn Butter, and Spicy Smoked Paprika Aioli
- SAUCE VERTE
- 1 cup parsley, chopped fine
- 1/2 teaspoon thyme, chopped fine
- 1 tablespoon finely chopped chives
- 1 small clove garlic, minced
- 3/4 cup olive oil
- 1 tablespoon capers, chopped

- 2 1/2 tablespoons lemon juice
- salt, to taste
- DRAWN BUTTER
- 8 ounces (2 sticks) high quality salted butter
- SPICY SMOKED PAPRIKA AIOLI
- 1 cup mayonnaise, preferably homemade
- 2 garlic cloves, grated on a microplane or minced
- 1-3 teaspoons lemon juice, depending on whether your mayo already has lemon or vinegar in it
- 3/4 teaspoon smoked paprika
- 1/4 teaspoon cayenne, or to taste
- pinch fine grain sea salt

Direction

- Cracked Crab with Three Sauces
- NOTES: -- If you would rather not cook live crab, you might be able to sweet talk your fishmonger into killing and cleaning it for you in the shop. Take it home and cook it immediately as the meat deteriorates quickly. Of course, you can always buy pre-cooked and cleaned crab from the store, but it's never as delicious as freshly-cooked. -- Some people serve whole crab and have their guests clean them at the table. I find this a little off-putting (read: gross) for those who are not die-hard crab lovers and seafood aficionados. I prefer to clean the crab and remove the innards before serving. -- The crab can be cooked up to 6 hours in advance. Store in the refrigerator until you're ready to serve it.
- Heat a large pot of generously salted water over high heat. If you do not have an extremely large pot, you will need to cook the crab in batches.
- While the water is heating, fill a large bowl or pot (or a clean sink) with ice. If you are cooking the crab in batches, be sure to save some of the ice for the rest of the crab.
- When the water comes to the boil, place as many crab as will fit in the pot. Be sure they are completely submerged. Bring back to the boil and cook for 15 minutes. Transfer the crab to the ice and cover with cold water. This will stop the cooking. Once completely cold, remove the crab from the ice water. Clean the crabs if you didn't have your fishmonger do it. Dry thoroughly and store in the refrigerator if not serving immediately.
- If you want to eat your crab cold (like we do), just take it out of the fridge about 20-30 minutes before you plan to serve it to let it warm up a bit.
- If you want to eat it hot, steam the crab for 5-10 minutes just before serving. The time will vary depending on how large your crabs are and how cold they are when they go in the pot. Taste the meat often as you steam the crab to be sure you don't overcook it.
- Serve crab accompanied by sauces and lemon wedges.
- Three Sauces - Sauce Verte, Drawn Butter, and Spicy Smoked Paprika Aioli
- SAUCE VERTE. Makes about 1 cup.
- Combine all the ingredients in a small bowl and stir to combine. Adjust seasonings to taste. Transfer to small bowls and serve alongside the crab. This sauce doesn't hold particularly well, so I recommend making it no more than an hour or two before you intend to serve it.
- DRAWN BUTTER. Makes about 3/4 cup.
- Melt the butter in a small saucepan over medium heat. Once melted, the butter will foam. Skim the foam then pour the butter into a clear heatproof container like a Pyrex measuring cup.
- Wait for the milk solids to fall to the bottom then carefully pour off the liquid butter, leaving the solids behind. You can use cheesecloth if you want your drawn butter to be extra clear. I usually don't fuss with the extra step since it wastes some of the butter.
- Heat the drawn butter in a small saucepan just before serving. Transfer to small serving bowls and serve alongside the crab.
- SPICY SMOKED PAPRIKA AIOLI. Makes about 1 cup.
- Combine all the ingredients in a small bowl and whisk to combine. Adjust seasonings to taste. Transfer to small bowls and serve alongside the crab.

- This aioli can be made up to 2 days in advance and will get spicier as it sits. Store, covered, in the refrigerator.

72. Cracking Bacon And Egg Breakfast Tortilla Cups

Serving: Serves 4 | Prep: | Cook: | Ready in:

Ingredients

- 4 strips of bacon
- 4 large eggs
- 2 flour tortillas
- 1 bunchChives
- 1 pinchpaprika powder
- 1 pinchsalt to taste
- 1 pinchsalt to taste

Direction

- Heat oven at 400 °F/ 200 °C
- Cook the bacon in a hot pan (no butter or oil required)
- Drain bacon
- Half the tortillas
- Fold the tortilla in a muffin tin
- Add the bacon to the tortilla
- Add an egg on top of the tortilla and bacon
- Cook in the oven for 20 minutes
- Take out of the oven add some chives, paprika powder and salt and pepper to taste
- Enjoy

73. Creamy Dijon Sweet Potato Salad

Serving: Serves 6 | Prep: | Cook: | Ready in:

Ingredients

- 3 Jumbo sweet potatoes, peeled
- 2 tablespoons olive oil
- 1/2 cup green onion, chopped
- 1/4 cup parsley, chopped
- 1/2 cup celery, chopped
- 2/3 cup mayonnaise
- 1/3 cup Dijon mustard
- 1 tablespoon paprika, divided
- 1 teaspoon salt
- 1 teaspoon fresh ground pepper

Direction

- Preheat oven to 400F
- Cut peeled sweet potatoes to 3/4" chunks Spread potatoes across 2 baking sheets, drizzle with olive oil Season with, salt, pepper and 1/2 the paprika Roast for 20-30 minutes or until just cooked through and beginning to color
- Meanwhile mix mayonnaise with Dijon and parsley, celery and green onion
- Let potatoes cool for 10 minutes
- Mix sweet potatoes with dressing and finish by sprinkling with the remaining paprika
- Chill for 2 hours or up to 24

74. Creamy Garlic Zoodles With Bursting Cherry Tomatoes

Serving: Serves 2 | Prep: | Cook: | Ready in:

Ingredients

- "Cream" sauce
- 1 tablespoon olive oil
- 1 shallot, diced
- 5 garlic cloves, minced
- 1 pinch sea salt
- 1 pinch freshly cracked pepper
- 2 tablespoons almond flour
- 1 teaspoon corn starch
- 1 1/4 cups coconut milk
- Zoodles + bursting cherry tomatoes
- 1 pint cherry tomatoes, halved

- 1 1/2 tablespoons olive oil
- 1 pinch sea salt
- 1 pinch freshly cracked pepper
- 2 large zucchini, spiralized
- 1 pinch paprika
- 1 pinch red pepper flakes

Direction

- Preheat oven to 400F
- In a medium sized bowl, toss tomatoes in 1/2 tablespoon of olive oil plus a little sea salt and freshly cracked pepper. Place on a baking sheet lined with parchment paper and roast for about 20 minutes!
- Heat one tablespoon of olive oil in a small/medium-sized sauce pan over medium-high heat. Add in the diced shallot and garlic cloves plus a healthy dash of sea salt and freshly cracked pepper. Stir frequently and cook for about 3-4 minutes (shallot and garlic should be fragrant and soft).
- Stir in the almond flour and corn starch then mix with a whisk. Once the flour and corn starch are incorporated into the oil, slowly whisk in the coconut milk! I add a little at a time and whisk very quickly so clumps don't form.
- Once all the coconut milk is whisked in, continue cooking for another 4-5 minutes to thicken. Then reduce heat to low and simmer the sauce until it reaches your desired thickness. Taste and adjust seasonings as you see fit! (Optional step: use an immersion blender to blend the sauce until creamy and smooth)
- Add one tablespoon olive oil to a large skillet over medium heat. Add zoodles plus a pinch of paprika then sauté for about 3-5 minutes or until zoodles are soft-ish but not limp.
- Stir in cream sauce (completed in step five) and bursting cherry tomatoes (from step one) then cook for another 3-5 minutes or until zoodles are soft and resemble spaghetti noodles.
- Divide zoodle mixture into two bowls, top with a pinch of red pepper flakes then eat

75. Creamy Mac N' Cheese

Serving: Makes one 9 x 13 pan | Prep: | Cook: | Ready in:

Ingredients

- 1 pound fusili pasta
- 1 ounce flour
- 1 ounce unsalted butter, melted
- 1/4 teaspoon mustard powder
- 1/2 teaspoon hot Spanish paprika
- 1/4 teaspoon nutmeg
- 1/4 teaspoon cayenne pepper
- 3 cups whole milk
- 3 cups gouda, shredded
- 6 ounces cream cheese, at room temperature
- 1/2 cup garlic bread crumbs
- 1 cup grated cheddar cheese, for topping
- 3 tablespoons grated Parmesan cheese

Direction

- Boil pasta according to package directions. Drain.
- Preheat oven to broil.
- Meanwhile, in a large, nonstick pot over medium high heat, add butter. Let it warm up and then whisk in flour, paprika, mustard powder, cayenne, and nutmeg. Cook for 1-2 minutes until it starts to turn a pale white. You've got the start of a white roux (except it'll be a tad red because of the paprika and the cayenne)!
- Slowly add little increments of the milk so the roux doesn't get lumpy, and once you have a smooth mixture, add the rest of the milk. Bring mixture to a simmer, whisking constantly. Cook until thick enough to coat the back of a wooden spoon. Remove from heat and whisk in cream cheese and the gouda. It will melt without being on the burner.
- Mix cooked pasta with sauce and place into a greased baking dish. Top with the shredded cheddar cheese, breadcrumbs and parmesan.

Broil until brown and bubbly, about 2-3 minutes.

76. Crispy (Fried) Chickpeas

Serving: Serves 2 to 3 | Prep: | Cook: | Ready in:

Ingredients

- olive oil
- 2 cups chickpeas
- 1/2 teaspoon sea salt, divided
- 1/4 teaspoon smoked paprika
- zest of 1 lemon
- 3 or 4 thyme sprigs

Direction

- Heat about ½ inch of olive oil over medium-high heat in a Dutch oven or large wide skillet.
- Meanwhile, dry drained chickpeas with paper towels.
- When the oil is hot, use a strainer to carefully place half of the chickpeas in the oil. Fry until crispy and golden, about 5 minutes, stirring frequently.
- Use a strainer or slotted spoon to transfer the hot chickpeas to a plate lined with paper towels. Transfer to a small owl and season and toss with ¼ teaspoon salt and paprika.
- Fry the remaining half of the chickpeas with the thyme, stirring frequently, and drain them on paper towels. Toss this batch in a small bowl with ¼ teaspoon salt and lemon zest. Serve immediately.

77. Croatian Bean Soup / Stew (Fažol I Testo)

Serving: Serves 6 | Prep: | Cook: | Ready in:

Ingredients

- Beans
- 3 cups romano beans (cranberry beans)
- 5 cups water
- 2 teaspoons salt
- Soup
- 3 teaspoons oil
- 1 shallot, finely chopped
- 2 cloves garlic, minced
- 2 tablespoons tomato paste
- 1 teaspoon paprika
- 1 teaspoon salt or to taste
- 1/2 teaspoon freshly ground pepper
- 4 cups stock or water
- Wide homemade noodles cut short (or 2 cups short pasta like elbow macaroni)
- Smoked sausage (one per person)

Direction

- In large saucepan place beans, water and salt. Bring to a boil and reduce heat to a simmer.
- Cook, uncovered, about 40 minutes or until tender.
- Turn off heat and let beans cool in liquid.
- Drain and use in soup or salads.
- For soup, heat oil in a big pot over medium heat.
- Add flour and cook 3-4 minutes, until it changes colour.
- Stir in shallot, garlic, tomato paste and paprika, and cook about 1 minute.
- Add stock and cooked beans and simmer another 20 minutes to blend flavours.
- If you do not want to use flour, just omit the flour and pure 1/3 of a soup.
- Make soup up to a couple days ahead and refrigerate.
- Just before serving, reheat soup and cook noodles for Fažol i testo or sausages in it (or if you prefer both).

78. Crunchy Tortilla Tostada With Tuna

Serving: Serves 2 | Prep: | Cook: |Ready in:

Ingredients

- 2 flour tortillas
- 340 gramssmall can of brown beans
- 2 tablespoonsvegetable oil
- 0.5 onion
- 1 cupwater
- 1 teaspoonpaprika
- 80 gramscan of tuna
- 1 cupsmooth roasted tomato salsa
- 0.5 cupsguacamole
- 0.5 avocado
- 1 Iceberg lettuce for decorating
- 30 brown beans for decorating
- 0.5 grated cheese

Direction

- Boil the egg (I boil them for 7 minutes so they are medium hard), drain and put into cold water
- Slice half of the avocado in thin slices
- Heat a small pan with 2 tbsp of vegetable oil
- First add the onion and fry them until soft and transparent. This takes about 3 minutes
- Then add the brown beans, the paprika and then the cumin and stir through before adding the cup of water
- Let the beans get to the boil
- Stir and reduce the heat to medium to let the brown beans simmer for about 10-15 minutes
- Take the beans of the heat. Drain the brown beans preserving about 30 brown beans for decorating and transfer to a bowl
- Mash the brown beans
- Preheat the oven at 350°F/175°C
- Spray the tortillas with cooking spray or vegetable oil on both sides
- Bake in the oven for about 10 minutes (turn at about 5 minutes in the oven).
- Start plating the tostada and start with the smooth roasted tomato salsa
- Then the mashed brown beans before adding the avocado and a tbsp of guacamole
- Drain the can of tuna from liquid and put about half of it on the tostada
- Decorate with cheese, corn, lettuce and brown beans
- Ready to serve

79. Crème De Radish Pancetta Soup

Serving: Serves 6 | Prep: | Cook: |Ready in:

Ingredients

- 2 tablespoons extra virgin olive oil
- 1/4 cup pancetta – finely cubed
- 3 cups radish cut in half moons – thickness your preference
- 1/2 cup finely chopped celery
- 1/2 cup grated carrot
- 2 cloves garlic, smashed and minced
- 1/2 cup sliced leek
- 2 tablespoons Wondra flour (or AP)
- 3 cups milk 2% or whole NOTE: I used ricotta whey because I had it on hand.
- 1 bay leaf
- 1/4 teaspoon dried thyme
- 1/4 teaspoon smoked paprika
- 2 tablespoons unsalted butter
- 15ozs. cannellini beans, drained & rinsed
- Fresh ground pepper to taste
- 1/2 teaspoon salt or to taste
- Crème fraiche for garnish
- 1/2 cup grated radish for garnish

Direction

- Wash and cut the radish, finely chop the celery, slice the leek, smash the garlic and mince. Grate carrot for soup and extra radish for garnish. Wash and drain the beans. Set aside until needed.

- In a 4-6 quart Dutch oven style pot; heat the olive oil, add the pancetta and sauté about 2 minutes to release the flavor; add the radish, celery, carrot, leek and garlic, sauté for a couple minutes more.
- Add the flour, stir, incorporate well, stir in the milk – one cup at a time; let simmer for 20 minutes, the soup will thicken a bit.
- Add the bay leaf, thyme paprika, butter, cannellini beans, salt & pepper to taste. Let simmer for 20-30 minutes, soup will thicken a little more.
- Add 2 tablespoons crème fraiche and grated radish for garnish and serve.

80. Cucumber Appetizers

Serving: Serves 5 | Prep: | Cook: | Ready in:

Ingredients

- 1 piece cucumber
- 20 teaspoons cottage cheese
- 100 grams smoked salmon
- 1 teaspoon paprika

Direction

- Slice the cucumber into 20 slices.
- Add a teaspoon of cottage cheese on top of each slice of cucumber then a small slice of smoked salmon.
- Finish off with a sprinkle of paprika then enjoy!

81. Cucumber Rounds With Savory Cores

Serving: Serves 15-20 rounds | Prep: | Cook: | Ready in:

Ingredients

- 5 English cucumbers
- 5 slices turkey bacon
- 1 plum tomato-seeded and diced small
- 1 small celery stalk-minced
- 1 shallot-minced
- 1/2 small jalapeno-seeded and minced
- 1/2 cup grated parmesan
- 1/4 cup parsley-minced, plus extra for garnish
- 2 teaspoons lime juice
- 2 tablespoons olive oil
- 1 tablespoon sherry vinegar
- 1.5 teaspoons smoked paprika
- salt to taste
- pepper to taste
- 15-20 sesame rice crackers

Direction

- Rinse the cucumbers and peel them using a channel knife-giving them zebra stripes (do so by peeling lengthwise, approximately a 1/8th of an inch apart). Once peeled, cut the tips off each end and cut each cucumber (crosswise) into 1.5 inch thick rounds. Using a melon baller, remove the centers; place a damp cloth over the cucumbers and reserve.
- Heat a pan over medium-high heat and add bacon; cook until golden and just crisp; remove from the pan, allow to cool, and mince.
- In a bowl, mix bacon, tomato, celery, shallot, jalapeno, parmesan, minced parsley, lime juice, olive oil, vinegar, paprika, salt, and pepper.
- Lay the crackers out on a plate; place one cucumber round on each cracker; fill each cucumber round with bacon mixture; garnish each with a parsley leaf.

82. Curried Chickpea Sandwich

Serving: Makes 4 sandwiches | Prep: | Cook: | Ready in:

Ingredients

- 1 cup dried chickpeas (you could also use a can of chickpeas)
- 1 handful cilantro, chopped
- 1 avocado
- 3 scallions, chopped
- 1 lime, juiced
- 1 tablespoon curry powder
- 1 teaspoon smoked paprika
- 2 tomatoes, sliced
- 1 cup arugula
- 8 slices hearty bread

Direction

- If you are using dried chickpeas (I recommend this method -- you won't regret it), cover the chickpeas with a couple inches of water in a large bowl. Let them sit overnight. In the morning, rinse the chickpeas, then transfer them to a large heavy-bottomed pot and cover them with a few more inches of water. Bring to a boil, then cover and simmer for about 2 hours, until the chickpeas are soft.
- In a large bowl (or a food processor), mash (or process) the chickpeas, cilantro, avocado, scallions, lime juice, curry powder, and smoked paprika.
- To serve, spread the chickpea mixture on a slice of bread. Top with arugula, a couple tomato slices, and a second piece of bread. Cut your sandwich in half and enjoy!

83. Dad's Chorizo And Egg Breakfast Tacos

Serving: Serves 3 | Prep: 0hours15mins | Cook: 0hours20mins | Ready in:

Ingredients

- Chorizo and Eggs
- 1 clove garlic
- 1/2 small to medium onion
- 6 eggs
- 1/2 piece any good Mexican Chorizo, or Trader Joes Soy Chorizo if you don't eat pork
- 2 pinches Mexican oregano
- 1 dash salt
- 2 pinches pepper
- 3 tablespoons olive oil
- Breakfast Potatoes
- 3 potatoes (regular or sweet potatoes)
- 1 pinch any chili powder (optional)
- 1 teaspoon salt
- 1 teaspoon pepper
- 1 tablespoon paprika
- 2+ tablespoons olive oil

Direction

- Chop up potatoes, onions, and garlic. Set potatoes aside in a separate bowl and mix together onions and garlic
- Coat potatoes in about two tablespoons of olive oil and toss with salt, pepper, and paprika. Make about one small-medium potato per person.
- Put coated potatoes in a cast iron pan and cook until softened and fully cooked inside but still firm enough to hold their shape. Make sure to check frequently and move the potatoes around the pan so they cook evenly and don't stick to the pan, if they start sticking add a bit more olive oil. These can also be made earlier and heated through in the oven.
- Scramble about two eggs per person with a bit of salt and whisk in a generous amount of black pepper. You're going to use more than you think you need but it gives a really nice bite, you'll want enough to just about cover the surface of the eggs. Add two generous pinches of Mexican oregano. This is similar to traditional oregano, but has a slightly different flavor which works particularly well for dishes like this.
- If you are using a pre-cooked or soy chorizo you should prepare the chorizo now by removing it from the casing. If you are using uncooked chorizo you will want to fry it off until cooked, but not too crispy.

- Using about 1 tablespoon of olive oil for every two eggs begin to fry off the onions and garlic on a medium to high heat.
- Once the onions are transparent turn the heat to low and add the eggs. To get the best scramble cook at a low temperature, folding from under as the egg cooks. Also, don't skimp on the oil!
- Before the eggs are cooked, while they are still quite soft and large curds are starting to form add the chorizo and continue cooking until the eggs are cooked but still soft and the chorizo is a bit crispy on some edges. You won't want to leave it in the pan very long as it will continue cooking.
- Serving Suggestions: Serve eggs alone on a corn tortilla with avocado, salsa verde, hot sauce, and sharp cheese. Serve eggs and potatoes in a burrito with avocado/guacamole, salsa verde, hot sauce, sharp cheese, and anything else you fancy. Serve eggs and potatoes separately with a slice or two of buttered toast

84. Dark Chocolate Chili

Serving: Serves 6-8 | Prep: | Cook: | Ready in:

Ingredients

- 2 tablespoons olive oil
- 1/2 medium/large yellow onion diced
- 1/4 teaspoon salt
- 3 cloves of garlic minced
- 12 ounces mild italian sausage
- 2 teaspoons chili powder
- 2 teaspoons italian seasoning
- 1 teaspoon paprika
- 2 cups diced red/green/yellow bell peppers
- 15 ounces can tomato sauce
- 10 ounces can rotel tomatoes
- 6 ounces can tomato paste
- 2 15 ounces cans black beans
- 12 ounces water
- 1.5 ounces dark chocolate

Direction

- Heat the olive oil in a Dutch oven over medium heat. Add the onion and salt and sauté until soft and translucent.
- Add the garlic and stir. Let the garlic cook about 2 minutes and then add in the sausage. Break up the sausage as it cooks. Once the sausage begins to brown add the chili powder, paprika & peppers. Stir everything together and let cook about 3 minutes.
- Now add in the tomato sauce, rotel tomatoes, tomato paste, black beans, Italian seasoning and the water. (I used the tomato paste can, filling it up twice to add the water. This helps to get more of the tomato paste out of the can). Stir everything together and let come to boil. Once the mixture has come to a boil reduce the heat to simmer and stir in you dark chocolate. Continue stirring until the dark chocolate has completely melted and has been thoroughly mixed in.
- Let the chili sit about 10min to let the flavors really come together. After 10min it is ready to serve!

85. Deep Fried Green Beans

Serving: Makes as much as you want | Prep: | Cook: | Ready in:

Ingredients

- 1 pound Green beans (or Haricot Verts), topped & tailed
- Stale white bread, blitzed to make 1 cup crumbs (alternative - Japanese panko)
- 1-2 tablespoons fine yellow cornmeal
- 4 tablespoons all-purpose flour
- 1 tablespoon cornstarch
- Salt, to taste
- Red pepper flakes, to taste
- Freshly crushed black pepper, to taste

- 1 egg, beaten with 2 tablespoons of milk
- Vegetable/Canola oil, to fry
- Smoky paprika, to taste
- Onion powder, to taste
- To serve: Ranch/buttermilk dressing

Direction

- Blanch green beans in salted boiling water for 2 - 3 minutes and refresh in a bowl of (ice) cold water. Drain but don't dry beans as the water will allow the flour (1st step of battering) stay on.
- Heat up oil in deep fryer (165 degrees Celsius) or a deep pan of oil.
- Set up three bowls: the first with a mixture of the cornmeal. all-purpose flour and cornstarch, seasoned with garlic, onion powder, paprika, salt and pepper (black and chili flakes); the second with the beaten egg, lightly seasoned with salt and pepper and the final bowl with the freshly ground breadcrumbs, and spices
- In batches, dip the dried green beans into the flour mixture, to coat. Follow that with dipping in the egg wash and then the final roll in the bread crumbs. You can repeat if you'd like a double coating.
- Fry in the oil till golden and a crisp outer coating forms, 2-3 minutes, till golden. Be careful not to overcrowd the pan. Drain on kitchen tissue, and repeat for the other batches till done.
- Serve as you wish....a bowl of ranch is wonderful, if not traditional 'Thanksgiving'.....

86. Dev Aiolied Eggs

Serving: Serves 6 | Prep: | Cook: | Ready in:

Ingredients

- Aioli
- 1 egg yolk, room temperature
- 2 tablespoons lemon juice
- 1 garlic clove, mashed
- 1 teaspoon salt
- 3/4 cup grapeseed oil
- 1/4 cup olive oil
- Egg Filling
- 6 hard boiled eggs
- 2 tablespoons aioli, plus extra to top eggs
- 1 tablespoon lemon juice
- 1 tablespoon tomato paste
- 1 garlic clove, mashed
- 1/2 teaspoon smoked paprika
- 1 tablespoon chives, minced, plus extra for garnish
- salt and pepper to taste

Direction

- Whisk the egg yolk, lemon juice, garlic and salt together. Add the grapeseed oil slowly and whisk quickly to incorporate. Next whisk in the olive oil, slowly adding and incorporating. Makes 1 cup. You will have aioli leftover from this recipe, so save the extra to enjoy with grilled veggies or fish.
- Peel the hardboiled eggs and slice in half lengthwise. Arrange the whites on a serving platter. In a small bowl, mash the egg yolks. Add the aioli, lemon juice, tomato paste, garlic, paprika, chives, salt and pepper and mix until smooth.
- Spoon the egg filling into a small Ziploc bag and snip a tiny hole in one corner. Pipe the filling into the egg whites.
- Spoon a little bit of aioli into another small Ziploc, snip the corner and squeeze little dollops on top of eggs. Garnish with reserved chives and serve.

87. Deviled Egg Potato Salad

Serving: Serves 10 to 16 | Prep: | Cook: | Ready in:

Ingredients

- 4 pounds red potatoes

- 1 teaspoon sea salt
- 6 hard-boiled eggs
- 6 stalks celery, chopped
- 1 cup mayonnaise
- 1/4 cup dijon mustard
- 1 teaspoon freshly ground black pepper
- 1/2 teaspoon sea salt
- 1/2 teaspoon celery seed
- 1/2 teaspoon sweet hungarian paprika
- finely chopped chives
- sweet hungarian paprika

Direction

- Peel the potatoes, and then dice them into equal sized chunks.
- Place the potatoes and 1-teaspoon sea salt in a large pot, and then cover with water by two inches.
- Bring the potatoes to a boil over high heat, and cook until tender.
- Drain the potatoes and rinse with cold water for two minutes.
- Halve the hard-boiled eggs, and separate the white from the yolk, roughly chopping the egg whites and placing the yolks into a large bowl.
- Use a fork to mash the egg yolks, and then mix in the mayonnaise, mustard, pepper, salt, celery seed, and paprika.
- Gently fold in the hard-boiled egg whites, celery, and potatoes.
- Garnish with finely chopped chives and a sprinkle of paprika.

88. Deviled Eggs

Serving: Makes 16 halves | Prep: | Cook: |Ready in:

Ingredients

- 8 Hard boiled eggs
- 4 Slices Applewood Smoked Bacon, cooked, drained, crumbled
- 1/4 cup mayonnaise
- 4 teaspoons yellow mustard
- 1/4 teaspoon Paprika
- 1/4 teaspoon ground black pepper
- 1/2 tablespoon diced fresh parsley

Direction

- Remove egg yolks from whites and smash, leaving small chunks.
- Mix with remaining ingredients except the parsley, slowly adding the mayonnaise and mustard until you get a proper consistency. You can always add more if needed (but remember, you can never take it away, so be careful). Mixture should be smooth but not runny!
- Refill egg halves with yolk mixture.
- Garnish with parsley.
- Bacon can be omitted to make them vegetarian. Use Smoked Paprika instead to add a bacon like flavor to the eggs.

89. Devilish Hogwart Eggs

Serving: Makes 12 | Prep: | Cook: |Ready in:

Ingredients

- 6 organic eggs boiled
- 1/4 cup sour cream
- 2 tablespoons mayonnaise
- 4 pieces basil leaves finely chopped
- 2 tablespoons Dijon Mustard
- 1 pinch sea salt
- 1 pinch black pepper
- 1 ounce Feta Cheese Crumbled
- 1 pinch Paprika

Direction

- Let eggs cool, remove shell, carve out yolks and mix yolks with wet ingredients and basil in bowl.
- Using a melon ball scoop refill egg cavern with yolk mixture and sprinkle with paprika & Feta Cheese crumble. Serve room temp.

90. Devils On Horseback In A Pool Of Blood

Serving: Serves 2 | Prep: | Cook: | Ready in:

Ingredients

- 1/2 onion, diced
- 4 garlic cloves
- 1/2 teaspoon crushed red pepper flakes (optional)
- 1 tablespoon smoked paprika
- 1/2 cup dates, pitted and chopped (I used Halawy dates b/c they were on sale but I think Deglet Noors would hold up better)
- 1 pound tomatoes
- 1 teaspoon miso (I used a mixture of red and white miso)

Direction

- Prepare tomatoes for sauce. For me, this means pureeing it in a food processor. For most, skinning and seeding tomatoes prior to pureeing.
- Sautee onions until fragrant. Add garlic and crushed red pepper flakes if using. Sautee for a few minutes more.
- Add tomato puree and smoked paprika. Stir and cook until thickened to SLIGHTLY SOUPIER THAN desired consistency.
- Add chopped dates and cook until thickened to desired consistency.
- Lower heat to barely a simmer and add the miso. Stir to combine all flavors. Adjusting seasoning.
- For a "meatier" versions while remaining vegan, add 8 ounces of chopped chanterelles with the garlic.
- For a non-vegan/vegetarian recipe, top with cheese of choice.
- For an omnivore version, use pancetta and skip the smoked paprika and miso. I'd render the pancetta first, using the left over fat to sauté the onions and garlic. Top the sauce with the pancetta.

91. Double Sweet Corn And Lobster Chowder

Serving: Serves 6-8 | Prep: | Cook: | Ready in:

Ingredients

- 4 uncooked lobster tails, meat removed and sliced into large chunks, briefly sauté in butter (slightly undercooked), cool and refrigerate until ready to add to the chowder.
- 3 ears yellow and white corn, roasted (I oven roast in the husks)
- 1/2 lb diced sweet potatoes
- 2 lbs diced white or yellow potatoes
- 1/2 cup light cream
- 1 cup heavy cream
- 3 cups lobster corn stock
- 1 cup shrimp stock
- pinch of saffron
- 8 slices pancetta, diced
- 3 small shallots, minced
- 1 leek, white part diced
- 2 small Bay leaves
- 2 Sprigs of thyme, leaves removed and minced
- 2 tablespoon unsalted butter
- 1/2 teaspoon sweet paprika
- 1/4 cup white wine or sherry
- White pepper and salt to taste
- Pinches of saffron
- 3 large diced tomatoes sauteed in the lobster butter

Direction

- I am not wedded to any one particular lobster stock so feel free to use any version that you like, but I like to sauté the corn cobs with the other ingredients, fennel fronds, leek, carrot, celery, bay leaves, fresh thyme sprigs, black peppercorns, saffron. Sauté until shells turn bright red, toss in ¼ white wine stir, slightly reduce and add the water (6 cups) and 1 cup shrimp stock, reduce to 4 cups and strain. Whenever I clean shrimp I make shrimp stock so I have a pretty good amount in the freezer and use at least a cup in the chowder.

- 4 uncooked lobster tails, meat removed and sliced into large chunks, briefly sauté in butter, cool and refrigerate until ready to add to the chowder. Saute the diced tomatoes in the remaining butter in the pan, add into chowder.
- Sauté pancetta in about ½ tablespoon olive oil and 2 tablespoons butter until crisp, add onion, shallot, bay leaf, paprika, saffron, and minced thyme leaves until the leeks and onions are soft. Stir in wine simmer for a minute or so, add the sauteed tomatoes, potatoes, corn and stock to cover. Bring to a low boil, cover until the sweet potatoes are soft. I remove about 2 full cups potatoes and corn and stick blend the soup in the pot to thicken. I make it a few hours ahead to this point and slowly reheat stirring in the cream. Don't boil, but get good and hot adding the lobster meat. When lobster meat is heated through (a couple of minutes), serve the chowder in heated bowls or toasted bread bowls, garnish with a little fresh parsley and additional crispy pancetta. Serve with fresh rolls or crusty bread.
- This recipe is difficult in that my husband likes "thick" and that I have to figure out how to thicken it not too much for me... more taters. Play with it...

92. Drunken Chicken Paprika

Serving: Serves 5 | Prep: | Cook: |Ready in:

Ingredients

- 5 chicken leg quarters
- 1 yellow onion sliced in half moons
- 8 ounces button mushrooms sliced
- 3 garlic cloves sliced
- 3 ounces sour cream
- 1 cup white wine
- 1/4 cup marsala wine
- 1 tablespoon paprika
- 2 tablespoons flour
- 3 tablespoons oil
- salt
- pepper
- 1 1/2 cups chicken stock

Direction

- Season chicken with salt and pepper, dust pieces with 1 tbs. flour. Pour oil in a large metal pot and put in chicken pieces and brown, do in 2 batches if necessary. Remove from pot and set aside. Preheat oven to 350 degrees.
- Add onions to the pot and cook until caramelized. Add in garlic and sliced mushrooms. Cook until all of the liquid has cooked out of the mushrooms.
- Add paprika and cook for a minute, now add in the remaining tablespoon of flour and stir.
- Pour the marsala wine in and deglaze the bottom of pan and scrape up all of the yummy brown bits. Now add the wine and reduce by 1/2. Once wine is reduced add in the chicken stock.
- Arrange chicken back in the pot, cover partially with a lid or foil and cook in oven for around 1 hr. and 15 min. When it's done take out chicken pieces and set aside. Skim fat off the top and reduce liquid by 1/4. Turn off heat whisk in sour cream. Season to taste with salt and pepper. Add chicken pieces back in and serve.

93. Dukkah

Serving: Serves makes about 2 1/2 cups | Prep: | Cook: |Ready in:

Ingredients

- 2/3 cup sesame seeds
- 1/2 cup hazelnuts, with or without skins
- 1/2 cup roasted chickpeas
- 1/2 cup coriander seeds
- 3 tablespoons cumin seeds
- 1 teaspoon dried thyme
- 1 teaspoon kosher salt
- 1/2 teaspoon black peppercorns
- 2 tablespoons mild Hungarian paprika
- 1 teaspoon Spanish smoked paprika, optional
- extra virgin olive oil, for dipping
- flatbread or crusty bread, your choice, preferably warm

Direction

- Toast the sesame seeds in a dry skillet until golden. Remove and set aside. Roast the hazelnuts and chickpeas, separately, in the same hot pan for about 4-5 minutes each or until aromatic. Remove and set aside. Reserve two tablespoons of the roasted hazelnuts. Dry toast the coriander and cumin seeds until aromatic. Remove from pan and let cool.
- Mix all the Dukkah ingredients except the paprika and reserved hazelnuts in a bowl. In a spice grinder or small food processor, grind the dukkah, leaving a little texture if you'd like. Transfer to a serving bowl and stir in the paprika and the reserved hazelnuts.
- To serve, place the olive oil in a separate bowl, and put the dukkah and oil side by side on a large serving platter with flatbread or crusty bread. The bread is dipped first into the oil, then into the dukkah.
- Store in an airtight container at room temperature for up to 2 weeks or in the freezer for 3 months.

94. Easiest And Yummiest Burger Ever!

Serving: Serves 2 | Prep: | Cook: | Ready in:

Ingredients

- 1 pound ground beef
- 1 small brown onion
- salt
- ground black pepper
- 1/4 pound feta cheese
- ground paprika
- 1 glove garlic
- 1/2 cup sour cream
- 2 pieces thick pita bread

Direction

- Finely dice and salt the onion, squeeze all the water out by hand
- Mix the onions into the meat, salt and pepper to taste
- Form 2 large patties about 1/2 inch thick
- Grill about 2 to 3 minutes on each side until done
- OPTIONAL TOPPING: crumble feta into sour cream, add finely minced garlic and paprika to taste, mix with a fork until smooth
- Warm pita bread, top each patty with some of the feta mix and place on the bread (can also be eat with a knife and fork alongside the bread or the patty with topping can be put in the pita - all personal preference)

95. Eat Your Greens! Rainbow Chard With A Maple Vinegar Drizzle

Serving: Serves 4 | Prep: | Cook: | Ready in:

Ingredients

- 1/3 cup raw, unsalted cashews
- 2 pounds rainbow chard, washed and ends trimmed
- 2 tablespoons olive oil
- 1/2 large red onion, chopped
- 1/4 teaspoon smoked paprika
- 1/2 cup golden raisins

- 1/2 cup low sodium vegetable stock
- Kosher salt and/or ground black pepper
- 1 tablespoon pure maple syrup
- 1 tablespoon Sherry vinegar

Direction

- Using a small dry skillet, toast the cashews over medium heat, stirring until toasted, about 3 to 5 minutes. When cooled, roughly chop and set aside.
- Take the chard and remove center ribs with a sharp knife. Cut the ribs into 1/2-inch pieces and set aside. Coarsely chop the chard leaves and set aside.
- Using a large, heavy-bottomed pot, heat the oil. Add the onion, paprika, and chard rib pieces. Cook over medium heat for 5 minutes.
- Add the chard leaves and cook, stirring, until leaves wilt, about 3 minutes.
- Add the raisins and stock, cover and cook over medium-low heat for 5 minutes, stirring once or twice.
- Transfer the chard to a serving dish. Add the maple syrup and vinegar. Toss. Top with toasted cashews and serve.

96. Egg Tartines With Romesco And Greens

Serving: Serves 1 | Prep: | Cook: | Ready in:

Ingredients

- Egg Tartines
- 2 eggs, soft boiled, scrambled, or fried
- 2 piece of crusty, toasted, or grilled bread
- 1/4 cup Romesco Sauce
- olive oil
- 1/4 cup chopped, toasted almonds
- Romesco Sauce
- 1/4 cup extra-virgin olive oil, plus more to taste
- 1 slice of sourdough or country bread
- 1/3 cup skinless Marcona almonds
- 3 cloves garlic
- 1 16-ounce can piquillo peppers, drained and roughly chopped
- 1/2 teaspoon smoked paprika or pimentón
- Fine sea salt
- 3 tablespoons sherry vinegar, plus more to taste

Direction

- Egg Tartines
- Make the eggs and toast, and set aside. Rinse and dry the greens. Spread the Romesco on the toast and lay the eggs on top. Top with greens and drizzle olive oil on top. Finish with toasted almonds.
- Romesco Sauce
- Cover the bottom of a large sauté pan with about a tablespoon of the olive oil and heat over medium-high heat. Add the bread and toast it until browned on both sides, 30 seconds to 1 minute per side. Set aside to cool. Cut into ½-inch cubes. (You should have about 1 cup.)
- Wipe the pan clean with a paper towel and place back over medium-high heat. Add enough olive oil to coat the bottom of the pan again, about 2 tablespoons.
- When the oil begins to shimmer, add the almonds and garlic. Cook, stirring occasionally, until the garlic cloves are golden but not too brown and the almonds are aromatic, 1 to 2 minutes.
- Stir in the piquillo peppers and paprika. Season with salt and sauté for an additional minute or so.
- Transfer all ingredients—including the cooking liquid, the bread cubes, and the sherry vinegar—to a food processor. Blend until you achieve the desired consistency, 30 seconds to 1 minute. Some people like their romesco super-smooth and creamy, while others like a bit more texture and bite.
- Add more salt, vinegar, or olive oil as desired for taste and texture. Refrigerate for 3 to 4 hours to let the flavors meld before serving.

Store in an airtight container in the refrigerator for up to 1 week.

97. Eggnog Chicken & Waffles

Serving: Serves 6 | Prep: | Cook: |Ready in:

Ingredients

- Chicken
- 4 Chicken Wings, whole
- 1/2 cup Pancake Mix
- 1/2 cup All Purpose Flour
- 1 teaspoon Creole Seasoning
- 2 Large Organic Brown Eggs
- 1/2 tablespoon Allspice Seasoning
- 1/2 tablespoon Paprika
- 1/2 tablespoon Ground Thyme
- 1/2 teaspoon Garlic Powder
- 1/2 teaspoon Ground White Pepper
- 1/2 cup Eggnog
- dash Red Cayenne Pepper
- Waffles
- 1 cup Pancake Mix
- 1 cup Eggnog
- 2 Large Organic Brown Eggs
- 1/2 teaspoon Ground Nutmeg
- 1/2 teaspoon Ground Cinnamon
- 2 tablespoons Sugar
- 1/2 tablespoon Vanilla Extract
- 2 tablespoons Melted Butter

Direction

- To begin the waffles, add 1 cup of pancake mix to a bowl.
- Add ground nutmeg, sugar, vanilla extract and cinnamon into bowl with pancake mix and slightly stir.
- In a separate bowl, separate the 2 egg yolks from the egg whites and add the yokes into the bowl with other ingredients.
- Whip the leftover egg whites until it begins to rise and foam.
- Add eggnog to bowl with ingredients and stir until slightly smooth.
- Add melted butter and whipped egg whites into bowl with ingredients and lightly fold. Do not over blend.
- Pre-heat your waffle maker to default temperature.
- Once the waffle maker is ready, add waffle mix into waffle maker for 3 to 4 minutes or until done and place onto plate.
- To begin the chicken, rinse chicken and cut the wings in half.
- Season your wings and drumettes with creole seasoning and coat with 2 tbsp. or more of all-purpose flour.
- In a separate bowl, add 2 eggs and eggnog. Stir until smooth.
- Add the chicken pieces to the bowl and allow to sit for a few minutes while you prepare the flour and seasoning bag.
- Pre-heat your pan to medium heat and add enough olive oil to cover the bottom of the pan completely.
- Get a large zip lock bag and add flour, pancake mix, ground allspice, paprika, garlic powder, red cayenne pepper, white ground pepper and ground thyme and shake until mixed.
- Add chicken from the eggnog and egg mix into the zip lock bag and shake until each piece is coated well.
- Fry chicken pieces for 7 to 8 minutes on each side and set to side to cool.
- Serve with warm syrup.

98. Eggplant Chips With Honey

Serving: Serves 2 people | Prep: | Cook: |Ready in:

Ingredients

- 1 eggplant that's firm to the touch
- salt
- extra virgin olive oil

- cayenne pepper
- paprika
- honey

Direction

- Cut the aubergine in slices of no more than 2mm thickness. If you can use a mandoline it's best but you can also use a sharp knife that's not serrated.
- Lay the slices on a board or clean surface and salt them heavily.
- Let them rest for at least 10min or until you see that they have released water. Along with this water comes their bitterness.
- Rinse thoroughly and don't season with salt again, they don't need it.
- Paint with very little olive oil. If you add too much they will take longer to dry in the oven.
- Lay them one next to the other on an oven tray lined with baking paper.
- Drizzle extremely lightly and carefully with cayenne pepper as it's really spice and then a larger amount of paprika. At this point you could add other spices such as dried oregano, powdered onion or powdered garlic if you like.
- Take to a preheated oven at 125C for 45min.
- At 45min check if the smallest or thinnest ones are ready to come out of the oven and return the rest until done. Most of them will most likely take 1 hour to be done but check often starting from the 45min mark to make sure they don't go too dark in color.
- Let cool completely and the drizzle slightly with honey right before serving. If you add the honey a long time before eating they will become slightly soggy.

99. Eggplant And Cabbage Pitas

Serving: Serves 4-6 | Prep: | Cook: | Ready in:

Ingredients

- 1/2 cup olive oil, divided
- 1 1/4 pounds Japanese eggplant, sliced into 1 inch thick rounds
- 2 cups green cabbage
- 1/4 teaspoon tumeric
- 1/2 teaspoon Spanish paprika
- 1 teaspoon kosher salt
- 1 large cucumber, chopped
- 5 mint leaves
- 4 pitas, toasted
- For the sauce
- 1/2 cup tahini
- 2 garlic cloves, minced
- 1/2 cup water
- 2 tablespoons lemon juice

Direction

- Heat olive oil in a heavy bottomed pan over medium high heat. Add eggplant and cook for about 10 minutes, until eggplant softens. Add additional olive oil if eggplants start to burn. Stir in cabbage, turmeric, paprika, and salt. Cook for an additional 10 minutes, stirring frequently, until cabbage wilts. Adjust salt to taste.
- Meanwhile, prepare sauce. Using an immersion blender or small food processor, blend tahini, garlic, water, and lemon juice.
- To serve, stuff pitas with eggplant and cabbage, cucumbers, mint, and top with tahini sauce.

100. Eleanor's Vinegarette

Serving: Serves 3-4 | Prep: | Cook: | Ready in:

Ingredients

- 3 teaspoons any kind of salt
- 1 teaspoon any kind of pepper, not white
- 2 teaspoons Coleman's mustard
- 2 teaspoons Hungarian Hot Paprika or Regular
- 1 ounce cold water

- 3 ounces vinegar, whatever your choice [I use cider]
- 6 ounces first-pressed, virgin olive oil, or whatever oil you choose to use
- 3-4 pieces smashed and minced, fresh garlic

Direction

- 1. With some sort of "implement" [I use a chop-stick], stir all the ingredients well until all the lumps from the mustard and the paprika are completely ground finely. Slowly stir in the cold water until you have a "paste.
- "Then add remaining liquids, one-at-a-time, and stirring constantly until all particles are thoroughly dissolved. You can also make this dressing in a name-brand, glass "salad dressing shaker" using the measurements on the sides of the glass. Simply shake well when you add each liquid. After last stir/shake, then add the garlic pieces, and stir/shake once again.
- Refrigerate promptly after use, and during storing when unused.

101. Everyday Chicken Curry

Serving: Serves 6-8 | Prep: | Cook: | Ready in:

Ingredients

- 1 medium onion, minced
- 1 red or green chilli (optional)
- 1 tablespoon minced garlic
- 1 tablespoon oil (olive or cooking)
- 1 chicken, skinless and cut into small pieces
- 1 tablespoon cumin powder
- 1 tablespoon coriander powder
- 1/2 teaspoon turmeric powder
- 1 tablespoon paprika
- 1/2 tablespoon salt
- 1 tablespoon lemon juice (preferably fresh)
- 2 cups crushed tomatoes
- 2 tablespoons tomato paste
- 3 cups water
- Chilli powder, to taste

Direction

- Place minced onion and oil into a large saucepan and sauté over medium heat until brown.
- Add garlic, ginger and chicken to pot and continue to sauté.
- Using a blender, mix cumin powder, coriander powder, turmeric, paprika, salt, lemon juice, crushed tomatoes, tomato paste and 1 cup water.
- Add the blended mixture to the pot.
- Add 1 cup of water to the pot. As the curry cooks, you may want to add a second cup to get the desired consistency or to allow it to cook longer.
- Add chili powder.
- Simmer the curry on low heat until chicken is cooked, stirring occasionally (approximately 30 minutes).
- Peel 3 potatoes, cut into half lengthwise and then cut each half into quarters, ensuring they are all equal in size.
- Parboil potatoes in a separate pot until fork tender (or just before).
- When chicken is cooked (or close), add potatoes and let simmer for an additional 3-5 minutes.
- Serve with rice (cauliflower or regular) or roti and enjoy!

102. Everything Bagel Spiced Nuts

Serving: Makes about 2 1/2 cups | Prep: | Cook: | Ready in:

Ingredients

- 1 cup raw cashews
- 1 cup raw almonds
- 2 tablespoons canola oil
- 1 tablespoon sugar

- 2 teaspoons kosher salt
- 1/2 teaspoon smoked paprika
- 1 tablespoon sesame seeds, toasted
- 1 tablespoon poppy seeds
- 1 teaspoon onion powder
- 1 teaspoon garlic powder
- 1/2 cup bagel chips (broken up if large)

Direction

- Preheat your oven to 375° F. In a medium-sized bowl, toss the cashews and almonds with the oil and sugar. In a separate bowl, mix together the salt, smoked paprika, sesame seeds, poppy seeds, onion powder, and garlic powder. Set aside. Line a baking sheet with a silpat mat (or parchment) and place the nut mixture on the sheet. Bake for 15 to 17 minutes, tossing it three times during baking. As soon as the nuts come out of the oven, mix in the spices and the bagel chips. Let them cool completely before serving (or move to an airtight container for storage).

103. Fake Snow Day Baked Beans

Serving: Serves 4-6 | Prep: | Cook: | Ready in:

Ingredients

- 2 cups dried navy beans, soaked overnight
- 1 cup chopped white onion
- 1 tablespoon smoked paprika
- 2-4 tablespoons olive oil (more gives a richer taste)
- 1 tablespoon chipotle chili in adobo sauce, smooshed
- 1 teaspoon fresh ground black pepper
- 1/2 cup light brown sugar
- 1/2 teaspoon ground cloves
- 2-3 dashes Liquid Smoke
- 1 tablespoon dijon mustard
- 2 teaspoons kosher salt (adjust to your taste)
- 1 1/2 cups boiling water

Direction

- Pre-heat oven to 250 degrees. Place drained beans into an ovenproof pot or casserole dish with a lid.
- In a pan on medium heat, sauté onion in olive oil until soft. Add paprika, chipotle, and black pepper. Cook 30 seconds.
- Add to beans along with water, brown sugar, ground cloves, mustard, Liquid Smoke and salt. Taste liquid for seasoning and adjust salt and pepper to taste if needed.
- Bake covered in the oven for 5 hours at 250 degrees. Check and see if you need to add any water along the way. Beans should be very soft, caramelized and absorbed all the flavors.

104. Farro With Eggs And Mushrooms

Serving: Serves 2 | Prep: | Cook: | Ready in:

Ingredients

- 1/2 cup farro
- 1 1/2 cups water
- 10 crimini mushrooms, sliced
- 1 shallot, chopped
- 2 cloves garlic, minced
- 2 1/2 tablespoons butter
- 2 eggs
- 1/4 cup sour cream
- 1 teaspoon paprika
- 1 tablespoon fresh thyme
- salt and pepper, to taste

Direction

- In a small bowl, mix sour cream and paprika together, set aside.
- Rinse the farro and pick out any stray stones or debris. Place in a large, heavy bottomed pot and add water. Place over medium high heat and bring to a boil. Reduce heat and simmer, covered for 30-40 minutes.

- In a large saucepan over medium high heat, melt two tablespoons butter. Once foam subsides, add shallot and garlic. Cook for two minutes, until shallot starts to become translucent and add mushrooms. Sauté, stirring until mushrooms are fully cooked, about four minutes. Season to taste. Remove from heat
- In your favorite egg pan, melt the remaining tablespoon butter over medium heat. Fry your eggs (I like them over-medium).
- In a bowl, place one cup of farro. Top with half the mushroom shallot mixture, a dollop of sour cream, one egg and half the fresh thyme. Season with salt and pepper to taste. Devour!

105. Fattet Hummus (Mid Eastern Savory Chickpea Bread Pudding)

Serving: Serves 6 | Prep: 0hours0mins | Cook: 0hours0mins | Ready in:

Ingredients

- 2 cups chickpeas, dry
- 3 cups natural yogurt
- 2 tablespoons tahini
- 1/2 lemon, juiced
- 1 to 2 garlic cloves, crushed
- 1 pinch cumin
- 1 pinch white pepper (optional)
- 1 pinch salt
- 4 to 5 small pita loaves
- 1/2 cup olive oil
- 2 tablespoons pine nuts, more to taste
- 1 pinch paprika or cayenne pepper (optional for garnish)
- 3 to 4 mint leaves (optional for garnish)

Direction

- Soak the chickpeas overnight. Rinse well several times under cold running water, then place them in a large pot.
- Cover the chickpeas with about twice their own volume of fresh cold water, bring to a boil, and then lower the heat. Simmer them for one hour until tender. Add the cumin and a small dash of olive oil. Keep the pot covered to make sure the liquid remains simmering-hot and ready for use later. (Contrarily, you could use canned chickpeas, and skip to the next step. Make sure to have some hot water ready.)
- Put the yogurt in a large glass mixing bowl. Add the tahini, lemon juice, and crushed garlic. Whisk well. Bring two inches of water to a rolling boil in a pot and place the glass bowl on top. Heat the yogurt mix gently, whisking the whole time. Make sure it does not come to a boil; the idea is to just warm it up and blend the flavors together. If the yogurt mixture thickens too much, add a little of the chickpea broth until you get a soupy consistency. Add salt and white pepper to taste.
- Separate the pita loaves into two thin layers, then cut them into bite-sized pieces with kitchen scissors. Heat half the olive oil in a frying pan and shallow-fry the pita until crunchy and golden. Alternatively, brush the separated pita rounds with olive oil, toast them well in a hot oven, then break them into bite-sized pieces by hand. You could even simply use day-old bread, if you're in a hurry.
- Spread the bread in an even layer in a deep serving platter or bowl. Ladle out about a cup or so of the reserved hot chickpea broth, and drizzle it on top of the bread pieces until they are just soaked.
- Set aside 1 to 2 tablespoons of the chickpeas for garnish. With a ladle, scoop the remaining hot chickpeas out of the broth and spread them evenly on top of the bread. Pour the warmed yogurt mixture over the chickpeas. Gently stir the layers together with a large slotted spoon. Top with the reserved chickpeas.
- Heat 3 tablespoons of olive oil and fry the pine nuts until golden, then pour them, along with the hot oil, over the chickpea-yogurt mixture.

Sprinkle paprika, cayenne pepper, and the torn mint leaves on top for garnish, and enjoy immediately!

106. Faux Bouillabaisse

Serving: Serves 4 | Prep: | Cook: | Ready in:

Ingredients

- 1 Onion
- 3 Garlic cloves
- 1 Fennel bulb
- 3 tablespoons Olive Oil
- 3 Lemon slices
- 1/2 cup cooked Potato
- 1 teaspoon Paprika
- a pinches Saffron
- 1/2 teaspoon Kosher Salt
- Ground Black Pepper
- 1/4 cup Parsley
- 3 cups Chicken Stock
- 4 Tomatoes, blanched and pulped
- Parsley to garnish
- 1/2 pound Tilapia or Cod

Direction

- Cut onion and garlic into thin slivers. Trim and cut fennel into 1/4 inch slices.
- Heat olive oil in deep saucepan. Add onion, garlic and sauté for 3/4 minutes till onion starts to color,
- Add fennel and lemon slices to onion and sauté for a minute. Add potatoes, paprika, saffron, salt, pepper, parsley, chicken stock and tomatoes. Let the soup come to slow boil, lower heat and simmer for 10 minutes.
- Cut fish into bite size pieces and add to soup. Let fish cook and flake. It should take 5 to 7 minutes.
- Remove the lemon slices, garnish with remaining parsley and serve soup with a hunk of bread!

107. Fennel & Green Garbanzo Polo

Serving: Serves 5-6 | Prep: | Cook: | Ready in:

Ingredients

- Rice
- 1 cup Basmati rice, cleaned, rinsed & drained
- 2 tablespoons Ghee
- 1/4 teaspoon Kosher salt
- 2 cups boiling water
- Polo
- 1 Large Fennel bulb
- 1 cup shallots cut into thin strips or thin slices
- 1 cup sweet mini peppers cut into strips
- 2-3 tablespoons Olive oil
- Salt & freshly cracked peppercorn to taste
- 1 1/2 cups Fresh green garbanzo (or frozen edamame)
- 1 tablespoon ghee
- 1 teaspoon Green fennel seeds
- 1/4 cup Fennel leaf fronds
- 1 pinch Paprika or cayenne pepper powder (optional)

Direction

- Rice
- Melt the ghee in a heavy bottom pan. Add Basmati rice and toast in the ghee until it begins to emit a characteristic fragrant aroma.
- Add the boiling water along with the salt, give the mixture a good stir to dislodge the grains that are holding on to the bottom of the pan. Lower the heat to barely above a simmer, cover with a lid and allow the rice to cook & absorb all the liquid. (~ 20 minutes), Fluff and set aside.
- Polo
- Using a mandolin, slice the fennel bulb into thin slices. Reserve the fronds. Combine fennel with the shallots and the sweet pepper in a large bowl. Drizzle with the olive oil, and season with Salt & fresh crushed pepper.

Using clean hands, toss the vegetables to coat evenly with the olive oil. Layer evenly on a baking sheet and roast in a 450 F oven until the shallots turn translucent and begin to caramelize. (~ 30 min)
- Steam the Fresh green garbanzo (or edamame) until done and set aside.
- In a large mixing bowl add 2 cups of rice, the steamed garbanzo and the roasted fennel, Shallot & pepper mix.
- Heat the ghee until almost smoking and add the fennel & nigella seeds. Once the fennel seeds 'split' (like cumin under similar conditions) pour this tempering into the rice mixture. You may add the paprika if you choose into the oil just before pouring it into the rice. Gently fold the mixture to combine the ingredients. Taste and adjust for seasoning with the salt & pepper. Garnish with the Fennel fronds & serve warm with tsatziki, raita or plain yogurt.

108. Feta Stuffed Grilled Poblano Peppers In A Sesame Peanut Sauce

Serving: Serves 4 | Prep: | Cook: | Ready in:

Ingredients

- stuffed poblano peppers
- 4 Poblano peppers
- 1 cup grated paneer
- 1 cup Crumbled Feta cheese
- 1/8 teaspoon paprika or cayenne powder
- Gravy
- 1/2 cup dry roasted peanuts (unsalted)
- 1/4 cup white sesame seeds
- 2 teaspoons cumin seeds
- 1 tablespoon Tamarind pulp or pomegranate molasses
- 1/2 cup grated frozen fresh coconut
- 2 arbol chiles
- 1 Large vidalia onion cut into pieces
- 2 cloves garlic
- 1 tablespoon fresh ginger root, minced
- 2 tablespoons Finely chopped Cilantro for garnishing
- 2 tablespoons ghee
- 1/4 teaspoon turmeric
- Salt to taste

Direction

- Grill the poblano peppers directly over the flame on the stove top. When the skin is blistered and blackened, wrap in plastic wrap and set aside. When cool, rub off the charred skin off the peppers. (Use gloves if your fingers are sensitive to capsaicin). Make a slit and carefully scoop out the seeds from the cavity & discard.
- Combine the feta, paneer & the cayenne/paprika. Carefully stuff this filling into the cavity in the roasted poblano peppers. Place the peppers into a rectangular ceramic baking dish.
- Ina hot skillet, toast the cumin & sesame seeds till they turn a golden brown color, remove from heat, combine with the peanuts, arbol chile, tamarind/pomegranate molasses and coconut and grind to a paste. Set aside. Clean out the blender jar with a cup of water and add to the paste.
- In the same blender jar add the onion, ginger & garlic & blend into a smooth paste. Heat the ghee in a skillet and add the onion paste & fry on medium/low heat till the paste turns a light brown.
- Add the sesame/peanut blend to the onion paste, add salt & turmeric and simmer on medium heat till the gravy for 10 minutes.
- Pour the gravy over the stuffed poblano peppers, cover the baking dish with aluminum foil (with holes pierced through for the steam to escape). Place in a 300 F oven for 30 minutes.
- Remove from the oven, garnish with fresh cilantro and serve with Naan, Biryani or plain Basmati rice.

109. Fish "Meatballs" In Spicy Red Pepper Sauce

Serving: Serves 2 | Prep: | Cook: | Ready in:

Ingredients

- For the "Meatballs"
- 1 slice white bread, crusts removed
- 1/2 lb white fish (I used tilapia, but whatever is on sale), coarsely chopped
- 1 shallot, coarsely chopped
- 1 clove garlic
- 1/3 cup parsley leaves
- 1 egg, beaten
- 1/2 teaspoon salt
- dash of cayenne
- 2 cups spicy red pepper sauce (recipe follows)
- Spicy Red Pepper Sauce
- 1 small yellow onion, diced
- 1 small red bell pepper, diced
- 1/2 teaspoon hot smoked paprika
- dash cayenne
- 1 garlic clove, minced
- 1/2 teaspoon salt
- One 15-ounce can crushed tomatoes

Direction

- For the "Meatballs"
- In a small food processor, pulse the bread until it resembles crumbs. Set aside in a medium mixing bowl. Add the fish to the processor and pulse until resembling the texture of ground beef. Remove to the bowl. Add the shallot, garlic, and parsley and mince in the processor. Toss together with the bread crumbs, fish, egg, salt, and pepper. Form the mixture into balls, about 1 1/2 inches wide, and set aside on a cutting board. You should have about 8 balls.
- Coat a large lidded skillet or sauté pan with olive oil and set it over medium-high heat. Brown the fish balls in batches until seared on both sides. Set aside.
- Clean out any burnt bits from the pan. Either add premade Spicy Red Pepper sauce, or follow the directions below to make it. When the sauce is finished and simmering, add the balls back to the pan. Cook for 5 minutes, covered, then turn the balls in the sauce and cook for another 3 to 5 minutes, until the balls are cooked through completely.
- To serve, place a forkful of spaghetti on each plate and top with a spoonful of sauce and 4 meatballs. Garnish with parsley.
- Spicy Red Pepper Sauce
- In a large skillet over medium heat, sauté the onion and red pepper in enough olive oil to coat the pan. Cook until the vegetables have softened, about 6 minutes. Add the paprika, cayenne, garlic, and cook for another 2 minutes, until the mixture is very fragrant. Add the salt, and carefully stir in the tomatoes. Simmer until the sauce has thickened and the vegetables are very tender, about 5 minutes. Turn off the heat and taste again for seasoning. Puree in a food processor or with an immersion blender until smooth. (This can be made up to a week in advance).

110. Flatiron Chicken

Serving: Serves 4 | Prep: | Cook: | Ready in:

Ingredients

- 1 Whole Chicken (3#) cut into 8 peices
- 1 head garlic, cut in half
- 3 tablespoons Olive Oil
- 1 tablespoon Paprika
- 1 tablespoon Cumin
- 2 Bay leaves
- 2 cups onion cut in chunks
- 1 pound Yukon Gold POtatoes cut in 2 " chunks or equivalent in smaller potatoes
- 1 cup Thick sliced Spanish (dry) Chorizo
- 2 cups Red & Yellow Pepper cut in 2" chunks or use mini peppers

- 1 bunch Dandelion greens, washed & chopped
- Salt & Pepper
- 2 tablespoons Sherry Vinegar
- 1/2 cup Chicken Stock
- Garnish: Chopped Fresh parsely, toasted almonds lemon zest- Optional

Direction

- Mix together Cumin, Paprika + 1 teaspoon each Salt & Pepper
- Season both sides of Chicken (you can do this early in the day or even the day before)
- Pre heat oven to 400Heat 1 Tablespoon Olive oil in a LARGE oven proof pan or Shallow Dutch Oven
- Brown Chicken on Both Sides, making sure skin in brown & crunchy
- Remove Chicken from Pan add in Chorizo Potatoes, Onions, Peppers & Garlic
- Toss to coat, Season with Cumin, Paprika mix well, tuck bay leaves into the veg, Lay Chicken on Top
- Roast in oven @ 40 minutes until veg is tender and chicken in cooked
- Place pan back on low burner, Remove Chicken & Veg to serving platter
- Deglaze pan with Vinegar & Stock
- Wilt Greens briefly in hot pan
- Add Greens to serving platter ...Drizzle chicken & Veg with remaining Olive oil Serve, garnished with fresh parsley or not and a sprinkled of toasted almonds & lemon zest or not.

111. Floribbean Shrimp And Grits

Serving: Serves 4 | Prep: | Cook: | Ready in:

Ingredients

- 1 pound Shrimp, peeled and deveined
- 1 teaspoon Brown Sugar
- 1/2 teaspoon Allspice
- 1/2 teaspoon Paprika
- 1/4 teaspoon Cayenne Pepper
- 1/4 teaspoon Ground Ginger
- 1/4 teaspoon Salt
- 1/4 teaspoon Black Pepper
- 2 cups Water
- 2 cups Chicken (or Seafood) Stock
- 1 cup Grits
- 1/2 teaspoon Onion Powder
- 1/2 teaspoon Black Pepper
- 1/4 teaspoon Salt
- 2 tablespoons Butter
- 2 cups Grated Cheddar Cheese
- 6 Bacon Slices, chopped
- 2 tablespoons Lemon Juice
- 1 Garlic Clove, minced
- 2/3 cup Chopped Green Onions
- 2 tablespoons Chopped Fresh Cilantro

Direction

- Combine the brown sugar with your dry spices; allspice, paprika, cayenne, ginger, salt and pepper. I like to use a Ziploc bag to combine the spices and coat the shrimp, but a medium sized bowl works just fine. Make sure the shrimp is patted dry before shaking into the spice mixture, seal up the bag (or bowl) and refrigerate until needed.
- Using a medium saucepan, bring water and stock to a boil and add the onion powder, salt and pepper. Stir in the grits, cover and reduce heat to a low simmer. Stir the grits occasionally to prevent them from sticking to the bottom of the pan. Stir in the butter and cheese when the consistency is thickened and keep at low heat.
- Bring a large skillet to medium heat and add the bacon. Stirring occasionally, cook for 7-8 minutes until the bacon is firm but not crispy. Pour off the excess bacon grease and return the skillet to medium heat. Add the shrimp and toss for 5-6 minutes, until the shrimp is turning pink. Add the lemon juice, garlic clove, green onions, and cilantro, and stir

- together to combine. Cook for an additional 3-4 minutes.
- Plate the grits onto plates or bowls, and top with the shrimp.

112. Foolproof Rolled Sandwiches Party Tray With Tomato Dip & Deviled Eggs

Serving: Serves 8-10 | Prep: | Cook: | Ready in:

Ingredients

- Rolled Sandwiches
- 7 large flour tortillas (room temp.)
- 8 ounces low-fat cream cheese, softened
- 1/2 cup mayonnaise (I use half-fat)
- 1/2 cup Ranch Dressing
- 1/4 cup dried minced onions
- 1 tablespoon minced garlic
- 1 envelope dried Vegetable Soup mix
- 1 package spinach leaves
- 1/2 package of romain lettuce, torn small
- 1/2 pound thin-sliced smoked turkey
- 1/2 pound thin-sliced deli smoked ham
- 1/2 cup brown mustard
- colored toothpics (at least 60)
- Tomato Dip & Deviled Eggs
- 1 large fat, red, ripe tomato, cold!
- 1/2 cup low-fat sour cream
- 1/2 cup low-fat mayo
- 1 tablespoon dried minced oion
- 1/2 teaspoon dried dill
- 1/4 teaspoon white pepper
- 1/2 teaspoon minced garlic
- 1/3 cup shredded cheese (cheddar & Monterrey jack)
- 1 dozen eggs
- 1/4 cup lo-fat mayo
- 1 tablespoon brown mustard
- 1 tablespoon DILL relish (NOT sweet!)
- 1/2 tablespoon curry powder
- 1/2 tablespoon minced garlic
- paprika to garnish
- baby carrots to garnish

Direction

- First boil your eggs for 30 minutes, as this makes them good and firm. Set the timer then take them off and immediately pour out the hot water and fill the pot with cold water--let it run over the eggs a minute, then leave them to sit in the cool water until you're ready for them--this rapid cooling prevents the dark sulfur coating on the yolk.
- Next take out the flour tortillas and make sure they are room temperature for easy rolling. In a medium bowl add the cream cheese, mayo, minced onion and garlic, dried vegetable soup mix, dill and Ranch dressing--mash and mix with a fork until smooth. Spread this mix on the tortillas almost to the edges, leaving about a half-inch clear. Lay the spinach leaves and a little romaine lettuce, flattening it slightly (for easier rolling). Lay on the meats (separately or some of each, as you prefer), then spread with a little brown mustard. Take the edge of the tortilla and carefully roll it tightly and turn the seam side down--secure it with 3-4 toothpicks, set aside, covered in the fridge to let them firm up, about 30 minutes.
- Carefully peel the eggs, cutting each in half (wipe the knife clean after each egg so you don't spread the soft yolk around), and set the halves on a separate plate and dump the yolks into a small bowl. Add the mayo, brown mustard, curry powder, dill relish, minced garlic and salt and white pepper to taste, stir well to blend them with the yolks, then spoon into a large zip-lock bag. Cut a very small corner off the bag, and use this to pipe the mix into the egg halves; sprinkle with paprika and set aside. I sometimes use an olive half to garnish as well.
- Make sure the tomato is firm and cold, then taking a small serrated knife, cut the top off (about 2/3 up) using little v-shaped cuts, lift off top and scoop out the tomato insides.
- Mix the sour-cream, mayo, white pepper, dill, minced garlic and garlic--add the tomato

- insides (minced) if you like, stir well and fill the tomato--top with shredded cheese.
- Take the sandwiches from the fridge and carefully cut into 5 portions each and secure with the colored toothpicks. Garnish the tray with a little romaine lettuce and lay the sandwiches as shown, nestle the deviled eggs around them, then a handful or so of baby carrots. The tomato goes in the middle. Cover with clear Saran wrap and store in the fridge until the party is ready!

113. French Bread Eggs Benedict With Asparagus

Serving: Serves 2 | Prep: | Cook: | Ready in:

Ingredients

- 4 eggs (at room temp)
- 1 egg yolk
- 2 tablespoons butter, melted
- 1 tablespoon butter
- 1/2 tablespoon lemon juice
- 10-12 Asparagus Stems, bottom removed
- 1/2 red onion, diced
- 6 thin slices of french baguette
- 1/8 teaspoon chili powder
- 1/4 teaspoon smoked paprika
- 1 tablespoon vinegar
- salt
- pepper

Direction

- Preheat oven to 350.
- For hollandaise sauce, add lemon juice and yolk to metal bowl and beat until doubles in size. Place bowl over double boiler or over a pot with boiling water. Ensure water does not touch bottom of bowl. Pour in melted butter and whisk until incorporated. Careful not to allow egg to cook. Remove from heat, add chili powder and smoked paprika and cover, mix and set aside.
- Add about 4 inches water to a high rimmed skillet or small pot. Place French Baguette into oven on middle rack and let heat for about 10 minutes. Watch to prevent burning.
- In medium pan, add onion and cook for about 7 minutes, remove from pan. Add remaining 1 tablespoon butter to pan and add asparagus, season with salt, pepper. Add 1 tablespoon water and cover and cook about 5-7 minutes.
- While asparagus is cooking, add vinegar to boiling water and then carefully add eggs. I used silicone eggs cups to make it a bit easier. Cover and cook for 3 minutes.
- Top bread with eggs, onions and asparagus. Spread onions around and top with sauce. If sauce is thick, add 1 teaspoon water.

114. Fresh Corn Salsa

Serving: Serves 4 | Prep: 0hours15mins | Cook: 0hours20mins | Ready in:

Ingredients

- 2 ears of fresh corn on the cob, shucked and ready to go
- 2 tablespoons olive oil
- 3 shallots, finely chopped up
- 1 fresh red chili pepper, finely chopped up
- 1/2 red paprika, finely chopped up
- Finely grated zest and juice of a lime
- 1 -2 tablespoons sweet chili sauce
- 1 tablespoon fresh coriander, finely chopped
- A handful fresh basil, finely chopped
- Optional - green scallions to garnish and basil leaves
- 1 tablespoon chopped mint

Direction

- Heat up a grill pan on medium. When hot, brush on some oil and place corn on. Let cook lightly and turn around after 30 seconds, till the corn changes color from yellow to just

- golden - you know what I mean, about 3-4 minutes.
- Remove from pan and using a sharp knife, strip the cobs of their kernels, cutting as close to the cob as possible, without getting the cob itself!
- Heat up remaining oil in another pan (sorry) and gently cook the shallots, chili pepper, paprika, lime zest for a couple of minutes till soft but not colored.
- Add the corn kernels, stir well and take off the heat. Stir in the chili sauce and herbs. Season to taste.
- Also delicious served on top of light toasts, Brie, eggs, crostini style

115. Fresh Stuffed Red Pepper Shells With Pearl Couscous, Forbidden Rice, Kamut Or Red Quinoa

Serving: Serves 4 or even 8 (with half portions) | Prep: | Cook: | Ready in:

Ingredients

- 4 sweet select red peppers
- 2-3 cups whole grains, soaked and then cooked accordingly, such as forbidden rice, pearl couscous, kamut, or red quinoa
- 2 teaspoons cumin, optional
- 1/4 teaspoon tumeric, optional
- 1 cup feta or similar cheese
- 1 ounce toasted pinion pine nuts, almonds, or pecans
- 4 tablespoons fresh chopped mixed herbs, such as mint, basil, parsley and cilantro
- 1 teaspoon pink or kosher salt
- 1-2 tablespoons chopped scallions
- 1-2 tablespoons dried currants, yellow raisins or cranberries, optional
- 2 tablespoons grated carrot and fresh ginger
- 4 tablespoons EVOO
- juice of a fresh lemon or lime
- 1 tablespoon champagne vinegar
- 1 teaspoon dijon mustard
- 1 tablespoon sweet or hot pepper jelly, or honey
- salt, paprika and pepper to taste
- paprika for garnish
- fresh herbs for garnish

Direction

- Cut the tops of the peppers and take out all the seeds as well as the white fleshy interior bits. Cut triangles out of the top of the pepper saving the cuts for use in the filling. (You can bisect or even trisect the remaining triangle border of the pepper shell for effect if desired. This can also make eating easier with these pre-cuts).
- Mix your cooked grains of choice with feta and whatever other fillings and seasonings you want to include in a bowl. Be sure to add the leftover red pepper triangles diced further into the filling. I have used turmeric and cumin with the pearl couscous in one version, but not in the forbidden rice version.
- Mix the oil, juice, mustard, jelly or honey, vinegar with salt, paprika, and pepper to taste for the dressing. Pour this over the grain salad filling and lightly toss. Adjust the seasoning if needed.
- Fill each cut pepper with the grain filling. Garnish with fresh herbs and paprika. You can serve whole or even consider slicing these in half.

116. Friday Night Garlicky Roast Chicken And Potatoes

Serving: Serves 4-6 | Prep: | Cook: | Ready in:

Ingredients

- 1 3-3 1/2 lb. broiler chicken
- 1/4 cup crushed garlic cloves (about 6-8 cloves)

- 1/2 teaspoon paprika
- 1/4 teaspoon tumeric
- 1/2 teaspoon kosher salt
- 1/8 teaspoon black pepper
- 1 tablespoon olive oil
- 1 celery stalk cut in quarters
- 1 small onion cut in quarters
- 1 parsnip cut in quarters
- 1 carrot cut in quarters
- 1/4 cup frozen orange juice concentrate
- 1/4 cup water
- 8-10 red potatoes cubed
- 1/2 teaspoon paprika
- 1/4 teaspoon tumeric
- 1/2 teaspoon kosher salt
- 1/8 teaspoon black pepper
- 1 1/2 tablespoons olive oil

Direction

- Mix the garlic, paprika, turmeric, salt and pepper with the olive oil to form a paste. Rub the chicken all over with the garlic rub, including in the cavity and under the skin.
- Place chicken in roaster with quartered vegetables around it and pour the frozen orange juice concentrate on top and add water to bottom of roaster. Roast covered in 400 degree oven for 1 hour. Remove cover and continue to roast chicken 30 minutes longer uncovered, basting frequently. Then flip the chicken so the breast is sitting in the juices and roast another 30 minutes uncovered or till done.
- To make the potatoes, toss the cubed potatoes with the paprika, turmeric, salt, pepper and olive oil and transfer to an oiled baking tray or roasting pan. Roast uncovered for 1 hour or till done in 400 degree oven. If desired you can add 2 tablespoons of the roast chicken pan juices to the potatoes.
- To serve, assemble the roast chicken on a platter with the vegetables and potatoes around it.

117. Fried Stuffed Zucchini Blossoms

Serving: Makes 8 | Prep: | Cook: | Ready in:

Ingredients

- 8 squash blossoms, rinsed well
- 1 large ball fresh mozzarella cheese, sliced into thin strips
- 1 egg
- 1/4 cup water
- 1/4 cup all-purpose flour
- 1/2 teaspoon kosher salt
- 1/2 teaspoon hot paprika
- 1/4 teaspoon freshly ground black pepper
- 1/4 teaspoon cayenne pepper
- oil for frying

Direction

- Fill a large frying pan up to about 1/2 inch with oil.
- Heat the oil over medium-high heat. While the oil is heating, stuff the blossoms with the strips of mozzarella.
- Make an egg wash by beating the egg and water together.
- Mix together the flour, salt, paprika, black pepper and red pepper in a shallow dish.
- When the oil is hot enough for frying, dip each blossom first in the egg wash, then in the flour mixture, and gently place it in the oil. Avoid crowding the blossoms - if the pan isn't large enough, do this is two batches of four.
- Cook each blossom approximately two minutes on each side, then let rest on a paper towel.
- Eat the entire thing while it's hot!

118. Fried Shrimp Cakes Tortillitas De Camarones

Serving: Serves 6 | Prep: | Cook: | Ready in:

Ingredients

- 1.5 cupschickpea flour
- 1 cupsmall pink shrimp or dried shrimp
- 1 tablespoonparsley
- 3 spring onion or scallions cut finely in small rings
- 1 tablespoonpaprika powder
- 1-2 cupsvegetable oil for pan frying (add more when needed)
- 1 cupwater

Direction

- Put 1½ cup chickpea flour in a bowl
- Add the paprika powder and parsley
- Stir thoroughly the flour mixture before adding the water and stir some more
- Then add the scallion and stir
- Add the shrimp and stir as well
- Heat a skillet on medium to high heat
- Take two spoons and scoop the batter into the oil. Press them down in the oil so it becomes a think crisp small pancake
- Pan fry for about 2 minutes or when golden brown then turn the tortillas de camarones
- When done take the tortillas out of the pan and drain on a paper towel
- Serve immediately

119. Gandule Rice (Arroz Con Gandules)

Serving: Serves 4 | Prep: 24hours15mins | Cook: 0hours30mins | Ready in:

Ingredients

- 1 cup gandules (pigeon peas), soaked overnight
- 1 pound lean pork (tenderloin is best)
- 1 whole onion
- 6 cloves garlic
- 1 pinch or more pepper, to taste
- 1 (8-oz) can tomato sauce or tomato puree
- 4 stalks green onion
- 1 bunch cilantro
- 4 cups chicken broth
- 2 cups rice, uncooked
- 1 pinch or more salt, to taste
- 1 tablespoon achiote seeds (substitute: 1 1/2 tsp paprika + 1 1/2 tsp turmeric)
- 1 tablespoon vegetable oil (or Crisco)

Direction

- Bring gandules to a boil; drain in colander and set aside.
- Slice pork into thin, short, narrow strips. Chop onions. Fry pork with onions, pepper, and garlic until browned. Add can of tomato sauce and allow it to simmer, uncovered, for a few minutes. Add chopped green onions, cilantro, gandules, broth, and uncooked rice. Add salt to taste.
- In a separate pan, melt the achiote seeds (or paprika + turmeric) in oil. Strain seeds, if using. Add the infused oil to the other ingredients.
- Bring mixture to a boil then lower heat and place foil on top, folding in the edges. Place pot lid on foil. Simmer until the rice is cooked, about 15 minutes.

120. Ganoush Is The New Guacamole

Serving: Serves 8 | Prep: | Cook: |Ready in:

Ingredients

- 1 medium sized Japanese eggplant (the long skinny kind)
- 3-5 garlic cloves, peeled
- 1 drizzle of olive oil
- 2 tablespoons low sodium tahini (check out Artisana tahini packets at Whole Foods - less commitment than a huge tub!)
- 1/4 teaspoon low sodium (20 mg per teaspoon) horseradish

- 1 tablespoon water
- 1/4 teaspoon smoked paprika
- 1/4 teaspoon ground black pepper
- 1 meyer lemon, just the juice
- 1 handful of chopped parsley for flare

Direction

- Turn oven to 400 degrees F.
- Peel eggplant (with a vegetable peeler) and chop in half. Place the eggplant and garlic cloves on tinfoil and drizzle with olive oil. Wrap up the tinfoil and place the aromatic veggie package into the oven for 1 hour.
- While the eggplant and garlic are roasting, mix the tahini and the water with a spoon in a deep bowl or a tall plastic container (like the kind that comes with an immersion blender) until it is smooth.
- Add the lemon juice, the horseradish, the pepper, and the smoked paprika to the tahini/water mixture. Wait.
- When the eggplant is soft to the touch, add the garlic and eggplant to the tahini/water/lemon juice mixture. Use an immersion blender, Cuisinart, or stand-up blender to mix all the ingredients, adding a few more drizzles of olive oil as it blends to make it silky smooth.
- Garnish with roughly chopped parsley and a bag of chips. Touch. Down.

121. Garlic Brad Sticks With Garlic Infused Olive Oil

Serving: Serves 4-6 | Prep: | Cook: | Ready in:

Ingredients

- 1 1/3 cups Warm water
- 1 packet Active dry yeast
- 2 teaspoons salt
- 5 cups flour
- 3 tablespoons olive oil
- 1/4 cup garlic olive oil
- 1 tablespoon Garlic powder
- 1 tablespoon Paprika

Direction

- Add warm water into a bowl of dry active yeast and let set for 10 minutes. Note: the water should be warm to the touch. Too warm of water and the yeast will die. And you don't want to be known as a yeast murderer. No, no you do not.
- In a separate bowl add the flour and the salt and whisk together to combine.
- In one cup increments; add the flour/salt mixture to the yeast/water mixture. After the first cup of flour, add the 3 tablespoons of olive oil. Now mix, mix, and mix until dough forms.
- Put dough on well-floured surface and knead for a minute. Note: It's not need as in "I need your love". Remember a very important rule of baking; dough can't love. Put dough in a greased bowl and place bowl in the oven turned off with a towel over the bowl for 45 minutes
- After 45 minutes, take your dough out of the oven, place it on well-floured surface, divide in half, and roll out. Preheat the oven to 450°F (232°C)
- Roll the dough out into a square shape (about a ½ inch thick). Take a pizza cutter or sharp knife and cut the dough into 1 inch strips long ways. Take your strips of dough and cut them in half
- With your half cut dough strips; fold them in half long ways (like a hot dog bun). Twist away all those bad feelings away until you get something twisty and fun.
- Sprinkle some corn meal on a cookie sheet. Lay the spiral strips of dough on the sheets, about ¼ inches apart
- Take a brush and gently brush your olive oil along the dough. Sprinkle some garlic powder and paprika over the dough. Take your brush again and brush over the sticks to evening coat the seasonings. Put your breadsticks in the oven for 12 to 14 minutes or until golden brown

122. Gazpacho With Peaches And Jalapeño

Serving: Serves 4 | Prep: | Cook: |Ready in:

Ingredients

- 3 tomatoes (they should feel heavy for their size)
- 1 ripe peach
- 1 Kirby cucumber
- 1 small purple onion, divided
- 1 garlic clove
- 1/2 a jalapeño pepper
- 1 shallot
- 1 pinch dried oregano
- 1 pinch paprika
- 3/4 teaspoon sea salt
- black pepper
- 2 tablespoons sherry (or red wine) vinegar
- 3 tablespoons olive oil
- 1/2 cup cherry or grape tomatoes (as garnish)
- 1/2 a ripe avocado (as garnish)
- 1 ear of corn (as garnish)

Direction

- Boil a medium pot of water. While you are waiting for the water to heat up, prepare an ice bath. Use the tip of a knife to draw an X into the bottoms of the tomatoes and the peach. (This will make removing the skins a breeze.)
- Peel the skins off the tomatoes and the peach; they should slide right off. Also remove any stems from the tomatoes. Discard the skins and stems. (You could also save them for a stock.)
- Dice up the tomatoes and the peach, making your best effort to keep the juices on the cutting board. It doesn't have to look pretty. Move everything to a large bowl.
- Next, dice the: cucumber, 1/2 the purple onion, the garlic clove, the jalapeno half (seeds removed), and the shallot. Toss everything into the bowl with the tomatoes and the peach.
- Into the bowl goes the: oregano, paprika, sea salt, a healthy crack of black pepper, the peach balsamic vinegar, the sherry vinegar, and the olive oil. Give everything a good stir.
- Move the contents of the bowl to a blender or a food processor. (If you don't have one, you could always enjoy what you've made as a salad.) Blend the gazpacho to your desired texture. (I blend mine about 30 seconds, because I like it to be smooth, but still to retain a little texture. If you want it totally smooth, blend for about 1 minute.)
- Empty the gazpacho back into the large bowl. Cover it with plastic, and move it to the fridge for 1-3 hours. (Of course you can eat it right away, but it's better to give the flavors a chance to meld. It's good in the fridge, covered, for about 2 days.)
- While the gazpacho is chilling in the fridge, prepare the garnishes. With the second 1/2 of the red onion, I like to create wispy slices with my mandolin, but you could also do a fine dice. The cherry tomatoes just need to be washed, and cut into quarters. The avocado can be sliced or diced. You can grill, simmer or steam the corn. Just cut the kernels off the cob before you're ready to serve.
- Ladle the gazpacho into 4 bowls. Generously scatter each with red onion, cherry tomatoes, avocado, and corn.

123. Gipsy Lunch

Serving: Serves 1 | Prep: | Cook: |Ready in:

Ingredients

- 1 Slice of fresh bread.
- 1 pinch Smoked paprika
- 1 splash Extra virgin olive oil
- 1 pinch Sea salt

Direction

- If you can get your hands on still warm bread, I urge you to try spicing it this way! It is so simple but so so satisfying!
- Cut a slice of bread, sprinkle with the smoked paprika and a little sea salt, drizzle with olive oil and squash with your fingers to marry the ingredients! Enjoy!

124. Gluten Free Pot Pie With Brown Rice Crust

Serving: Serves 4-6 | Prep: | Cook: | Ready in:

Ingredients

- Rice crust
- 1 cup cooked brown rice (or wild and brown mix)
- 1/4 cup Parmesan cheese
- 2 teaspoons paprika
- 1 tablespoon fresh parsley, chopped
- 2 teaspoons dried thyme
- Salt and pepper, to taste
- Filling
- 1 tablespoon butter
- 1 onion, yellow or white, chopped
- 1 cup sliced button mushrooms
- 4 large carrots, thinly sliced
- 2 pieces celery, thinly sliced
- 1/2 cup frozen peas
- 2 teaspoons dried thyme
- 1 cup chicken broth
- 1 cup low-fat or non-fat milk
- 1/4 cup gluten-free flour (brown rice recommended; can use all-purpose if not allergic to gluten)
- Salt and pepper, to taste

Direction

- Preheat oven to 400 degrees F. Spray or lightly oil a 9 inch pie dish.
- Heat butter in a large skillet over medium high heat. Add all the vegetables and thyme; and cook until just tender, about 8-10 minutes.
- Add flour and stir constantly for 1 minute until all vegetables coated. Add broth and milk, stir well and bring to a simmer. Reduce heat to medium and simmer until very thick, about 10 minutes.
- While veggies are cooking, combine rice, cheese, paprika, thyme, salt and pepper in a medium bowl.
- Stir peas into vegetable mixture and season with salt and pepper before transferring to prepared dish. Scatter rice mixture evenly over the top. Place dish on a baking sheet to catch drips. Bake until bubbly and crust is crisp, about 30 minutes.

125. Goat Cheese Croquettes

Serving: Serves 2-4 | Prep: | Cook: | Ready in:

Ingredients

- 1 log of goat cheese (you can use either seasoned or plain)
- 1/4 cup all purpose flour
- 1 egg
- 1/2 cup Panko bread crumbs
- 1 tablespoon salt (I use Maldon flakes)
- 1 tablespoon black pepper
- 1 tablespoon smoked paprika
- 1 tablespoon dried oregano

Direction

- Freeze goat cheese for about 10 minutes (so it's easy to work with), then divide into round balls.
- Roll the balls in a bowl with 1/4 cup flour, then dip them in a bowl with the beaten egg, and roll in another bowl of a mixture of panko, salt, pepper, oregano and paprika - coat evenly.
- Heat 1 inch of vegetable oil in a large skillet over medium-high heat. Gently drop the chilled croquettes into the oil and fry until

- golden brown on all sides. It should take about 2-4 minutes.
- Transfer to paper towels to drain, serve hot.

126. Golden Onion Dip

Serving: Makes about 1 cup | Prep: | Cook: | Ready in:

Ingredients

- 1 medium yellow onion
- 1 tablespoon butter
- 1 tablespoon olive oil
- 1/2 teaspoon paprika
- 1/2 teaspoon salt
- 1/2 teaspoon freshly ground black pepper
- 2 ounces cream cheese, softened
- 2 tablespoons mayonnaise
- 1/3 cup sour cream

Direction

- Peel the onion and cut in half. Slice the onion into very thin half-moon slices. Heat the butter and oil over medium heat in a large skillet. Add the onion and sauté about 10 minutes, stirring every so often. Add the paprika, salt and pepper. Reduce the heat to low and cook 10 minutes more. Remove from the heat and cool.
- Meanwhile, beat the cream cheese, mayonnaise, and sour cream together with an electric mixer. Stir in the onions. Refrigerate for at least 30 minutes and up to two days. Serve with potato chips for dipping.

127. Gourmet Orange Cashew "Chicken"

Serving: Serves 12 to 15 nuggets | Prep: | Cook: | Ready in:

Ingredients

- "Chicken"
- 7 ounces Extra-Firm Tofu
- 4 ounces chopped portobello mushrooms
- 5 tablespoons nutritional yeast
- 2 teaspoons paprika
- 1 teaspoon cardamom
- 0.5 teaspoons onion powder
- 0.5 cups cashews
- 0.125 cups (1/8) almond milk
- Marmalade, Batter, and Finishing
- 1 cup orange juice
- 1 cup water
- 1/4 cup apple cider vinegar
- 1 cup cane sugar, granulated
- 1 tablespoon fresh minced ginger
- 1 tablespoon fresh minced garlic
- 1 thinly sliced jalapeno (adjust according to taste)
- 1 teaspoon citrus zest, orange or lemon would work best
- 2 cups tempura flour
- 2 teaspoons oil
- 1 teaspoon cracked black pepper

Direction

- "Chicken"
- Heat oven to 325' F.
- In a blender, combine cashews and almond milk and blend until consistent texture.
- Cut tofu into 1"x1"x1" cubes and add all ingredients (paprika, mushrooms, cardamom, onion powder) including cashew mixture, into food processor and combine until everything is well mixed. Depending on the size and quality of your food processor, you may have to finish mixing with a spatula in order to create a malleable nugget. Add nutritional yeast as necessary.
- Scoop out individual and uniquely shaped nuggets and place them onto a butter-lined baking sheet.
- Cook for 30-40 minutes, or until you start to see browning on the outside.

- Stick into freezer and let's move on to the marmalade and batter!
- Marmalade, Batter, and Finishing
- Combine liquid ingredients into large sauce pan and bring to a boil.
- Once boiling add in the garlic, ginger, zest, and sugar.
- Boil for about 15 minutes, or until it reduces by about 25%. Remove from heat and add thinly sliced jalapenos.
- For the batter we need to just mix together the tempura batter, oil, and 3/4 cup marmalade with the crushed black pepper.
- Bring deep-fryer to 350' F, or heat 2" of oil in a pan to a near highest heat (9).
- By now the nuggets should be quite close to freezing, if not, take a break, Kemosabe. Once they are (or are nearly) frozen, take out, roll in batter, and then plop into the fryer!
- Now, depending on how long you had to wait for these guys to cool, you may need to quickly reheat the marmalade. That's fine. Once it's heated take the fried nuggets and plate them next to rice and veggies, pouring the marmalade on the nuggets. Enjoy!

128. Grandma's Hungarian Pork Stew (a/k/a "Sertesporkolt")

Serving: Serves 4 | Prep: | Cook: | Ready in:

Ingredients

- 2 pounds Pork Loin, Cut Into 1-inch Pieces
- 1 Large Onion, Finely Chopped
- 1 14.5 oz Can Diced Tomatoes
- 2 Green Peppers, Seeded and Cut into 1/2 Inch Strips
- 4 tablespoons Salted Butter
- 1/2 teaspoon Hot Hungarian Paprika
- 1 pinch Salt (to taste)
- 1/4 teaspoon Caraway Seeds, crushed w-back of spoon
- 1/2 cup Water

Direction

- In 3 qt covered flame-proof casserole, sauté onion in butter over medium-high until it wilts (about 3 minutes.) Remove from pan and place in a large bowl.
- Return pan to stove-top and add the pork. Cook until pork is browned on all sides, then remove the pork from the casserole and add to the bowl with the onions.
- Add 1/2 cup water to pan and scrape-up the juices and cooking detritus.
- Add the salt, paprika and caraway seeds. Stir. Put meat and onions back into casserole, then add enough water to just-barely cover the meat. Simmer on low, covered for 30 minutes.
- Add green pepper strips, tomatoes and their juices to casserole. Cover and simmer for an additional 60 minutes, adding water whenever needed, to keep the meat just barely covered with sauce.
- Remove from heat, let cool and skim fat from surface of the sauce. Taste and correct seasonings to taste. (A pinch of red pepper flakes can kick this up a notch!)
- Place spaetzle or egg noodles in bottom of individual bowls, then spoon the stew over these and enjoy.

129. Greek Style Chickpea Soup

Serving: Serves 6-8 | Prep: | Cook: | Ready in:

Ingredients

- 1/2 cup Greek Olive oil
- 2 medium onions, diced.
- 4 cloves garlic, minced.
- 2 ribs celery, diced.
- 2 carrots, peeled, diced.
- 1 2 russet potato (medium), peeled, diced.
- 2 15 oz cans chickpeas, drained, rinsed.

- 1 15 oz can San Marzano tomatoes, crushed.
- 1 quart good stock, Vegetable or chicken.
- 1 teaspoon smoked paprika
- 1 teaspoon cracked ground pepper
- 2 teaspoons kosher salt
- 2 teaspoons dried oregano, preferably Greek
- 2 tablespoons Fresh dill
- 2 tablespoons Fresh parsley
- Pinch of red pepper flakes
- 2 cups Water
- 1 lemon, cut into wedges

Direction

- Pour half the oil into a Dutch oven or whatever vessel you cook your soup in, over medium heat, when oil is starting to bubble, add onions, red pepper flakes and garlic.
- Caramelize over medium low heat 30 minutes or until soft, golden, and sweet.
- Add carrots, celery, stir. Add chickpeas, potato, tomatoes, water, oregano, paprika, salt, pepper and stock.
- Turn heat to medium high, when the soup begins to simmer, turn heat to low and cook 1 hr.
- Add fresh parsley and dill, drizzle remaining oil over the top of each serving and serve with lemon wedges. I like to blend mine with an emulsion blender, making sure to leave some texture, this leaves the soup with a velvety finish. I served mine with Chevre smeared baguette slices, but you can choose your own breadventure.

130.   Green Hot Chili Peppers In My Backyard BBQ

Serving: Serves 6 | Prep: | Cook: |Ready in:

Ingredients

- 1 cup parsley chopped finely
- 1/2 mint chopped finely
- 6 garlic cloves minced finely
- 1/2 cup shallots, chopped finely
- 1 green chilli, seeds removed and chopped finely
- 1/2 cup red pepper, seeds and white fibre removed, chopped finely
- 2 teaspoons paprika
- 1/2 cup white wine vinegar
- 1 cup Extra Virgin Olive Oil
- Salt to taste

Direction

- Chop the herbs very finely. Put in a glass container that has a good fitting lid.
- Add the garlic, shallot, green chili, red pepper, vinegar and mix. Add some salt and the paprika and mix to dissolve both in the liquid. You can put the lid on the container and shake it.
- Finally add the olive oil and mix well.
- Keep in the fridge for a minimum of 1 day and check the seasoning again - at this point the flavours will have blended and you will have a much better taste.
- The sauce will keep well in the fridge for 1 or 2 weeks.
- Serve with grilled meat or as a marinade.

131.   Grilled Beef Fajitas

Serving: Serves 2 | Prep: | Cook: |Ready in:

Ingredients

- 9 ounces beef (such as flank steak)
- 1 garlic clove
- 1 lime
- 2 tablespoons olive oil
- 1 teaspoon paprika (hot)
- 1 pinch dried thyme
- 2 red bell peppers (about 400 grams)
- 2 onions
- 4 ounces sour cream
- salt, pepper
- 1 bunch cilantro

- 1 large tomato
- 4 tortillas (preferably whole-grain)

Direction

- Cut beef into strips, about 1 cm wide. Peel and finely chop garlic. Squeeze 3 tablespoons juice from lime. In a bowl, mix together garlic, 1 1/2 tablespoons lime juice, 1 tablespoon oil, the paprika and thyme.
- Add meat to lime-garlic mixture and turn to coat. Marinate in the refrigerator for at least 1 hour. Meanwhile, rinse bell peppers, wipe dry, remove seeds and cut peppers into thin slices. Peel onions and cut into wedges.
- Heat the remaining oil in a heavy pan over medium-high heat. Add onions and bell peppers. Cook, stirring frequently, until tender, about 20 minutes.
- In a bowl, combine sour cream and remaining lime juice, then season with salt and pepper. Rinse cilantro, shake dry, pluck leaves and coarsely chop. Mix half with the sour cream.
- Rinse tomato, wipe dry, cut into quarters and remove seeds, if desired. Slice tomato thinly. About 2 minutes before peppers and onions are finished cooking, add tomato to pan and cook until slightly softened. Heat tortillas in the oven or microwave until warmed through.
- Heat a grill pan over high heat. Add beef and cook until medium-rare, 3-4 minutes. Divide beef and vegetables among tortillas. Top with remaining cilantro, then roll up fajitas and serve immediately with cilantro-sour cream on the side.

132. Grilled Butterfly Chicken With A Paprika And Herb Dry Rub

Serving: Serves 2-4 | Prep: 0hours20mins | Cook: 0hours40mins | Ready in:

Ingredients

- 1 tablespoon good quality paprika
- 1 teaspoon dried oregano
- 1 teaspoon dried marjoram
- 1 teaspoon onion powder
- 1 teaspoon sea salt
- 1 teaspoon fresh ground black pepper
- 1/2 teaspoon garlic powder
- 1/2 teaspoon cayenne pepper

Direction

- Mix all of the ingredients together in a bowl. Make sure none of them are clumped together (especially the onion and garlic powder). Taste and adjust as you see fit. Make sure you are comfortable with the consistency. If you like more herbs in your rubs then go with a tbsp. of oregano and marj. Be quite generous with the paprika. It smells great when grilled and gives the chicken wonderful color.
- Next, prepare the bird. Butterflying a chicken is pretty easy. It is best done with a set of really sharp kitchen shears. But, simply put, starting from the rear, cut down each side of the spine. Stay as close to the bone as you can so as not to waste any meat. This will effectively remove the spine. After the spine has been removed, open up the bird as far as it will go, but be gentle, you don't want to break the skin. You will notice that there is a small tendon near the top that prevents the bird from opening flat. Once you see that just nick it with a sharp knife. This should allow the bird to open up. But again, be gentle. Slicing too deep here could mess with the cooking time and leave a part of the chicken dry and a big bummer. After this, pat the chicken dry with some paper towel. Then apply the rub to the bird on both sides. Rub the rub into the bird gently but firmly. I suggest using a spoon to scoop the rub onto the chick then rub it in with your hands. If you can keep your raw chicken hand out of the rub you can save it for another day. Drizzle the bird with some olive oil. Have a small bowl and brush with more oil (or melted butter) for basting throughout the grilling process.

- Let the chicken rest, and take in all that flavor from the rub as you prepare the grill. I always use wood charcoal but gas would obviously work fine. At this point in the process, it's absolutely imperative that you have 1-4 beers. Arrange the coals in your grill so that you have two different heat zones going on. One very hot, the other medium. Start by cooking the bird for 5 minutes or so over the hot coals, meaty side down. The idea is to get a nice sear on this. Little bit of char is alright. Flip it over and do the same on the other side. Then move the bird to the more tame side of the grill and cook until done. Flip and baste frequently to avoid burning and drying out. This usually takes about 40-60 minutes - depending on the size of the bird. The best way to tell if it's done is to use a thermometer. You're looking for 165F or 75C.Pull the chicken off and allow to rest for at least 10 minutes before carving and serving. As I mentioned above. The sides are up to you but I like an onion-garlic couscous and a simple tomato-cucumber salad.

133. Grilled Lamb Chops & Garlic Scapes With Romesco Sauce

Serving: Serves 4 to 6 | Prep: | Cook: | Ready in:

Ingredients

- 2 red bell peppers
- 1 ancho chile
- 1/4 cup sun-dried tomatoes
- 1/2 cup hazelnuts, toasted and brown skins removed
- 2 tablespoons sherry vinegar
- 2 cloves garlic
- 1 teaspoon smoked paprika
- 1/4 teaspoon red pepper flakes
- Kosher salt and freshly ground black pepper
- 1/2 cup extra-virgin olive oil, plus 3 tablespoons
- 16 rib lamb chops

Direction

- Adjust oven rack to 4 to 5 inches from heat element and preheat oven to broiler setting. Place peppers on parchment lined baking sheet and broil until skins, turning peppers occasionally until all sides charred and flesh is tender, about 20 minutes. You want your peppers to be completely charred (black) on the outside. Oven temperatures (especially broilers) vary, so be sure to keep an eye on them since some might cook faster or slower. Transfer to bowl and cover with plastic wrap, then let stand cool for 20 minutes. When peppers are cool enough to handle, peel off skin and discard seeds. Strain and reserve any accumulated juices.
- Meanwhile, soak ancho chile and sun-dried tomatoes in bowl covered with hot water until softened, about 15 minutes. Drain ancho and tomatoes and pat dry with paper towel. Remove stem and seeds from ancho and discard.
- Process hazelnuts and garlic in food processor until finely ground. Add the roasted peppers, ancho, sun-dried tomatoes, sherry vinegar, paprika, and red pepper flakes, ground pepper and salt to food processor with hazelnuts and process to a coarse meal. With the motor running add 1/2 cup of olive oil in a slow steady stream. Taste for seasoning.
- Prepare charcoal grill (or heat gas grill to high). Set the cooking rack in place, cover the grill with the lid, and let the rack heat, about 5 minutes. Use a wire brush to scrape clean the rack.
- Toss the garlic scapes in 1 tablespoon oil and season with salt and pepper. Place the scapes in a grill basket and place basket on grill over the coals. Grill, flipping and moving them around until they're soft (you'll notice they're limp when you pick them up) and charred in spots, about 10 to 12 minutes. Remove them from the grill, and toss them with a little more salt.

- Rub the chops with remaining 2 tablespoons oil and sprinkle with salt and pepper to taste. Grill the chops, uncovered if using charcoal and covered if using gas over the hottest part of the grill, until well browned, about 3 minutes per sides. (If the chops start to flame, drag them to the cooler part of the grill and/or extinguish the flames with a squirt bottle.) Remove the chops from the grill and let rest for 5 minutes. Serve immediately with garlic scapes and Romesco sauce.

134. Grilled Pork Tenderloin With Roasted Red Pepper Sauce

Serving: Serves 4 | Prep: | Cook: | Ready in:

Ingredients

- 1 1/4- pounds pork tenderloin
- Sea salt and freshly ground pepper
- 1 tablespoon butter
- 1 cloves garlic, peeled
- 2 ounces Pecorino cheese
- 1/4 cup toasted pumpkin seeds
- 1 roasted red bell pepper, (fresh or from a jar), peeled and seeded
- 1 teaspoon Sherry vinegar
- 1 teaspoon paprika
- Pinch cayenne
- 1/4 cup extra virgin olive oil

Direction

- Preheat the oven to 400°F or the grill to medium high heat. Season the pork with salt and pepper.
- If cooking in the oven, heat a large ovenproof skillet over medium-high heat. Add the butter. Add the pork to the skillet. Cook until browned, 3 to 5 minutes. Turn and repeat until browned on all sides. Transfer to the oven and cook until a thermometer inserted into the center reaches 135°F, about 20 minutes. Transfer to a cutting board and let sit for 5 minutes.
- If grilling, put the pork on the grill over direct heat, cover and cook for 6 minutes. Turn, cover and cook for 6 minutes. Turn again, cover and cook 6 more minutes. Until a thermometer inserted into the center reaches 135°F. Transfer to a cutting board and let sit for 5 minutes.
- While the pork is cooking, put the garlic in a food processor and pulse until chopped. Add the pecorino and pulse until finely chopped. Add the pumpkin seeds and pulse until finely chopped. Scrape down the sides with a spatula. Add the pepper, vinegar, paprika and cayenne. Pulse until almost smooth. With the machine running, gradually add the olive oil. Season to taste with salt.
- Slice the pork and arrange on a platter. Serve with the red pepper sauce on the side.
- To roast a pepper: Place the red pepper under the broiler and cook until the skin begins to brown. Turn and cook until all of the sides are browned. When it's cooked on all sides, put in a plastic bag and seal it. Let rest 20 minutes before peeling.

135. Grilled Summer Squash With Charred Chickpeas, Raisins + Garlic Yogurt Sauce

Serving: Serves 4 | Prep: | Cook: | Ready in:

Ingredients

- 3 medium, mixed summer squash (such as zucchini, yellow, pattypan), cut lengthwise into 1-inch wedges
- 3 tablespoons olive oil, divided
- 1/2 teaspoon lemon zest plus lemon wedges for serving
- Kosher salt and freshly ground black pepper
- 2 (15-ounce) can chickpeas, drained and rinsed

- 4 garlic cloves
- 1/4 teaspoon cayenne pepper
- 1/2 teaspoon smoked paprika
- 1/2 teaspoon ground cinnamon
- 2 tablespoons chopped parsley
- 1/4 cup golden raisins
- 1 cup whole milk Greek yogurt

Direction

- Preheat grill to medium-high. While grill heats, combine 2 tablespoons olive oil and lemon zest in a large rectangular dish; add squash and turn to coat. Season squash with salt and pepper.
- Finely grate garlic cloves (you should have about 1 teaspoon). Toss chickpeas with 1 tablespoon oil, 1/2 teaspoon garlic, cayenne, paprika and cinnamon. Season with salt and pepper. Place a large square of foil on a work surface; place chickpeas in the center. Crinkle and gather the edges of the foil to create a packet. (Reserve bowl.)
- Add squash to one side of the grill and packet on the other. Grill, turning squash and shaking packet occasionally, until squash is tender and chickpeas are lightly browned, about 8 to 12 minutes. Transfer squash to a serving platter and return chickpeas to reserved bowl. Toss chickpeas with parsley and raisins; scatter over squash. In a small bowl, stir together yogurt and remaining 1/2 teaspoon garlic; season with salt and pepper. Spoon yogurt over vegetables, drizzle with olive oil if desired, and serve with lemon wedges.

136. Gumbo Z'Herbes II

Serving: Serves 4 | Prep: | Cook: | Ready in:

Ingredients

- 1 link andouille sausage, cut into approximately 1/2 inch dice
- 2 tablespoons grapeseed or other vegetable oil
- 1/2 teaspoon kosher salt
- 1 cup chopped onions
- 1/2 cup chopped celery
- 1/2 cup chopped bell or red pepper
- 2 cloves garlic, minced
- 4 cups chicken stock
- 2 pounds assorted greens: collards, turnip, beet, mustard, chard, kale, spinach, celery leaves, coarsely chopped
- 1 tablespoon fresh thyme leaves
- 1 teaspoon onion powder
- 1 teaspoon garlic powder
- 1 teaspoon smoked paprika
- 1 teaspoon dried oregano (use dried instead of fresh; it's a classic ingredient in Cajun spice blends.)
- Optional 1 cup of lentils
- salt, black pepper and cayenne to taste
- 1 tablespoon Worcestershire sauce (or to taste)
- a little Tabasco or Louisiana hot sauce if you like
- 2 cups Cooked white or brown rice for serving

Direction

- Cook the sausage in a large Dutch oven over medium heat, turning once or twice until nicely browned. Scoop it onto a plate and set aside.
- Heat grapeseed (vegetable) oil over medium heat till shimmering. Add onions, celery, bell pepper and salt, and sauté, stirring occasionally till softened but not browned. Stir in garlic and let it sweat with the other vegetables for a minute or two. Add stock to the Dutch oven. Raise heat till it comes to just below boiling. Add greens a little at a time until they are all wilted into the soup. Add thyme, onion and garlic powders, smoked paprika, oregano and andouille into soup. Stir in 1 tablespoon Worcestershire sauce. Reduce heat to low, and simmer soup, uncovered, for at least 1 hour and up to 3 hours. (Throw the lentils in here if you're using them.) The vegetables will become mushy and the soup will be very green. This is what you're going

for. Taste and add salt, fresh ground black pepper, cayenne, and more Worcestershire sauce to your taste. (I like a little Tabasco or other Louisiana hot sauce, too.)
- To serve, place a scoop of rice into a bowl and pour soup over the rice.

137. Hash Browns, Spinach, And Froached Egg Stack

Serving: Serves 1 | Prep: | Cook: | Ready in:

Ingredients

- 1 cup frozen shredded hash browns
- 1/2 tablespoon butter
- Paprika, ground black pepper, and salt to taste
- 1 teaspoon olive oil
- A large handful of fresh spinach
- Squeeze of lemon juice
- A pinch of crushed red pepper flakes
- 1 egg
- More ground black pepper, to taste
- 1/8 cup water
- Spray oil, as needed

Direction

- Start off by adding the frozen hash browns to a glass measuring cup to the one cup line (give or take). Add the butter on top then microwave for one minute. Add the paprika, pepper, and salt to taste and mix
- Add the teaspoon of olive oil to a medium-hot skillet and plop the hash browns onto it and smoosh it down with a spatula and make it pretty and round, or so. Cook it until nice and crisp on the bottom until it holds its shape. Once it is crisp enough on the bottom to flip, spray some olive oil on the top of it, and then flip it over with a wide spatula. Cook until crispy on that side, then remove to a plate and tent with a piece of foil to keep warm.
- Spritz the pan with more olive oil and throw in a really large handful of fresh spinach. Squeeze some lemon juice over it and then cook it until wilted. Add a pinch of crushed red pepper flakes. Once the spinach is all wilted, spoon it on top of your hash browns patty and re-tent with the foil.
- Spray a bit more olive oil into the pan, and gently crack an egg into it and grind a whole bunch of black pepper over it.
- Cook until the egg white is solid all the way through and the edges of the whites start to sizzle. Now pour the 1/8 cup of water all around the edges of the egg, then immediately put a tight-fitting lid on the skillet. Let it "steam" for one minute exactly. Do not peek. Do not pass go. At the one minute mark, lift up the lid and you should see a fine example of a "froached" egg. Now take a slotted spatula and lift the egg out of the pan to drain a bit, then place on the hash browns and spinach stack.
- Grab your utensils and cut into the egg and watch mesmerized as the yellow runny yolk spreads its goodness down the stack. EAT IT NOW!

138. Hearty Spicy Kale And Pork Soup With White Beans

Serving: Serves 6 | Prep: | Cook: | Ready in:

Ingredients

- 1 tablespoon olive oil
- 1 pound boneless pork loin or chops, trimmed and cut into bite-size pieces
- Mrs. Dash Table Blend, or salt, to taste
- Ground Black Pepper, to taste
- 1 cup chopped onion
- 2 garlic cloves, minced
- 1 teaspoon Hungarian paprika
- 1 teaspoon Ancho chile powder
- 1 or 2 pinches of crushed red pepper flakes
- 1/4 cup red wine
- 4 Roma (plum) tomatoes, chopped

- 4 to 5 cups chicken or turkey broth, homemade or low sodium
- 1 bunch of kale, ribs removed and chopped
- 1 can of white beans, drained and rinsed

Direction

- Heat the oil in a Dutch oven or soup pot on medium high.
- Generously season the pork with the Mrs. Dash and black pepper, then add to the pot. Brown the pork on all sides, then remove to a bowl and set aside.
- Add the chopped onion to the pot, and cook for about five minutes until starting to soften.
- Add the minced garlic, Hungarian paprika, Ancho chile powder and crushed red pepper flakes, and stir for about a minute longer.
- Add the red wine and chopped tomatoes, stirring to scrape up any browned bits on the bottom.
- Add the broth, then bring to a boil. Add the kale (it looks like a lot, but it all wilts down just like spinach) until it's mixed in, then turn down the heat to a low simmer.
- Add the pork back in and the white beans (I used cannellini) and continue simmering until ready to eat.

139. Herbed Soft Scramble

Serving: Serves 2 | Prep: | Cook: | Ready in:

Ingredients

- 4 happy, farm fresh eggs, at room temperature
- 1 tablespoon real mayonnaise, best quality
- 1 tablespoon whole milk, (goat or cow)
- 1/2 tablespoon unsalted butter
- dash of Maldon salt flakes or sea salt
- two turns of fresh milled mixed peppercorns
- 1 teaspoon snipped fresh chives
- small handful of torn cilantro leaves (or Italian parsley if you prefer)
- finishing dash of sweet paprika or Aleppo pepper

Direction

- Gently whisk eggs with mayonnaise and milk until smoothly blended. Add the salt and ground peppercorns.
- Heat butter in the frying pan. Then slowly pour in the egg mixture. Using a fork, gently fluff the eggs.
- As soon as they are scrambled, transfer to warmed plates. Season with a little more salt and pepper if needed. Garnish with the fresh chives and cilantro leaves. Finish with a sprinkle of either sweet paprika or Aleppo pepper. Serve while still warm so you can savor each bite. And don't be one bit afraid of the mayo-you will not taste it.

140. Honey Roasted Chicken With Garlic, Lavender, And Roasted Vegetables

Serving: Serves 4-6 | Prep: | Cook: | Ready in:

Ingredients

- 4 pounds roasting chicken, spatchcocked
- 10 whole garlic cloves, crushed
- 1/3 cup runny honey, or any good-quality honey
- 1 1/2 tablespoons lavender honey (if you have)
- 1 teaspoon dried thyme, or 3 sprigs of fresh thyme
- 1 small onion, chopped
- 1 lemon, juiced
- 3 tablespoons olive oil
- 2 bay leaves
- 1/4 teaspoon smoked paprika
- 1 teaspoon Kosher salt
- 1/2 teaspoon ground black pepper

- 3 medium potatoes, rinsed & skin-on, quartered (1 red, 1 yukon gold, 1 purple, if possible)
- 1 broccoli crown, florets cut small
- 1 cauliflower head, florets cut small (purple or yellow if available, for color)
- 1 large carrot, peeled & sliced
- 1 1/2 tablespoons dried culinary lavender

Direction

- In a bowl, make your marinade. First, crush your dried lavender to release their oils. You can do as I do: Crush and roll the dried lavender back and forth in your hands, or you can use a mortar and pestle for this. (A wooden spoon, bottom of a cup, etc., also work fine.)
- Once the lavender is crushed in your bowl, add in the honey (both regular and lavender, if you have it), olive oil, lemon juice, smoked paprika, thyme, crushed garlic cloves, chopped onion, kosher salt and black pepper. Give it a good stir until all are combined, and add then add in the bay leaves.
- TIME TO MARINATE: In a large Ziploc refrigerator storage bag or plastic tupperware, place in the spatchcocked chicken and pour in the marinade. Make sure the pieces are completely coated. (I like to best do this by sealing the Ziploc bag, and massaging the chicken with the marinade. Less mess!) The chicken will be best marinated overnight, or for at least 5 hours.
- When the chicken is done marinating, remove the bay leaves and discard. Remove the chicken and set aside; reserve the marinade. Preheat your oven to 425° F.
- In a roasting pan, place in your chopped and colorful vegetable medley (potatoes, carrot, broccoli, and cauliflower). Douse them with a bit of olive oil and the reserved chicken marinade (garlic, onions, and all), a dash of both salt and pepper, and toss until all are coated. Spread out on the bottom of the pan.
- Lay the chicken flat, skin-side down (not up), on top of the vegetables. Season the chicken with a bit of kosher salt & pepper, and put the entire roasting pan into the oven to cook for about 30-minutes.
- After the 30 minutes are done, take the roasting pan out of the oven and carefully flip the chicken over with tongs, so it is now skin-side up. Season the surface of the chicken skin with salt and pepper, and put the roasting pan back into the oven to cook for another 25-30 minutes, or until the meat on the chicken thigh reads 165° on a meat thermometer (150° F on the breast meat). Or, if you don't have a meat thermometer, pierce the thickest part of the meat with a fork and see if the juices run clear (and not bloody).
- Once the chicken is done, take the roasting pan out of the oven and carefully remove the chicken to rest on a plate for about 10-15 minutes. Take this time to stir around the pan-dripped roasted vegetables and season them to your liking. Remove from the roasting pan, and to a serving plate.
- Once the chicken is rested, carve up to your liking (half, quarter, however you want). Serve atop the roasted vegetables.

141. Hot Chicken Recipe And Jalapeño Bacon Cheddar Waffle

Serving: Serves 4 | Prep: 4hours0mins | Cook: 0hours40mins | Ready in:

Ingredients

- FOR THE CHICKEN:
- 4 boneless chicken breasts, pounded out to an even thickness
- ½ cup pickle juice
- 1 large egg, beaten
- ½ cup milk
- 1 teaspoon cayenne pepper hot sauce
- 1 cup all-purpose flour
- 1 teaspoon kosher salt
- vegetable or peanut oil for frying the chicken

- FOR THE MAPLE HOT SAUCE:
- 1 cup maple syrup
- 3-4 tablespoon cayenne pepper hot sauce
- 1 teaspoon cayenne pepper powder
- 1 teaspoon chili powder
- 1 teaspoon garlic powder
- 1 teaspoon paprika
- FOR THE WAFFLES:
- 1 ¼ cup all-purpose flour
- 1 teaspoon baking powder
- 1 teaspoon sugar
- ¾ teaspoon kosher salt
- ☐1 egg , beaten
- 1 to 1 ¼ cup milk
- 4 tablespoon butter , melted
- 1 cup sharp cheese , shredded
- ¼ cup bacon (about 4 slices), cooked and crumbled
- 3 tablespoon fresh or pickled jalapeño , minced

Direction

- FOR THE CHICKEN:
- Marinate the chicken breasts in the pickle juice in the refrigerator in a covered container for 4 hours.
- After marinating the chicken, remove container from refrigerator and allow to sit at room temperature for 30 minutes. Set up a breading station with two shallow dishes. In one dish, combine the beaten egg, whole milk, and hot sauce. In the other dish, combine the flour and salt.
- Remove the chicken from the pickle juice and dip into the egg-milk mixture first, then dip into the flour mixture.
- Pour 2-3 inches of oil into a large cast iron pot or pan and heat the oil to 350F/176C degrees over medium-high heat. Fry each chicken breast for about 8 minutes on each side, or until internal temperature registers 165F/74C degrees. Drain on a wire rack over a sheet pan.
- FOR THE MAPLE HOT SAUCE:
- In a small pan over medium heat, combine the maple syrup with the cayenne pepper hot sauce, cayenne powder, chili powder, garlic powder, and paprika. Reduce to low and keep warm.
- FOR THE WAFFLES:
- Pre-heat the waffle iron to the desired waffle setting (I used a soft waffle setting at 4.5)
- Whisk together the flour, baking powder, sugar, and salt in a large bowl. In a small bowl, mix together the egg, milk, and melted butter until well combined. Add the egg mixture to the flour mixture and mix together just until the batter comes together. Fold the cheese, cooked bacon, and jalapeños into the batter.
- Lightly grease the waffle iron, if needed, and cook per the iron's directions. Mine took about 3-4 minutes.
- To assemble the dish, place one waffle on a plate, one fried chicken breast on top of the waffle, and pour a ¼ cup of the maple hot sauce over it all.
- Grab a big fork and knife and dig in!
- Recipe Notes & Tips:
- Extra waffles can be refrigerated for 1-2 days and frozen for up to 1-2 months.

142. Hummus With Sesame Seeds (no Tahini)

Serving: Makes 2 1/2 cups | Prep: 0hours0mins | Cook: 0hours0mins | Ready in:

Ingredients

- 2 cups cooked* chickpeas (Garbanzo beans)
- 1/4 cup sesame seeds
- 3 cloves of garlic
- 2 tablespoons lime juice
- 1/4 cup olive oil (plus extra to top with)
- 1/2 teaspoon sesame oil (optional)
- A pinch of cumin
- A pinch of paprika
- Salt

Direction

- *If using canned chickpeas, just drain the liquid and use.
- *If using dried chickpeas : soak ¾ cup of dried chickpeas in plenty of room temperature/cold water and soak them overnight, at least 6 - 8 hours. They will expand to more than double their size, so make sure to cover by several inches of water. Rinse and discard the water.
- Place them in a pot and cover with at least 2 inches of cold water. Bring the water up to the boil, then simmer for 50 - 60 minutes until they soften (cooking time of dried chickpeas varies vastly; some might take up to 2 hours). A good trick to check their doneness is to take one out and smash it between your fingers. You want them to be just tender, not completely falling apart. Once done, drain the chickpeas and drop them in an ice bath. Remove their skins and discard.
- Place the sesame seeds in a small pan and toss them until lightly colored and toasted, about 1 minute. Reserve 1 tsp for garnish, and toss the rest into a blender. Pour over olive oil and sesame oil and blend until smooth.
- Add the chickpeas, garlic, lime juice, and salt to the sesame paste and blend until smooth. Add water to loosen out the hummus to get your desired consistency.
- To serve, decant the hummus into a bowl. Pour over a generous glug of olive oil, and sprinkle with cumin, paprika and reserved sesame seeds.
- FREEZING INSTRUCTIONS: Hummus freezes very well; spoon into air-tight containers or zip-lock bags. To thaw, let it sit in the refrigerator for a few hours.

143. Hungarian Pork Paprikash

Serving: Serves 4 | Prep: | Cook: | Ready in:

Ingredients

- 1 1/2 pounds boneless pork shoulder, trimmed of fat and cut into large chunks
- 2 tablespoons sunflower oil, plus extra if needed
- 1 large onion, finely chopped
- 1 1/2 pounds baby bella mushrooms, sliced
- 1 tablespoon smoked paprika
- 1 tablespoon dry dill
- 1 tablespoon cornstarch
- 1 cup condensed cream of mushroom soup, low sodium
- 2 red bell peppers, halved lengthwise, seeded, and diced
- 4 tablespoons Greek yogurt
- 10 ounces dry egg noodles
- 2 tablespoons butter
- salt
- fresh ground black pepper
- chopped chives, to serve

Direction

- Season the pork with salt and pepper. Heat the oil in a large skillet over high heat. Lower the heat to medium, add the pork and fry 3 to 5 minutes until brown on all sides, working in batches to avoid overcrowding in the pan, and adding extra oil if necessary. Use a slotted spoon to transfer the pork to the slow cooker as it browns.
- Add the onion to the skillet and fry, stirring, 3 to 5 minutes until soft. Add the mushrooms, sprinkle with salt, and fry 5 to 8 minutes until all the liquid is absorbed. Sprinkle the paprika and dill over the mushrooms and stir 30 seconds.
- Put the cornstarch and 2 tablespoons cold water in a small bowl and whisk until smooth. Add the cornstarch paste and mushroom soup to the pan and bring to a boil, scraping the bottom of the pan. Pour the mixture into the cooker and stir well. Season lightly with salt and pepper.
- Cover the cooker with the lid and cook on LOW 8 hours. Stir in the peppers and yogurt. Switch the cooker to HIGH, re-cover and cook

- 30 minutes until the pork and peppers are tender.
- Twenty minutes before serving, bring a large pot of salted water to boil, add the egg noodles and cook to package directions. Drain well, shaking off any excess water, then return the noodles to the hot pot, add the butter, and stir until it melts.
- Spoon the paprika over the noodles and season with a little more salt and pepper, if you like. Sprinkle with chives and serve.

144. Hungarian Stuffed Reds With Red Quinoa

Serving: Serves 4-6 | Prep: | Cook: | Ready in:

Ingredients

- 1/2 cup whole red quinoa, uncooked, soaked in water
- 1/2 pound farm quality ground beef
- 1/2 pound farm fresh quality ground pork
- 1/4 cup finely chopped red cabbage
- 1/4 cup finely chopped red onion
- 1/4 cup grated carrot
- 1/2 teaspoon fresh chopped thyme leaves
- 1/2 teaspoon fresh chopped marjoram leaves
- 1/2 tablespoon premium quality Hungarian smoked (or sweet) paprika
- dash of kosher salt
- pinch of pepper
- 4-6 plump red sweet bell peppers
- 2-4 cups fresh vegetable broth, made from fire roasted as well as uncooked red pepper, tomatoes, carrots, onions and herbs (see photo) with canned stewed tomatoes as alternative
- 1/2 tablespoon sweet red Hungarian paprika
- 1 bay leaf
- 1 bouquet garni of fresh herbs (thyme, marjoram, parsley, even some basil)
- sweet paprika for garnish
- dollop of sour cream, creme fraiche, or fage for serving
- fresh chopped parsley for serving
- 4 cups red pepper semolina soup as a richer alternative to the vegetable broth

Direction

- Soak the quinoa in water for an hour and then drain off the water. Mix gently the next ten ingredients on the recipe list together with the quinoa for the filling.
- Cut a border of triangles out of the top edge of the peppers, about an inch in height. Clean out their seeds and interior membranes. Take the cut out triangles and dice smaller. Add these into the filling mixture.
- Stuff the peppers up to the beginning of the triangular border. The quinoa will expand when cooking.
- Arrange these in a large Dutch oven and add the broth. Make sure to add sweet paprika to the broth. Bring to a boil, then simmer for 40 minutes. While cooking ladle some broth over the peppers. Make sure the quinoa is fully cooked. Remove the peppers carefully to a bowl and peel off their skins, if desired. Replace back into the broth to keep warm until serving. If you do not mind the skins, you can simply skip this step.
- Serve with a generous ladle-ful of broth in a bowl, or alternatively for a richer meal with my red pepper semolina soup. Fold the triangles inwards. Garnish with sour cream, crème fraiche or fage, chopped flat leaf parsley and sweet paprika.

145. Instant Pot Uzbek Plov

Serving: Serves 4-6 | Prep: | Cook: | Ready in:

Ingredients

- 1 tablespoon Olive Oil or Neutral Cooking Oil
- 1 pound Beef or Lamb Stew Meat

- 2 Onions, chopped
- 4-5 Carrots, julienned
- 1 teaspoon Cumin
- 1 teaspoon Paprika
- 3 teaspoons Salt, Divided
- 3 Bay Leaves
- 2 tablespoons Dried Currents
- 2 cups Rice, rinsed
- 1 Head of Garlic

Direction

- Using the "Sauté" mode brown the meat in the Instant Pot with the olive oil.
- Once the meat is browned, add the chopped onions and cook until softened (3-5 min). Then add the carrots, cumin, paprika, 1-1.5 teaspoon of salt, dried currants, and the bay leaves. Cook for another 5 minutes, until carrots are softened.
- Add enough water to cover the meat and vegetables.
- Press the "Off" button, then press "Manual" and set the time for 45 minutes on high pressure.
- After 45 minutes, release the pressure.
- Add the 2 cups of rice evenly over the top of the dish, the rice should be covered by the cooking water and no extra water should be needed.
- Evenly distribute 1.5 teaspoons of salt across the rice
- Press the whole garlic head into the middle of the pot, so it is covered by the water/rice.
- Press the "Off" button, then press "Rice" and set the time to 12 minutes.
- After 12 minutes, release the pressure and take off the lid. Allow the setting to change to "Keep Warm".
- Using the handle of a spatula or stir spoon, poke multiple large holes all the way to the bottom of the pot. This will allow the extra water to evaporate.
- Allow pot to stay on "Keep warm" for 15-20 minutes, or until all the water is evaporated.
- Remove garlic head and bay leaves.
- Serve with salted plain yogurt or cacik (Turkish yogurt dip).

146. Jalapeño Cream Cheese Dip

Serving: Makes 1 large serving bowl | Prep: | Cook: | Ready in:

Ingredients

- 16 ounces softened cream cheese
- 1 cup sour cream
- 2 cups shredded sharp cheddar cheese
- 1/2 cup chopped jalapeño (jar, drained)
- 4.25 ounces chopped black olives
- 2 teaspoons onion powder
- 1 teaspoon garlic powder
- 1/2 teaspoon smoked paprika
- 1/2 teaspoon white pepper

Direction

- Place all ingredients in a bowl and mixed with a hand held mixer until mixed thoroughly. Place in a serving bowl and garnish with jalapeños, shredded sharp cheddar cheese and smoked paprika! Serve with crackers!

147. Juicy Vegan Meatballs And Gravy

Serving: Serves 2 | Prep: | Cook: | Ready in:

Ingredients

- For the meatballs
- 2 Slices of gluten-free vegan bread, crusts removed and finely crumbled
- 1 Brown onion, grated
- 300 grams Organic plain tempeh, grated
- 4 Sprigs thyme, stems discarded

- 2 teaspoons Nutritional yeast
- 1 pinch Salt
- For the gravy
- 1 tablespoon Garlic powder
- 1 teaspoon Cumin powder
- 1 teaspoon Vegetable stock powder
- 1/4 teaspoon Smoked sweet Hungarian paprika
- 1/2 cup Chickpea flour
- 1 1/2 cups Water
- 2 tablespoons Gluten-free soy sauce

Direction

- Preheat oven to 220 degrees C.
- Mix the crust-less bread and grated onion. Let sit for five minutes before adding the tempeh, thyme, nutritional yeast and pinch of salt. Mix until combined and shape into meatballs.
- Cook in the oven for 15 minutes before flipping and cooking a further 10 minutes.
- While the meatballs are cooking, heat one teaspoon of olive oil in a pan and add garlic, cumin, powdered stock and paprika. Stir to avoid spices catching on the pan and once fragrant, add the chickpea flour. Continue to stir to avoid it catching. After a minute or two, add 1/2 cup water and whisk to remove the lumps. While whisking continuously, add the next 1/2 cup water as it thickens, and repeat for the last 1/2 cup water. Once it has reached the consistency of gravy, turn off the heat and stir through 2 tbsp. gluten-free soy sauce. Season to taste.
- Serve meatballs in bowls with steamed carrots and pour gravy on top.

148. Julie's Almost Famous Stuffed Fish

Serving: Makes about 4 servings | Prep: | Cook: | Ready in:

Ingredients

- one large (around 4 pounds) whole fish which is suitable for baking, filleted in one piece leaving the head and tail intact.(or use 2 large fillets of your favorite fish for baking) I suggest whitefish, flounder, salmon, lake trout or snapper
- 6 tablespoons butter, divided (3/3) plus more for buttering the pan
- 1/3 cup finely diced onion
- 1/3 cup finely diced celery
- 8 ounces king crab meat
- 1/4 cup chopped fresh parsley
- 1/2 cup fresh bread crumbs
- 1/4 cup light cream
- 1/3 cup dry vermouth
- Sweet Hungarian paprika

Direction

- Melt 3 tablespoons of the butter in a sauté pan, add the onion and celery and gently sauté until the vegetables have softened. Remove from the heat and stir in the crab meat, bread crumbs parsley and cream.
- If using a whole fish, open it up and press the stuffing over one side. Fold the other side over and secure with toothpicks if necessary. If using two fillets, press the stuffing over the flesh of one fillet and place the second over the stuffing. And again, secure with a few toothpicks.
- Butter an appropriate size baking dish and place the fish in. Generously sprinkle the top side with the paprika.
- Melt the remaining 3 tablespoons of butter and then stir in the vermouth. Pour this over the entire fish. Roast the fish for 40 to 45 minutes at 400F basting with the pan juices frequently. Remove any toothpicks, slice and serve!

149. Jägerschnitzel (Pork Schnitzel With Red Wine Mushroom Sauce)

Serving: Serves 4 | Prep: 0hours30mins | Cook: 0hours15mins | Ready in:

Ingredients

- Schnitzel
- 4 boneless pork loin chops
- 1 tablespoon or more vegetable oil, for frying
- 3/4 cup flour
- 1 tablespoon salt
- 1 teaspoon freshly ground black pepper
- 1 egg
- 3 tablespoons water
- 1 cup breadcrumbs
- 1 tablespoon dried parsley
- 1 teaspoon paprika (sweet or smoked)
- 3/4 teaspoon garlic powder
- Mushroom Sauce
- 1/4 pound bacon, diced
- 1/2 large yellow onion, diced
- 2 cups sliced mushrooms
- 1/4 cup red wine
- 1 cup chicken stock
- 2 tablespoons chicken stock
- 2 tablespoons cornstarch
- 1 pinch or more salt, to taste
- 1 lemon, to finish dish

Direction

- Schnitzel
- Preheat oven to 200° F so you can keep schnitzel warm while preparing the mushroom sauce.
- Set up your breading stations. Lay out two plates and one shallow bowl, with the bowl in the middle. Mix flour with salt and pepper on the first plate. Whisk egg with water in the bowl. Mix breadcrumbs with dried parsley, paprika, and garlic powder on the second plate.
- Place one of the pork chops in a Ziploc bag but don't seal the bag. Using a meat pounder or the bottom of a heavy pan, pound pork until it's 1/8" thick, which is thinner than you think! If using a pan, try to land the bottom of the pan square on the chop each time to help create a more uniform thickness and even surface. Repeat with remaining chops.
- One at a time, dredge pork chop in flour. Coat both sides and shake off excess. Then dip into the egg wash. Flip chop in egg mixture to coat both sides. Pull chop out and let excess drip off for a moment before laying chop onto the breadcrumb mixture. Push chop down completely into the breadcrumb mixture and then flip to push down on the other side, to ensure both sides are fully covered in breadcrumbs. Use your hands if necessary. If using tongs to move chops from one station to another, these will work as well.
- Let chops rest for at least 5 minutes on a wire rack to let the crumbs dry out a little bit. This helps the crust be crispier.
- Pour oil into fry pan so it's about 1/2-inch deep and warm over medium high heat. When oil shimmers, add one or two chops depending on the size of your pan. Let cook 1-2 minutes on each side. The chops are thin so they will cook quickly. You're looking for a nice golden brown color on them. When schnitzel is finished, move to the oven to keep warm and repeat with remaining pork chops.
- Mushroom Sauce
- Cook bacon in skillet over medium heat until golden, but not black and too crispy, about 3 minutes. You'll want a little bit of chew rather than crunch for your sauce. Remove bacon and drain on paper towels.
- Add onions to the pan and cook 3 minutes in the bacon fat until onions become a bit translucent. Add mushrooms and continue cooking for another 4 minutes until mushrooms are properly sautéed.
- Add red wine and allow mixture to reduce by 2/3, just a minute or two. Add broth and simmer until mixture is reduced by a 1/3. While sauce is cooking down, make slurry to thicken the sauce. Whisk together cornstarch and 2 tablespoons stock off the heat until well

combined and no lumps remain. Once stock has reduced, add slurry and stir constantly for a minute or two until sauce thickens and any taste from the cornstarch has cooked off. Cook too long and the slurry will lose some of its ability to thicken the sauce.
- Remove sauce from heat and season with salt. Add a squeeze of lemon to brighten the sauce.
- Remove schnitzel from the oven and serve with mushroom sauce and additional lemon wedges if desired.

150. Kadu Ki Subzi

Serving: Serves 5-6 | Prep: | Cook: |Ready in:

Ingredients

- 4 cups diced cheese or calabaza pumpkin
- 1 cup onions, thinly sliced
- 1 cup crushed or diced tomatoes
- 1-2 serrano chillies diced
- 1 tablespoon minced ginger root
- 3 tablespoons oil
- 1 tablespoon cumin
- 1/4 teaspoon turmeric
- 1/2 teaspoon paprika or Kashmiri chili powder (the non heat variety)
- 1 pinch Asafetida
- 2 tablespoons blend of coriander and cumin powder
- Salt to taste
- slices of lime
- cilantro for garnish
- water as needed

Direction

- In a coffee grinder combine 2 tablespoons of coriander seeds and 1 tablespoon of cumin, crush to a powder and use 2 tablespoons for spicing
- Heat oil in a pan and add the cumin when it gets to smoking. When the cumin 'splits' add the diced serrano & ginger and give it a stir.
- Add the onions and fry until the onions turn translucent.
- Add the tomatoes along with the asafetida, paprika and turmeric and tip in the diced pumpkin, salt. Add water, bring to a boil and then lower the heat. Cover and cook until the pumpkins are cooked to a 'fork tender' consistency. Add the cumin coriander spice blend and allow to simmer for another 10 minutes till the flavors combine. Taste and adjust for salt.
- Transfer to a serving dish and garnish with cilantro. Serve warm with roti, naan or poories. Add lime juice as per personal taste.

151. Kale Salad With Blood Oranges, Almonds And Cured Black Olive Dressing

Serving: Serves 4-5 | Prep: | Cook: |Ready in:

Ingredients

- For the salad
- 6 oz baby Red Russian kale (about 7-8 cups), thoroughly washed, dried and roughly chopped
- 8 oz lacinato kale (about 24 leaves) - also called Dino or Tuscan kale, thoroughly washed and dried
- 2 tablespoons olive oil, divided
- 1 teaspoon Spanish paprika, divided
- 2 blood oranges plus 1 T juice for dressing, if desired
- 1/3 cup cup sliced almonds (from bulk bins), toasted
- For the dressing
- 1/2 cup cured small black olives (dry cured or oil cured from the olive bar), pitted
- 1 1/2 tablespoons extra virgin olive oil
- 2 tablespoons Sherry vinegar

Direction

- Preheat your oven to 350 ° Fahrenheit. Arrange your racks in the middle and bottom third of your oven.
- Make sure your lacinato kale leaves are as dry as you can get them. This will ensure crispy roasted kale rather than soggy roasted kale. Line a large rimmed baking sheet with a single layer of lacinato kale. I fit about 12 whole leaves. Repeat with another pan and remaining kale. I've found that roasting whole leaves rather than cut pieces reduces the chance of uneven roasting or burning. On each sheet, toss leaves with 1 T olive oil and 1/2 t Spanish paprika until evenly coated. Resist the urge to add a pinch of salt (you won't need it with the dressing). Roast for 7 minutes, setting a timer.
- Make your dressing by combining pitted olives, olive oil and sherry vinegar in a mini-prep or similar appliance (food processor and blender should also work). Pulse until well combined. Taste dressing and if too salty, add up to 1 T blood orange juice (start with 1 t). Pulse again
- By this time your roasted kale timer should be buzzing. Swap pan positions, front to back and top to bottom. Set your timer for 6 minutes.
- Place chopped baby kale in a large bowl for mixing. Using a small spatula or spoon, add ½ of dressing by folding and pressing the dressing into the kale until evenly coated. Knowing that the dressing will begin to wilt the raw leaves a little as it sits, taste dressed kale and use your best judgment to determine if you need more dressing. Add as needed
- Prep oranges by trimming off very top and bottom of each with a sharp paring knife. Set the fruit on end and very carefully cut the skin from its flesh, following the curve from top to bottom with your knife. Slice fruit crosswise into wheels (or half-moons), and push out any seeds. Add to dressed baby kale.
- Remove roasted kale from oven. Leaves should be crisp and a golden dark green. Allow to cool and using shears, stack multiple leaves and thickly cut crosswise into bowl. My stems were tender so I included all but the very end (about 1 inch). If your stems are too thick and tough, slice kale lengthwise on either side of stem before stacking and cutting with shears.
- Toss salad gently but thoroughly with tongs, making sure to pull up the dressed kale from the bottom of the bowl. Add more dressing to taste if desired. Plate on a platter and top with toasted sliced almonds. Enjoy immediately.

152. Kale Salad With Spiced Chickpeas & Herbed Yogurt Dressing

Serving: Serves 3 - 4 | Prep: | Cook: | Ready in:

Ingredients

- For the dressing
- 1 cup plain whole milk yogurt
- 2 tablespoons extra virgin olive oil
- 2 tablespoons fresh lemon juice
- 1 teaspoon honey
- 2 teaspoons freshly grated lemon zest
- 1 small garlic clove
- 1 serrano chile, seeds & veins removed, roughly chopped
- 1/2 teaspoon sea salt
- 1/2 cup cilantro leaves
- 1/2 cup fresh mint leaves
- 1 bunch chives
- For the salad
- 1 1/2 teaspoons ground cumin
- 1 1/2 teaspoons ground coriander
- 3/4 teaspoon ground fennel seed
- 1 teaspoon smoked paprika
- 1/4 teaspoon ground cinnamon
- 1 teaspoon sea salt
- 1 1/2 tablespoons extra virgin olive oil
- 1 14-ounce can chickpeas, drained
- 4 cups curly kale, shredded
- 1/2 small red onion, thinly sliced
- 1 large avocado, diced

Direction

- Preheat oven to 425°F.
- To make the dressing, combine all the ingredients in a blender and blend until smooth. Pour into a bowl and set aside.
- In a medium bowl, add the ground cumin, coriander, fennel, smoked paprika, cinnamon and salt and stir to combine. Add the drained chickpeas and olive oil and toss to evenly coat.
- Spread the spiced chickpeas in an even layer on a large rimmed baking sheet. Bake, stirring halfway through, until crispy and golden brown, about 15 - 20 minutes.
- To assemble, toss kale with your desired amount of dressing in a large serving bowl. Top with warm spiced chickpeas, red onions and avocado, and enjoy!

153. Kentucky Derby Mini Hot Browns In Grana Padano Frico "Hats"

Serving: Makes 12 | Prep: | Cook: | Ready in:

Ingredients

- Grana Padano Frico "Hats"
- 1-2 cups shredded Grana Padano
- Filling
- 12 cherry tomatoes
- 1/2 tablespoon olive oil
- 6 strips of bacon, cooked and diced
- 4 ounces smoked turkey breast, diced
- 1 green onion, thinly sliced
- 3 tablespoons butter
- 3 tablespoons flour
- 1 cup whole milk
- 1/2 teaspoon salt
- 1/2 teaspoon white pepper
- 1 pinch smoked paprika
- 1/2 cup grated Grana Padano

Direction

- To make the frico cups/hats: Preheat oven to 350 degrees. Line a baking sheet with parchment paper and put about a tablespoon or two of the shredded Grana Padano in a thin layer, about two to three inches in diameter, depending on the size of your muffin tin. Repeat leaving about 3/4 inch between each circle, working in batches of 6 at a time. Bake, keeping a close eye, until golden brown, about 3-5 minutes. Remove from oven and gently transfer each circle onto an upside down muffin tin, gently pressing down the sides of the muffin cups. Let cool for 5-10 minutes then remove.
- When the cups are finished, bump up oven temperature to 400 degrees. Gently toss tomatoes in olive oil and spread out on a sheet tray lined with parchment paper. Bake until wilted and wrinkly.
- Meanwhile, combine bacon, turkey and green onions in a small mixing bowl and set aside.
- To make the mornay sauce, melt butter over medium-low heat in a small sauce pan. Whisk in flour until smooth and combined, heating for a minute or two to cook off raw floury taste. Whisk in milk over heat until sauce is thickened. Remove from heat and stir in salt, pepper, smoked paprika and Grana Padano.
- Spoon turkey mixture into each frico cup, top with mornay sauce and a cherry tomato and serve!

154. Lamb Burgers With Double Paprika Feta Spread, Cherry Peppers, And Kale

Serving: Serves 2 | Prep: | Cook: | Ready in:

Ingredients

- For the Double-Paprika Feta Spread:
- 1 ounce feta cheese
- 1 tablespoon mayo (I used light)

- 1 small garlic clove, microplaned or finely minced
- 1/4 teaspoon regular (sweet) Hungarian paprika
- 1/4 teaspoon hot Hungarian paprika
- salt and pepper to taste
- For the burgers and assembly:
- 6 ounces ground lamb
- 2 teaspoons chopped fresh parsley
- 1/4 teaspoon salt
- 1/8 teaspoon ground pepper
- 1/8 teaspoon dried oregano
- 2 hamburger buns (I used whole wheat)
- 2-4 jarred cherry peppers, wiped dry with a paper towel
- 2 leaves of kale

Direction

- For the Double-Paprika Feta Spread:
- Crumble the feta. Use a fork to mash it up with the mayo, garlic, and both paprika. Season to taste with salt and pepper.
- For the burgers and assembly:
- Preheat a ridged grill pan to medium-high heat and brush with a little vegetable oil. (Or use a cast iron skillet, but I liked using the ridged pan because it let some of the grease drip off.)
- Mix together the lamb, parsley, salt, pepper, and oregano. Shape into 2 patties.
- Cook the patties until desired doneness, about 4 minutes per side for medium-rare.
- While the patties are cooking, toast the buns if you want. (I did.)
- When the burgers are done cooking, remove the pan from the heat. Wait a few minutes, then rub some of the lamb drippings into the 2 kale leaves until they're soft and shiny.
- To assemble the burgers, top each one with the spread you already made, some cherry peppers, and a drippings-rubbed kale leaf.

155. Lamb Stuffed Pattypans

Serving: Makes 4 | Prep: | Cook: | Ready in:

Ingredients

- 1/3 cup short grain rice
- 1 cup water
- 4 pattypans
- 1 pound lamb or your favorite meat
- 1 medium onion
- 2 medium carrots
- 3-4 garlic cloves
- 1-2 tablespoons cooking fat (I used tallow)
- few sprigs of thyme
- 1 teaspoon ground cumin
- 1/2 teaspoon paprika
- 1/2 teaspoon salt + more for rubbing pattypans
- 1-2 tablespoons fresh chopped herbs

Direction

- In a small sauce pan, cook 1 cup water + 1/3 cup rice for about 10 minutes. Drain excess water and set aside.
- Cut off the top portion of the pattypan (where the stem is), just about 1? thick. Using a small knife create an outline of the opening in the pattypan around the "rim" at the top, leaving about 1/2? margins. Using a regular tablespoon, scoop the pattypan's flesh out along the margins and hollow it out throughout. You will have to reach further into the pattypan to scoop out the sides, but it doesn't require a huge effort — pattypan's flesh is quite tender. Reserve the scooped flesh, and sprinkle some salt inside the hollowed out pattypans, and rub it into the sides and the bottom.
- Cut the meat into small cubes and grind in a processor.
- Chunk pattypan scooped flesh, onions, garlic and carrots and pulse them in a processor until small crumbs form. The mix will be quite liquid at that point.

- Melt some butter or vegetable oil in a skillet over medium heat.
- Add ground meat and vegetables all at once. Stir well until combined in a uniform way. Add thyme sprigs, cumin, paprika and salt, stir well, and sauté for about 7-8 minutes, until all juices are evaporated and meat is nicely browned, but not too dry. Remove thyme sprigs at this point.
- Add rice and chopped herbs to the meat and stir.
- Fill the pattypans with stuffing quite tightly. It won't expand anymore since we precooked the rice.
- Cover the stuffed pattypans with the cut off top portions, using them as lids.
- Wrap each pattypan in a square sheet of foil, gathering the four corners of the sheet above the top of the pattypan.
- Bake stuffed pattypans in a 375F degree oven for about 45-50 minutes, or until pattypan is fork tender. In the last few minutes of baking, open up the foil slightly to allow outside of the pattypans lightly brown. You can use the broiler for this, if desire.
- Serve hot, with an [optional] dollop of sour cream or plain yogurt on top.

156. Lecso (Hungarian Summertime Stew)

Serving: Serves 1 | Prep: | Cook: | Ready in:

Ingredients

- 1 Large beefsteak tomato
- 1 Large green bell pepper
- 1 Scallion
- 1 teaspoon Vegetable oil
- 1/2 teaspoon Sweet paprika
- Pinch Hot paprika and caraway seed
- Salt and pepper to taste
- 1/2 cup Cooked rice
- 4 ounces Favorite protein, cooked

Direction

- Cut the tomato and pepper into 1-inch cubes; slice the scallion finely. Have all ingredients prepared and ready to cook.
- In a skillet over medium-high heat, warm the oil. Heat the scallion, caraway, and paprika until the scallion just starts to wilt. Add the tomato and pepper, and sauté, stirring constantly, until the peppers brighten and the veggies just start to become tender.
- If you're going to eat promptly, stir in your chosen protein, heat through, and serve over hot rice.
- If you want to freeze the lecso, continue to cook until the peppers are soft and the tomato has released its juices. Chill, the pack into freezer safe containers or freezer bags, removing as much air as possible. To later add lecso to a dish such as pörkölt, substitute a generous cup of lecso for the tomato and pepper mixture in the recipe.

157. Lemon Cranberry Quinoa Salad

Serving: Serves 4 people | Prep: | Cook: | Ready in:

Ingredients

- 1 cup raw quinoa (yellow or tri-color)
- Water
- 2 tablespoons fresh lemon juice
- 1/2 tablespoon ground coriander
- 1/2 tablespoon ground cumin
- 1 teaspoon paprika
- Table Salt
- Freshly ground black pepper
- Half a red bell pepper, deseeded and finely chopped
- 1/3 cup sweetened dried cranberries
- 1/3 - 1/2 cups of any 1-2 of the following ingredients: halved grape tomatoes, chopped walnuts, chopped cucumbers, OR crumbled goat cheese

- 3 green onions, white and green parts, thinly sliced
- 1/4 cup chopped fresh cilantro leaves

Direction

- Pour quinoa into a mesh strainer and rinse with tap water. Rinse the quinoa a few times, rubbing the quinoa between your fingers to remove bitter taste on outside of quinoa grains.
- Pour quinoa into a small pot with water (about 2 inches of water above quinoa) and cover saucepan to bring to a boil. Once pot comes to a boil, reduce the heat to low and allow to simmer for 6-10 minutes, or just until quinoa is tender and slightly firm still. Do not overcook quinoa; drain any excess water in the saucepan and transfer the cooked quinoa to a large bowl.
- Add lemon juice, ground coriander, ground cumin, paprika, ½ teaspoon salt, and ¼ teaspoon ground black pepper, and toss quinoa until evenly mixed. Add chopped bell pepper, sliced green onions, cranberries, cilantro, and your preferred optional ingredients, and mix with quinoa until combined. If necessary, adjust for seasoning by adding additional spices, lemon juice, ¼ teaspoon salt, and pepper. Serve quinoa salad at room temperature or chilled.

158. Lemon Scented Linguine With Scallops, Cauliflower And Lemon

Serving: Serves 6 | Prep: | Cook: | Ready in:

Ingredients

- 2 Cloves garlic, minced
- 8 Tbs olive oil, divided
- 1 cauliflower, cut into florets
- 1 cup fresh parsley, minced
- 1 tablespoon grated lemon zest
- 1 tablespoon capers, drained
- 1/2 teaspoon red pepper flakes
- 1/2 cup pecorino romano cheese, grated
- 2 tablespoons fresh lemon juice
- 1/4 cup pine nuts, toasted
- 1 pound whole wheat linguine
- 3/4 pound Bay Scallops, rinsed and patted dry
- salt and freshly ground pepper
- 1 tablespoon unsalted butter
- 1 pinch cayenne pepper
- 2 1/2 teaspoons sweet paprika
- 1 tablespoon Minced parsley leaves

Direction

- Place oven rack in highest position and preheat oven to 475 degrees. Bring a pot of salted water to boil and add pasta. Cover a baking sheet with parchment paper.
- In a large bowl, toss cauliflower with 4 TBs olive oil and season with salt and pepper, place on prepared baking sheet and roast for 15-18 minutes, adding minced garlic halfway through the cooking time. Cauliflower should be nicely browned around the edges when done.
- In a large bowl, toss the scallops with the paprika and cayenne pepper.
- In a sauté pan large enough to hold the scallops, melt butter and 1 TB olive oil over medium-high heat. When hot but not smoking, add the scallops, stirring constantly, until scallops are translucent; about 4 minutes. Remove from heat.
- In a serving dish, combine parsley, lemon zest, juice, capers and red pepper flakes with remaining 3 TBs of olive oil. Add cooked pasta, roasted cauliflower and scallops, toss to combine. Top with toasted pine-nuts. Sprinkle with pecorino and remaining tablespoon of parsley.

159. Lentil Arugula Range Salad

Serving: Makes 2 side salads | Prep: | Cook: |Ready in:

Ingredients

- 1/2 cup dried lentils
- 1/4 cup wild rice
- 1/4 cup prepared black beans (canned or re-hydrated)
- 1/4 cup diced sweet yellow onion or shallots
- 1+ cups arugula
- 1+ cups spinach
- 3 medium sized tabasco peppers or similar
- 1/4 cup apple cider vinegar
- 1/8 cup soy sauce
- 2 tablespoons tahina (tahini)
- herbs and spices: paprika, sage, salt, pepper, lemon juice, and parsley

Direction

- Begin by bringing water to a boil in a medium sauce pan. Add in rice and lentils and cook for about 7 minutes. Remove from heat. Let sit for 10 minutes and then move on.
- In a large wok add apple cider vinegar, soy sauce, black beans, (1 tbsp.) lemon juice, (1 tsp ea.) salt and pepper, and bring to a simmer. For better texture and flavor, add a bit of vegetable margarine.
- Once well combined, mix in the rice and lentils, and then add the onions and sliced tabasco peppers. You may find you want to turn the heat up a little and stir fry, that's fine! Just make sure to keep stirring.
- Once the sauce we made in the wok is mostly gone, add (1 tbsp.) of your favorite oil and continue to mix until the onions have browned.
- Once onions have browned on the edges turn the heat off and drizzle tahina onto the lentils and rice. Add a bit more lemon juice for extra flavor. Stir well.
- In a large bowl add arugula together with the lentils and rice. Drizzle some extra oil and vinegar on top. Mix well and add to a smaller or salad bowl.
- Pack a nice layer of spinach onto the top of the bowl and compress it a little. This is going to give us a means to spear our food with forks and still pick up all of the ingredients.
- Place a plate, inverted, onto the bowl and invert the assembly, removing the bowl after. Garnish with parsley, sage, paprika, and black sesame seeds.
- As always I recommend adding nutritional yeast flakes but it isn't in the core of this recipe.

160. Linguini With Corn, Potatoes, Shrimp And Herbs

Serving: Serves 6 | Prep: | Cook: |Ready in:

Ingredients

- For the Shrimp
- 1 pound large shrimp, peeled and deveined
- 3 tablespoons olive oil
- 2 garlic cloves, crushed
- 1 tablespoon fresh parsley
- 3 tablespoons crisp white wine
- 1 teaspoon smoked paprika
- salt and pepper
- For the Pasta, Corn and Potatoes
- 1 pound linguini
- 3 youkon gold potatoes
- 4 ears corn
- 1 tablespoon extra virgin olive oil
- 2 tablespoons unsalted butter
- 2 tablespoons fresh rosemary, chopped
- 1 tablespoon fresh thyme
- 1 tablespoon fresh oregano
- 1 leek
- 2 tablespoons fine quality extra virgin olive oil
- salt and pepper

Direction

- In a large bowl, combine shrimp, garlic, olive oil, smoked paprika, the wine and parsley. Allow to marinate for about 1 hour - it does not need much time in the marinade. Drain shrimp from marinade. Discard marinade.
- Peel and julienne the potatoes.
- Remove the corn from the cob.
- Slice the leek into thin slices.
- Bring a large pot of water to the boil. Salt as desired. Add the pasta and the potatoes to the pot. After 5 minutes, add the corn. Cook the pasta to al dente. Remove and drain.
- Meanwhile, heat the butter and the extra virgin olive oil in a small skillet. Add the leek and the herbs. Sauté for 5 minutes, stirring often, until the leek is soft. Remove from heat.
- Drain the linguini, potatoes and corn. Place on a large serving platter. Arrange the shrimp on top of the pasta. Pour the contents of the skillet over the pasta and vegetables. Pour the fine extra virgin olive oil over the pasta. Season with salt and pepper and toss well. Serve immediately.

161. Littleneck Clams With Sherry, Garlic And Smoked Paprika

Serving: Serves 2-4 | Prep: | Cook: | Ready in:

Ingredients

- 50 littleneck clams
- 1 tablespoon olive oil
- 6 cloves garlic, chopped
- 1 tablespoon smoked paprika
- 1/4 teaspoon cayenne pepper
- 3/4 cup dry sherry
- 1/4 cup clam juice
- 2 tablespoons fresh lemon juice
- 1 tablespoon cold unsalted butter, cubed
- 4 scallions, white and green parts sliced

Direction

- Scrub clams, checking to make sure they are all closed. If any are open, gently tap - if they close immediately, keep; if they stay open, discard. Place closed clams in colander set inside large bowl. Rinse until the water runs clear, changing water as necessary.
- Heat large sauce pot over medium-low heat; when hot, add olive oil. Heat 1 minute; add garlic and cook 2 minutes, or until tender, stirring constantly. Add smoked paprika and cayenne pepper; cook 1 minute more, stirring constantly. Add sherry, clam juice and lemon juice; increase heat to high and bring to a boil. Boil mixture 4 minutes.
- Gently add clams to boiling mixture, stirring to coat. Cover pot. Cook clams 6-9 minutes, or until clams start to pop open. As clams open, remove to a serving bowl or individual bowls, using slotted spoon. Tent with foil to keep warm.
- Boil liquid in pot 3 minutes, or until reduced slightly. Stir in the cold butter cubes in two batches, stirring each time until the butter dissolves completely. Season with salt and pepper to taste, if desired. Add scallions and cook 1 minute, or until the scallions have softened. Pour sherry mixture over clams.

162. MB's Infamous Pea Salad

Serving: Serves 4-6 | Prep: | Cook: | Ready in:

Ingredients

- 12 ounces Frozen green peas, thawed to barely room temperature
- 4 ounces Sliced pimiento or roasted red peppers, drained well
- 1/4 cup Sweet pickle relish
- 1 Small white onion, finely chopped
- 1 teaspoon Coarse ground salt
- 1 tablespoon Coarse ground black pepper
- 1-1/2 cups Shredded sharp or extra sharp Cheddar cheese
- 3/4 cup Mayonnaise

- 1 tablespoon Paprika [optional garnish]

Direction

- In a medium mixing bowl, gently stir together peas, pimientos, pickle relish, onion, salt and pepper. Add cheese and 3/4 cup mayonnaise; fold together just until ingredients are moistened, adding more mayonnaise as needed. Place salad in serving bowl. If desired, sprinkle 1-2 tablespoons cheese and paprika over top to garnish.
- Notes: This salad can be prepared up to 1 day ahead. Garnish just before serving. No, the peas are NOT cooked; they just need to be thawed to facilitate easy mixing. [This is usually the first question asked when I give out this recipe.]When recipe is doubled or tripled, it can serve a crowd.

163. Madeira Braised Oxtail Montaditos

Serving: Serves 8-10 | Prep: | Cook: | Ready in:

Ingredients

- Oxtail braise
- 1 tablespoon olive oil
- 3 ounces Pancetta, chopped in small pieces
- 4 pounds meaty oxtails
- salt and freshly ground black pepper
- 2 large onions, quartered and thinly sliced
- 1 stalk celery, finely diced
- 1 carrot, finely diced
- 4 cloves garlic, minced
- 1 cup red wine
- 3/4 cup Madeira
- 1 tablespoon sweet paprika (Hungarian or Spanish, not smoked)
- 2 tablespoons tomato paste
- 2 bay leaves
- 1 teaspoon dried thyme
- beef or chicken stock (low salt, if canned) or water
- 1 tablespoon Sherry vinegar
- Montaditos
- 36 1/2" baguette slices, cut on bias to make ovals
- olive oil
- 1/2 pound Mahon cheese (alternately, a young Manchego; Trader Joe's 'Basque Cheese' works well too)

Direction

- Preheat oven to 300 degrees.
- Lightly salt and pepper the oxtails on both sides. Heat olive oil in a large Dutch oven. Add Pancetta and cook until browned, just shy of crisp. Remove and set aside, leaving rendered fat in the pan.
- Brown the oxtails well on all sides, 10-15 minutes. (Do in batches if they don't all fit in the pan without crowding.) Remove to a plate.
- Sauté the onion, stirring a few times, 10-15 minutes or until they start to turn golden. Add celery and carrots and cook another 5-10 minutes. When they begin to soften, add the garlic, cook for another minute, then stir in the tomato paste and paprika and cook for a minute more.
- Pour in the wine and Madeira and bring to a simmer, scraping up any browned bits. Add the cooked pancetta, thyme, bay leaves, a half teaspoon salt and a few grinds of pepper (adjust salt if stock is salty.) Put back the oxtails back, and stock or water if necessary, so they're ¾ covered.
- Put the pot in oven for 3-4 hours, turning the oxtails in the sauce a few times. Add a little stock or water if it dries out too much.
- When oxtails are very tender, remove from the sauce and pull the meat from the bones, discarding them. (While doing this, you can reduce the sauce over a medium-high flame to thicken, if necessary.) Shred and return the meat to the sauce, stir in the Sherry vinegar and simmer a few minutes.
- Keeps well (actually improves) after a day or so in the fridge. When chilled, the fat will

- harden on the surface and is easily removed. ***
- For the Montaditos:
- Preheat oven to 375 degrees.
- Arrange baguette slices a foil lined baking sheet and brush with olive oil. Bake for 15 minutes, or until lightly browned.
- Spread about 2 T of the meat on each piece and cover with slices of cheese. Place in oven for 5-10 minutes, until cheese is melted. Serve hot.
- ***This recipe will probably yield more of the braised oxtail than needed for 8 people, depending on what else you're serving and so on. But it freezes well - great to have on hand for future tapas feasts.

164. Magic Mushrooms With Egg Noodles And Ricotta

Serving: Makes a pint or more of mushrooms, depending how many pounds you start with, and about 1 1/2 pints vinaigrette | Prep: 0hours25mins | Cook: 0hours30mins | Ready in:

Ingredients

- For the Smoky Tomato Vinaigrette
- 1 15 oz can fire-roasted diced tomatoes and their juice, or 1 lb small fresh tomatoes, such as cherry, blistered in a dry, hot pan
- 1/2 cup fresh basil leaves, packed (from the typical 3/4-1 oz package found in most grocery stores)
- 2 tablespoons sherry vinegar
- 2 tablespoons extra virgin olive oil
- 1 tablespoon honey, preferably smoked if you can find it (see note above)
- 2 teaspoons smoked salt
- 3/4 teaspoon sweet smoked paprika
- 3/4 teaspoon sweet Hungarian paprika
- 1/2 teaspoon Aleppo pepper
- pepper to taste

- For the mushrooms and finished pasta dish (quantities per 1 lb of mushrooms):
- 1 tablespoon olive oil
- 2 tablespoons unsalted butter, plus extra for the pasta
- 1 shallot, thinly sliced
- 1 pound cremini or button mushrooms, trimmed and quartered (or halved if very small)
- 1 pinch chipotle pepper flakes or powder (I just buzz a few dried chipotles in a spice grinder and store in a jar so I always have some on hand)
- 1/4 cup pickled jalapeno pepper brine
- 1/4 cup smoky tomato vinaigrette
- 1 small or half a larger garlic clove, peeled
- a big pinch of chopped fresh marjoram or oregano
- egg noodles
- fresh ricotta cheese
- salt and pepper to taste

Direction

- Make the smoky tomato vinaigrette: If using canned tomatoes, just whiz all the ingredients in a food processor until completely smooth. If using fresh tomatoes, blister them all over in a hot, dry pan, then continue as above, but take the extra step of putting the puree through a fine-mesh sieve to remove skins and seeds. Taste and adjust for seasoning, then set aside until ready to use. You'll have quite a bit leftover--use it as Giada does, to dress a bowl of orzo, with lots of fresh grated parmigiano and some more basil.
- Make the mushrooms: For each pound of mushrooms, heat 1 tbsp. olive oil and 2 tbsp. unsalted butter over medium heat in a large skillet. When butter smells nutty and has begun to brown, add shallot and cook until it begins to brown as well, about a minute. Be mindful it doesn't burn. Add a pinch of chipotle flakes and sauté another 30 seconds or so, until fragrant, then add mushrooms and toss to coat in fat and aromatics. Sauté mushrooms until they have given up their

liquid and are golden-brown. Deglaze with pickled jalapeno brine, stirring to scrape up any browned bits and delighting in the heady aroma now enveloping your nostrils. When the brine has mostly evaporated, hit the mushrooms with a couple spoonfuls (2-4 tbsp.) of the tomato vinaigrette. Stir to coat, and cook until the vinaigrette caramelizes a little and the mushrooms take on a glazed appearance. Dump the mushrooms in a bowl and micro plane the garlic over the top. Hit it with a pinch of chopped fresh marjoram and toss a few times. Set aside until ready to use, or wipe out the skillet and repeat the process for each additional pound of mushrooms.
- Bring a pot of water to the boil and salt it well. Cook egg noodles according to package directions. Drain, reserving a cup of pasta cooking water for finishing the dish. Heat a large skillet over medium-low heat and melt some butter. Add the noodles and toss to coat. Add the mushrooms, the ricotta, a little of the pasta cooking water, and another pat of butter if you please. (I please.) Toss. Finish with a smattering of chopped fresh marjoram or oregano and perhaps a sprinkle of paprika or Aleppo pepper, and serve.

165. Magical Pomegranate Molasses Chickpeas

Serving: Serves 6-8 | Prep: | Cook: | Ready in:

Ingredients

- 1 medium red onion, sliced
- 2-3 pieces garlic
- 1 tablespoon black cumin seeds
- 1 tablespoon paprika
- 1 cup cooked chickpeas
- 2 tablespoons pomegranate molasses
- 1 red bell pepper, diced
- 1 bunch fresh basil
- 10 kalamata olives, sliced

Direction

- In a T. of olive oil, sauté the chopped garlic and the thinly sliced onions until translucent.
- Add the black cumin seeds and the paprika. Cook them until you can smell the fragrance as the fragrance oils are released.
- Add the cooked chickpeas into the pot with about half a cup of water. Simmer on a medium to low heat until the water has completely evaporated.
- Take off the flame
- Add the uncooked red pepper, the chopped Kalamata olives, and the fresh chiffonade of basil. Add the pomegranate molasses. Season with salt and pepper to taste. Can also add red chili flakes.
- Serve with a garnish of basil.

166. Mamere's Tourtier

Serving: Serves variable | Prep: | Cook: | Ready in:

Ingredients

- 1.5 pounds Ground Pork Butts (I grind my own)
- 1 Large Russet Potato (largest you can find)
- 1 Large onion minced (I grind with the pork)
- 1 teaspoon *Each, Kosher salt, black pepper, ground clove, ground cinnamon, and ground allspice
- 1/2 cup Water
- 1 Egg
- 1 Pastry recipe for 9" double crust
- 1/4 teaspoon Paprika (for dusting)

Direction

- Bake the potato until done, 30 - 45 minutes in a preheated 400 degrees F (205 degrees C) oven. Peel and mash the potato
- Place the potato, ground pork, onion, spices and water in a large pan and simmer until

very thick, for about one hour. Let cool to lukewarm.
- Meanwhile, prepare your pastry and line a deep-dish pie plate with one crust.
- Spoon in filling, spreading evenly. Cover with top crust.
- Brush with beaten egg and sprinkle with paprika, if desired. Cut steam vent. Bake for 50 minutes at 350 degrees F (175 degrees C). If edges brown too fast, cover with a strip of foil. Serve warm.
- *When it comes to the spices…..start with above then adjust to taste

167. Maple Sweet Potato Cakes With Curried Greek Yogurt

Serving: Makes 6 cakes | Prep: | Cook: | Ready in:

Ingredients

- Curried Greek Yogurt
- 7 ounces 2% Greek yogurt
- 1/2 teaspoon curry powder
- 1/4 teaspoon salt
- 1/4 teaspoon ground black pepper
- Maple Sweet Potato Cakes
- 1 large sweet potato, peeled and shredded
- 1/2 teaspoon kosher salt
- 1 egg
- 1 1/2 tablespoons maple syrup
- 1/2 teaspoon ground white pepper
- 1/2 teaspoon paprika
- 1 pinch of cinnamon
- 1/3 cup minced yellow onion
- 1/3 cup panko breadcrumbs
- Nonstick cooking spray

Direction

- Make Curried Greek Yogurt: In a small bowl, stir together all ingredients.
- Make Maple Sweet Potato Cakes: Place shredded potato in a large bowl and toss with salt. Let stand 5 minutes.
- Meanwhile, in a second large bowl, whisk together egg, maple syrup, white pepper, paprika and cinnamon. Using your hands, squeeze all excess liquid out of potato; discard liquid. Add potato, onion and breadcrumbs to egg mixture; toss to combine well.
- Form potato mixture into 6 cakes (they should be about 3 1/2-inches diameter and 1/2-inch thick). Heat a griddle or large nonstick pan over medium high-heat. Spray griddle with nonstick spray; place potato cakes on griddle. Cook 8 to 10 minutes or until golden brown and crispy on the outside, flattening with spatula as they cook and flipping occasionally. Serve immediately with Curried Greek Yogurt.

168. Mediterranean Roasted Chickpea And Spinach Salad

Serving: Serves 2 | Prep: | Cook: | Ready in:

Ingredients

- For the Roasted Chickpeas and Salad
- 13.5 ounces can chickpeas, drained and rinsed
- 1 teaspoon smoked paprika
- 1/2 teaspoon ground coriander
- 1/2 teaspoon ground cinnamon
- 1 tablespoon oil
- 2 handfuls fresh baby spinach leaves
- 1/2 cup sliced cucumber
- 1/2 cup deli-sliced roasted red bell pepper
- 1/3 cup thinly sliced red onion
- 2 tablespoons feta cheese
- 2 tablespoons toasted walnuts
- For the Balsamic Vinaigrette
- 1/4 cup extra virgin olive oil
- 2 tablespoons balsamic vinegar
- 1 teaspoon honey
- 1 pinch salt

- 1 pinch black pepper
- 1 pinch onion powder
- 1 pinch dried oregano
- 1 pinch dried minced garlic

Direction

- Preheat oven to 350 degrees Fahrenheit (F).
- Drain and rinse chickpeas, then spread them on a rimmed baking sheet. Add the spices (smoked paprika, coriander, and cinnamon) and oil. Toss to combine.
- Roast chickpeas at 350 F for approximately 15-20 minutes, or until chickpeas are browned and crisp but not burnt. Set aside and allow chickpeas to cool.
- Meanwhile, toast walnuts over the stove top. Place them in a skillet over medium heat and toast until fragrant (takes only a few minutes). Let cool on a plate.
- To prepare the balsamic dressing, combine all ingredients in a small bowl and whisk to combine (you can also add dressing ingredients to a small jar with lid and shake to combine).
- To assemble the salad, place spinach leaves on a plate and top with roasted chickpeas, roasted red bell peppers, sliced cucumbers, sliced red onions, crumbled feta cheese, and toasted walnuts.
- Top with homemade balsamic dressing right before eating.

169. Mel's Bean Pie

Serving: Serves 8 | Prep: | Cook: | Ready in:

Ingredients

- For the Pie
- 1-2 pounds ground beef
- 1/2 medium sized white onion- diced
- 2-3 garlic cloves- minced
- 1-2 cups sliced mushrooms
- 1 cup sour cream
- 1/2 cup milk
- 1 cup canned or stewed tomatoes
- 2 teaspoons hot sauce (your choice, I like Tapatio)
- 1/4 cup cornstarch
- 1 tablespoon chopped fresh parsley
- 1 teaspoon paprika
- salt and pepper to taste (about 1 teaspoon of each)
- 1 can kidney beans- rinsed and drained
- 1 can black or pinto beans- rinsed and drained
- 2 cups shredded cheddar cheese
- 1/2 cup sliced green onions
- Pastry for double crust pie (just pick your favorite pie crust recipe)
- For the Garnish
- sour cream
- shredded cheese
- black olives
- green onions
- salsa

Direction

- Preheat oven to 425. In a skillet, cook beef, onion, mushrooms, and garlic until beef is browned, drain.
- In a large bowl, sour cream, milk, tomatoes (with their sauce), cornstarch, parsley, paprika, salt & pepper; mix well.
- Fold in beans, cheese, green onions and beef mixture.
- Line deep dish pie plate with pastry; fill with bean mixture. Top with remaining crust; seal and flute edges. Cut slits in the top crust.
- Bake for 30 –35 minutes or until lightly browned. Let stand for 5 minutes before cutting. Garnish with sour cream, olives, salsa, cheese & onions.

170. Michael Ruhlman's Rosemary Brined, Buttermilk Fried Chicken

Serving: Serves 6 to 8 | Prep: 24hours20mins | Cook: 0hours30mins | Ready in:

Ingredients

- Brine
- 1 small onion, thinly sliced
- 4 garlic cloves, smashed with the flat side of a knife
- 1 teaspoon vegetable oil
- 3 tablespoons kosher salt
- 5 branches rosemary, each 4 to 5 inches long
- 4 1/2 cups water
- 1 lemon, halved
- Fried Chicken
- 8 chicken legs, drumsticks and thighs separated
- 8 chicken wings, wing tips removed
- 3 cups all-purpose flour
- 3 tablespoons freshly ground black pepper
- 2 tablespoons paprika
- 2 tablespoons fine sea salt
- 2 teaspoons cayenne pepper
- 2 tablespoons baking powder
- 2 cups buttermilk
- 6 cups Neutral, high-heat oil for deep-frying (like canola)

Direction

- Make the brine: In a medium saucepan over medium-high heat, sauté the onion and garlic in the oil until translucent, 3 to 4 minutes. Add kosher salt after the onion and garlic have cooked for 30 seconds or so. Add the rosemary and cook to heat it, 30 seconds or so. Add the water and lemon, squeezing the juice into the water and removing any seeds. Bring the water to a simmer, stirring to dissolve the salt. Remove from the heat and allow the brine to cool. Refrigerate until chilled. To speed this process up, chill over an ice bath, stirring.
- Place all the chicken pieces in a large, sturdy plastic bag. Set the bag in a large bowl for support. Pour the cooled brine and aromatics into the bag. Seal the bag so that you remove as much air as possible and the chicken is submerged in the brine. Refrigerate for 8 to 24 hours, agitating the bag occasionally to redistribute the brine and the chicken.
- Remove the chicken from the brine, rinse under cold water, pat dry, and set on a rack or on paper towels. The chicken can be refrigerated for up to 3 days before you cook it, or it can be cooked immediately. Ideally, it should be refrigerated, uncovered, for a day to dry out the skin, but usually I can't wait to start cooking it.
- Combine the flour, black pepper, paprika, sea salt, cayenne, and baking powder in a bowl. Whisk to distribute the ingredients. Divide this mixture between two bowls.
- Pour the buttermilk into a third bowl. Set a rack on a baking sheet/tray. Dredge the chicken in the flour, shake off the excess, and set the dusted pieces on the rack. Dip the pieces in the buttermilk, then dredge them aggressively in the second bowl of flour and return them to the rack.
- Heat oil in a pan for deep-frying to 350°F/180°C. Add as many chicken pieces as you can without crowding the pan. Cook the chicken, turning the pieces occasionally, until they are cooked through, 12 to 15 minutes depending on their size. Remove to a clean rack and allow them to rest for 5 to 10 minutes before serving. For legs, thighs and wings, Ruhlman says, "I like to finish them in a 250? F/120? C. oven, to make sure they're super tender and to further crisp them. This lets me serve it whenever I want, no last minute frying if guests are invited."

171. Mini Frybreads With Smoked Paprika Aioli

Serving: Serves 8 as an appetizer | Prep: | Cook: | Ready in:

Ingredients

- Smoked Paprika Aioli
- 6 cloves roasted garlic
- 1 heaping tablespoon lemon zest
- 1 tablespoon Dijon mustard
- 2 egg yolks
- 1 cup extra virgin olive oil
- 2 teaspoons smoked paprika
- salt and lots of freshly ground pepper, to taste
- Frybread
- 2 cups all purpose flour
- 1 tablespoon baking powder
- 1 teaspoon salt
- 1/4 cup butter, melted and cooled slightly
- 1/2 cup warm water, or as needed
- oil, as needed for frying
- coarse salt, as needed for garnish

Direction

- Smoked Paprika Aioli
- Make a smooth paste from the garlic, lemon zest, and mustard. Transfer the mixture to a small bowl, and whisk in the egg yolks.
- Gradually add the olive oil to the yolk mixture in a thin, even stream - whisking constantly. Continue to whisk until all the oil has been incorporated and the aioli is light and fluffy.
- Season the aioli with the smoked paprika, salt, and pepper. Chill until ready to serve.
- Fry bread
- In a medium bowl, combine the flour, baking powder, and salt. Make a well in the center of the mixture, and add the warm butter and water. Mix to combine, the mixture will look like a shaggy mass. Knead the dough until it is smooth, 1-2 minutes.
- Divide the dough into about 16 pieces (this makes for mini flatbreads to give everyone one or two...you can also make larger ones or cut them into strips, etc.), and round the dough slightly. Cover with a damp paper towel and let sit for 10 minutes. Meanwhile, heat the oil for frying.
- When the dough has rested and the oil is hot, fry the breads until it is golden brown and slightly puffed up on both sides.
- Drain on absorbent paper towels and garnish with coarse salt. Serve warm with the aioli.

172. Minted Beans And Ham

Serving: Makes about 6 servings | Prep: 0hours0mins | Cook: 0hours0mins | Ready in:

Ingredients

- 1 pound dried Great Northern beans
- 1 very meaty ham bone and 2 cups of cubed ham (one inch cubes) Note: If you can't get your hands on a ham bone just add another cup of ham cubes.
- 1 large onion
- 2 medium carrots
- 2 stalks celery
- 3 large cloves of peeled garlic
- 1 tablespoon dried mint leaves
- 1 tablespoon sweet Hungarian paprika
- 1 teaspoon crushed red pepper flakes(or less if you're not a heat freak)
- 6 cups low sodium chicken broth
- Salt and pepper to taste (optional)

Direction

- The night before making, soak your beans by placing them in a bowl and covering with water. The next day drain and rinse them before starting your soup.
- Place the soaked beans in a six quart slow cooker. Chop the onion, carrots and celery in large pieces and place them in a food processor along with the garlic cloves and process until the mixture is finer than a small dice. Stir this into the beans.

- Stir the mint, paprika and crushed red pepper into the chicken broth. Add the ham and ham bone to the beans and pour the broth mixture over.
- Set your slow cooker on low for 8 hours and enjoy your day. Once the eight hours has elapsed, check to make sure your beans are nice and creamy. Remove the ham bone from the pot to cool a bit and then remove the meat from it and return (the meat) to the pot.
- Scoop out about 1 to 1 1/2 cups of the beans, place in a shallow bowl and take a fork and smash them until creamy. Return the beans to the pot. Taste to see if you need to season with salt and/or pepper.

173. Mom's Potato Salad With A Twist (of Lemon)

Serving: Serves 4 | Prep: | Cook: | Ready in:

Ingredients

- The salad
- 3 hard boiled eggs
- 1 bunch scallions
- 1 bunch radishes (6-8)
- 1 pound (approximately) new potatoes, boiled and cooled enought to handle
- 2 tablespoons Vermouth
- Good paprika or red pepper flake du jour (right now I tend to reach for the Gochugaru)
- The dressing
- 1/4 cup mayo
- 1/4 cup greek yogurt
- 1/2 tablespoon mustard
- 1/2 tablespoon horseradish
- 1 teaspoon tabasco or other hot pepper sauce to taste
- 1/2 tablespoon capers
- 1 tablespoon Cain's sweet pepper relish (a sweet element is necessary; I have used mango chutney at times)
- 1/2 lemon, grated rind and approx. 1 tsp juice

Direction

- Peel potatoes (unless the skins are beautiful, in which case retain them) and chop up into a large bowl. Sprinkle cut-up potatoes with vermouth and toss. Let them sit and absorb the vermouth while you peel eggs and chop them and chop the scallions, radishes and eggs.
- Mix all dressing ingredients together. If it seems too thick add another teaspoon or two of vermouth.
- Add to the potato bowl the chopped radishes, scallions and 2/3 of chopped eggs along with dressing and mix gently but thoroughly.
- Garnish with the rest of the chopped egg and paprika over all.

174. Monterey Jack & Macaroni With Spinach And Roasted Tomato

Serving: Serves 6 | Prep: | Cook: | Ready in:

Ingredients

- 8 ounces quinoa macaroni
- 2 tablespoons butter
- 2 tablespoons flour
- 4 cloves garlic, minced
- 2 cups milk
- 1 onion, diced
- 8 ounces fresh spinach, chopped
- 2 pounds compari tomatoes, halved and seeded
- 1/4 teaspoon paprika
- 1/2 teaspoon dried parsley
- 1/2 teaspoon salt, and more to taste
- 2 tablespoons vegetable oil
- 1 pinch pepper, more to taste

Direction

- Set the oven to 400 degrees.
- Cut the tomatoes in half, and push out the seeds. Place them on a lined baking sheet, skin side up, and coat them with a little olive oil, salt and pepper. Put the baking sheet into the oven on the top rack, and roast for 10 - 15 minutes, just long enough for the skins to brown a little and the "meat" to soften.
- Boil and drain the macaroni according to package directions. Rinse the macaroni with cold water to stop it from cooking, then toss it with a little olive oil and salt & pepper. That will help keep the macaroni from sticking together while you are preparing the rest of the dish.
- In a large sauce pan, combine the butter, and half of the garlic. Set the heat to medium, and stir the butter and garlic until the butter melts completely. Raise the heat just a little bit, then add the flour. Whisk together. Keep whisking the butter and four. As the roux cooks, the butter will foam, and the garlic will sweat. Cook the roux, while whisking continuously for about 5 minutes. Slowly add the milk, whisking to avoid any lumps. Bring the sauce to a simmer, then reduce the heat to low.
- Add the cream cheese, and let it melt completely. Slowly add the shredded cheese, stirring as you drop it in, letting it melt. When the cheese has totally melted, add the paprika and the parsley.
- Add 1/2 teaspoon of salt and a pinch of pepper, then taste it to see if it needs some more. The key to cheese sauces is salt. If it tastes bland to you, try adding a little more salt. Taste, and add, then taste again. Adding the salt little by little will help you get the flavor just right.
- Heat 2 tablespoons of oil in a large frying pan over medium heat. Add the onion, and the remaining garlic to the pan. Cook until the onions clear. Raise the heat to medium-high or high, then add about 1/3 of the spinach. Use a pair of tongs to toss the spinach in the pan. When it wilts, add another 1/3 of the spinach, and repeat until all the spinach is cooked.
- You can serve the pasta with the toppings and sauce over it, or you can mix all of the ingredients together in a big pot. It will taste great either way, so the choice is up to you. I find that the dish looks prettier when the sauce is draped over the noodles, and the spinach and tomatoes are plopped on top. However, mixing it all together has a much more hearty, classic mac n' cheese feel to it, so without considering looks, I prefer it that way.

175. Moroccan Carrot Salad By Way Of Israel

Serving: Serves 4 to 6 as a side/appetizer/mezze | Prep: 1hours20mins | Cook: 0hours10mins | Ready in:

Ingredients

- 6 carrots, peeled
- 2 cloves garlic, minced
- 1 teaspoon chili powder or cayenne pepper
- 3 tablespoons freshly squeezed lemon juice
- 1 teaspoon ground cumin
- ½ teaspoons hot paprika
- ¼ cups chopped cilantro or parsley
- 1/2 teaspoon harissa or chopped chili pepper (optional, more to taste)
- 1 pinch salt, more to taste

Direction

- Cook the carrots in boiling water until just tender, about 10 minutes.
- Drain the carrots and rinse under cold water. Slice on a bias into thin coin-shaped slices.
- Mix together the garlic, chili powder, lemon juice, cumin, paprika, parsley, and harissa (if using) and toss with the sliced carrots. Season with salt.
- Let stand at room temperature or in the fridge at least 1 hour, or in the fridge up to 2 days (the carrots will only get more flavorful with time). Serve cold or at room temperature.

176. Moroccan Chickpea Pockets

Serving: Serves 4 | Prep: 0hours10mins | Cook: 0hours15mins | Ready in:

Ingredients

- 2 cups cooked chickpeas
- 2 tablespoons olive oil
- 1 teaspoon kosher salt
- 1 teaspoon Hungarian sweet paprika
- 1/2 teaspoon ground coriander
- 1/4 teaspoon ground cayenne pepper
- 1/4 teaspoon ground ginger
- 1/8 teaspoon ground cinnamon
- 2 large garlic cloves, minced
- 1/2 large orange, juiced
- 1 tablespoon dried currants
- 1 cup crushed tomatoes (this time of year I use canned Italian tomatoes)
- 1 handful cilantro (around 1/3 cup)
- 4 whole wheat pita pockets

Direction

- I keep a stash of freshly cooked chickpeas in the refrigerator and freezer as I prefer the flavor of freshly cooked to the ones that are canned. To cook garbanzo beans (chickpeas), I rinse the beans, and soak them overnight in enough water to cover them by two inches. The following morning, I drain them, recover them with vegetable broth, and simmer for about one hour to an hour and a half. They can be stored in the refrigerator for four to five days or frozen for a few months.
- Combine the salt, paprika, coriander, cayenne, ginger, and cinnamon in a bowl for the spice mix. Set aside.
- Warm up the olive oil in a large sauté pan over medium heat and add the chickpeas, minced garlic, and 2 teaspoons of the spice mix. Sauté for 5 minutes until the garlic is very fragrant, but not browning.
- Add the orange juice and currants, and simmer for a couple of minutes.
- Add the tomatoes and cook for 5 to 7 minutes until the sauce thickens.
- Stir in the cilantro. Warm the pita bread in the microwave for 1 minute.
- Spoon the chickpea mixture into the pockets of the pita bread and serve with a side salad for a great, healthy meal.

177. Moroccan Onion Flatbread

Serving: Serves 3 large flatbreads | Prep: | Cook: | Ready in:

Ingredients

- Dough
- 1 packet active dry yeast
- 1 3/4 cups lukewarm water
- 4 1/2 cups all-purpose flour
- 1 teaspoon salt
- 1/3 cup olive oil
- Spicy Onion Filling
- 4 medium onions, thinly sliced
- 2 tablespoons olive oil
- 2 tablespoons butter
- 1 teaspoon cumin seeds, toasted and ground
- 1 teaspoon coriander seeds, toasted and ground
- 1/2 Rocoto chili pepper, seeds removed and finely chopped
- 2 teaspoons paprika
- 1 teaspoon Spanish smoked paprika
- 1 teaspoon black pepper
- Pinch salt
- 2 tablespoons chopped parsley
- 2 tablespoons chopped cilantro
- 1/4 cup dry white wine

Direction

- Dough

- In the bowl of a large stand mixer mix the yeast, 3/4 cup warm water, and 1/2 cup of flour together with a whisk. Let sit until foamy, about 3-5 minutes, and the yeast has been activated before adding the remaining 4 cups of flour, salt, olive oil, and the remaining 1 cup of warm water. Use the dough hook attachment and, on speed two, mix until the dough comes together in a smooth ball, about 4 minutes, adding more flour if needed. Cover and let rest in the refrigerator for two hours or overnight.
- Spicy Onion Filling
- Preheat the oven to 400 degrees Fahrenheit. In a large, heavy skillet over high heat place add the olive oil and sliced onions and cook, stirring occasionally, until the onions are soft and light golden brown, about 25-30 minutes. De-glaze the pan with the 1/4 cup of white wine and add the cumin, coriander, chopped red chile, paprika, Spanish paprika, black pepper and salt. Remove the onions from the heat and sprinkle and toss with the chopped parsley and cilantro.
- Divide the dough into six equal-sized balls and cover and let rise for an additional 10 minutes. Roll out 2 of the dough balls into 6-8 inch rounds and, using a spoon, place 1/3 of the onion mixture on one of the rounds. Cover with the other round and pinch the edges together. Flatten out the dough a little bit with your hands and then, with a rolling pin, carefully roll out into a 12-inch circle, taking care so that the onion filling does not spill out the sides. Repeat the process with the remaining dough and onion mixture to make two more flatbreads.
- Using a wide spatula and your hands carefully transfer the flatbreads to three separate lightly greased baking sheets and bake them two at a time for about 20-25 minutes, flipping the bread halfway through. Brush with olive oil and sprinkle with coarse salt and serve either hot or at room temperature.

178. Muscovado Baked Beans

Serving: Serves 4-6 | Prep: | Cook: | Ready in:

Ingredients

- Baked Beans
- 1 splash olive oil
- 1 onion, finely chopped
- 2 large cloves of garlic, crushed
- 2 teaspoons paprika
- 1 can chopped tomatoes
- 10 ounces dried haricot beans, soaked and cooked as per packet instructions
- 3 tablespoons dark muscovado sugar
- 2 tablespoons ketchup
- 1 tablespoon dijon mustard
- 150 milliliters beer
- a few sprigs fresh thyme
- Salt and freshly ground pepper
- Crumble Topping
- 4 ounces butter
- 4 ounces flour
- 3 ounces porridge oats
- 4 ounces cheddar cheese

Direction

- Pre-heat the oven to 200degreesC/350degreesF.
- Heat olive oil in a heavy based pan and sauté the onion and garlic till soft.
- Add paprika, beans and tomatoes. Stir well then add the sugar, ketchup and mustard.
- Add beer to thin the sauce a little.
- Season with thyme, a few grinds of black pepper and a hefty pinch of salt.
- Allow to simmer gently for around 20 minutes to allow the flavors to combine. Add a little water if too thick.
- For the crumble: Rub the butter into the flour with your fingertips until the mixture resembles breadcrumbs, then stir in the oats and cheese.
- To assemble: Put the beans into an ovenproof dish and top with the crumble mixture.

- Bake in the oven for 20 minutes until golden and bubbling.

179. Mushroom Goulash

Serving: Serves 4 | Prep: | Cook: |Ready in:

Ingredients

- 10 ½ ounces oyster mushrooms
- 3 ½ ounces shiitake mushrooms
- 3 ½ ounces mixed dry mushrooms
- 3 ½ ounces tomato purée (or passata di pomodoro)
- 2 pieces bigger carrots
- 1 piece big parsley root
- 1 piece big parsnip root
- ½ pieces celery root
- 2 pieces red onions
- 1 teaspoon mustard
- 2 tablespoons spelt flour
- 2 tablespoons sweet smoked paprika powder
- 2 pieces bay leaves
- 3 tablespoons olive oil
- salt, pepper, chili powder, turmeric, basil, oregano, parsley leaves to taste
- few slices of sundried tomatoes

Direction

- Take the carrots, parsnip, parsley and celery and grate it on a grater, or in food processor to approximate size as if they were grated by hand.
- Cut red onions into small cubes.
- Take large heavy bottom pan, put it on a stove – low heat, and add olive oil and spelt flour in it. Stir it with wooden spoon for one – one and a half minute, or until it becomes golden, then add a smoked paprika in and stir for another minute or so, until paprika darkens to make a kind of roux.
- Pour in about ½ cup (120 ml) warm water, while constantly stirring. The mixture should be smooth, with no lumps. Add the onion and shredded vegetables into the pan, season with one teaspoon of salt, add additional water if needed to cover vegetables, put the lid on, bring it to a boil and cook on a low heat, stirring occasionally for about 15 minutes.
- Slice the mushrooms stems into smaller pieces, and the caps into strips. Add sliced and dry mushrooms into the pan; cook additional 15 minutes, with the lid on.
- Add the tomato purée, mustard, bay leaves, good pinch of basil and oregano, and good pinch of chili and turmeric powder; add about 2/3 teaspoon of pepper, taste it and (if needed) add more salt (this depends on how salty the tomato purée was, but additional 2 teaspoons of salt should do it).
- Leave it covered to cook for about half an hour on low heat. From time to time stir with wooden spoon, taste it, and (if needed) add some of the seasoning. Before the end add about one tablespoon of chopped parsley leaves.
- Serve hot with a few slices of rustic bread or boiled potatoes and a glass of red vine.

180. Mushroom Stroganoff

Serving: Serves 4-6 | Prep: | Cook: |Ready in:

Ingredients

- 1 pound button mushroom, stems removed and sliced
- 1/2 large onion, diced
- 1 cup water or veg stock, up to 1 cup*
- 2-3 cloves of garlic, minced
- 1/2 cup white wine
- 1 splash worcestershire sauce
- 1 tablespoon dijon mustard, heaping
- 1/4 cup vegan yogurt
- 1 splash olive oil
- 1-2 tablespoons AP flour
- 2 teaspoons smoked paprika, really amount to taste

- 1/4 cup flat leaf parsley, rough chopped
- 1 packet noodles, cooked according to package instructions

Direction

- In a large pan, heat up a healthy splash of olive oil (medium high). Add in the onion and garlic, sauté until fragrant, anywhere from 5-10 minutes, you're not aiming to caramelize it, though if it does, don't freak out, it just adds another layer of flavor. *season with salt*
- Add in the mushrooms and sauté. The mushrooms will brown and release a lot of liquid. Don't be alarmed.
- At this point, boil noodles according to package instructions
- Add in the white wine and scrape the bottom of the pan to get all the good brown bits. Next, add in the Dijon mustard and healthy splash of Worcestershire sauce.
- Allow the mixture to reduce down, scraping the pan periodically.
- Spoon the flour over the mushrooms, minimum 1 tablespoon, or up to 2 tablespoons. Stir the mushrooms until the flour has been incorporated into the oils/liquid/onions. Slowly add in the water or stock, liquid amount at your discretion, depending on how saucy you it to be.
- Allow for the mixture and flour to warm though and thicken.
- Add in the yogurt and paprika, stir until fully incorporated.
- By this point, the noodles should be done. The dish can be served with the sauce ladled over the noodles, or the noodles can be added into the pan and mixed through with the mushrooms.
- Garnish with parsley and more paprika. Serve.

181. My Favorite Fried Egg On Toast

Serving: Serves 1 | Prep: 0hours5mins | Cook: 0hours10mins | Ready in:

Ingredients

- 1 thick piece of a good rustic country-style bread
- 1 tablespoon good-quality mayonnaise, adjusted to taste
- 2 pinches smoked paprika
- 1 generous pat of butter
- 1 large egg (or 2 if you're hungry)

Direction

- Toast your bread until it is nicely golden brown and crisped around the edges. Smear on a thin, but still decidedly noticeable, layer of mayonnaise. Sprinkle a couple of pinches of smoked paprika over the toast.
- Place a small pan—I much prefer to use a pan that is not non-stick, like cast iron—over medium high heat. Add the butter and wait until the butter has melted, foamed up, settled back down and has started to brown. You want the pan to be hot enough that the egg really sizzles when it hits.
- When the pan is hot, crack the egg in. Sprinkle the egg with a good bit of salt. Now, turn the heat down to medium-low, cover the pan and let the egg fry. This will help the white to cook through while the yolk stays runny. When it has reach this stage (cooked white, runny yolk) transfer the egg onto your toast. If there is any remaining browned butter in the pan, scrape that on top too. Sprinkle with some freshly ground pepper and eat.

182. My Favorite Vegan Mac And Cheese

Serving: Serves 4 to 6 | Prep: | Cook: | Ready in:

Ingredients

- 2/3 cup (about 3 ounces) raw cashews, soaked in water for at least 2 hours (and up to 8), drained
- 1/2 cup cooked cannellini, great white northern, or navy beans
- 2 tablespoons freshly squeezed lemon juice
- 1/2 teaspoon smoked paprika
- 1 teaspoon ground turmeric
- 2 tablespoons white miso
- 1/4 cup nutritional yeast
- 1 small clove garlic, crushed
- 1 dash cayenne pepper
- 1/2 cup water
- 12 ounces elbow pasta or mini shells (whole wheat, gluten-free, and regular pasta are all fine)
- 1 cup cooked green vegetables, such as chopped broccoli or cauliflower florets, blanched peas or chopped asparagus spears, or steamed spinach (optional)
- Salt, to taste

Direction

- Place the cashews, beans, lemon juice, paprika, turmeric, miso, nutritional yeast, garlic, cayenne, and water into a blender or a food processor and blend/process until totally smooth. Set the sauce aside.
- Bring a pot of salted water to boil and add the pasta. Cook the pasta according to package instructions, till it's to your liking.
- Drain the pasta and return it to the pot. Add the sauce and fold everything together gently, until the pasta dish is creamy and evenly coated. Adjust seasoning to taste. You may not need to use all of the sauce: If you have some leftover, use it as a dip or as dressing for a grain bowl.

183. My Oh So Buttery, Crispy & Moist Ritz Cracker Brined Chicken

Serving: Serves 4 to 6 | Prep: | Cook: | Ready in:

Ingredients

- For the Brine:
- 8 cups Cold Water
- 1/4 cup Table (not Kosher) Salt
- 1/4 cup Sugar
- For the Chicken:
- 3 pounds Skinless and Boneless Chicken Breast (if you buy chicken breast halves like me, I like to further cut each into 2 pieces)
- 2 Large Eggs
- 2 Rolls of Ritz Crackers, crushed (with some pieces looking like breadcrumbs and others being a bit bigger)
- 1/4 teaspoon Garlic Powder
- 1/4 teaspoon Sweet Smoked Paprika
- 1/2 teaspoon Black Pepper
- 1 Stick (4 oz or 8 tbsp) unsalted butter cut into bits (not margarine)
- NOTE: No salt is added to the chicken since it is brined; however, if you choose not to brine the chicken you will of course need to add some salt.

Direction

- TO BRINE: In a big bowl, mix the water with the salt and sugar and add the chicken, making sure it is covered with the water. Place in refrigerator for 1 hour (not more, not less) then rinse in cold water 4 to 5 times to wash the extra salt. This step renders a chicken that is more tender and juicy.
- Preheat the oven to 375*F.
- Place the eggs into a shallow bowl. In another bowl, place the crushed Ritz crackers and add the garlic powder, black pepper and smoked paprika. Please do NOT add any more salt.
- Dip the chicken pieces first into the eggs and then roll them in the Ritz cracker crumb mixture, making sure they are well coated.

- Place them in a baking dish, like a 15 inch Pyrex; then drop the pieces of butter all around, in between and over the chicken. I like to cut the butter in several tiny pieces (maybe 20-30 pieces).
- Bake for 35 minutes in the preheated oven until the chicken is no longer pink inside, the juices run clear and the crumbs are nicely browned. Note that if you prepared the chicken overnight and it was thus in refrigerator, it may take a bit longer to cook.
- For a touch of color, feel free to sprinkle some more paprika over the chicken prior to serving. You can also even sprinkle some chopped chives or scallions. I like to serve this rich dish with steamed broccoli, and my salt & vinegar maple glazed potatoes or Thai Basil Asiago stuffed potatoes.

184. NW Applewood Smoked Pork & Sauce

Serving: Serves 20-30 | Prep: 1hours15mins | Cook: 0hours0mins | Ready in:

Ingredients

- NW Applewood Smoked and Braised Pulled Pork
- 8 pounds bone-in pork shoulder or butt
- 1 tablespoon kosher salt
- 2 teaspoons ground black pepper
- 2 teaspoons brown sugar
- 1 teaspoon smoked paprika
- 1 teaspoon crushed brown or yellow mustard seeds
- 1 teaspoon dried thyme
- 1 teaspoon dried and crumbled rosemary
- 1 teaspoon granulated garlic
- 2 large apples, cored and diced but not peeled
- 1 large sweet onion, sliced pole-to-pole
- 1/4 cup apple cider vinegar
- 1/4 cup Calvados or similar oak-aged apple brandy (or Bourbon if you can't find apple brandy)
- 10 lightly crushed juniper berries
- additional salt to taste
- Caramelized Apple and Onion Barbecue Sauce
- 2 medium apples, cored and finely chopped but not peeled
- 1/2 medium sweet onion
- 2 tablespoons butter
- 2 dashes ground white pepper
- 1 pinch baking soda
- 1/2 teaspoon smoked paprika
- 1 dash allspice powder
- 3 tablespoons brown sugar, divided
- 1/3 cup apple cider vinegar
- 1/2 cup smoked/pulled pork braising juices (from the accompanying recipe or substitute prepared stock with the addition of a little liquid smoke or more smoked paprika)
- 2 tablespoons molasses (or honey, maple syrup, etc.)
- 2 tablespoons ketchup (optional)
- salt to taste

Direction

- NW Apple wood Smoked and Braised Pulled Pork
- Set up smoker per manufacturer's directions. Include water in the liquid pan if it has one. Place a full charge of apple wood chips (pre-soaked in water) in the smoke box. Preheat to 225°F.
- Combine the measured salt, pepper, brown sugar, smoked paprika, mustard seeds, thyme, rosemary, and garlic in a small bowl and stir together to make a dry rub.
- Apply the dry rub (reserving 2tsp for later use) all over the pork and place it fat-side-up in a low-sided pan that will just fit it. I use disposable foil pans or a quarter sheet pan lined with parchment paper for this.
- Place the meat on a middle rack in the smoker and smoke at 225°F for about 4 hours, pausing to refill the water pan and recharge the smoke tray with fresh wood chips about three times (I

do this on the hour). After 4 hours, the pork should have an internal temperature of 150°F, but it isn't necessary.
- Prepare a large (at least 7 quarts) enameled cast iron Dutch oven or a large crock pot for the braise: Place the sliced onion and apples in the bottom, sprinkle on the reserved 2tsp of dry rub and crushed juniper berries (use a mortar and pestle or the side of a chef's knife) and pour in the vinegar and Calvados. Place the pork on top of the bed of apples/onions and pour in any juices that collected in the pan while in the smoker.
- Cover with the lid and braise for at least 4 hours and up to 20 hours over low heat on the stovetop or high heat in a crock pot. Aim for a constant low boil. If you want to speed the cooking process for a shorter braise, cut the large chunk of meat into 4-8 smaller chunks in the pot.
- After about 4 hours, the meat should be tender enough to "pull" by simply stirring it with tongs. Remove the bone at this point. If it isn't soft enough yet to separate, give it more time and heat. If a lot of liquid has built up, crack the lid for the final hour of cooking and stir often to reduce and concentrate the juices. This is harder to accomplish in a crock pot because most products don't supply enough heat to keep a boil with the lid cracked. That's the main reason I prefer stovetop preparation. If you just can't get the juice reduced, pull some off with a ladle and keep it for another use such as a soup or the accompanying barbecue sauce.
- Adjust the salt, acid, and sweet seasoning as desired before serving. I often mix in half a cup of barbecue sauce to further moisten and flavor the meat.
- Caramelized Apple and Onion Barbecue Sauce
- Melt butter in a 1-2 quart saucepan over medium-high heat. Add onion, white pepper, a few pinches of salt, baking soda, and 1 tsp of the brown sugar. Stir and let it cook uncovered until the onions start to brown and stick to the pot a little (7-10 minutes).
- Have some water handy in a small cup. Pour in about 2 tsp of water, and deglaze the browned bits from the bottom of the pan using a flat-tipped wooden spoon. Let the onions cook and brown again undisturbed (but watch carefully--don't let them burn!) for about 5 minutes. Repeat the water deglazing. Again repeat the browning rest and deglazing a third time until a deep brown-colored paste is achieved. If you think it can get darker without burning, go for a fourth rest and deglaze.
- Now add half the apples with a little salt, stir, add a little water and quickly close the lid. This rapidly steams a portion of the apples and speeds up the breakdown process.
- After 5 minutes, remove the lid, add the remaining apples, cider vinegar, remaining brown sugar, smoked paprika, and allspice. Stir and continue to cook over medium-high heat while watching carefully to prevent burning.
- Once the apples are browned and starting to disintegrate (5-10 minutes later), add the pork braising juice or stock and cook for another 5-10 minutes. For a sweeter sauce, add molasses (my favorite), honey, maple syrup or any combination thereof. A tablespoon of ketchup or two is optional but really ties the flavors together well. Remove from heat and puree with an immersion blender then try a taste test. Adjust with salt, cider vinegar, or brown sugar as needed.

---

185. New Orleans Style Barramundi Fish Cakes With Creole Remoulade

Serving: Makes 20 | Prep: | Cook: | Ready in:

Ingredients

- For the Remoulade
- 1/2 cup mayonnaise

- 2 tablespoons Creole mustard (substitute stone ground dijon if unavailable)
- 2 teaspoons hot sauce (Suggested: Crystal or Tabasco)
- 1 1/2 teaspoons Worcestershire sauce
- 2 teaspoons prepared horseradish
- 1 tablespoon ketchup
- 1/8 teaspoon garlic powder
- 1/2 teaspoon paprika
- 1/4 teaspoon cayenne pepper (use less if sensitive to heat)
- 1 tablespoon fresh lemon juice (about 1/2 lemon)
- For the Barramundi Fish Cakes
- 1/2 cup mayonnaise
- 1 large egg
- 1 tablespoon Creole mustard (substitute stone ground dijon if unavailable)
- 1 tablespoon Worcestershire sauce
- 2 teaspoons Cajun or Creole seasoning
- 1 teaspoon hot sauce (Suggested: Crystal or Tabasco)
- 1/2 small red, yellow or orange bell pepper, finely chopped
- 2 scallions, finely chopped
- 20 saltine crackers, finely crushed
- 1 pound cooked barramundi, flaked apart
- 1 tablespoon olive oil
- 4 tablespoons tablespoons butter
- 8 lemon wedges, for serving

Direction

- To make the remoulade, whisk together the mayonnaise, Creole mustard, hot sauce, Worcestershire, horseradish, ketchup, garlic powder, paprika, cayenne pepper and lemon juice in a small bowl. Taste and adjust seasoning as needed. Cover and refrigerate until ready to serve.
- To make the barramundi cakes, whisk together the mayonnaise, egg, Creole mustard, Worcestershire sauce, hot sauce, Cajun seasoning, bell pepper and scallions in a large bowl. Add the crushed saltine crackers and flaked barramundi, then gently mix until combined. Form the mixture into about 20 small patties and set aside.
- Preheat the oven to 325 degrees. Heat the olive oil and butter in a large sauté pan over medium high heat. Sauté the barramundi cakes in batches, being sure not to overcrowd the pan. Cook until golden brown on one side, flip, and cook until golden on the other side. Remove the cakes to a rack or paper towels to drain, then transfer to a baking sheet and place in the oven to keep warm. Repeat until all of the cakes.
- Arrange the barramundi cakes on a platter and serve with Creole remoulade and lemon wedges on the side. Serve hot.

186. No Tato Salad

Serving: Serves 3 | Prep: | Cook: | Ready in:

Ingredients

- 1 head cauliflower
- 2 stalks celery
- 1/4 - 1/2 cups yellow onion (~ 1/4 of an onion, preferably Vidalia or some other sweet variety)
- 2 tablespoons fresh parsley
- 2 eggs
- 2 tablespoons mayo (I use the type made with olive oil)
- 2 tablespoons capers (or good old green Spanish olives)
- 1 tablespoon dijon mustard
- 1/4 teaspoon celery salt
- 1/4 teaspoon garlic powder
- Salt & pepper to taste
- Sprinkle sweet paprika (optional)

Direction

- Place the eggs in a small pot. Cover with water and put over a burner on high. Bring to a boil, let go 4 minutes and cut the heat. Remove pot to the sink, drain, and fill with cold water.

- While your eggs are cooking, chop/snap the cauliflower into small florets. When this is complete, add to a large pan over medium high heat with a splash or 2 of water. Cook until softened – if you want to go a little brown here, have at it. I went for just steamed to taste as close as possible to potatoes, but brown would be nice, too. Remove from the heat when done. Add to a large bowl to cool.
- While that is working, dice the celery, onion, capers and parsley. Add to the bowl with the cauliflower.
- When the eggs are done, cool, peel and dice. Add to the bowl.
- Add the mayo, mustard, celery salt & garlic powder. Combine. Taste & add salt and pepper if needed. Dust with paprika as an optional old school garnish.
- Serves 2 for dinner with a nice steak and 1 for lunch beefed up with a little chicken and the gift that keeps on giving: hazelnut gremolata (yes, this is the same gremolata that's been kicking around the back of my fridge and popping up here and there since Easter).

187. North African Grilled Chicken Salad

Serving: Serves 2 to 3 | Prep: | Cook: | Ready in:

Ingredients

- For the marinade:
- 1 pound boneless, skinless chicken breast
- 2 teaspoons paprika
- 2 tablespoons olive oil
- 2 teaspoons balsamic vinegar
- 1/2 teaspoon salt
- 1 garlic clove, smashed
- For the salad:
- 1/4 cup plain, whole-milk yogurt
- 1 tablespoon olive oil
- 1/2 lemon, juiced
- 1/2 teaspoon ground ginger
- 1/4 teaspoon ground cinnamon
- 1/2 teaspoon ground turmeric
- 1 teaspoon paprika
- 1/4 teaspoon cayenne pepper (optional)
- 1/4 teaspoon salt
- 1 garlic clove, minced
- 1/4 cup green olives, pitted and chopped
- 1/4 cup dried apricots, chopped
- 1/2 Granny Smith apple, cored and diced
- 1/4 cup toasted walnuts, chopped
- 2 tablespoons chopped fresh mint

Direction

- Combine the marinade ingredients in a bowl. Add the chicken and turn over to coat evenly. Let marinate for at least 3 hours.
- Heat up your grill or grill pan to medium and cook chicken for about 5 minutes on each side, or until fully cooked. Remove from grill and, using two forks, shred the chicken into bite-sized pieces.
- In a medium bowl, whisk together the yogurt, olive oil, lemon juice, ginger, cinnamon, turmeric, paprika, cayenne (if using), salt, and garlic. Add in the chicken, olives, dried apricots, apple, walnuts and mint. Toss to combine. Add salt and pepper, to taste.

188. North African Lamb Stew (Boktoff)

Serving: Serves 6-8 | Prep: | Cook: | Ready in:

Ingredients

- 1 lamb shoulder, cut in chunks
- 2 cups cooked fava beans, white beans, or chick peas
- 2 onions, diced
- 3 tablespoons paprika
- 3 tomatoes, cut in chunks
- 1 bunch greens, cut in thin strips (or 2 zucchini, diced)
- 1 bunch cilantro, chopped

- 1 bunch mint, chopped
- 1/2 cup small form pasta
- 2 tablespoons lemon juice

Direction

- If using fava beans, remove the skins.
- Brown the lamb chunks in 2 Tbsp. olive oil, until dark golden.
- Add the onion and cook until golden, salt and pepper liberally. Add the paprika, and stir and cook until well caramelized.
- Add the tomatoes, cook until they have blended with the rest. Add the beans, cover with water, add 1 tsp salt, one half of the mint and one half of the cilantro. Cook about 1 hour, or until the meat is tender.
- Add the greens or zucchini and the pasta and cook 15 minutes. Serve garnished with the remaining mint and cilantro and a squeeze of fresh lemon juice.

189. OMFGoulash!

Serving: Serves 8-10 | Prep: | Cook: |Ready in:

Ingredients

- For the Pork:
- 1.5 pounds pork neck bones
- 1/2 pound fresh pork belly, cut into 1.5-2-inch pieces
- 2 pounds fresh pork butt or shoulder, cut into 1.5-2-inch cubes
- neutral oil, such as sunflower, canola, or vegetable, for browning
- 1 teaspoon (each) kosher salt, whole black peppercorns, fennel seed, & caraway seed
- 1/2 teaspoon (each) cumin seed, coriander seed, dill seed, dried rosemary, dried thyme, & dried marjoram
- 12 juniper berries
- 1 tablespoon sugar, or to taste
- 2 tablespoons sweet Hungarian paprika
- 1 teaspoon hot Hungarian paprika
- 1/4 cup tomato paste
- 3/4 cup lecso, pureed (or substitute a drained can of stewed tomatoes pureed with one roasted red pepper)
- 1/2 cup cider vinegar
- 1 tablespoon worcestershire sauce
- To finish the goulash:
- 2 tablespoons neutral oil, such as sunflower or canola
- 1 large yellow onion, chopped
- 4 garlic cloves, chopped (remove and discard any green shoots)
- 1/2 teaspoon caraway seeds, crushed
- 1 teaspoon sweet paprika
- 1/2 cup water
- 15 ounces can stewed tomatoes with their juice, roughly chopped (OR: omit, along with the peppers, and substitute an equivalent amount of lecso)
- Reserved pork and de-fatted sauce
- 1 pound sauerkraut, rinsed and drained (use the bagged variety)
- 1/2 pound banana or cubanelle peppers, stemmed, seeded, and chopped (OR: omit, along with the stewed tomatoes, and substitute lecso)
- sour cream, for garnish
- cooked egg noodles, boiled potatoes, or spaetzle for serving

Direction

- For the Pork:
- Set oven to 400 F. Rinse the neck bones and pat dry. Line a rimmed baking sheet with foil and set a wire rack in it. Season the bones with salt and pepper and set on the rack, then roast in the oven 60 minutes, turning the bones over halfway through. Remove from oven, cover with foil, and set aside. Lower heat to 250 F.
- Toast whole seeds briefly in a dry skillet. Let cool, then transfer to a mortar or spice grinder. Blitz with the remaining herbs, the kosher salt, the juniper berries, and the sugar. Combine with the sweet and hot paprika, then whisk in a large bowl with the tomato paste, lecso, vinegar, and Worcestershire sauce. Set aside.

- Rinse the pork butt and pat dry. Do the same with the belly. Season with salt and pepper. Heat oil in a large, heavy-bottomed skillet or sauté pan. Brown butt/shoulder and belly pieces all over, working in batches and transferring browned pieces to a large bowl to catch all their juices. When all the pork is browned, toss the belly, butt/shoulder pieces, and any accumulated juices in the bowl with the spice paste. Spread the roasted neck bones in the bottom of a large casserole or 9 x 13 baking dish. Smother with the spice-paste-coated pork, scraping down the sides and bottom of the bowl so every last bit of paste makes it into the baking dish. Cover the dish tightly with foil, secure with the lid, and braise in the oven 4 hours. At about the halfway mark, your kitchen will start to smell amazing.
- Remove the casserole from the oven. Uncover (taking care to avoid steam-burning yourself!). Remove the pork from the sauce with a slotted spoon or tongs and prepare each component for storage separately. You can also take this opportunity to separate the neck meat from the bones--either discard or reserve them for stock. When both pork and sauce have cooled to room temperature, refrigerate them until ready to use again.
- To finish the goulash:
- If the sauerkraut is very fresh, simmer in water until tender, then drain and set aside. Take the pork and its sauce from the refrigerator. Let the pork come to room temperature. (The reserved sauce should have congealed and have a consistency like that of refrigerated gravy.) If a fat cap has formed on the surface of the sauce, remove it. (If there is a significant amount of fat, reserve a little for sautéing and discard the rest, or reserve for another use.)
- Heat 2 tbsp fat or oil (or a mix of both) over medium-low heat until shimmering. Add the onions and garlic and sauté until tender and translucent and turning golden. Remove from heat and add the paprika, caraway, and water, and whip to integrate. Return the pan to heat and add the tomatoes and their juice, the pork, and the sauce. Mix in the sauerkraut and the peppers and bring to a simmer. Then cover, lower the heat, and stew for 30 minutes.
- Toss warm noodles, potatoes, or spaetzle with a spoonful of the reserved fat or some butter or oil and divide among bowls. Spoon the goulash over and top each with a dollop of sour cream and a sprinkle of paprika.

190. Okinawan Taco Rice Bowls

Serving: Serves 4 | Prep: 0hours10mins | Cook: 0hours35mins | Ready in:

Ingredients

- For the taco bowls
- 2 cups short-grain sushi rice or arborio rice
- 2 cups shredded cheese (cheddar or a mild white cheese like Gruyère, asiago, or mozzarella)
- 2 cups shredded iceberg or romaine lettuce
- 1 pound ground beef
- 2 tablespoons olive oil
- 1/2 teaspoon chili flakes
- 1 teaspoon ground cumin
- 1/2 teaspoon ground coriander
- 1 teaspoon sweet paprika
- 1   clove garlic, minced
- 2 tablespoons soy sauce
- 2 teaspoons sweet miso paste, dissolved in 1/2 cup water
- For the salsa
- 3/4 cup diced fresh tomatoes
- 2 tablespoons rice vinegar
- 1 tablespoon mirin
- 1 tablespoon soy sauce
- 2 teaspoons minced fresh ginger
- 1   small red chili, minced (optional, only if you like heat!)

Direction

- Put the rice with 2 cups cold water and a pinch of salt in a medium pot. Bring to a boil, then

reduce to a low simmer, cover, and cook until tender and the water is absorbed, about 20 minutes. Fluff with a fork and set aside.
- To make the beef, heat the oil in a large saucepan over medium-high heat. Add beef and stir to break up any lumps, cooking for about 4 minutes until well-browned.
- Add the chili flakes, cumin, coriander, and paprika, and cook for 1 minute, stirring constantly.
- Add the soy sauce and miso/water blend. Cook for about 4 minutes, until the beef is cooked through and the liquid is mostly cooked off. Remove from the heat.
- To make the salsa: Combine all the ingredients in a medium bowl and mix well.
- Divide the rice between four bowls. Top with the seasoned beef, lettuce, shredded cheese, and salsa. If you want a more filling meal, add sliced avocado and/or an egg.

191. One Pot Pasta Bolognese Style

Serving: Serves 6 | Prep: | Cook: | Ready in:

Ingredients

- 3 carrots
- 2 garlic cloves
- 2 onions
- 150 grams celeriac
- 4 tablespoons olive oil
- 500 grams minced meat
- 3 tablespoons fresh oregano
- 2 tablespoons tomato paste
- 850 milliliters chopped tomatoes, canned
- 500 grams vegetable broth
- 150 grams ribbon noodles, Mafaldine or Reginette
- 150 grams Ricotta, Italian cream cheese
- 200 grams crème fraiche
- 75 grams Parmesan
- 6 sprigs basil
- sweet paprika powder
- salt
- pepper
- sugar

Direction

- Peel the carrots, garlic, celeriac and onions and dice very finely.
- Wash and pluck fresh oregano. Then cut very small with a very sharp knife or a chopping-knife.
- Heat the olive oil in a large pot or crockpot and fry the minced meat.
- Add the onions, garlic, carrots and celery, and sauté them briefly.
- Add the oregano and season with paprika powder, salt and pepper.
- Stir in the tomato paste and simmer briefly.
- Then add the vegetable broth and chopped tomatoes.
- Bring to the boil, then stir in the noodles.
- Leave to simmer for 8 to 10 minutes or until the pasta is al dente.
- Mix the ricotta and cream fraiche. Season with salt and pepper.
- Season with salt, pepper, sugar and paprika powder.
- Wash the basil, dry and pluck the leaves from the stalks.
- Cut the leaves of five stems.
- Put the one-pot pasta in a large bowl. Serve with one to two spoons of ricotta cream fraiche mixture.
- Now sprinkle and garnish with basil and serve with the remaining cream.

192. Onion And Red Pepper Confit

Serving: Serves never enough | Prep: | Cook: | Ready in:

Ingredients

- 2 generous tablespoons good olive oil

- 1 large vidalia or other sweet onion, cut into approximately 1 inch pieces
- 3 red (and yellow) bell peppers, roasted, skins removes, and cut into 1 inch by 1/2 inch (approx) pieces
- 2 cloves garlic, finely chopped (but not too fine)
- 1 generous pinch of salt
- 2-4 tablespoons sherry or red wine vinegar
- 1/2 teaspoon smoked paprika
- salt and pepper to taste

Direction

- In a large skillet, heat olive oil over medium heat. Add onions, peppers and garlic, and sauté, stirring frequently, until softened. You might need to raise the heat somewhat, because you want everything to brown.
- Once the vegetables have started to brown, stir in just enough vinegar to deglaze the pan and scrape up the fond on the bottom of the pan. Stir in paprika, reduce heat to very low, cover, and continue to cook, stirring occasionally, until the vegetables are browned and caramelized. Taste and add salt and pepper as needed.
- You can keep any leftovers in the refrigerator for a few days. (It never lasts more than a few days in my house.)

193. Orzo With Butter & Parmesan A La Chicken Fritz

Serving: Serves 4-6 | Prep: | Cook: | Ready in:

Ingredients

- ORZO
- 1 pound Orzo
- 4 ounces Unsalted butter (8 oz or 1/2 cup). I have also successfully used light butter.
- 1 cup Grated Parmesan cheese
- Salt and black pepper to taste
- CHICKEN
- 3 cups Cooked chicken cut or shredded into small pieces (I use storebought rotisserie chicken)
- 1/4 cup Vegetable oil, preferably extra virgin olive oil
- 1 Large onion, chopped
- 3 Small to medium Garlic Cloves crushed mixed with 1/2 tsp lemon or lime zest and 1/2 tsp Sriracha sauce
- 1 teaspoon Sweet smoked paprika (I use McCormick Smoked Paprika)
- 1/4 cup Chopped parsley or cilantro
- Salt and black pepper to taste
- Optional - 1/4 tsp turmeric

Direction

- Boil orzo according to package instructions but more on the al dente side. You don't want it mushy. Drain well and place back into pot. Add butter, parmesan, and some ground black pepper. Taste to see if it still needs salt. Spread/place on a nice, large serving plate; and cover with aluminum foil to keep it warm.
- In the same pot in which you cooked the pasta but that is now empty, add the oil and the onions, and cook for 12-15 minutes or until the onions are cooked and golden brown. You want to stir often because they can burn. When they get golden brown, add the garlic (mixed with the lemon zest and Sriracha sauce) and stir for 20-30 seconds. Add the chicken and toss to coat with the oil and onions. Add the paprika and (optional) turmeric. Taste and add salt and black pepper as needed. Cook for another 10-15 minutes, stirring occasionally, until the chicken has browned quite a bit and is crispy around the edges.
- Spread the chicken all over the orzo. Sprinkle with cilantro or parsley. You can also choose to place orzo and chicken on individual plates; and add droplets of sriracha sauce all around the orzo.

194. Oven "Fried" Chicken With Paprika & Tarragon

Serving: Serves as much as you want | Prep: | Cook: | Ready in:

Ingredients

- Chicken legs and/or thighs (as many as you need)
- Peanut oil
- Sweet Hungarian paprika (or a combination of sweet and hot)
- Dried tarragon leaves
- Kosher or sea salt (optional)

Direction

- Lightly coat a baking pan with peanut oil. Trim off excess blobs of fat from the chicken, but leave the skin on. Place chicken in the pan and turn to coat with oil.
- Sprinkle both sides of the chicken with paprika and dried tarragon leaves (crush them lightly with fingers as you sprinkle them over the chicken).
- Arrange chicken skin-side up on the baking sheet. Sprinkle with salt (optional, to taste).
- Bake in a preheated 350 degree oven, without turning, until completely cooked and skin is crispy, about 40- 45 minutes.
- Variation: Mix equal amounts of sweet Hungarian paprika, hot Madras curry powder, freshly ground cumin seed, and chili powder. Sprinkle on both sides of chicken pieces and bake as above. Use a neutral oil. (Because ground cumin tends to lose potency rather quickly, make smaller batches of this blend to keep on hand for quick dinner preparation.)

195. Paella

Serving: Serves 3-4 | Prep: 0hours0mins | Cook: 0hours0mins | Ready in:

Ingredients

- 2/3 quart chicken stock from cube or fresh
- a few strands of saffron
- 1 chicken breast
- 1 chicken thigh, skin on, bone out (or just thighs or breasts)
- 1 tablespoon vegetable oil
- salt and pepper
- 1 medium onion, diced
- 2 garlic cloves, chopped finely
- 1 teaspoon (heaped) tomato purée
- 1 red pepper, cored and roughly chopped
- 1 teaspoon smoked hot paprika
- 2-3 ounces sliced chorizo
- 1 cup paella rice (Bomba or Calasparra)
- 1/2 cup dry white wine
- 8-12 raw large shrimp, shelled, shell-on or a mix
- 1/2 cup frozen peas, thawed

Direction

- Heat up the stock or dissolve the cube in boiling water; add the saffron and stir.
- Chop each chicken thigh and breast into 4 or 5 pieces and season them with salt and pepper.
- Heat up the oil in the largest pan you have (25cm will be good) and brown the chicken pieces on all sides.
- Push them to the sides and add the onion and garlic into the middle of the pan.
- Fry it hard for a couple of minutes, then stir in the tomato puree, keeping it away from the chicken.
- Add the red pepper; fry it together with the onion and garlic for a minute.
- Turn down the heat a little and mix the chicken pieces in. Sprinkle over the smoked paprika and add the chorizo pieces.
- Pour the stock into the pan, all at once and turn up the heat. Let it bubble vigorously for two-three minutes.
- Sprinkle the rice evenly over the surface of the stock – DO NOT STIR from now on.
- Cook it for 10 minutes until the rice appears through the liquid. Gently displace any dry

grains sticking to the chicken but DO NOT STIR. If it looks too dry too soon, add the white wine.
- Sprinkle the peas over the surface and arrange the prawns on top.
- Turn the heat down and simmer the paella for 10 minutes until the rice has absorbed all the liquid; you may cover the pan at this stage so the prawns cook through. If you don't have a lid to fit the pan, cover it with a large baking sheet.
- After the 10 minutes turn the heat right up for 1 minute until you can hear the rice start to pop and crackle. Keep it on for 30 seconds and take the pan off the heat.
- Cover it with a clean dry tea towel to absorb the steam, keep it like that for 10 minutes and serve in the pan placed in the middle of the table.
- If you're lucky, the mixture has stuck to the bottom of the pan; crispy and almost-burnt. This is socarrat, a characteristic of good paella. Well done – the socarrat is truly scrumptious.

196. Paella Manantiales Calientes

Serving: Serves 6-8 | Prep: | Cook: | Ready in:

Ingredients

- 1 pound chorizo or andouille sausage, cut in 1/2 inch slices
- 1 pound chicken (I used boneless thighs), cut in 1-inch cubes
- 6 cloves garlic, mashed or minced, divided
- 1 tablespoon smoked paprika
- 1/4 teaspoon saffron, powdered in a mortar
- kosher salt and freshly ground black pepper
- 4 tablespoons olive oil, divided
- 1 cup lima beans
- 1 cup fresh green beans, broken in 1/2 inch pieces
- 1 1/2 cups artichoke hearts, quartered
- 1 cup finely diced tomato, drained
- 1 1/2 cups Arborio or Bomba or other short-grain, glutinous rice
- 5 cups chicken broth

Direction

- Sprinkle the chicken with half the paprika and garlic, and set aside while you gather and prep everything else.
- Put chicken stock on to simmer, and add powdered saffron. Preheat oven to 425.
- In a large, flat bottomed fryer or paella pan over medium high heat, sauté the chicken in half the olive oil until no pink shows. Add the sausage and sauté until it starts to brown. Add the veggies, and sauté until they, too, start to brown. Push the mixture to the outside edges of the pan, where it's cooler.
- In the center of the pan, add remaining oil and garlic, and sauté until it's fragrant. Add paprika and tomatoes. Cook until tomatoes begin to break down. Stir everything together and add the rice, stirring to coat it nicely with pan juices.
- Add four cups of simmering chicken stock. DO NOT STIR! Cook, uncovered, until liquid is just above level of rice and veggies (5-7 minutes). Move to oven and bake for 15 minutes, uncovered, adding more stock if top starts to look dry.
- Remove from oven and cover, and wait 20 minutes for flavors to blend and for the rice to finish steaming tender. (Note: This is the ideal time to open a bottle of Tempranillo and sit down with it, some Manchego and a tad of honey to whet your appetite!

197. Paella, Paella, Paella!

Serving: Serves 8 hungry, hungry hippos | Prep: | Cook: | Ready in:

Ingredients

- Paella!
- 7 1/4 cups shrimp stock (recipe follows)
- 1 teaspoon saffron threads
- 1/8 cup olive oil (don't use extra-virgin—the sweet flavors will be ruined by the heat)
- 8 chicken thighs (bone-in and skin-on, please!)
- 2 small onions, diced
- 4 cups arborio rice
- 4 cloves garlic, smashed and minced
- 1 dash fish sauce (really, a tiny dash is all that is required)
- 1 pound andouille sausage, cut into ½ inch chunks
- 2 teaspoons Spanish paprika
- 1 glass dry white wine
- 1 can stewed tomatoes, diced (the stewed part here is important)
- 1 cup frozen peas
- 1 jar pimento or slices
- 1 pound peeled shrimp (but buy the ones with heads and shells on for the stock)
- 1 pound clams or mussels
- 8 2 oz cuts of monkfish (I buy the 4 ounce fillets and cut them myself)
- 1 bunch parsley, roughly chopped

Direction

- Paella!
- Heat oven or grill to 450°F.
- Warm the shrimp stock in a sauce pan until hot to the touch, add the saffron, and set aside.
- Heat two cast iron pans (or paella pans if you've got 'em) with ½ of the oil and sear the chicken on all sides (make sure you've patted the chicken dry and salted it with kosher salt to get a good sear).
- Add the remainder of the oil and the onions, split between the two pans, along with a pinch of kosher salt and cook until translucent on a medium-low heat.
- Add the arborio rice to each pan, turn up the heat, and cook for about 3 minutes.
- Add the garlic, fish sauce, sausage, paprika, wine and tomatoes and cook for 5-7 minutes.
- Add the peas and pimentos or olives, pour in 7 cups of the warm shrimp stock, reserving ¼ cup, and stir thoroughly once.
- Top each pan with the fish and shellfish and put in the hot oven (or on the grill and close the cover).
- Leave it alone for 15-20 minutes and check to see that the rice is done and the shellfish have opened (if some don't open be sure to toss them out).
- Pour in the remaining ¼ cup shrimp stock to each paella and top with parsley.
- Let sit, covered, for 5-10 minutes and serve.

198. Paprika Roast Chicken

Serving: Serves 4 + | Prep: | Cook: | Ready in:

Ingredients

- 1 Whole chicken (3.5-4 lbs)
- i Large onion
- 3/4 teaspoon Salt
- 3/4 teaspoon Pepper
- 1 1/2 teaspoons Paprika (I use a mix of hot and smoked)
- 4 teaspoons Olive oil
- 1 1/2-2 pounds Small roasting potatoes

Direction

- Cut the onion into 1/2 inch rings and lay in the bottom of a roasting pan.
- Heat oven to 400 degrees
- Rinse chicken and pat dry. I sometimes butterfly the chicken at this point if I want it to cook faster. Sprinkle the inside cavity with 1/4 tsp of salt and 1/4 tsp of pepper.
- Mix the remaining salt and pepper with paprika in a small bowl. Loosen the skin of the breast with your fingers. Rub chicken breast under the skin with a tsp of olive oil and most of the spice mixture.

- Place chicken on top of the onion in the roasting pan. Rub outside of chicken with 2 tsp of olive oil and remaining spice mixture.
- Roast chicken for 30 minutes. Meanwhile cut your potatoes in half or quarters depending on size. You want about 1 1/2-2 inch pieces.
- After 30 minutes, baste with remaining olive oil, reduce heat to 350 and toss the potatoes into the roasting pan. Continue to cook for another hour or more, basting every 15 minutes with pan juices and stirring the potatoes, until juices run clear or a thermometer reads 175, and potatoes are soft.
- Let rest for 5-15 minutes depending how hungry you are for dinner!
- Serve with a salad and crusty bread to soak up the yummy onion gravy!
- Remove potatoes and serve in a separate bowl with onion gravy from the roasting pan

199. Paprika Scented Manchego Chorizo Puffs

Serving: Makes 24 | Prep: 0hours20mins | Cook: 0hours40mins | Ready in:

Ingredients

- 3/4 cup chorizo, finely diced
- 3/4 cup manchego cheese, finely diced
- 1/4 cup scallions, thinly sliced
- 1 cup water
- 1 stick unsalted butter, cut into cubes
- 1/4 teaspoon iodized salt
- 1 cup flour
- 4 large eggs
- 2 tablespoons sweet paprika
- 1/2 cup sea salt

Direction

- Preheat oven to 375° F. In a bowl, combine chorizo, cheese, and scallions. Set aside. In a heavy saucepan, bring water, 1/4 tsp. salt, and butter to a boil until butter is melted. Remove from heat and add flour. Stir with a wooden spoon until the dough comes together. Return the saucepan to medium heat and stir with the wooden spoon until a film develops on the bottom of the pan, about 3 minutes. Transfer dough to an electric mixer. Add eggs one at a time, beating well after each addition. Continue to beat the dough for 5 minutes. Stir in the chorizo mixture. Transfer to a pastry bag. Pipe dough into 1-inch balls onto a parchment-lined baking sheet. Bake for 20-25 minutes or until lightly browned. While the puffs are cooking, combine paprika and sea salt. Remove puffs from the oven and immediately sprinkle with paprika mixture. Serve warm.

200. Passover Brisket, Inspired By Libbie Miller

Serving: Serves 8 to 10 people | Prep: | Cook: | Ready in:

Ingredients

- 3 1/2 pounds brisket
- Canola oil
- 2 tablespoons sweet paprika
- 2 tablespoons light brown sugar
- 2 tablespoons tomato paste
- 4 dashes Tabasco sauce
- 4 dashes Worcestershire sauce
- 2 yellow onions, sliced
- 4 garlic cloves, smashed
- 1 cup water
- 1 bay leaf
- 1 tablespoon cider vinegar

Direction

- Season the brisket aggressively with salt on all sides. Set a large Dutch oven or pot over high heat, and add just enough canola oil to cover the bottom of the pot. When the oil begins to lightly smoke, add the brisket and let it cook undisturbed until it browns nicely on one side.

- Flip it and brown the other side. Remove the brisket to a large plate or rimmed baking sheet. Discard the excess oil from the pot, and set the pot aside for a moment. Do not wash the pot.
- Preheat the oven to 300° F. In a mixing bowl, add the paprika, brown sugar, tomato paste, Tabasco, and Worcestershire sauce. Mix to form a paste. Cover the outside of the brisket in this paste. Return the brisket to the pot. Scatter the onions and garlic on top of the brisket. Add the water, bay leaf, and cider vinegar. Set the pot over high heat. When the water begins to boil, place a lid on top of the pot and transfer the pot to the oven.
- Cook the brisket with the lid on for 90 minutes. After 90 minutes, flip the brisket over in the pot and then continue cooking with the lid on for an additional 90 minutes. When the brisket is finished cooking, it should be soft and very tender.
- Remove the brisket from the oven. Transfer the brisket to a cutting board. Discard the bay leaf. Transfer the remaining contents of the pot (cooked onions and cooking liquid) to a blender, and blend on high until the mixture becomes a smooth purée. Taste this sauce, and adjust the flavor with salt and/or cider vinegar as necessary. Slice the brisket against the grain, pour the pureed sauce over the brisket, and serve.

201. Passover Puffs

Serving: Makes 12 puffs | Prep: | Cook: | Ready in:

Ingredients

- • 1 cup water
- • 1/2 cup canola or grapeseed oil
- • 1/2 teaspoon kosher salt
- • 1 tablespoon sugar
- • 1 cup matzo meal
- • 1/4 teaspoon paprika
- • 1/4 teaspoon freshly grated nutmeg
- • 4 large eggs, room temperature
- • 1 cup shredded Gruyere or a blend of Parmesan, Asiago, Fontina & Mild Provolone (optional)

Direction

- Preheat oven to 375 degrees. Line a baking sheet with parchment paper; set aside.
- In a medium saucepan over medium-high heat, combine oil, sugar, salt, and water. Bring to a boil and immediately remove from heat. Using a wooden spoon, quickly stir in the flour until combined.
- Return pan to medium heat and cook, stirring vigorously, until mixture pulls away from the sides and a film forms on the bottom of the pan, about 3 minutes.
- Remove from heat and transfer dough to a bowl to cool slightly, about 3 minutes. Add eggs, one at a time, stirring vigorously after each addition, and waiting to add the next egg until the previous one is entirely incorporated. Mix in cheese (if using), paprika and nutmeg.
- Transfer dough to a pastry bag fitted with a 1/2-inch round tip; pipe 1 1/2-inch puffs about 1 inch apart. You can also deep an ice cream scoop in cold water and form balls. Using a lightly moistened finger, smooth tops.
- Transfer to oven and bake until they are puffy, about 15 minutes. Reduce heat to 350 degrees and continue baking until golden brown, about 30-35 minutes.

202. Patas Bravas With Smoked Paprika Tomato Sauce

Serving: Serves 4 as part of tapas | Prep: | Cook: | Ready in:

Ingredients

- For the potatoes:
- 3 large maris piper potatoes
- 100 milliliters rapeseed oil (or olive oil)

- Pinch Sea Salt
- For the paprika sauce
- 2 Shallots
- 2 Garlic
- 2 tablespoons Mayonnaise
- 5 tablespoons Good tomato sauce (or ketchup)
- 1 teaspoon Sherry, such as Manzanilla (or good quality sherry vinegar)
- 2 teaspoons Paprika
- 2 teaspoons Smoked Paprika
- 1 teaspoon Cayenne Pepper
- 1 teaspoon Tabasco
- 1 Lime, Juice of
- 1 tablespoon Olive oil or rapeseed
- Pinch Sea salt and Black Pepper

Direction

- Bring a large pan of salted water to the boil on the hob and pre-heat the oven to 190 degrees C. Add 100-150ml rapeseed or olive oil to a high sided baking tray and place in the oven to heat up.
- Peel the potatoes and cut them in half. Place in the boiling water for 4 minutes to part boil them.
- Drain and cool. When cool slice the potatoes into half a centimeter thick discs.
- Add the potatoes to the hot oil in the oven, turn so they are sufficiently coated, and season with a few pinches of sea-salt. Cook for approximately 35 minutes, turning half way through, until they are crisp and golden.
- Whilst they are cooking make the sauce. Peel and finely chop the shallots and garlic and shred the thyme leaves. Heat a tablespoon of olive oil in the small pan over a medium heat and add the garlic, shallots and thyme. Cook for 3 minutes until soft and remove to cool.
- Mix all the remaining sauce ingredients together and add the cooled shallots, garlic, and thyme. Taste and adjust to your preference.
- When the potatoes are a golden color remove from the oil and drain on kitchen paper. Lay out on a flat serving plate and dollop the paprika sauce all over the top.

203. Patatas Bravas

Serving: Serves 4 | Prep: 0hours45mins | Cook: 0hours30mins | Ready in:

Ingredients

- For the Sauce
- 4 Potatoes
- 2 cups Canola or vegetable oil
- 1 Egg
- 1 Clove garlic
- .5 cups Canola or vegetable oil
- 1 tablespoon Lemon juice
- 1 teaspoon Paprika
- 1/4 teaspoon red pepper flakes
- 1/2 teaspoon cayenne pepper
- 1 tablespoon tomato paste (you can substitute for tomato sauce)
- salt
- Potatoes
- 4 Potatoes
- 2 cups vegetable or canola oil

Direction

- Make the sauce first: In a food processor, add the garlic, egg, lemon juice and a 1/4 cup of olive oil and blend well on high speed. Then, while the food processor is still blending, slowly (very slow!) add the rest of the 1/2 cup of vegetable or canola oil. Mix until it has a nice thick consistency. Place in a bowl and add the paprika, cayenne, red pepper flakes and the tomato paste and mix well with a spoon or spatula. This recipe has a mild spicy profile. If you like it spicier, add more cayenne and red pepper flakes. Add less if you don't enjoy spicy foods.
- For the potatoes: Peel the potatoes and cut them into bite-sized chunks. Heat the oil on a high temperature. Once the oil is hot, cook the potatoes until golden brown, stirring them occasionally. Remove the potatoes, and place

on a paper towel-lined plate to drain the excess oil. Season with salt. You may need to cook the potatoes in several batches if your pan is not big enough.
- Place the potatoes in a bowl or plate and pour some of the sauce on top. That's it! Ready to serve! Eat with a fork or with a toothpick which is typical in Spain.

204. Peekytoe Crab Dip

Serving: Serves 6-8 as a hors d'oeuvre | Prep: | Cook: | Ready in:

Ingredients

- 1 pound Peekytoe crab meat (or substitute another kind of crab)
- 1 tablespoon mayonnaise
- 3 ounces cream cheese, softened
- 1 teaspoon Dijon mustard
- 3 tablespoons creme fraiche
- 1/4 cup freshly grated parmesan cheese, plus additional
- pinch of cayenne
- salt and pepper
- 2 scallions, finely chopped
- sweet paprika
- crackers or toast points for serving

Direction

- Heat the oven to 350 degrees. Check the crab meat for shells, being careful not break it up too much. Squeeze handfuls of the crab meat gently to get rid of any excess moisture and set aside in a medium bowl.
- In another bowl, combine the mayonnaise, cream cheese, mustard, crème fraiche, 1/4 cup parmesan, cayenne and salt and pepper to taste. Stir until smooth. Stir in the scallions and gently fold in the crabmeat until just combined. Taste and add more salt if necessary.
- Spoon the crab mixture into a shallow oven-proof serving dish. Sprinkle more parmesan over the top to cover, followed by a dusting of paprika. Cover with foil and bake for 15 minutes, until warmed through. Uncover the dip, turn on the broiler and broil until the top is golden brown, watching carefully. Let sit for a few minutes to cool slightly before serving with water crackers, Triscuits or toast points.

205. Pimento Cheese Biscuits

Serving: Makes 8 | Prep: | Cook: | Ready in:

Ingredients

- 2 cups all-purpose flour, plus more for dusting
- 1 tablespoon baking powder
- 1 teaspoon salt
- 1/2 teaspoon sweet paprika
- 1/2 teaspoon garlic powder
- 3/4 cup cold butter
- 1/2 cup cold, well-shaken buttermilk, plus a little more for brushing
- 1 egg
- 1 teaspoon Worcestershire sauce
- 4 ounces jarred diced pimentos, drained and patted dry
- 1 cup grated extra-sharp cheddar cheese
- Sea salt, for sprinkling

Direction

- Preheat the oven to 425° F. Line a baking sheet with parchment paper.
- Put the flour, baking powder, salt, paprika, and garlic powder in the bowl of a stand mixer and stir together with a fork. Cut the butter into small cubes and drop them in the flour. Using the paddle attachment, blend the butter and flour on low speed until the butter is the size of small peas. You want some butter blended in, but the visible small pieces of butter help make the biscuits fluffy.

- Measure the buttermilk in a measuring jug, crack in the egg, add the Worcestershire sauce, and beat it with a fork until the egg is well blended. Keep the mixer on low, dump in the buttermilk mixture, and blend just until everything is moist. Toss the cheese with a little flour, and do the same to the pimentos. This step keeps the cheese and pimentos from clumping together, so they blend throughout the dough. Drop them both in the mixer and, still on low, beat until everything just starts to come together.
- Dump the dough onto a well-floured surface and gently bring it all together, kneading just a few times. Handle with care and don't overwork the dough, or the biscuits will get tough. A few pimentos may stick to the board or fall out—just stick 'em back in. Pat the dough into a rectangle, about 6 by 10 inches, using the back of a large knife or bench scraper to square off the ends. Flour the knife or scraper and cut the dough into eight squares. Place the biscuits on the prepared baking sheet, lightly brush the tops with a little buttermilk, and sprinkle with sea salt.
- Bake the biscuits for 15 to 20 minutes, until lightly browned and cooked through. Serve warm, or wrap tightly and store in an airtight container, gently reheat before serving.

206. Piri Piri Chicken Meatballs With Crispy Potatoes

Serving: Serves 6 | Prep: 0hours0mins | Cook: 0hours0mins | Ready in:

Ingredients

- Piri piri sauce
- 10 tablespoons olive oil, divided
- 2 red bell peppers, finely diced
- 2 red onions, finely diced
- 1 1/4 teaspoons salt, plus more to taste
- 4 garlic cloves, smashed, peeled, and roughly chopped
- 1 piri piri chile, roughly chopped
- 6 tablespoons red wine vinegar
- Meatballs and potatoes
- 1 pound ground chicken, preferably a combo of white and dark meat
- 2 piri piri chilies, minced
- 2 large eggs
- 5 tablespoons olive oil, divided, plus more for pan-frying
- 1/2 cup potato chip crumbs
- 6 garlic cloves, minced
- 2 tablespoons minced parsley
- 2 tablespoons minced cilantro
- 1 tablespoon grated lemon zest
- 1/4 teaspoon smoked paprika
- 2 teaspoons salt, divided plus more to taste
- 6 russet potatoes, scrubbed

Direction

- Start the sauce. Add 4 tablespoons olive oil to a very wide skillet—big enough to get the peppers and onions as spread out as possible. Set the skillet over medium-high heat. When it's shimmery and hot, add the peppers and onions. Add the salt and stir to combine. Cook, stirring occasionally, for about 20 minutes until soft and caramelized.
- When the vegetables are done, transfer half to a blender and half to the freezer (to speed cooling for the meatball-mixing). Add the garlic and chile to the blender and process until mostly smooth. Add the vinegar and rest of the olive oil and process until as smooth as possible. Season with salt to taste.
- Add the ground chicken, chilies, eggs, 3 tablespoons olive oil, potato chip crumbs, garlic, parsley, cilantro, lemon zest, paprika, and 1 teaspoon salt to a big bowl. When the vegetables in the freezer are cool, add those, too. Mix until just combined. You don't want to overwork it, or you'll end up with dense meatballs. Stick the mixture in the fridge to set.
- Meanwhile, preheat the oven to 425° F. Cut each potato in half lengthwise. Cut each half in half lengthwise. Now cut each half in half lengthwise again. This will yield 8 wedges

from each potato. Add to a sheet pan. Drizzle with the remaining 2 tablespoons olive oil and 1 teaspoon salt. Toss. Lay each potato flat on one side. Bake for about 30 minutes, flipping the potatoes halfway through, until both sides are very colorful and crusty.

- After the potatoes have been in the oven for 10 or so minutes, get going on those meatballs. Set a very large skillet (maybe the same one you used for the peppers and onions) over medium-high heat. Add enough olive oil to reach a 1/4-inch or so depth. When the oil is shimmery and hot, use a cookie scoop (figure about 1 1/2 tablespoons) to dollop the meatball mixture into the hot oil. If you don't have a scoop, you can use two spoons. The mixture is too wet to roll in your hands (because we don't want dry meatballs!). And you'll need to do this in batches — don't overcrowd. Cook for about 8 minutes — progressively turning as they brown on each side — until cooked through and crusty all over. Transfer to a paper towel-lined plate to drain. Repeat with the remaining meatballs.
- Serve the meatballs and potatoes together with lots of piri piri sauce.

207. Pollo Asado

Serving: Serves 4 | Prep: | Cook: |Ready in:

Ingredients

- 1 whole chicken
- 1 tablespoon salt
- 2 teaspoons pepper
- 2 teaspoons Smoked paprika
- 1 teaspoon garlic powder
- 1 tablespoon Canola oil
- 2 ripe large tomatoes
- 2 tablespoons queso fresco
- 1 tablespoon olive oil
- 1 teaspoon salt
- 4 Poblano peppers or similar
- 4 corn tortillas
- 1 lime
- 1 cup greens

Direction

- Clean chicken and butterfly it in half (cut lengthwise not all the way through).
- Mix salt, pepper, paprika, garlic powder and oil and create a rub. Rub the chicken with the mixture.
- Prepare grill for direct heat over medium high heat. Place chicken breast side down and cook for 6 minutes. Turn over and do the same.
- Change chicken to indirect heat and cook chick3n 35-40 minutes or until reaches 165 degrees.
- Chard peppers. Slices tomatoes, place greens and drizzle olive oil, queso fresco, salt, lime.
- Warm tortillas and enjoy!

208. Poor Man's Paella

Serving: Serves 8-12 | Prep: | Cook: |Ready in:

Ingredients

- 3 cups short grain rice, soaked overnight
- 1 red bell pepper
- 1 ear of summer corn, husk removed
- 3 vine-ripened tomatoes
- 2 tablespoons olive oil
- 1 link of spicy chorizo, sliced
- 1 fat garlic clove
- 1 tbsp each smoked paprika, ground tumeric
- 1 tablespoon fish sauce
- 4 1/2 cups water
- 1 pound frozen mixed seafood (shrimp, calamari, octopus, clams, etc), do not thaw
- 1 pound frozen raw mussels on the half shell, do not thaw

Direction

- First, char the bell pepper, corn, and tomatoes on an open flame. You can just put them

- directly on a gas element, or on the grill, until blackened and blistered.
- When cool enough to handle, thinly slice the pepper, slice off the corn kernels, reserving any juices in the process, and dice the tomatoes. Reserve until needed.
- Heat the oil in a large roasting pan. Sweat the onion and chorizo on medium heat until the onions are translucent and the chorizo is browned.
- Add the garlic, paprika, turmeric, and fish sauce and fry until fragrant. Add the prepared vegetables and cook on high heat until the tomatoes lose their raw flavour, about 5-7 minutes.
- Stir in the soaked rice and water, then season well. Cover and bring to the boil.
- Meanwhile, preheat the oven or grill to 450 degrees F, with the rack placed in the lower third of the oven.
- Once boiling, remove it from the heat, stir well, and arrange the frozen seafood on top. Do not stir once you add the seafood!
- Cover and bake in the preheated oven or grill for 1 hour, or until the liquid has been completely soaked up by the rice. Turn off the heat and leave the paella in the oven to rest for a further 10 minutes, undisturbed so the juices can get soaked up by the rice.
- Serve with a bit of chopped parsley and squeeze of lemon.

209. Pork Loin And Butternut Squash With Fresh Herbs And Cider

Serving: Serves 4 | Prep: | Cook: | Ready in:

Ingredients

- Pork loin with butternut squash and herbs
- 2 tablespoons olive oil
- 1 1.5 lb pork loin
- 1 cup sweet onion cut in chunks
- 2 cups butternut squash - peeled seeded and cubed
- 3-4 cloved garlic - chopped
- 2 large shallots - chopped
- 1 handful fresh thyme
- 1 cinnamon stick
- 3-4 fresh sage leaves
- 1 1/2 cups apple cider
- 1 cup low salt chicken broth
- 1 teaspoon sweet paprika
- Mashed red skinned potatoes
- 12 small red skinned potatoes
- 1/2 cup sour cream
- 1/2 stick unsalted butter
- salt and pepper to taste

Direction

- Pork loin with butternut squash and herbs
- Cut the pork loin into medium sized chunks, season with salt and pepper. Heat the olive oil in the tagine to medium high, and then brown the pork on all sides. Remove the pork and set aside. Turn heat to medium, add the onions and brown for 2-3 minutes. Add the shallots and the garlic and brown another 2-3 minutes.
- Lay the pork loin on top of the onion mixture. Distribute the squash cubes evenly in the pan. Tie the thyme into a bundle with kitchen string and lay it on top. Add the cider, broth, cinnamon stick and sage. Sprinkle the paprika on top and cover - cook on medium low for 1 1/2 - 2 hours, until pork and squash are very tender. Serve over mashed red skinned potatoes.
- Mashed red skinned potatoes
- Boil the potatoes until very tender. Drain and let them sit in the pan for a few minutes. Put the pan back on the heat and add the butter. When it is melted, remove from heat and add sour cream. Hand mash until they are mashed but retain a bit of texture. Salt and pepper to taste.

210. Porotos Granads With Polenta Dumplings

Serving: Serves 8 | Prep: | Cook: | Ready in:

Ingredients

- 2 tablespoons Olive Oil
- 8 ounces Slab Bacon
- 1 Medium Yellow Onion, medium dice
- 2 Carrots, small dice
- 2 Celery Stalks, small dice
- 4 Garlic Cloves, minced
- 1 14.5-oz Can Diced Tomatoes, strained – juice reserved
- 1 Bay Leaf
- 1 tablespoon Paprika
- 1/2 cup Red Wine
- 1 1/2 pounds Butternut Squash, cut into 1 ½ inch cubes
- 32 ounces Low Sodium Chicken Broth
- 1 cup Red Quinoa
- 2 15-oz Cans of Pinto Beans, do not strain or rinse
- 3 tablespoons Fresh Basil, chopped
- 2 cups Water
- 1 cup Polenta *Do not use quick cooking polenta
- 1/2 teaspoon Salt

Direction

- Heat large heavy bottom soup pot (a Dutch oven works well) over medium high heat, add olive oil. Sauté bacon until brown and crispy. Remove bacon with slotted spoon and set aside on a paper towel to drain excess fat.
- Sauté onions and carrots in the bacon fat until well caramelized. Add the garlic, celery and tomatoes, sauté until all the moister has evaporated and the tomatoes have taken on a dark red almost rusty color (approx. 7-10 minutes). Add paprika and bay leaf.
- Deglaze the plan with red wine and reduce until almost dry. Add reserved tomato juice and broth. Bring stew to a boil and add butter nut squash. Reduce heat to low and cover. Let simmer for 20 minutes. Add quinoa and simmer covered for an additional 10 minutes.
- While the quinoa cooks, brings 2 cups of water and ½ tsp salt to a boil in a small saucepan. Turn of the heat and whisk in polenta. Using two spoons form polenta into 2 inch dumplings.
- Return the stew in a simmer and gently drop the dumplings on top (do not stir). Cover and let dumplings steam for an additional 10 minutes over low heat.
- Garnish with the crispy bacon and fresh basil. *Garnish with the crispy bacon and fresh basil.
- QUINOA FUN FACT: Quinoa is native to Chile and completes the stew's already well rounded nutritional profile. It is great source of protein (12-18%) and is the only plant based food source that contains all 8 essential amino acids.

211. Portobello Mushroom Tacos

Serving: Serves 2 | Prep: | Cook: | Ready in:

Ingredients

- Salsa
- 4 Ripe, juicy tomatoes
- 2 Cloves garlic, crushed
- 1 teaspoon Chipotle
- 1 teaspoon Cumin
- 1 Fresh serrano chili
- 1 splash EVOO
- 1 pinch Salt & Pepper
- Mushrooms & Taco Filling
- 1 pound Portabello mushrooms, sliced
- 2 teaspoons Paprika
- 2 Cloves of crushed garlic
- 1/2 red onion, finely chopped
- 1 Ripe avocado
- 1 Pack mini corn tortillas
- 1 bunch Cilantro
- 1 pinch Feta cheese

- 1 Lime

Direction

- Start by making the tomato salsa. Preheat the oven to 400F. Blanch the tomatoes in boiling water to remove the skins and chop into quarters. Season with a good lug of extra virgin olive oil, salt, pepper, crushed garlic, cumin and chipotle. Roast in the oven for about 40 mins or until the tomatoes are soft, squishy and smelling delicious.
- Once done, transfer to a blender, add the chili (seeds and all), check the seasoning and blend to a smooth sauce-like consistency.
- Next, start the mushrooms - in a good skillet add the remaining two cloves of crushed garlic, onion, a lug of olive oil and the paprika. Cook on a medium heat until the onions soften and brown slightly (about 10 minutes). Then add the mushrooms and cook for another 10 mins or until the mushrooms turn dark and start oozing juices. Season to taste.
- Serve with a wedge of fresh lime, slices of avocado, cheese and garnished with fresh cilantro. Side of corn on the cob. Lashings of red wine optional, but highly recommended.

212. Pot Sticker Hash Browns With Greens And Cheese

Serving: Serves 4 as a side dish | Prep: | Cook: | Ready in:

Ingredients

- 2.5 cups Diced potato (any kind you like can even mix in sweet potatoes)
- 1 cup Diced yellow onion
- 2 Cloves sliced garlic
- .05 cups Diced red, yellow, orange an/or red pepper
- 1 tablespoon Minced jalepeno
- 3 tablespoons Vegetable oil
- 1 tablespoon Smoked paprika
- Salt & pepper to taste
- 2 cups Julienned lacinato (dinosaur) Kale
- 1 cup Shredded cheese of Choice (I like Fontina or Monteray Jack)
- 1 tablespoon Fresh thyme leaves, chopped

Direction

- Heat oil in pan over medium heat
- Add potatoes, peppers, garlic and onions, best if they can cover the pan in one layer, buy if they can't it's not tragic, season with smoked paprika, salt & pepper
- Pour 1 cup cold water into pan
- Pour 1 cup cold water and let it come to a boil
- Add kale on top of potatoes (Don't stir) Lower heat and cover, cook 10-15 minutes (it will depend on your pan and if they are in one layer or not
- Check to see if the water has evaporated, and that the potatoes are brown and they are tender. If that has occurred, take a spatula and flip everything over so it browns on the other side.
- Cover with Cheese & Thyme leaves, then run under the broiler until a brown/bubbly cheesy top, if you have no broiler or don't care to deal with it you can just cover the pan again until the cheese melts
- Sausage or any other smoky meats (chunks of pancetta, pulled pork, brisket) make a great add-on. Mushrooms are a great add-in as well, I like them with mushrooms and Gruyere but no peppers. I like to top these with fried egg.

213. Prawn And Coriander Crostini

Serving: Makes 20 - 24 | Prep: | Cook: | Ready in:

Ingredients

- 20 ounces cooked prawns
- 2 tablespoons mayonnaise
- 1 handful fresh coriander
- 1 tomato

- 1/4   red onion
- 1/2 teaspoon hot smoked paprika
- 1 teaspoon sea salt
- 1/4 teaspoon black pepper
- 1/2 cup extra virgin olive oil
- 1   clove garlic
- 1   baguette
- 1   lime (juice)

Direction

- Slice your bread thinly, and lay out the pieces on a baking tray.
- Turn on your oven griller, and grill/broil your bread on one side for about a minute until just golden. Flip them over and repeat the process.
- While still hot, brush them with the olive oil, and rub the peeled garlic clove onto the hot bread. At this point your kitchen will smell like garlic bread!
- To make the mixture, peel and devein your prawns, chop them into small pieces, and add them to a large mixing bowl.
- Deseed your tomato, and chop it up into small pieces. Add that to the bowl, along with the roughly chopped coriander and finely chopped onion.
- Stir in the mayonnaise, paprika, lime juice, salt and pepper, until it's all evenly coated. Check the seasoning, it should be slightly salty and tart, with a kick of heat.
- Spoon over the mixture onto the crostini, and serve immediately. Enjoy with champagne!

214. Preserved And Fresh Lemon Hummus

Serving: Makes 1 pint (.5 litre) | Prep: | Cook: |Ready in:

Ingredients

- 2   quarters preserved lemon, rinsed
- 1   small onion
- 2   large cloves garlic
- 1 teaspoon cumin powder
- .5 teaspoons paprika
- .5 teaspoons hot paprika (or omit, use 1 tsp paprika total)
- 2 tablespoons fresh lemon juice
- .25 cups olive oil
- 1.5 cups cooked chick peas (or 1 can), drained
- Garnish options -- paprika, sumac, cilantro, drizzle of olive oil.

Direction

- Put all the ingredients in a food processor and blend until smooth.
- Garnish with sprinkled paprika or sumac, or chopped cilantro, and/or a drizzle of olive oil.

215. Pucker Up Lemon Sumac Chicken With Lemon Herb Board Sauce

Serving: Serves 6-8 | Prep: 0hours35mins | Cook: 1hours0mins |Ready in:

Ingredients

- 1   whole chicken, spatchcocked
- 2   garlic cloves, smashed
- 1   onion, sliced
- 2   lemons, sliced
- 1 tablespoon salt
- 1 tablespoon oregano
- 1 tablespoon turmeric
- 2 teaspoons sumac
- 1 teaspoon paprika
- 1/2 teaspoon ras el hanout (more if you like it spicy)
- 1/2 teaspoon freshly ground black pepper
- 2 teaspoons fresh thyme
- 4 tablespoons cooked chicken juices
- 2   garlic cloves from the roasting pan, chopped
- 4   slices cooked lemons from the roasting pan
- 1   bunch fresh parsley, chopped
- 1   handful fresh mint, chopped

- 2 tablespoons honey

Direction

- For the chicken: Have the butcher spatchcock the whole chicken, or do it yourself by cutting out the backbone, then flattening the chicken until you hear the breastbone pop. A whole chicken cooks much faster this way!
- Combine salt, oregano, turmeric, sumac, paprika, ras el hanout, black pepper and fresh thyme.
- Rub spice blend into chicken thoroughly, including under the skin.
- In a large baking dish, place the smashed garlic cloves, sliced onions, and the sliced lemons on the bottom. Place the chicken on top of the lemons.
- Bake at 350° F for approximately 1 hour, or until the internal temperature reaches 160-165° F. Check at the 20 minute mark and tent with foil if the skin is already browned.
- When the chicken is done, remove from the oven to rest and make the board sauce. Board sauce is made on a cutting board with the juices from cooking and other ingredients. The juices from the cooked chicken or meat combine with the other ingredients to make a fantastic sauce.
- For the board sauce. On a cutting board with channels (less messy), chop the cooked lemons and garlic from the chicken dish. Mix with the parsley and mint. Remove 4 tablespoons of juices from the bottom of the cooked chicken dish and combine them with the honey. Add salt and pepper to taste, then add to the lemon-herb mixture, and place the chicken on top to complete resting.
- After 15 minutes of resting, carve chicken and serve with the board sauce.

216. Pulled Pork Baps With Apple Slaw And Tangy BBQ Sauce

Serving: Serves 6-8 | Prep: | Cook: | Ready in:

Ingredients

- For the Pork and Slaw
- 3kg Pork Shoulder Joint, bone in
- 2 tablespoons Olive Oil
- 1/2 tablespoon Smoked Paprika
- 1 Dried Ancho Chile
- 2 Cloves of Garlic
- 1 tablespoon Dark Brown Sugar
- 1/2 Red Cabbage, Shredded
- 2 Carrots, peeled and grated
- 2 Sticks of Celery, finely sliced
- 1/2 Red Onion, finely sliced
- 1 Apple, such as Braeburn/ Granny Smith, peeled and grated
- 2 tablespoons Mayonnaise
- 4 tablespoons Buttermilk
- 2-3 tablespoons Cider Vinegar
- Salt & Pepper, to taste
- Bread Baps, to serve
- For the BBQ Sauce
- 1 White Onion, diced
- 4 Cloves of Garlic, finely grated
- 1 tablespoon Olive Oil
- 1 tablespoon Mustard Seeds, ground to powder
- 500 milliliters Tomato Ketchup, I used Heinz
- 150 milliliters Cider Vinegar
- 8 tablespoons Dark Brown Sugar
- 3 tablespoons Honey
- 1 tablespoon Smoked Paprika
- 1 Dried Chipotle Chilli
- 2 tablespoons Dark Soy Sauce
- 2 tablespoons Worcestershire Sauce
- 1 tablespoon Cayenne Pepper

Direction

- Preheat your oven to 220 degrees Celsius. Line a roasting tin with tin foil and place the roasting joint in it. If your butcher has not already scored the crackling skin, do so with a sharp knife, with lines 1cm apart. Drizzle the olive oil over the meat, sprinkling the paprika with some salt and pepper over. Rub the mixture into the meat, coating all over and into the crevices. Cut the garlic cloves in half and rub over the meat, before pushing the pieces into gaps in the meat and underneath during cooking. After soaking the dried ancho chile in hot water until soft, rub it over the meat, massaging the flavours in. Pop it into the oven for half an hour at the high heat for the crackling to crisp. Remove from the heat and turn the oven down to 170 degrees Celsius. Take what cooking juices have come from the meat and place in a saucepan with the sugar. Stir on a high heat until the sugar has melted and pour over the meat. Cover the joint with tin foil and return to the oven. Continue to cook for 5 hours, occasionally basting the meat, making sure to always cover with tin foil before returning to the oven.

- While the meat is cooking, make the barbecue sauce. Heat the olive oil in a large saucepan, tossing in the onions and garlic with some salt, before reducing to a low heat. Cook until the onions become translucent. Add the ground mustard seeds and cook for one minute to gain fragrance. Next, add three tablespoons on the sugar, allow to caramelize for a moment, before adding the ketchup and vinegar. The sharp aroma of the vinegar will hit the back of the nose with a punch, so stand back.

- Bring the heat down to let the mixture simmer, and stir in the paprika, cayenne pepper, two tablespoons of the honey and the chipotle chili. Allow the mixture to simmer for a further ten minutes to cook off some of the vinegar. Add another three tablespoons of sugar, all of the soy sauce and Worcestershire sauce. Keep on a low heat for another twenty minutes, by which time the sauce should have thickened and darkened, the vinegar now a pleasant undertone when tasted. The rest of the honey and sugar should be added to taste, as the taste of the sauce depends on the quality of ketchup and vinegar used. Set aside and allow to cool before pouring into jars. It will keep in the fridge for up to a month.

- Next, prepare the coleslaw. Put the cabbage, onion, celery, apple and carrot into a large bowl. In a separate bowl, combine the mayonnaise, buttermilk and two tablespoons of the vinegar. Season to taste with salt and pepper, before adding to the vegetable mixture. Stir to combine, and taste. Depending on the sweetness of your apple, you may add the extra tablespoon of cider vinegar. Chill in the fridge until serving.

- After five hours of cooking and basting, take the pork from the oven. Remove the foil from the meat and return to the oven for 20 minutes at 200 degrees Celsius to crisp the crackling. Remove from the oven and allow to rest, tin foil replaced, for 15 minutes. This will moisten the meat, making it easier to pull apart. Remove the crackling and serve separately. Pull the meat apart, shredding with two forks, putting pieces of fat to the side.

- Slice the bread baps in half and toast under the grill. Pile the meat in a large serving dish and serve on the table, letting your group serve themselves and pile those baps high!

217. Pulled Pork Sandwiches With Stone Fruit Salsa

Serving: Makes 12 large sandwiches | Prep: | Cook: | Ready in:

Ingredients

- Boston Butt
- 1 tablespoon Dijon mustard
- 1 tablespoon Worcestershire sauce
- 1/2 tablespoon hot pepper paste
- 5-6 garlic cloves, divided, peeled
- 3 tablespoons light brown sugar
- 1 tablespoon dried oregano
- 1 tablespoon ground thyme
- 1 tablespoon smoked paprika

- 1 tablespoon sea salt
- 1 tablespoon cider vinegar
- 3 tablespoons olive oil
- 4-5 pound Boston butt (pork shoulder)
- 1 small white onion
- 2 medium carrots
- 2 cups beef or veal stock
- Stone Fruit Salsa
- 1 small red onion
- 1 serrano pepper
- juice of 1 lime
- 1 teaspoon honey
- 1 tablespoon white vinegar
- 1 tablespoon olive oil
- 4 nectarines
- // 12 large buns, or 24 mini ones. Potato works well, but brioche does too. Any soft bun will work.

Direction

- Boston Butt
- Rinse the pork, pat it dry, and set it on a cutting board. Check "the top" (the side with a layer of fat covering it); if the fat layer seems too thick, trim it down a little. Score the fat by cutting a diamond pattern; this will help the marinade better penetrate the meat, resulting in more flavor.
- Add the following to a food processor: the mustard, the Worcestershire sauce, the hot pepper paste, 2-3 garlic cloves, the brown sugar, the oregano, the thyme, the paprika, the salt, the vinegar, and the olive oil. Press the "stir" button, and let the ingredients blend together, 30 seconds-1 minute. You want a loose paste.
- Rub the marinade all over the Boston butt. Really get in there, on all sides, into every hidden space. (If you have the time, apply the marinade the night before. Cover and refrigerate overnight.)
- Heat the oven to 325F.
- Lift the Boston butt into a Dutch oven (or a heavy pot with a good lid). Peel and halve the carrots, and then peel and quarter the onion. Distribute the carrot pieces, the onion, and the remaining garlic around the Boston butt. Pour the stock on top of the vegetables.
- Set the range to medium-high, and let the stock come to a boil. When it does, put the lid on and move the pot to the oven.
- Remove the pot from the oven once an hour to flip the Boston butt. At this temperature, it should take about 1 hour per pound to cook. (For a more exact measurement, wait until your meat thermometer registers 190F-195F; mine only took 3 1/2 hours, so it's always good to check. You're looking for meat that falls away from the bone.) During the last 10-15 minutes of cooking, flip the Boston butt so that the "top" (the fat side) is facing up. Raise the oven temperature to 425F. Cook until the top becomes crispy and golden.
- Take the pork out of the pot, and let it rest on a cutting board for 10-15 minutes. (You can lightly tent it with foil.)
- The pan juices: During the last 10-15 minutes of cooking at 425F, I could see my pan juices happily boiling away and reducing. However, if you find yourself with an abundance of jus, you can further reduce the sauce on the stove top while your pork is resting. When it reaches the consistency of runny gravy, take it off the heat.
- Run the juices and vegetables through a sieve, and then let the strained sauce rest in a cup or bowl for about 10 minutes, until the fat rises to the top. Remove as much of the fat as you can. Reserve the rest to pour over the pork, once it has been pulled apart.
- After the pork has rested, use two forks to "pull" the meat apart. (It should come apart quite easily.) Discard any fatty bits, or gristle. If you like, save the bone for stock.
- Return the pulled pork to a clean pot and pour the strained pan juices on top. Using tongs or a large spoon, gently toss the pork until the juice is evenly distributed.
- The pork is ready. You can turn the range to the lowest setting to keep the pork warm as you serve. (I keep the lid on, to help prevent the pork from drying out.)
- Stone Fruit Salsa

- Using a knife or mandolin, cut the red onion into thin slices. Seed and finely dice the serrano.
- In a medium bowl, blend the lime juice with the honey, the white vinegar, and the olive oil. Add the red onion and the serrano, and stir to incorporate. Let the onion and the serrano sit in the liquid for 10-20 minutes.
- Just before serving, slice up the nectarines however you like, and stir them into the onions and serrano.
- Assemble the sandwiches // I toasted the buns, although it isn't mandatory. Scoop some of the shredded pork onto the bottom layer of each sandwich. Finish with a spoonful of stone fruit salsa. Enjoy warm.

218. Pulled Pork With Chile Barbecue Sauce

Serving: Serves 10-12 | Prep: | Cook: | Ready in:

Ingredients

- Pork Shoulder
- 8-10 pounds bone-in pork shoulder (butt over picnic, but picnic will do)
- 1 cup kosher salt
- 1 cup granulated sugar
- 1 tablespoon garlic powder
- 1 tablespoon onion powder
- 3 tablespoons hot paprika powder
- Chile Barbecue Sauce
- 3 guajillo or puya chiles
- 2 ancho chiles
- 2 pasilla chiles
- 2 tablespoons oil
- 1/2 cup minced onion
- 1 teaspoon kosher salt
- 1 teaspoon minced garlic
- 1/2 teaspoon fresh ground black pepper
- 1/4 teaspoon cinnamon
- 28 ounces tomato puree
- 1/2 cup cider vinegar
- 1/3 cup brown sugar
- 1/3 cup dark molasses
- 1/2 cup your favorite bottled barbecue sauce
- 1/4 cup bourbon

Direction

- Pork Shoulder
- In large, shallow bowl mix together salt, sugar, garlic, onion, and paprika. Add pork shoulder and coat with the mixture. Cover with plastic wrap and leave in fridge 6 hours to overnight.
- When ready to cook, heat oven to 300 degrees. Remove pork from bowl, place in roasting pan and slide into oven. Discard all juices remaining in the bowl. Cook pork for 6 hours. After first hour, baste every hour with the juices in the pan. You know the meat is done when it starts to collapse and yields easily to a fork. At this point you can remove from the oven and let rest for a maximum of 1 hour.
- When ready to serve, turn heat up to 450, coat pork with a slathering of the barbecue sauce and cook for 15 minutes or until the sauce has caramelized.
- If pork did not rest prior to the last step, let pork rest at least 20 minutes before pulling the meat off the bone and apart with two forks.
- Cover pulled pork with 1/2 cup of the barbecue sauce and toss to coat.
- Top each portion of pulled pork with generous spoonful of barbecue sauce. Pork can be eaten on buns, white bread, or by itself with any sides you like.
- Chile Barbecue Sauce
- Chop stems off of chiles, place in bowl and cover with bowling water. Let rest 20 minutes or until chiles have softened.
- Meanwhile, heat oil on medium-low and sauté onion with salt until softened.
- Add garlic and black pepper. Sauté until fragrant.
- Remove chiles from water, reserving water. Slice chiles open and remove the seeds.
- Place chiles and reserved water into blender and process until smooth.
- Add cinnamon and sauté for 30 seconds.

- Add tomato puree, dark brown sugar, molasses, cider vinegar, bottled barbecue sauce, bourbon, and blended chiles. Stir to combine.
- Bring mixture to a boil and then reduce to simmer for 30 minutes or until thickened.
- Pour sauce into blender and process until smooth. Sauce can be stored in the fridge for up to a month.
- Reheat sauce before serving over pulled pork.

219. Pumpkin & Butternut Squash Soup

Serving: Makes 1 large pot | Prep: | Cook: | Ready in:

Ingredients

- 1 yellow onion (diced)
- 1 medium carrot (peeled & diced)
- 2 stalks celery (diced)
- 6 cloves garlic (rough chop)
- 1/2 cup dry white wine
- 2 bay leaves
- 1 teaspoon Hungarian paprika
- 1 butternut squash (halved, peeled & seeds removed)
- 15 ounces can pumpkin puree
- 15 ounces can Cannellini Beans
- 1 spring rosemary
- 4 cups homemade or low sodium chicken broth
- 4 cups water
- 1 cup cream
- 1/2 cup Parmesan (grated)
- salt and pepper
- olive oil

Direction

- Heat a Dutch over or soup pot over medium heat and add olive oil. Add in onion, carrot, celery, salt and pepper. Let soften for 5 minutes. Add garlic and cook for 1 more minute.
- Deglaze pan with dry white wine and let reduce for 2-3 minutes. Now add paprika and bay leaves.
- Now add in previously peeled and cubed butternut squash, can of pumpkin puree, and drained Cannellini beans. Add a big pinch of salt, pepper and add rosemary. Put the rosemary in a spice bag if you have it. Mix and let cook together for 5 minutes.
- Add in chicken broth and water, with another generous pinch of salt and pepper. Bring to a boil and then reduce to a simmer. Cover and let simmer for 45 minutes.
- Turn off heat. Using a spider or slotted spoon, remove about 1/4 - 1/2 of the chunks to a bowl. Set aside. With an immersion blender, puree everything left in the Dutch oven, until very smooth.
- Add back in the un-pureed hunks of veggies and beans. Add the cream and parmesan as well. Stir everything together and taste. Adjust seasoning as necessary. Serve warm with toasted bread or a grilled cheese.

220. Pureed Mustard Greens (Sarson Da Saag)

Serving: Makes ~2.5 cups | Prep: | Cook: | Ready in:

Ingredients

- 2 bunches Mustard greens
- 1 bunch spinach
- 2 large shallots finely diced
- 2-3 green Serrano peppers
- 2 tablespoons fresh minced ginger
- 3 cloves garlic
- 4 tablespoons butter
- 1/4 cup heavy cream
- 1/2 teaspoon Paprika
- 2 tablespoons dried fenugreek leaves
- Salt to taste

Direction

- Trim the veins off the mustard greens and shred them with your hands into pieces. Combine with the spinach leaves and cook down until they're completely wilted, and then a bit more. Allow to cool and then puree the leaves using an immersion blender.
- Crush the ginger, garlic and the serrano chiles in a mortar & pestle and make it as smooth as possible (Yes, you can run it thru a blender if you choose too).
- Heat 2 tablespoons of the butter and add the ginger garlic paste, Fry until the paste begins to turn brown. Add the shallots and fry until it turns translucent and then add the dried fenugreek leaves. Allow the leaves to bloom until they emit their signature aroma.
- Add the mustard/spinach puree along with the paprika and salt. Allow the mix to simmer until the liquid evaporates enough for the dish to almost acquire a paste like consistency. Add the remaining butter, simmer for 5 minutes more
- Drizzle the cream just prior to serving. Serve warm with Naan or Pita

221. Purple Cauliflower Soup

Serving: Serves 4 | Prep: | Cook: | Ready in:

Ingredients

- 1 1/2 pounds purple cauliflower
- 2 small shallots
- 2 garlic cloves
- 3 - 4 cups veggie stock
- 2 tablespoons olive oil
- kosher salt, to taste
- good quality olive oil, garnish
- ezpeletako bipera or smoked paprika, garnish

Direction

- Remove outer leaves of cauliflower. Wash and cut cauliflower into chunks.
- Cut shallots and garlic into medium sized pieces.
- Heat olive oil over medium heat in a large saucepan or Dutch oven. Add shallots, cook over low heat, until soft. About 5 minutes.
- Add cauliflower. Stir to coat with olive oil. Cook for about 5 minutes over low heat.
- Add stock and garlic. Bring to boil. Do not cover with a lid.
- Bring heat to a low simmer. Season to taste with salt.
- Cook until cauliflower is soft, about 25 - 35 minutes. It all depends on how large you cut the pieces of cauliflower.
- Remove from heat and let cool about 10 minutes. Puree in batches, using either a blender or food processor. Return to cooking pan.
- Gently reheat over low heat. If necessary season with a bit more salt.
- Ladle into serving bowl. Drizzle good quality olive oil over the top and sprinkle with ezpeletako bipera or smoked paprika.
- Serve. Eat.

222. Quick Chicken Paprika

Serving: Serves 4 | Prep: | Cook: | Ready in:

Ingredients

- 1 large vidalia onion
- 1 pound skinless boneless chicken thighs, cut up in bite size pieces
- 2 tablespoons good Hungarian sweet paprika
- 1 tablespoon cider vinegar
- 1/2 cup sour cream
- 1/4 cup butter
- 1/4 cup water, plus more as needed
- salt and pepper to taste

Direction

- Melt the butter in a pan. Slice the onion thinly and add to melted butter. Cook slowly over

low heat till the onion melts down and starts to turn brown, about 10 or 15 minutes.
- Toss in the paprika and stir. Turn up the heat, and keep stirring for a minute or so till it starts to smell good. Then add the vinegar. Keep tossing the onions with a spatula as the edge sizzles off the acid. Throw in the cut up chicken pieces, leaving them alone for a couple minutes until they brown on one side before moving them.
- When the chicken has browned (it will be a lovely reddish brown from the paprika) add a small amount of water, just enough so the chicken and onions don't stick to the bottom of the pan. This will form the beginning of a sauce. Cover the pan and let simmer five or ten minutes to cook the chicken through and let the flavors marry (more of a shotgun wedding in Vegas than a nice cathedral ceremony, but married they will be just the same).
- When sufficiently married remove from heat. Add sour cream and mix well with the sauce. Taste for salt and pepper. Serve with small boiled potatoes or boiled noodles.

223. Quick Curry | Gluten Free Vegan Yellow Curry

Serving: Serves 3 | Prep: | Cook: |Ready in:

Ingredients

- For the tofu
- 250 grams organic non-GMO tofu, cut into triangles
- 4 tablespoons vegan fish sauce (see note)
- 1/2 lemon, juiced
- 2 tablespoons dried wakame flakes
- 2 teaspoons garlic powder
- 1/4 teaspoon smoked sweet paprika
- 1 teaspoon salt
- For the curry
- 1 brown onion, halved and cut into even slices
- 1 mild red chilli, de-seeded and sliced longways
- 1 thumb-sized piece of ginger, sliced into matchsticks
- 1 clove fresh garlic, diced
- 1 teaspoon garlic powder
- 1 tablespoon ground cumin
- 270 milliliters coconut milk
- 2 tablespoons filtered water
- 1 teaspoon vegetable stock powder
- 200 grams baby spinach

Direction

- Preheat oven to 200 degrees C.
- Marinate the tofu in vegan fish sauce and lemon juice for at least 5 minutes in the fridge (the longer, the better, but who has time to wait?). Then, in a small bowl, combine the wakame, garlic, paprika and salt. Add each piece of tofu to the mix and evenly coat.
- Place tofu on a baking tray and put in the oven for 20 minutes.
- Cook onion in a wide-based saucepan over a medium heat. Once soft, add the ginger, chili and garlic (both fresh and dried) and cook until fragrant. Add the cumin and stir until mixed through.
- Add the coconut milk, water and vegetable stock powder and cook for a minute longer before adding the spinach. Cook until spinach has wilted then serve into bowls with some steamed rice and a couple of pieces of baked tofu on top.
- NOTE: Vegan fish sauce is available from Asian grocery stores. Look out for it in the vegetarian section. Otherwise, check out the internet. Not vegan? Use real fish sauce.

224. Red Cabbage Slaw With Honey Lime Cumin Vinaigrette

Serving: Serves 6 | Prep: 0hours15mins | Cook: 0hours5mins | Ready in:

Ingredients

- 1 whole red cabbage, cut into quarters and sliced into ribbons
- 1/2 cup Olive oil
- 1/3 cup Lime juice
- 2 garlic cloves, chopped then mashed with the side of the knife blade
- 2 teaspoons Ground cumin (plus a pinch just because I LOVE cumin!)
- 1 teaspoon Paprika ((smoked paprika is even better if you have it)
- 1 teaspoon salt
- 1 tablespoon black pepper
- 1 tablespoon honey (adjust to taste, add more honey if you prefer the dressing sweeter)

Direction

- Combine lime juice, honey, garlic, cumin, paprika in a mixing bowl.
- Slowly add olive oil as you whisk dressing together.
- Adding oil slowly while whisking helps emulsify the dressing so it won't separate (science, baby!).
- Add salt + pepper to taste as you go along, adjust as needed.
- Add dressing to cabbage and mix well.
- Let sit for 20-30 minutes. It gets better after it sits for a while.
- p.s. *It was even better the next day when we had the leftovers with chicken.

225. Red Chile Chicken And Hominy Soup

Serving: Serves 4 generously | Prep: | Cook: | Ready in:

Ingredients

- Soup
- 1 tablespoon olive oil
- 1 cup chopped tomatoes
- 1 medium onion, chopped
- 2 garlic cloves, minced
- 1 jalapeño pepper, seeded and finely chopped
- 2 teaspoons ancho chile powder
- 1/2 teaspoon ground cumin
- 1/2 teaspoon oregano
- 1/2 teaspoon smoked paprika
- 1/2 teaspoon salt
- 1/4 teaspoon cayenne pepper
- 1 tablespoon fresh lime juice
- 1 25 ounce can hominy, drained and rinsed well
- 4 cups chicken broth
- 2 cups cooked chicken (or turkey), chopped
- sliced avocado and hot sauce for serving
- Slaw
- 2 cups thinly sliced cabbage
- 1 medium carrot, peeled into ribbons using a vegetable peeler
- 1/4 cup cilantro leaves
- juice of 1 lime
- 1/4 teaspoon salt

Direction

- Start by making the soup. Heat the olive oil in a large pot over medium high heat, then add the tomatoes, onion, garlic, and jalapeno. Cook until vegetables start to soften, about 3-4 minutes, then add the chile powder, cumin, oregano, paprika, salt, cayenne pepper, and lime juice and cook for another 3-4 minutes.
- Add the hominy and chicken broth. Bring to a boil, then reduce heat to low and simmer for 20 minutes.
- While soup simmers, make the slaw by combining all slaw ingredients in a bowl and mixing well. Set aside while you finish the soup.
- After soup has simmered for 20 minutes, add the chicken, and bring back to a boil. Season to

taste with additional salt if needed. Serve soup hot topped with the slaw, as well as sliced avocado and hot sauce.

226. Red Pepper Chicken Paprika

Serving: Makes a lot | Prep: | Cook: | Ready in:

Ingredients

- Cooking oil
- 1 chicken breast, in chunks
- ½ (whole) chicken, in small bits
- 1 teaspoon sweet paprika
- 1 teaspoon hot paprika
- 2 cups chicken stock (some of this used to puree the roasted red pepper)
- ¼ cup passata, or 1 large fresh tomato, skinned and pureed
- 1 red pepper, roasted, seeded and pureed (with some of chicken stock)
- 1 fresh red pepper, seeded and cut into chunks
- 2 tablespoons sour cream
- Fresh (yellow) chili pepper (optional), to taste
- Salt, to taste

Direction

- Place a couple of tablespoons in a large oven-proof casserole dish and heat up. When hot, add the chicken (in batches) if the pan isn't large enough to fry them all at the same time. You want the pieces to brown - not necessarily cook.
- Once you're done with frying the chicken, remove from pan and set aside.
- Use the leftover oil, or add a couple more tablespoons to the same dish as you cooked the chicken in. Add the onions with a pinch of salt and cook on low heat till softened. Then add all the paprika powder and stir well, being careful it doesn't burn.
- After a minute or too, add the chicken stock to 'de-glaze' followed by the passata, pureed red pepper and red pepper chunks. Let cook for a few minutes then add the chicken. Stir well and hold back on the salt – once it cooks down and the flavours merge, you can then season it – too early and you'll end up with an overly salty dish
- Stir and then carefully put the dish into an oven at 180 degrees centigrade. Cook for 40 – 50 minutes and then remove.
- If you want to add the sour cream, remove about 2 tablespoons of sauce and stir that in with the sour cream, to 'temper' then gently stir the sauce-sour cream mixture back into the whole casserole and combine well.
- Serve with tarhonya (egg barley) or plain white rice, small pickled cucumbers and sour cream.

227. Reuben Cheese (and A Beet Reuben)

Serving: Makes 1½ cups spread; 1 sandwich | Prep: | Cook: | Ready in:

Ingredients

- 3 cups Swiss cheese, grated (12 ounces)
- 2 tablespoons sweet onion, finely grated
- 2 tablespoons ketchup
- 1/4 cup mayonnaise
- 2 tablespoons sweet pickle relish
- 1 teaspoon Sriracha (optional)
- 1/4 teaspoon sweet paprika
- 1 large beet, sliced (canned; or boiled or roasted if using fresh beets)
- 1 tablespoon butter, softened
- 2 slices bread (such as rye or pumpernickel bread)

Direction

- Combine the grated cheese, grated onion, mayonnaise, relish, paprika, and Sriracha (if using) in a mixing bowl with a spatula until

smooth and spreadable. Cover and refrigerate until ready to use. It will last for about 1 week.
- To make a Reuben sandwich, spread both sides of the bread thickly with the cheese spread (about 2-3 tablespoons, or to taste — there will be leftover spread for more sandwiches). Top with sliced beets (or other protein) and sauerkraut, as desired.
- Preheat a cast-iron griddle or skillet over medium-low heat. Spread each side of the bread with softened butter. Griddle on each side until deeply golden brown and the cheese is fully melted, about 5 minutes per side.

228. Rice And Ground Beef Stuffed Bell Peppers And Onions

Serving: Serves 6-8 | Prep: | Cook: | Ready in:

Ingredients

- Rice Stuffing
- 6-8 bell pepper (all color, though I prefer red, i think they are sweeter)
- • One very large onion (instead of some of the peppers, or other veggies like zucchinis or tomatoes)
- 1 cups of long grain rice
- 1/2-1 pounds of ground beef (depends on how much meat you want in your mix. I use meat with 15% fat)
- 2 grated tomatoes (or a cup of chopped canned tomatoes)
- 1 diced big onion (or 2 small ones)
- 2 minced cloves of garlic
- 1/4 cup toasted pine nuts (or almonds)
- 2 teaspoons Baharat (or mix cinnamon and cumin and if you have just a touch of clove and cardamom)
- (optional) 1/2 cups shredded carrot
- 2-3 tablespoons of chopped mix of parsley and dill
- 2 teaspoons salt
- pepper
- 2 tablespoons olive oil
- Sauce
- 1 diced big onion
- 5-6 sliced cloves of garlic
- 1/2 cup carrot diced to very small cubes
- 1 tablespoon sweet paprika
- 2 tablespoons tomato paste
- 1 can of tomatoes (pureed in the food processor)
- 1 tablespoon chopped parsley
- 1/2 cup of water
- 2 tablespoons of olive oil

Direction

- Prepare the stuffing: Put 2 tablespoons of olive oil in a pan that will fit all the peppers (or other veggies) in one layer. Add the diced onions and sauté for about 10 minutes on medium heat, until translucent and soft. Add the carrots and the garlic and sauté for another 2-3 minutes. Add the Baharat (or the mix of the spices) and sauté for 1-2 minutes while mixing, until fragrant. Add the ground beef and sauté for 5 minutes or so until it is not pink anymore. Make sure you break down all the big chunks.
- Add the rice, salt and pepper and a cup of water. Bring to a boil and then cover and lower the heat and simmer until all the rice absorbed all the liquid (it should be half cooked). Take out of the pan and put in a bowl to cool down.
- Make the sauce: add 2 tablespoons of olive oil to the pan. Add the diced onion and sauté for 10 minutes, until soft and translucent. Add the carrot and the garlic and sauté for few more minutes. Add the paprika and the tomato paste and sauté for 3 minutes while mixing, until the paste is caramelized a bit.
- Add the pureed tomatoes, 1/2 cup of water, 1/2 teaspoon of salt, pepper and parsley. Mix well and bring to a boil. Lower to a simmer.
- Once the stuffing is cooled (does not need to cool completely) add to the mixture pine nuts,

herbs and the pureed tomatoes. Mix gently but well.
- Stuff the peppers: cut the top of the peppers. The top needs to be thick enough so you can put it back on the pepper while it cooks. Take out the seeds and the membranes, gently without braking the peppers. Stuff the peppers with the rice mixture without pressing it down too much. Do not completely fill the pepper since the rice need some space to puff-up.
- For the onions: Peel the onion. Make a cut through some of the outer layers of the onion from top to bottom on one side. Put it in boiling water for about 2 minutes. Take it out and let it cool a bit. Once you can touch it, gently peel the outer bigger layers. The idea is to keep them whole. Put in the middle of an onion layer some of the rice mixture (2-3 tablespoons). Wrap the onion layer around the stuffing in a way that the edges will come one over the other to seal it.
- Arrange the veggies in the pan with the sauce (the peppers supposed to stand up and put the tops back). Spoon some of the sauce on top of them. If the sauce too thick or gets too thick while cooking add more water. Bring to a boil and then simmer for 30-40 minutes, until the veggies are soft and the rice is cooked through. Spoon some sauce on top of the veggies from time to time. Serve with some of the sauce.

229. Rich Taco Meat

Serving: Serves 3-4 | Prep: | Cook: | Ready in:

Ingredients

- 1 pound ground beef
- 1.5 tablespoons Brown fig balsamic vinegar (from San Saba Olive Oil Company)
- 1 tablespoon cumin seeds
- 1 medium red onion, diced
- 2-3 jalapeños, deseeded, cored and diced
- 4 cloves of garlic, minced
- 1/4 cup brewed coffee
- 1.5 tablespoons chili powder
- 1 tablespoon paprika
- 12 cherry tomatoes, quartered
- Salt and pepper

Direction

- In a medium mixing bowl, work the balsamic evenly into the ground beef. This will help tenderize the beef, and you can let it sit while you prep the vegetables.
- Heat a large skillet (or frying pan), and toast the cumin seeds until fragrant. Grind the cumin seeds with a mortar and pestle.
- Heat a large saucepan and coat both the saucepan and the skillet with a generous amount of olive oil.
- In the large saucepan, cook the onions, jalapeños and garlic on medium high heat, stirring regularly. It is okay if some of it sticks to the pan, because you will be deglazing.
- At the same time, sear and brown the beef in the skillet. It is important to do this in a separate pan, so that the steam and water from the vegetables do not boil the flavor out of the beef. You can remove it from heat if it is browned before the vegetable mixture is ready.
- Once the onions have caramelized, deglaze the saucepan with coffee and reduce heat to medium low.
- Add the beef, chili powder, cumin and paprika and mix thoroughly.
- Add water to almost cover the beef. Simmer and reduce to create a nice thick sauce.
- When it is nearly reduced but still has a few minutes to cook, add the cherry tomatoes and salt and pepper to taste.

230. Roast Cauliflower + Avocado Salad With Spiced Yoghurt

Serving: Serves 4 - 6 as a side | Prep: | Cook: | Ready in:

Ingredients

- cauliflower and avocado salad
- 1/2 cauliflower
- 2 tablespoons olive oil
- 2 or 3 handfuls of baby spinach leaves
- 3 tablespoons dried currants or raisins
- 1 avocado, cubed
- 1/2 bunch of chives, chopped (to yield about 1/4 cup)
- lemon wedges, to serve
- spiced yoghurt
- 2/3 cup full fat natural yoghurt
- 1 teaspoon turmeric powder
- 1/4 teaspoon sweet paprika
- big pinch of sea salt
- 1 small garlic clove, minced

Direction

- Preheat oven to 200 degrees Celsius. Start by chopping your cauliflower into thumb sized florets. Stir through olive oil and season well with salt and pepper. Spread evenly onto a roasting tray and roast for about 20 mins, or until tender. Allow to cool.
- Add to a large serving bowl and toss through the currants, chives, baby spinach and half of the avocado. Scoop the remainder of the avocado on top.
- Now prepare the spiced yoghurt by stirring through paprika, turmeric, salt and garlic into the yoghurt.
- Dollop large spoonfuls on top of the salad and serve.

231. Roasted Butternut Squash Queso

Serving: Serves 4-6 | Prep: | Cook: | Ready in:

Ingredients

- 2 cups butternut squash, cubed
- 2 tablespoons olive oil
- 1 teaspoon cumin
- 1/2 teaspoon smoked paprika
- 1/2 teaspoon chili powder
- Salt and pepper
- 3 tablespoons butter
- 2 cloves of garlic, chopped
- 3 tablespoons flour
- 2 cups whole milk
- 1 cup sharp yellow cheddar cheese, shredded
- 1/2 cup pepper jack or Monterey cheese, shredded
- 1-2 chipotle in adobo peppers (depending on how spicy you like it)
- Cilantro, chopped for garnish
- Scallions, chopped for garnish
- Serrano pepper, sliced thin, for garnish
- Sweet potato chips or tortilla chips, for serving

Direction

- Preheat oven to 400° F. In a bowl, toss the butternut squash with olive oil, cumin, smoked paprika, chili powder, 1/2 teaspoon salt and 1/4 teaspoon pepper. Once coated, pour onto a parchment lined sheet tray and roast for 20-25 minutes or until squash is tender. Set aside.
- To make to queso, melt the butter in a medium sauce pan. Once the butter is hot, add the garlic and cook for about a minute or two until garlic is fragrant. Next, add in the flour and cook until just toasted, about two minutes. Using a whisk, slowly incorporate the milk to make a béchamel. Bring the béchamel to a bubble and let thicken just a bit. Remove from the heat and pour it straight into a blender.
- To the blender, add the roasted squash, both cheeses, and the chipotle peppers. Blend for a few minutes or until the sauce is very smooth and silky. Taste and season with more salt, if necessary.
- Pour into a serving bowl and serve immediately or put into a fondue pot to keep warm. Garnish the top with chopped cilantro, scallions and serrano pepper slices.

232. Roasted Butternut And Red Quinoa Salad With Spicy Lime Vinaigrette

Serving: Serves 4 | Prep: | Cook: | Ready in:

Ingredients

- Vinaigrette
- 1 shallot, finely chopped
- 1 clove garlic, finely chopped
- 1 small jalapeño, seeded and finely chopped
- Zest of 1/2 lime
- Juice of 2 limes
- 1 teaspoon lemon juice
- 1/2 teaspoon crushed red pepper flakes
- 2 tablespoons olive oil
- 2 tablespoons canola oil
- Salt and pepper, to taste
- Quinoa Salad
- 1/2 cup pumpkin seeds
- 1/2 teaspoon olive oil
- 1 teaspoon smoked paprika
- 1 1/2 pounds peeled, seeded butternut squash cut into 1-inch cubes
- 1 tablespoon canola oil
- 1 cup red quinoa
- 2 cups water
- 15 ounces white beans or 1 can, drained
- 1/4 cup cilantro leaves, roughly chopped

Direction

- Vinaigrette
- In a small bowl, combine the shallot, garlic, jalapeño, lime zest and juice, lemon juice, salt, black pepper, and red pepper.
- Gradually whisk in the olive and canola oils in a slow steady stream until combined. Taste for seasoning, and set aside until ready to dress the salad.
- Quinoa Salad
- Set the oven to 350 degrees. On a baking sheet, combine the pumpkin seeds with the olive oil and paprika in one even layer. Toast for 8 minutes in the oven, or until browned and fragrant. Set aside to cool.
- Turn the oven temperature up to 400 degrees, and on the same baking sheet, combine the butternut squash and canola oil. Season with salt and pepper, and roast for 30 to 35 minutes, tossing halfway through to evenly brown and caramelize. Set aside to cool.
- In a saucepan over medium heat, toast the quinoa, stirring often, for 2 minutes, or until the grains are aromatic. Add the water and a pinch of salt. Stir well and bring to a boil. Lower the heat, cover the pan, and simmer for 15 to 20 minutes, or until quinoa is tender. Transfer to a large bowl and fluff with a fork.
- Add the squash, white beans, half of the pumpkin seeds, and half of the cilantro to the quinoa. Drizzle with the lime dressing and toss gently. Taste for seasoning, and add more salt and pepper. Garnish with remaining pumpkin seeds and cilantro.

233. Roasted Canela Cilantro Chicken

Serving: Serves 4 | Prep: | Cook: | Ready in:

Ingredients

- Roasted Chicken
- 4 Chicken thighs and legs
- 1/4 cup Cinnamon Pear Vinegar
- 1/8 cup Cilantro and Roasted Onion Oil
- 1/4 cup Chives, chopped
- 1 teaspoon Cinnamon
- 1/2 teaspoon Sweet Hungarian Paprika
- 4 teaspoons Mole' Sauce, from a jar
- Cilantro Rice
- 1 cup Rice, dry
- 2 cups Chicken Broth
- 1/4 Cilantro, fresh, chopped

Direction

- Add the chicken to a roasting pan (I used a glass pan). Pour the vinegar over the chicken, then drizzle the oil over the chicken. Sprinkle the cinnamon and paprika on, then spread the Mole' sauce evenly over each piece. Top with the chives. Cover and marinade over night.
- After marinating, cover the pan with aluminum foil. Bake in the oven at 350 degrees for 90 minutes.
- When the chicken has about 25 minutes left, add the rice and chicken broth to a pan, bring to a boil, then turn the heat down to a low and cover. Simmer for 20 minutes or until the rice is fully cooked. Remove from heat, fluff with a fork, and add the chopped cilantro.
- Serve the chicken over the rice, top with fresher cilantro if desired. Serving suggestion: top with Caramelized Onions; serve with a side salad of Mesclun topped with Goat Cheese and sliced pears in a vinaigrette. Cooking options: cook the chicken in a slow cooker or grill outside.

234. Roasted Carrots With Cauliflower Couscous

Serving: Serves 4 | Prep: | Cook: |Ready in:

Ingredients

- Roasted Carrots
- 12-15 small carrots
- 1 tablespoon ghee/ coconut oil
- 1 tablespoon honey
- 1 teaspoon lemon zest
- 1 teaspoon cumin powder
- 1 teaspoon paprika
- 1 teaspoon cardamom powder
- 1 tablespoon sessame seeds
- salt & pepper
- Cauliflower Couscous
- 1 head of cauliflower
- 2 tablespoons capers
- 1/2 cup fresh herbs - mint, cilantro and basil
- 1/4 cup raisins
- 1/4 cup toasted almonds
- 1 tablespoon ghee/ coconut oil
- 1/2 teaspoon turmeric powder
- juice of 1 lemon
- salt & pepper

Direction

- Roasted Carrots
- Preheat the oven to 350°F. Wash carrots thoroughly, wipe and chop in medium cubes if they are large in size.
- Make a marinade by combining ghee, honey, lemon zest, salt, pepper, cumin, paprika and cardamom powder.
- Rub the carrots with marinade and lay them on baking sheet. Sprinkle sesame seeds on top. Roast them in oven for 15-20 minutes until edges get golden brown.
- Cauliflower Couscous
- Cut the cauliflower in small florets, discard stalks. Place florets in food processor. Pulse food processor until florets become little grain like couscous.
- Heat ghee in sauce pan on medium heat. Add raisins and let them soak in hot ghee for 1-2 minutes. Add turmeric powder and cook for 10 seconds.
- Add cauliflower couscous to pan. Mix well until all couscous is covered with turmeric color.
- Remove from the heat and add fresh herbs, capers, almonds, lemons juice, salt and pepper and mix well. Serve warm with roasted carrots and yogurt.

235. Roasted Cauliflower With Paprika And Greek Yoghurt Dip

Serving: Serves 2 | Prep: | Cook: |Ready in:

Ingredients

- For the roast

- 1 medium size cauliflower, cut into florets or thick slabs
- 1 tablespoon coarsely ground sea salt
- 1 teaspoon paprika
- vegetable oil spray
- 1/2 cup white wine (chardonnay)
- 1/4 cup olive oil
- 2 garlic cloves, finely minced
- 1/4 teaspoon white ground pepper
- 1 teaspoon paprika
- extra paprika to garnish
- For the dip
- 1 cup sour cream cheese
- 1/2 cup greek yoghurt
- 1 tablespoon lemon juice
- salt and pepper to taste
- olive oil to drizzle

Direction

- Combine in a bowl the white wine, olive oil, finely minced garlic cloves, white ground pepper and paprika. Place the cauliflower florets or slabs in the bowl and marinate for an hour
- Spray a baking sheet with vegetable oil spray and place the cauliflower on top. Pour the marinade juices on the cauliflower, sprinkle the sea salt and the paprika on top
- Preheat oven to 220° C/ 430° F and bake for 20 minutes or until crispy and golden
- For the dip mix the sour cream cheese with the yoghurt and beat in the lemon juice. Season with salt and pepper and drizzle with olive oil. Garnish with the extra paprika. Serve the roasted cauliflower slabs or florets sprinkled with the extra paprika and the Greek yoghurt dip

236. Roasted Cauliflower With Za'atar And Lemons

Serving: Serves 4 (as a side dish) | Prep: | Cook: |Ready in:

Ingredients

- Zaatar Spice
- 1 tablespoon Tossed Sesame Seeds
- 1 tablespoon Thyme, fresh or dry
- 1 tablespoon Sumac
- Roasted Cauliflower
- 1 Lemon
- 1 teaspoon Butter
- 1 tablespoon Panko Breadcrumbs
- 4 tablespoons Olive Oil
- 1 Small cauliflower, torn or cut in 1-inch florets
- 1 teaspoon Salt
- 1 teaspoon red Pepper Flakes
- 1 tablespoon Smoked mushroom butter (or 1 tsp smoked paprika)
- 1 tablespoon Za'atar spice (recipe above) (or store bought)
- 1/4 cup Freshly grated Parmesan
- 2 tablespoons Chopped fresh parsley

Direction

- Zaatar Spice
- Combine all ingredients in a small bowl and mix well. Store in an airtight container (if the thyme is fresh let the container open for 2-3 days so the thyme dries).
- Roasted Cauliflower
- Grate and juice the lemon, place in separate bowls and set aside.
- Melt the plain butter in a large non-stick pan, add the bread crumbs and toast until golden-brown, about 30 sec. Set aside in a bowl.
- Return the non-stick skillet to the stove, heat it very well on high heat. When nice and hot, add the olive oil, the cauliflower and the salt. Stir well to coat the florets evenly, lower the heat to a medium-high and cook for 2-3 minutes until golden brown without disturbing. Turn (or stir) the florets on the other side and cook for additional 2-3 minutes, until nice and brown (the more charred on the sides tastier they will be). Add the red pepper flakes and the smoked butter (or smoked paprika) and cook for additional minute.

- Place the cooked cauliflower in a large bowl, add the lemon zest, half of the lemon juice, the Za'atar spice, bread crumbs, Parmesan and the parsley. Mix well to combine. Taste and add more lemon juice, Za'atar spice or seasoning if needed.

237. Roasted Cauliflower, Fennel And Farro Pilaf

Serving: Serves 4 as a main course, 6-8 as a side | Prep: | Cook: | Ready in:

Ingredients

- 1 head cauliflower, cut into florets
- 1 bulb fennel, sliced 1/4 inch thick
- 1.5 cups farro
- 3-4 green onions, white and dark green parts, sliced
- 1 lemon, juice and zest
- 1 can black beans, rinsed and drained
- 4 tablespoons olive oil, divided
- 1/2 teaspoon ground cumin
- 1/2 teaspoon pimente d'espelette
- 1/8 teaspoon ground nutmeg
- 1/4 teaspoon sweet paprika
- 1/4 teaspoon ground turmeric
- 1 tablespoon honey
- 1/2 teaspoon salt
- Freshly ground pepper

Direction

- Preheat the oven to 425 degrees F. Toss the cauliflower and fennel with the cumin, piment d'espelette, turmeric, paprika, nutmeg, olive oil, lemon zest and 1/4 tsp of the salt in a large bowl.
- Spread the cauliflower mixture on a baking sheet and roast until the cauliflower is brown and starting to caramelize on top, about 30 minutes.
- While the cauliflower is roasting, cook the farro: Bring a large pot of salted water to a boil and add farro. Cook until farro is tender but still chewy, about 35 minutes.
- When the cauliflower is done, transfer it to a large serving bowl and stir in the honey. Drain the farro when it is done and add to the cauliflower with the black beans and green onions and mix together.
- Stir the remaining 2 tablespoons olive oil and lemon juice in a small bowl. Pour over the pilaf and toss together. Taste and adjust for seasoning and serve. This is good hot or warm and I've even eaten it cold.

238. Roasted Corn, Poblano, And Bacon Salad With Maple Lime Vinaigrette

Serving: Serves 6-8 | Prep: | Cook: | Ready in:

Ingredients

- 3 tablespoons pure maple syrup
- 3 tablespoons fresh lime juice
- 2 teaspoons fresh lime zest
- 1 teaspoon hot sauce
- 2 tablespoons grapeseed oil
- 5 ears fresh white or yellow corn, shucked
- 1 medium poblano pepper, chop in ½-inch pieces, seeds removed
- 1 teaspoon smoked paprika
- 1/2 teaspoon garlic salt
- 1/2 teaspoon lemon & pepper seasoning salt
- 1/2 teaspoon ground cumin
- 5 slices of bacon, cut in bite size pieces
- 1 cup chopped red onion
- 1 cup chopped sweet red pepper
- 1/2 cup chopped cilantro, plus extra for garnish

Direction

- In a small bowl, whisk maple syrup, lime juice, lime zest, and hot sauce until well mixed. Set aside.

- Heat a large (11-inch or bigger) high walled skillet on medium-high for 3 minutes. Add 2 tablespoons grape seed oil, heat, and sprinkle with corn kernels and poblano pieces, paprika, garlic salt, lemon pepper, and cumin. Stir corn and poblanos every 2-minutes until corn is slightly roasted and brown, about 6-minutes total. Pour roasted corn and poblanos into a large salad bowl.
- Meanwhile, in a separate skillet or wait and use the same skillet over medium heat, cook bacon about 3 minutes or until limp. Add onion; cook 4-5 minutes longer or until bacon is browned, stirring occasionally. Add bacon and onions (I included the bacon fat), sweet red peppers, and cilantro to the corn mixture; stir well. Pour maple lime vinaigrette over roasted corn salad and mix well. Serve at room temperature or chilled. Optional: Line salad bowl with lettuce leaves.

239. Roasted Cornish Game Hens

Serving: Makes 2 cornish hens | Prep: | Cook: | Ready in:

Ingredients

- 2 Cornish Game Hens
- 1 cup White grape juice
- 2 sprigs Fresh basil (about 6 leaves each)
- 1/4 cup Olive oil
- 1/2 teaspoon Garlic powder
- 1 teaspoon Dried thyme
- 1 teaspoon Poultry seasoning
- 1 teaspoon Paprika

Direction

- Preheat oven to 375°.
- Line roasting pan with tin foil. Pour grape juice into pan. Place roasting rack in pan.
- Remove hens from package, rinse thoroughly, pat dry and place on roaster rack. Stuff 1 stem of basil into each hen cavity for added flavor.
- Combine oil, garlic powder, thyme, poultry seasoning, and paprika. Smear oil and herb mixture evenly on each hen.
- Roast for about 1 hour or until the internal temperature reaches 165°. Remove from oven and let rest a few minutes. Serve with roasted vegetables of your choice.

240. Roasted Dates & Honey Wings

Serving: Serves 4 to 6 | Prep: | Cook: | Ready in:

Ingredients

- ½ teaspoons ground ginger
- ½ teaspoons ground turmeric
- 2 teaspoons kosher salt
- ½ teaspoons ground black pepper
- 2 pounds chicken wings
- 1/4 cup all-purpose flour
- 3/4 cup pitted Medjool dates (about 8 dates)
- ½ cups tomato sauce
- 2 tablespoons olive oil
- 2 tablespoons apple cider vinegar
- 2 tablespoons lime juice
- 2 tablespoons honey, extra for garnish
- 1 tablespoon sweet paprika
- ½ tablespoons sesame seeds
- 1 tablespoon finely chopped chives

Direction

- Preheat oven to 400°F. Line a large sheet pan with parchment paper; set aside.
- In a small bowl, combine ginger, turmeric, salt and pepper; in a large bowl, season wings with salt/spice mix; coat wings with flour, tossing gently.
- Lay coated wings over prepared sheet pan; wrap dates in foil (slightly open) and place next to chicken wings on the side of sheet pan; bake for 20 minutes; remove dates; continue baking chicken wings till cooked through and skin is crispy (about 30 additional minutes).

- In a food processor, purée roasted dates, tomato sauce, olive oil, vinegar, lime juice, honey, and paprika; transfer to a large bowl.
- Toss hot baked wings in date sauce; transfer back to sheet pan and bake for another 15-20 minutes or till wings are sticky and caramelized.
- Drizzle with extra honey. Sprinkle with sesame seeds and chives; dig in!

241. Roasted Delicata Squash Stuffed With Autumn Farro

Serving: Serves 4 | Prep: | Cook: |Ready in:

Ingredients

- 2 large delicata squash, halved
- Salt and pepper, to taste
- Olive oil, as needed
- 1/4 teaspoon hot Hungarian paprika (optional)
- 1 teaspoon cumin
- 2 sprigs rosemary, cut into four halves
- 1 cup farro
- 3 cups water or vegetable broth
- 1 bulb fennel, shaved and chopped
- 1 bunch small scallions, white and green parts chopped
- 4 ounces winter greens or arugula
- 1/2 cup pistachio, crushed
- Seeds of 1 pomegranate
- 1/4 cup tahini
- Juice of 1 medium orange
- Zest of 1/2 orange
- 1 tablespoon Dijon mustard
- 1/2 teaspoon fresh thyme

Direction

- Preheat oven to 425° F. Remove the inner pulp and seeds from the squash (reserve for roasting if desired), drizzle and rub it in oil, and sprinkle it with salt and pepper. If using Hungarian hot paprika, mix it with the cumin; otherwise, sprinkle cumin over squash. Place squash on a large sheet pan, cut side down, and place one rosemary half beneath each squash (rosemary may either be discarded at the end or added to the farro salad). Bake for 20 to 25 minutes, or until a fork can be inserted into skin tenderly. Allow to cool slightly upon removal from oven.
- Assemble the farro salad: In a small saucepan, toast the farro over medium-high heat until fragrant and nutty. Add the water or vegetable broth and bring to a light boil. Cover and boil 15 minutes, until most of the liquid is absorbed and grain is cooked. If needed, drain any excess liquid.
- In a large bowl combine farro, fennel, scallions, winter greens or arugula, pistachio, and pomegranate.
- In a separate medium bowl, whisk together the tahini, orange juice, orange zest, mustard, and thyme.
- Serve squash halves filled with farro salad and topped with tahini dressing.

242. Roasted Eggplant With Cilantro Almond Salsa

Serving: Serves 4 | Prep: | Cook: |Ready in:

Ingredients

- 1 cup couscous
- 1 small garlic clove, peeled
- 1 teaspoon cumin seed
- 3/4 teaspoon paprika, divided
- 1/2 teaspoon coriander seed
- 1 teaspoon finely grated lemon zest and 1 tablespoon juice
- 4 tablespoons olive oil, divided
- Kosher salt and freshly ground black pepper
- 4 to 6 small eggplant, halved lengthwise
- 1/2 cup cilantro (leaves and stems)
- 1/4 cup roasted, unsalted peanuts
- Yogurt (preferably whole milk), for serving

Direction

- Preheat broiler, with rack in upper third of oven. Place couscous in a large heat-proof bowl. Cover with 1 1/2 cups boiling water, then place a plate over top of the bowl. Let stand 15 minutes, then fluff couscous with a fork.
- Meanwhile, combine garlic, cumin, paprika, coriander, lemon zest and 2 tablespoons olive oil in a mortar and use pestle to smash ingredients together to form a paste. Season generously with salt and pepper. Rub cut sides of eggplant with spice mixture and transfer to a broiler-proof baking dish. Broil 15 minutes, or until eggplant are tender and charred.
- While eggplant broils, chop cilantro and almonds and transfer to a bowl. Stir in 2 tablespoons oil, lemon juice and remaining 1/4 teaspoon paprika; season with salt and pepper. Serve eggplant with couscous, topped with a dollop of yogurt and a spoonful of salsa.

243. Roasted Grape And Butternut Squash Salad With Kale And Parmesan

Serving: Serves 6 | Prep: | Cook: | Ready in:

Ingredients

- For the vinaigrette:
- 1 clove garlic, smashed and minced
- 1 tablespoon sherry vinegar
- 1 tablespoon Dijon mustard
- 1 teaspoon honey
- 1/4 teaspoon paprika
- 1 pinch sea salt
- 1/4 cup extra-virgin olive oil
- 2 tablespoons finely shredded Parmesan
- For the salad:
- 1 small butternut squash, trimmed, peeled, halved, and seeded
- 1/2 teaspoon sea salt
- 1/4 teaspoon chipotle chili powder
- 1/4 teaspoon chili pepper flakes
- 1 pinch paprika
- 1 pinch black pepper
- 2 1/2 teaspoons extra-virgin olive oil, divided
- 2 cups seedless black grapes
- 8 ounces baby kale leaves
- 1/4 cup shaved Parmesan

Direction

- In a medium bowl, whisk together the garlic, vinegar, Dijon, honey, paprika, and sea salt. Slowly whisk in the olive oil until emulsified. Fold in Parmesan and set aside.
- Preheat oven to 400° F. Line 2 large baking sheets with parchment paper. (If you have a large oven, you can make arrangements to roast everything at once; otherwise, it's best to roast the squash first and then the grapes after.)
- Slice the butternut squash into 1/2-inch thick wedges or triangles, as evenly as possible.
- In a small bowl, combine the sea salt, chili powder, chili flakes, paprika, and black pepper. Set aside.
- In a large bowl, toss butternut squash wedges with 2 teaspoons olive oil and most of the spice mixture. Arrange the wedges with plenty of room on the prepared baking sheets. Slide into oven and roast for 20 minutes, then use tongs to turn each wedge and slide the baking sheet back into the oven to roast for another 15 to 20 minutes more, or until squash is tender and edges are lightly browned. Set aside to cool.
- In the same bowl used for the squash, toss grapes with 1/2 teaspoon olive oil and the remaining spice mixture. Spread a fresh layer of parchment on your baking sheet of choice, arrange the grapes, and slide the sheet into the oven. Bake, shaking pan once or twice, for 8 to 10 minutes total, or just until the grapes start to burst.
- Toss kale leaves with half of the dressing and arrange on a platter. Tuck squash wedges

throughout the kale, followed by the grapes. Scatter shaved Parmesan and then drizzle salad with remaining vinaigrette. Serve warm or at room temperature.

244. Roasted Pumpkin Seed Hummus With Gluten Free Rosemary Focaccia

Serving: Serves 6 | Prep: | Cook: | Ready in:

Ingredients

- 1 1/2 cups pumpkin seeds
- 3 cloves garlic
- 1 teaspoon smoked paprika
- 1 can white beans, drained
- 1/2 cup olive oil, plus more for drizzling
- 1 lemon, juiced
- 1 teaspoon salt

Direction

- Preheat oven to 350°F.
- On a parchment lined baking sheet add pumpkin seed and spread evenly.
- Roast for 10-15 minutes.
- In a food processor, add pumpkin seeds, garlic, olive oil, paprika, white beans, lemon and salt.
- Blend until smooth.
- Adjust salt/olive oil to desired taste.
- Serve, drizzled with olive oil and a sprinkle of smoked paprika.

245. Roasted Red Pepper Hummus

Serving: Makes 3 cups | Prep: | Cook: | Ready in:

Ingredients

- 2 large, sweet red peppers, roasted (if fresh, see note)
- 2 cans garbanzo beans(chickpeas) well rinsed and drained
- 1/3 cup fresh lemon juice
- 3 tablespoons Tahini
- 1 tablespoon Extra Virgin Olive Oil
- 3 garlic cloves, peeled
- 1 1/4 teaspoons kosher salt
- 1 teaspoon curry powder
- 1/2 teaspoon freshly cracked black pepper
- Extra Virgin Olive Oil and Paprika, for finishing

Direction

- If you're roasting your own peppers: (Simply broil them about 4 inches from the heat until skins are blistered, rotating and turning until all sides are blackened. Immediately place the peppers in a bowl, cover, and let stand for 15 minutes or so. Peel off and discard the blackened skin and remove stems and seeds.)
- Place the peppers in food processor. Add the remaining ingredients and process until blended and very fluffy, about 4 minutes, scraping down sides of bowl halfway through. Scrape into a container, drizzle liberally with olive oil and dust with paprika.
- Serve with fresh veggies, pita chips, or flatbreads, for dipping.

246. Roasted Red Pepper And Pomegranate Patatas Bravas

Serving: Serves 4 | Prep: 0hours30mins | Cook: 0hours30mins | Ready in:

Ingredients

- 1.5 pounds potatoes
- 5 tablespoons olive oil, divided
- 1 onion, diced
- 1 teaspoon ground coriander
- 1 teaspoon smoked paprika

- 1/4 cup blanched almonds
- 1/4 cup white wine
- 2 red peppers, well roasted
- kosher salt to taste
- pomegranate molasses, mayonnaise, and chopped parsley for garnish

Direction

- Heat oven to 400°. Toss potatoes with about 2 tablespoons of olive oil, sprinkled with sea salt and lay in a single layer on a baking sheet.
- Roast potatoes for 25-30 minutes, turning every 10, until potatoes are golden and easily pierced with a fork. You can turn off the oven and leave them inside to warm while you finish the sauce. When ready, move to a dish.
- Meanwhile, prepare the spicy red pepper sauce. Heat 3 tablespoons olive oil on medium high and sauté onion until golden.
- Add chopped garlic and sauté for a minute or so, then add salt, paprika, ground coriander, cayenne, and almonds, and cook, stirring, until spices are fragrant and almonds are slightly toasted. Add white wine and cook until liquid evaporates.
- Remove the mixture from heat and puree in a blender with the red peppers and enough water to thin it to a thick sauce, about 1/4 cup. Return to heat and gently heat through.
- Pour the sauce over warm potatoes. Garnish with a drizzle of pomegranate molasses and a drizzle of mayonnaise, and generous sprinkled of parsley. Serve hot.

247. Roasted Romesco Sauce

Serving: Makes two cups | Prep: | Cook: | Ready in:

Ingredients

- Two large beefsteak tomatoes, cored
- Two large red bell peppers
- 2 poblano peppers (you can use any chili which hits between 1000-2000 on the Scoville scale http://ushotstuff.com/Heat.Scale.htm , such as Rocotilla, Passila, Mulato or Ancho you just want a bit of heat)
- 1 head of garlic
- Olive Oil
- One one-inch thick slice of good white bread, cut in cubes
- ¼ cup almonds, blanched (whole, halved or slivered all work)
- ¼ cup hazelnuts, peeled
- ½ teaspoon Spanish smoked paprika
- ¼ cup oil (I use a mixture of hazelnut and almond oil because I happened to have them, but olive oil works well too.)
- 3 tablespoons red wine vinegar
- 1 tablespoon dry sherry
- 2-4 tablespoons water (if needed to thin the sauce)
- Kosher salt and ground black pepper to taste

Direction

- Set oven to 300 degrees. (I use the convection roast setting as it speeds things along.)
- Cut the top off the garlic bulb. Brush it with oil, wrap in foil and roast until the garlic is soft.
- Line a jelly roll pan with tin foil. Place the tomato halves cut side up, rub with olive oil. Roast until the tomatoes are roasted enough so that they slip out of their skins. That will take 30-40 minutes. Employ your favorite method for roasting the peppers so they can be peeled. I hold them over a gas flame until charred, then place them in a bowl covered with plastic wrap for 30 minutes. (Or in a pinch I open a jar and grab two already peeled ones!)
- In a dry skillet, lightly toast the almonds and the hazelnuts. Set aside to cool.
- Pour one tablespoon of olive oil into skillet and put over medium high heat. When oil is hot add bread cubes and sauté them until golden. Remove from pan and set aside to cool.
- When the roasted vegetables are cool enough to handle, slip them all out of their skins and into a food processor. Add the cooled nuts,

bread and paprika. Process until you have a smooth paste. Then pour in the oils, vinegar and sherry. Add water if the mixture is too thick. You want it thin enough to slide off a spoon.
- Season with salt and pepper to your taste. Sauce will keep refrigerated for about a week.

248. Roasted Spiced Carrots With Pistachios

Serving: Serves 4 | Prep: | Cook: | Ready in:

Ingredients

- 1 pound baby carrots
- 1/2 pound spring onions or regular onions
- 1 1/2 teaspoons smoked paprika
- 3/4 teaspoon ground cumin
- 1/4 teaspoon cayenne pepper
- 1/4 teaspoon cinnamon
- 1/2 teaspoon kosher salt
- 1/4 teaspoon freshly ground black pepper
- 1/2 teaspoon sugar
- 2-3 tablespoons canola, vegetable or grapeseed oil
- 2 tablespoons roughly chopped fresh mint
- 2 tablespoons roughly chopped fresh cilantro
- 1/3 cup shelled pistachios
- lemon wedges for serving

Direction

- Preheat the oven to 450°. Scrub the carrots to remove any dirt and trim the green parts. Depending on the size of the carrots, cut the large ones in half so that they're roughly the same diameter as the smaller carrots, for more even cooking times (I had lots of different sized ones). Trim the root and stem from the onions, peel and slice into wedges. Transfer carrots and onions to a large, rimmed baking sheet.
- In a small bowl combine the paprika, cumin, cayenne, cinnamon, salt, pepper and sugar. Drizzle the olive oil over the vegetables and toss with your hands until they are well coated. Sprinkle the spice mixture over the vegetables and toss again so that they are evenly coated. Spread the vegetables out on the baking sheet in a single layer.
- Bake the vegetables for 20 minutes or until tender. Remove from the oven and transfer to a serving platter. Sprinkle with the pistachios, mint and cilantro. Serve with lemon wedges to squeeze on the vegetables for a bright hit of citrus.

249. Roasted Stuffed Onion Gratin

Serving: Serves 12 | Prep: | Cook: | Ready in:

Ingredients

- 6 6 med.large round yellow onions, peeled
- 1/4 cup seasoned bread crumbs
- 3 tablespoons parmesan cheese
- vegetable oil
- salt & pepper to taste
- 2 teaspoons smoked paprika

Direction

- Drizzle some vegetable oil in a casserole dish large enough to hold all the onions. Cut onions in half crosswise and thinly slice off some of the bottoms of the onion so it can sit in the dish flat. Place all onions cut side up and drizzle with oil. In a small bowl mix breadcrumbs with cheese, pepper and paprika and 1-2 tbsp. of oil. Sprinkle over tops of onions. Season to taste Bake in a preheated 350F oven for approx. 40-45min until fork tender.

250. Roasted Sweet Potato Mac N' Cheese

Serving: Makes large dish | Prep: | Cook: |Ready in:

Ingredients

- 2 Sweet potatoes, diced into 1-inch pieces
- 2 tablespoons Canola oil
- Kosher salt
- Freshly ground black pepper
- 1/2 cup Unsalted butter
- 2 Cloves of garlic finely minced
- 1/2 cup Flour
- 1 tablespoon Powdered mustard
- 3 tablespoons Tomato paste
- 4 cups Whole milk
- 1 Bay leaf
- 1/2 teaspoon Smoked paprika
- 3 cups Shredded sharp cheddar cheese
- 2 cups Grated Parmesan cheese
- 1 pound Cellentani, cooked 2 minutes less than instructed for al dente
- 1 cup Panko bread crumbs
- 1/4 cup melted unsalted butter

Direction

- Preheat the oven to 450 degrees F. Toss the sweet potatoes with the canola oil along with 4 finger pinches of salt and ground black pepper. Evenly spread the pieces onto a baking sheet and roast in the oven for 20-25 minutes until tender on the inside and golden brown on the outside.
- In a large pot over medium heat, melt the butter. When the butter begins to bubble, stir in the minced garlic and cook for 60 seconds.
- Sprinkle the flour and powdered mustard over the butter and garlic and whisk for 90 seconds to cook out the raw flour taste. Whisk in the tomato paste and cook for about 2 minutes.
- Whisk in the milk, bay leaf and paprika and simmer until the mixture begins to thicken, about 5-10 minutes. Stir in the cheddar and Parmesan cheese until melted. Fold in the cooked pasta and roasted sweet potatoes.
- Transfer to a large baking dish. In a small bowl, toss the bread crumbs with the melted butter. Sprinkle over the pasta and bake for another 15-18 minutes, until golden brown on top. Serve and enjoy!

251. Roasted Tomato Eggplant Melts

Serving: Serves 2 | Prep: | Cook: |Ready in:

Ingredients

- 1 large ripe tomato, sliced 1/4 - 3/8 inches thick
- 2 Japanese Eggplant
- 4   slices Extra Sharp Cheddar Cheese
- 1.5 teaspoons smoked paprika
- 2 tablespoons Extra Virgin Olive Oil

Direction

- Preheat oven to 400 degrees
- Slice Japanese eggplant lengthwise so you have 4 pieces. Using a small knife cut diagonal slices into flesh of eggplant. Do not cut all the way through the eggplant.
- Coat eggplant with olive oil, gently rubbing it in the flesh along with the smoked paprika. Make sure the skin side gets coated with olive oil too.
- Bake until eggplant starts to soften - about 15-25 minutes. Take out of oven and top eggplant with tomato slices. Put cheddar cheese on top of tomato and cook until cheese is lightly melted 3-6 minutes.

252. Roasted Tomato And Carrot Soup

Serving: Serves 6 | Prep: | Cook: |Ready in:

Ingredients

- 3 tablespoons Extra Virgin Olive Oil
- 8 vine-ripened tomatoes, quartered
- 4 carrots, peeled and cut into thick biases
- 1 yellow onion, cut into large wedges
- 3 garlic cloves, chopped
- 1 tablespoon fresh thyme
- 1 teaspoon paprika
- 1/2 cup chopped fresh basil
- 2 cups chicken stock
- salt and pepper throughout

Direction

- Preheat oven to 400 degrees Fahrenheit.
- On an oiled baking sheet, toss the tomatoes, carrots, onions, generously with 2 T Extra Virgin Olive Oil, salt and pepper and thyme. Roast for 35-40 minutes or until the vegetables are tender and golden brown, turning occasionally.
- Heat a large pot on medium heat. Pour 1 T EVOO inside and add the garlic. Sautee for 1 minute then pour in the roasted vegetables, paprika, chicken stock, and bring to a simmer. When the baking sheet is cool enough, add the scraped roasting bits as well. Let simmer for at least 15 minutes, then add 1/4 c chopped basil. Puree the soup in a blender in multiple batches. When blending, fill the blender halfway with the vegetable mixture to create a smooth puree. Pour the pureed liquid into a large bowl and continue with the remaining soup. Return the pureed soup to the large pot and let simmer for 5 more minutes. Season with salt and pepper to taste. Ladle into bowls, sprinkle with remaining fresh basil and serve with Mini Grilled Cheese Croutons.

253. Rudy's BBQ Copycat Baby Back Ribs

Serving: Serves 4-6 | Prep: 0hours20mins | Cook: 4hours0mins | Ready in:

Ingredients

- For the Ribs
- 2 slabs baby back ribs, silver skin removed
- 1 teaspoon dry mustard
- 1 teaspoon smoked paprika
- 1 teaspoon salt
- 1 teaspoon fresh cracked pepper
- For the BBQ Sauce
- 8 ounces canned tomato sauce
- 1/2 cup ketchup
- 1/2 cup brown sugar
- 2.5 tablespoons white vinegar
- 2 tablespoons Worcestershire sauce
- 2 tablespoons lemon juice
- 1 teaspoon garlic powder
- 1 teaspoon fresh cracked pepper
- 1/4 teaspoon cumin
- 1/8 teaspoon cayenne pepper

Direction

- For the ribs: mix the dry mustard, smoked paprika, salt and pepper together and rub on the ribs. Put ribs in foil and tightly cover the ribs and bake on a cookie sheet at 250 degrees for three hours. This can be done over the weekend too for a quick weeknight meal.
- For the BBQ sauce: mix everything together in a pan and cook over medium low heat for 30 minutes. This can also be made ahead and keeps in the refrigerator for weeks.
- When you are ready to grill, light coals or heat up your gas grill. Brush both sides with the BBQ sauce and cook over medium heat until heated through, then I turn up the heat on high to get some char marks for an extra smoky flavor. These are fall off the bone ribs!

254. Rustic Muddy Duck Paella

Serving: Serves 4 | Prep: | Cook: | Ready in:

Ingredients

- 4 -4 1/2 cups heated, seasoned duck broth
- 7-9 Spanish saffron threads, toasted and steeped in 1/2 cup of the hot duck broth above
- 1 1/2-2 pounds succulent cooked roast duck, cut up
- 3/4 pound fresh chorizo
- duck skin, optional
- olive oil for pan
- 6-8 cloves garlic, peeled and minced
- 1 teaspoon fresh lemon zest
- 2 red cippolini onions, chopped
- 2 red heirloom tomatoes, grated, skinned, seeded and salted
- 2 ounces Cornelian cherry jam
- 2 teaspoons ground sumac (or more lemon zest)
- 2 teaspoons smoked paprika
- 4-6 ounces cherry fruit ale
- 1 1/2 cups bomba or arborio rice
- 1 red bell pepper, cored, seeded and cut into 1/2 inch strips
- 15 ounces cranberry beans (borlotti beans), fresh or canned
- 2 ounces Cornelian cherry jam
- a generous splash of cherry ale
- 1 teaspoon ground sumac
- 1/2 teaspoon smoked paprika
- 1 bay leaf
- kosher salt to taste
- fresh milled black pepper to taste
- lemon wedges for squeezing on each portion

Direction

- Heat the duck broth in a saucepan, bringing to a boil, then a simmer. Take out 1/2 cup of the liquid and add the saffron. After infusing, add this back to the broth. Taste for seasoning. Add salt and pepper if needed. Remove from heat until ready to add to the rice.
- Heat olive oil in the paella pan. Sauté the chorizo and optional sliced duck skin on medium high heat. Transfer to a plate and set aside. Have the remaining roasted duck meat cut into small pieces for later.
- Reduce heat to medium and add the red pepper, lemon zest, garlic and onion. Cook until limp, but not brown. Transfer the peppers to a plate and peel off their skin when cool.
- To make the sofrito add the salted, grated tomato, Cornelian jam mixed with sumac and smoked paprika to the onions and garlic in the pan Stir often. Cook until this turns burgundy. Add the cherry ale and reduce. Cook until this down to a compote consistency, about 20 minutes or more. Don't rush this. Make sure this is seasoned with enough salt because this is the flavor base.
- Set the paella pan over a larger burner on medium high. Add the rice, stirring until it is opaque, 1-2 minutes. Spread the rice out over the pan evenly. Pour in the hot broth. Arrange the duck, chorizo, beans, and red peppers in the pan. Do not stir the rice from this step forward. Vigorously simmer. When the rice reaches the same level as the liquid, about 10 minutes or less, reduce the heat to medium low. Continue to simmer gently rotating the pan if necessary. When the liquid is absorbed test a grain of rice. It should be al dente with a tiny dot in the center. If it is not done, then add a bit more liquid (broth or cherry ale) to the pan and cook a few more minutes. I used all 4 1/2 cups of broth in addition to the ale.
- To make the socarrat, increase the heat to medium high and rotate the pan. Cook for 2 minutes until the bottom layer of rice caramelizes. If you smell burning, remove the pan from heat right away. Let the paella rest; remove the pan from the heat (@ 5minutes), and cover.
- Simmer the Cornelian cherry jam with sumac, paprika, bay leaf, and reduced cherry ale, in a small sauce pan. Just before serving add this to the center of the paella pan (bay leaf removed). Set the paella pan in the center of the table. Invite folks to gather to eat, directly from the pan; provide enough lemon wedges for each portion.

255. Saffron And Paprika Rice With Smoked Andouille Sausage

Serving: Serves 6-7 | Prep: | Cook: | Ready in:

Ingredients

- 1 tablespoon olive oil
- 1 yellow onion, chopped
- 1 red bell pepper, chopped
- 3 garlic cloves, minced
- 2 cups long grain rice, dry
- 4 cups chicken broth
- 1 teaspoon salt
- 1/2 teaspoon saffron
- 1 cup green peas
- 4 smoked andouille sausage links, cooked (on grill or pan) and sliced into 1/2 inch pieces
- 1 teaspoon smoked Spanish paprika

Direction

- In a large Dutch oven, heat olive oil. Add onions and red pepper and cook until soft. Add in garlic and cook for additional minute.
- Stir in dry rice, coating in oil and juices from vegetables. Add chicken broth, salt, and saffron. Bring to a boil, reduce heat, and cover. Cook for 10 minutes, until most of the liquid is absorbed by the rice.
- Stir in sausage and peas. Cook an additional 5-10 minutes, until rice is soft and fluffy.
- Remove from heat and stir in paprika. Let cool for 5-10 minutes before serving.

256. Salmon Cakes

Serving: Serves 10 | Prep: | Cook: | Ready in:

Ingredients

- 12 ounces canned salmon
- 3 egg yolk
- 1/2 teaspoon sea salt
- 1 teaspoon black pepper
- 1/2 teaspoon paprika
- 1 garlic clove, minced
- 1/4 vidalia onion, minced
- 3 tablespoons duck fat, for frying

Direction

- Preheat the oven to bake at 350 degrees.
- Line a baking sheet with parchment paper.
- In a large mixing bowl, combine the salmon, egg yolks, salt, pepper, and paprika.
- In a mini chop food processor, mince the garlic and onion.
- Pour the garlic and onion into the salmon mixture, and stir to combine all ingredients.
- Using your hands, form the salmon mixture into 2 ounce patties, and place each cake on the parchment lined baking sheet.
- Bake salmon cakes for 15 minutes.
- Remove the cakes from the oven, and heat the duck fat in a cast iron skillet over high heat.
- Fry the cakes for about a minute on either side in the duck fat, or until they are golden brown and crispy on the outside.
- Serve with a squeeze of lemon.

257. Sausage Stuffed Mushrooms

Serving: Serves 2 generously, or 4 daintily | Prep: | Cook: | Ready in:

Ingredients

- 2 portobello mushrooms OR 6 cremini (baby bella) mushrooms
- 3 links raw Italian sausage (sweet or hot)
- Salt and freshly ground black pepper to taste
- Smoked paprika for sprinkling (optional)
- Finely grated Parmesan cheese for sprinkling

Direction

- Preheat oven to 350º F, and line a baking dish or deep-sided baking sheet with aluminum foil. Stem the mushrooms (save the stems–they're edible, and great in soups). Wipe the tops of the mushrooms clean with a damp cloth, and place stem-side up on the foil-lined baking vessel.
- Remove the casing from the sausage links. Distribute the sausage meat evenly into the mushroom caps–a link and a half for each Portobello mushroom, or half a link for each cremini. Pat the sausage meat down lightly to form a solid mass. Sprinkle with salt, pepper, and smoked paprika (if using), then top with Parmesan cheese.
- Bake for 35-40 minutes, until the sausage is cooked through and the juices are bubbling. Remove from the oven and let sit for 5-10 minutes before serving. Transfer the mushrooms to plates, and drizzle over the liquid from the pan. Serve with plenty of crusty bread for mopping up the juices.

258. Savory Lentil And Bok Choi Soup

Serving: Serves 3, give or take, depending on appetites | Prep: | Cook: | Ready in:

Ingredients

- 2 tablespoons olive oil
- 1 small onion, finely chopped
- 1-3 cloves garlic, minced
- 1/2 cup lentils, rinsed
- 4 cups liquid (I used 1-1/2 cups beef bone broth and 2-1/2 cups water
- 4 cups chopped bok choi
- 1/4 teaspoon smoked paprika
- 2 teaspoons Worcestershire sauce
- juice from 1/2 fresh lemon
- salt and pepper to taste

Direction

- In a large skillet, heat the olive oil over medium heat. Add the onion, garlic and lentils and stir to combine. Let cook for about 2 minutes.
- Add the liquid, turn up the heat and bring to a boil. Then lower the heat to a simmer. Add salt and a good grinding of black pepper, the paprika, stir, and cook uncovered for 15 minutes
- Stir in the bok choy. Cook for another 10 minutes and check the lentils for doneness. If still hard, cook for another 5-10 minutes and check again - the goal is to have the lentils be firm but not hard, and still have a good amount of broth.
- When done, add lemon juice and Worcestershire sauce, stir and taste. Adjust seasoning and Worcestershire sauce to taste.
- Enjoy.

259. Savoury Sausage And Butternut Squash Crepes

Serving: Serves 4 | Prep: | Cook: | Ready in:

Ingredients

- Crepe filling
- 1 pound Jimmy Dean's hot pork sausage
- 2 shallots (diced)
- 2 cups butternut squash peeled and cubed
- 1 tablespoon chopped sage
- 1/2 cup cream cheese
- Savoury Crepes
- 1 cup all purpose flour
- 2 eggs
- 1/2 cup whole milk
- 1/2 cup water
- 1/4 teaspoon salt
- 1/2 tablespoon chopped chives
- 1/2 tablespoon chopped parsley
- 1 teaspoon chopped basil
- 1 teaspoon hot paprika

Direction

- Crepe filling
- Cook sausage in skillet with shallots until sausage is completely browned.
- Meanwhile, place peeled and cubed butternut squash in shallow microwaveable bowl with ¼ cup water in the bottom, cover with kitchen towel, and microwave for about 7 minutes.
- Toss butternut squash in with sausage mixture and add sage, cook on medium for about 3 minutes.
- Turn off heat, stir in cream cheese
- Savoury Crepes
- 1. In a food processor, blend eggs, milk, water and butter. Mix salt and flour in small bowl, then add to processor and blend. Next add herbs and paprika and blend one more time.
- Heat a lightly oiled griddle or frying pan over medium high heat. Using ¼ cup to measure, scoop batter into pan for each crepe. Tilt the pan with a circular motion so that the batter coats the surface evenly.
- Cook the crepe for about 2 minutes, until the bottom is light brown. Shake pan and then loosen, then flip and cook until other side is also light brown. Fill with sausage filling and serve (I like to roll them up like burritos!)

260. Seafood Paella

Serving: Serves 4 to 6 people | Prep: | Cook: | Ready in:

Ingredients

- seafood stock
- 2-1/2 quarts water
- 1/2 onion, roughly chopped
- 2 stalks celery, roughly chopped
- 1 bay leaf
- several peppercorns
- paella
- 2 cups short-grain brown rice
- 1/2 cup extra-virgin olive oil
- 12 large shrimp, shells removed to use for stock
- 1 yellow onion, chopped
- 1/2 cup fresh or bottled tomatoes, puréed
- 1 teaspoon kosher salt
- 1 teaspoon turmeric or 1 teaspoon saffron threads
- 1 tablespoon smoked Spanish paprika
- 1 pound calamari steaks, cut into 1-inch pieces
- 1 quart fish stock, made with the leftover shrimp shells
- 1 pound monkfish or cod
- 1 pound fresh clams, scrubbed (discard any clams that don't close when tapped)
- a paellera (paella pan), at least 14 inches in width and 1-3/4 inches in depth

Direction

- (Note: On an electric stove with a standard 7-1/2 inch burner, you may need to adjust the cooking times and heat of each step to compensate for the smaller cooking area of the electric burner. What you want to avoid is either overcooking the seafood or burning the rice, or undercooking and ending up with too much liquid at the end).
- Remove the shells from the shrimp, and refrigerate shrimp until ready to use. Put the shells from the shrimp into a stockpot with 2-1/2 quarts of water. Add 1/2 roughly chopped onion, two chopped celery stalks, one bay leaf and a several peppercorns to the stockpot. Bring to a boil, then reduce heat and simmer for 25 minutes. After 25 minutes remove from the heat and strain the stock using a fine strainer and set aside.
- Put the 2 cups of brown rice and 1 quart of the seafood stock into a rice cooker and steam until most of the stock is consumed. Remove container from the cooker and remove the lid to let the steam escape so rice doesn't get soggy.
- Pour 1/4 cup of extra-virgin olive oil into a paella pan and heat over medium-high heat until shimmering. Add the shrimp and sauté briefly, about a minute on each side, then

remove and set aside. Add the onion to the pan and sauté until softened, about 10 minutes. Stir in the tomatoes and cook 2 minutes more. Mix together the salt, turmeric (or saffron), smoked Spanish paprika in a little dish to blend and stir into the pan with the onions and tomatoes. Add the calamari and cook until it starts to become a little firmer. Pour in the seafood stock, let it come to a boil, and let it cook for 5 minutes. Stir in the brown rice, spreading it evenly over the entire pan. If using monkfish, add it, along with the clams, dropping them evenly over the pan and pushing them down into the rice. If using cod, wait to add it with the shrimp. Let the stock come to a boil again and cook but do not stir for 10 minutes. Adjust the taste for salt, add the shrimp (and cod, if using), placing evenly over the pan and pushing them down into the rice. Let cook, still not stirring, until most of the stock has been absorbed, clams have opened, and fish is cooked. Adjust heat if needed; when done cooking there should be a nicely browned, caramelized crust on the bottom of the paella pan, but it should not be heavily charred or blackened. Remove pan from the heat and let stand until the liquid has completely absorbed, about 10 minutes. Serve immediately.

261. Semi Sweet Potato Mash With Spiced Caramelized Onions

Serving: Serves 10 | Prep: | Cook: |Ready in:

Ingredients

- 4-5 large sweet Vidalia onions, thinly sliced
- 2 1/2 pounds Russet potatoes, peeled and cut into 2 inch chunks
- 3 pounds Sweet potatoes, peeled and cut into 2 inch chunks
- 1/2 teaspoon cumin
- 1/2 teaspoon hot smoked paprika
- 1/4 teaspoon chili powder
- 1/4 teaspoon cayenne pepper (to taste)

Direction

- Sauté the onions over a medium flame, stirring very infrequently. Once they soften and begin to brown, return the flame to low and allow to slowly caramelize. During this time, it is important to make sure the onions are spread as evenly as possible across the pan. Every few minutes, scrape the bottom and redistribute the onions so each gains the maximum amount of surface area. The intention is to slowly crisp the onions by enticing the remaining liquids to sweat out, and for the onions to sweeten by condensing in their own juices. If you stir too often, the onions will turn to mush. This process takes about 40 minutes.
- In the meantime, place the sweet potatoes in a large pot of salted water and bring to a boil over high heat. Cook until tender and drain.
- When the onions are dark brown, but not burnt, add the cumin, paprika, chili powder, cayenne, and season with salt to taste. Set aside.
- When it comes to the mashing, use whatever technique your kitchen affords you. I find that the best texture is achieved by using a food mill. A ricer would work as well, or a masher for a coarser result. Once you've mashed your potato mixture, season with 1/2 to 1 tablespoon of salt, adding a dash of cayenne to give it some heat.
- Pour into a large baking or casserole dish and spread the onions evenly over the top of the pan. TIP: the dish can be stored in the refrigerator for up to two days before serving. To reheat, set the oven to 250 degrees and place the casserole dish inside 30 minutes or so before the meal.

262. Shakshuka

Serving: Serves 4-6 | Prep: | Cook: | Ready in:

Ingredients

- Shakshuka
- 3 tablespoons olive oil
- 28 ounces canned crushed tomatoes
- 9-10 garlic cloves, chopped small
- 1 1/2 tablespoons Pilpelchuma, store bought or recipe below
- 1 tablespoon sweet paprika
- 1/2 teaspoon salt
- 1/4 teaspoon cumin
- 1/4 cup cilantro, roughly chopped
- 4-6 eggs
- 1/4 cup feta cheese
- 4-6 warm pitas or grilled crusty bread
- Pilpelchuma
- 1 1/2 tablespoons olive oil
- 1 tablespoon sweet paprika
- 1/2 tablespoon hot paprika
- 1/2 teaspoon cayenne
- 1 pinch cumin
- 1 pinch salt

Direction

- If you can't find store bought Pilpelchuma: Mix ingredients together to form a paste. This will keep for 3 weeks in the fridge.
- Heat the oil in a large skillet or pan with lid over low heat.
- Add the chopped garlic, paprika, cumin, & pilpelchuma to the pan and sauté for 2-3 minutes until fragrant.
- Mix in the canned tomatoes & salt. Cover with lid and simmer for 15 minutes. At this point, you can cool the sauce and store to use another day. Just heat it back up in the same pan and continue from here.
- Add and mix in the cilantro leaving a bit out of the pan to garnish with later.
- Make pockets in the sauce with a wooden spoon or spatula and very carefully crack the eggs into them. Make sure to space the eggs out. There should be sauce in between each egg for them to cook properly (and prettily).
- Immediately cover the pan, turn the heat up a bit to medium and cook without lifting the lid for 5-8 minutes depending on how you like your egg yolks. 5 for runny and 8 for cooked.
- Eat right away while it's piping hot. Sopping up all the sauce with the pita. Enjoy!

263. Shakshuka Spicy Israeli Tomato Stew

Serving: Serves 2 | Prep: | Cook: | Ready in:

Ingredients

- 3 tablespoons olive oil
- 3 Anaheim chiles
- 1 yellow onion
- 1.5 teaspoons cumin, ground
- 28 ounces can of San Marzano tomatoes, whole
- 1 tablespoon paprika
- 5 cloves garlic
- 2 bell peppers, diced
- several slices haloumi cheese
- 4 eggs

Direction

- Heat olive oil over medium heat in a large heavy-bottomed skillet or Dutch oven (make sure there is room for all ingredients!)
- Add diced onion and chopped chiles and cook until softened.
- Add minced garlic, cumin, and paprika and cook for a minute or two while stirring often so as to not burn ingredients.
- Add tomatoes and bell peppers and 1/2 cup water. Slightly crush the tomatoes with the back of a wooden spoon and let simmer until the mixture reduces and thickens, 12-20 minutes depending on heat and preference of texture.

- Gently crack eggs over the surface of the stew. Cover and let poach for several minutes --- baste the whites carefully. Add sliced haloumi cheese and a sprinkle of sea salt before serving.

264. Shakshuka Focaccia

Serving: Serves 8 | Prep: 0hours0mins | Cook: 0hours0mins | Ready in:

Ingredients

- 1 recipe Saltie's Focaccia dough, not cooked: https://food52.com/recipes...
- 3 tablespoons canola oil
- 2 medium yellow onions, chopped
- 1 large green bell pepper, cored, seeded, and chopped
- 1 large jalapeño chile, cored, seeded, and chopped
- 7 garlic cloves, finely chopped
- 1/4 cup tomato paste
- 1 (28-ounce) can crushed tomatoes
- 1 bay leaf
- 1 1/2 tablespoons sugar
- 1 1/2 teaspoons kosher salt
- 1 tablespoon paprika
- 1 tablespoon ground cumin
- 1 1/2 teaspoons freshly ground black pepper
- 1 teaspoon ground caraway
- 8 large eggs

Direction

- At least 8 hours or up to 2 days before you plan to bake, make step 1 of the focaccia recipe—up until the dough rises in the fridge.
- Make the shakshuka. This can be done up to two days before you bake.
- Heat the canola oil in a large skillet. Add the onions and sauté over medium heat until translucent, 5 to 10 minutes. Add the bell peppers and jalapeño and cook just until softened, 3 to 5 minutes. Stir in the garlic and tomato paste and sauté for another 2 minutes.
- Slowly pour in the tomatoes. Stir in the bay leaf, sugar, salt, paprika, cumin, pepper, and caraway and let the mixture simmer for 20 minutes. This mixture can also be made 2 days in advance.
- When you're ready to bake (or the night before brunch), oil an 18 x 13-inch baking sheet. Remove the focaccia dough from the refrigerator and transfer to the prepared pan. Using your hands, spread the dough out on the prepared pan as much as possible, adding oil to the dough as needed to keep it from sticking. Place the dough in a warm place and let it rise until it about doubles in bulk. The rising time will vary considerably depending on the season. (In the summer, it might take just 20 minutes; in winter, it can take an hour or more.) When the dough is ready, it should be room temperature, spread out on the sheet, and fluffy feeling.
- Preheat the oven to 450°F. Use your knuckles to make a well in one corner of the dough. You'll be making eight wells total, so make sure to allow enough space for them all. Add a heaping 1/3 cup shakshuka sauce into the well you've just massaged. Continue until you have 8 sauce-filled wells. Sprinkle with salt.
- Bake the bread for 15 minutes, until the bread is just starting to brown. Crack an egg in a bowl with a spout and gingerly pour the egg into the shakshuka. Repeat with the remaining 7 eggs. Sprinkle the eggs with salt and freshly ground pepper and put the pan back into the oven until the eggs are set, about 5 minutes.
- Allow the bread to cool until you can touch it, then cut into 8 squares.

265. Sheet Pan Chicken And Cauliflower Bake

Serving: Serves 4 to 6 | Prep: 0hours15mins | Cook: 0hours45mins | Ready in:

Ingredients

- Neutral oil, for greasing
- 1 large head cauliflower (about 2.5 lbs pre trimming), cut into florets, large florets halved or quartered if necessary (see photo above as a reference)
- 1 large onion, sliced
- 5 tablespoons olive oil, divided
- Kosher salt and fresh pepper, to taste
- 1 tablespoon whole cumin seeds or ground cumin, see notes above
- 1 tablespoon whole coriander seeds or ground coriander, see notes
- 2 teaspoons smoked paprika
- 1/2 teaspoon cayenne
- 2 cloves garlic, minced
- 6 boneless, skinless chicken thighs, about 1.5 lbs.
- Lemon wedges, flatbread, and yogurt sauce (see notes) for serving

Direction

- Preheat the oven to 425°F and position a rack in the center. Rub a sheet pan with about a teaspoon of neutral oil. Place cauliflower florets and onion on top. Season all over with a teaspoon of kosher salt and pepper to taste, and 3 tablespoons of the oil.
- In a small bowl, stir together the cumin, coriander, smoked paprika, and cayenne. Pour half (about 1 tablespoon and a scant teaspoon) of this mixture over the cauliflower. Use your hands to toss the cauliflower and onions evenly with the oil and spice mix. Transfer pan to the oven and roast for about 30 minutes, tossing once after about 20 minutes.
- Meanwhile, place chicken thighs in a large bowl. Season all over with salt (at least another teaspoon). Add the remaining spice mix, remaining 2 tablespoons of oil, and minced garlic. Toss to coat. Let sit at room temperature while vegetables roast.
- Remove the sheet pan from the oven. Toss everything around. Nestle the thighs around the vegetables. Return pan to the oven and cook for 10 minutes — if thighs are large, they may need 5 more minutes or so. Cut into one to check. Remove pan from the oven and let everything rest on the sheet pan for 10 minutes.
- Meanwhile, stir together the yogurt sauce, warm up some bread, cut the lemons, etc. When chicken has rested, transfer it to a platter to cut or cut directly on the sheet pan, taking care not to ruin your pan. The chicken should be in 1- to 2-inch cubes or so — about the same size as the cauliflower. Return chicken to sheet pan or to a serving platter along with the cauliflower. Toss everything together. Taste. Adjust with more salt and pepper if necessary and squeeze a lemon over everything, if desired. To serve, spread flatbread with yogurt sauce, nestle chicken and cauliflower inside, and eat taco-style. Alternatively, serve the flatbread on the side and eat with a knife and fork. Serve lemon wedges on the side.

266. Sherried Potatoes Au Gratin

Serving: Serves 12 | Prep: | Cook: | Ready in:

Ingredients

- 10 cups Potatoes (approximately 6 large russets)
- 4 tablespoons Butter
- 4 tablespoons Flour
- 2 cups Milk (either whole or 2%)
- 1 teaspoon Salt
- 1 teaspoon Pepper
- 2 cups Grated Sharp Cheddar Cheese (for sauce)
- 1/2 cup Sherry
- 2/3 cup Grated Sharp Cheddar Cheese (for topping)
- dash Paprika for topping

Direction

- Preheat oven to 350
- Peel potatoes & chop into cubes. Boil for 10 minutes.
- In separate saucepan, melt butter. Once melted, add flour & whisk until it forms a paste. Then add milk, salt & pepper; whisk until smooth. Cook over medium heat until sauce thickens, whisking as needed. Once the sauce is thick, add 2 cups grated cheese and stir with spoon until melted. Remove from heat & stir in sherry
- Drain potatoes & place in large oval casserole dish. Pour sauce over potatoes. Sprinkle 2/3 cup cheese over top. Sprinkle with paprika. Bake covered for 30 minutes.
- For Thanksgiving, you can prepare this dish the night before & wait to bake them until Thanksgiving Day. Just double the cooking time, since it's cold from the fridge.

267. Short Rib & Pumpkin Chili

Serving: Serves 8 | Prep: 0hours30mins | Cook: 4hours0mins | Ready in:

Ingredients

- 2 tablespoons chili powder
- 1 tablespoon ground coriander
- 2 teaspoons ground cumin
- 1 teaspoon dried oregano (preferably Mexican)
- 1 teaspoon dried thyme
- 1 teaspoon hot Spanish pimentón (or other hot, smoked paprika)
- 3 tablespoons vegetable oil
- 5 pounds short ribs (bone-in, or 3 pounds boneless)
- 1 large sweet onion, diced
- 2 cloves garlic, minced
- 1/4 cup gochujang (Korean chili paste)*
- 2 tablespoons tomato paste
- 1 tablespoon soy sauce
- 1/2 teaspoon Maggi seasoning (or 1 teaspoon Worcestershire sauce)
- 2 12-ounce bottles oatmeal stout beer
- 1/2 cup espresso (or strong coffee)
- 1 ounce unsweetened chocolate (or 1 tablespoon unsweetened powdered chocolate)
- 1 tablespoon masa harina (or corn meal) mixed into 1/2 cup hot water
- 1 28-ounce can crushed tomatoes
- 1 15.5-ounce can black beans
- 3 cups more or less cubed, peeled cooking pumpkin (1/2-inch cubes). Can substitute butternut squash.
- 1 tablespoon brown sugar
- Salt
- Freshly ground black pepper
- Hot sauce of choice, jalapeño rings, sour cream/Mexican creme, shredded cheese, chopped cilantro (for garnish)

Direction

- *In place of gochujang, you can use another Asian chili paste, or use the peppers from a can of chipotles en adobo: Finely chop 2 of the chipotles and mix together with 1 tablespoon of the adobo sauce. It's a totally different flavor profile but more common to find.
- Combine the chili powder, ground coriander, ground cumin, dried oregano, dried thyme, and pimentón (smoked paprika) in a small bowl.
- Season the ribs with salt and pepper.
- Heat the oil in a large Dutch oven or large ovenproof braising pan over medium-high heat. Working in batches as needed, brown the ribs, transferring them to a platter as they are done.
- Preheat oven to 400° F.
- Add the onions to the oil, stirring to coat and scraping the pan to release any browned bits from the searing. Cook for about 4 minutes, until lightly browned, then add the garlic; cook for about 30 seconds, then stir in the gochujang, tomato paste, soy sauce, Maggi seasoning, and the chili powder-spice mixture.

Cook for about 1 minute, then stir in 1 1/2 bottles of the beer into the chili; drink the other half of the second bottle. (A total of 16 to 18 ounces of beer should end up in the chili.) Add the coffee, chocolate, masa harina, and tomatoes. Add the seared ribs and cook, stirring a few times, until the mixture reaches a brisk simmer. Transfer the covered pot to the oven and cook for 3 1/2 hours or until the meat is tender and falling apart.

- Stir pumpkin, black beans, and brown sugar into the chili. Continue cooking until the pumpkin is tender, about 30 minutes. Remove from the oven. Remove the ribs from the pan and allow to cool enough to handle. Remove meat from ribs (if using bone-in ribs). The meat should be fall-apart tender. Discard bones or save them for your dog. Using two forks, coarsely shred the meat and return to the chili. Season to taste with salt.
- Spoon chili into bowls and garnish with hot sauce, shredded cheese, sour cream, jalapeno rings, and cilantro (or some combination thereof, depending on tastes).

268. Short Ribs Braised In Red Wine And Vanilla

Serving: Serves 4 | Prep: 0hours0mins | Cook: 0hours0mins | Ready in:

Ingredients

- 4 beef short ribs
- 1 tablespoon kosher salt
- 1 pinch black pepper for seasoning meat
- 4 cloves garlic, peeled and thinly sliced
- 1 tablespoon extra-virgin olive oil
- 1 tablespoon balsamic vinegar
- 1 handful fresh herbs like thyme, rosemary, tarragon, sage (no need to remove from stems)
- 1/2 lemon, thinly sliced (remove seeds)
- 3 anchovy fillets, packed in oil
- 1 tablespoon tomato paste
- 2 teaspoons good quality vanilla extract
- 1 teaspoon paprika
- 1 tablespoon vegetable oil
- 1 yellow onion, diced
- 2 cups red wine, more to taste
- 1 pinch Parsley and cilantro for garnish

Direction

- Generously season the short ribs with salt and pepper. Place in a bowl or a zip-top bag. Whisk together garlic, olive oil, balsamic, whole herbs, and lemon. Use your hands to smash the marinade into the meat. Store in the fridge for a few hours or overnight.
- Remove short ribs form the fridge and heat oven to 250°F. Discard the herbs and lemon slices. Reserve the marinade. With a mortar and pestle, make a paste out of garlic from the marinade, anchovies, tomato paste, vanilla extract, and paprika. Set aside.
- Place a large ovenproof pot over high heat. Add vegetable oil. When it's just starting to smoke, place short ribs in the pan. No need to jiggle or shift the meat around. Just let them do their thing. After 2 minutes, take a peek. When the meat is a gorgeous dark brown, turn to sear on the other side. Remove from pan and set aside. Pour off excess oil, leaving a small splash for the onions you'll sauté next.
- Turn heat down to medium. Add the diced onion. Use a wooden spoon and the onions to get all of the meat goodies up off of the bottom of the pot. Once the onions are soft and translucent, turn the heat down to low and add the garlic/anchovy/paprika purée. Stir for a minute. Add wine and reserved marinade. Add ribs. Bring to a boil. Turn off the heat. Put on the lid and place in the preheated oven. The ribs don't have to be completely immersed in the liquid, just flip them every hour or so to make sure they get some love from the wine.
- Depending on the size of the ribs, they can take anywhere from 4 to 6 hours to become fall-off-the-bone tender. Sometimes a bit longer.

- When the ribs are tender and feel about ready to slide off the bone, take the meat out and reserve on a plate. Taste the sauce. Add salt if needed, or a splash of balsamic. Or a bit more vanilla. Using your hands, slide meat off of the bones and place back into the sauce. Pick out any large pieces of fat that are unappealing (small ones will melt into the braise). Shred the meat as best you can.
- Serve over polenta or quinoa. Garnish with chopped cilantro and parsley.

269. Shrimp Cooked In Smoked Sausage And Roasted Red Bell Pepper Jam Sauce

Serving: Serves 4 | Prep: | Cook: | Ready in:

Ingredients

- For the Red Bell Pepper Jam (makes 1 full cup)
- • 4 meaty red bell peppers+ 1 red jalapeño pepper washed, halved, seeds and membranes removed
- • 1 large garlic clove, peeled and diced
- • 1/3 cup brown sugar
- • 1/4 cup sherry vinegar
- • 1/4 cup soy sauce
- For the Smoked Sausage and Red Bell Pepper Jam sauce
- • 1 tablespoon olive oil
- • 4 ounces any good quality smoked sausage, roughly chopped
- • 2 garlic cloves, minced
- • 1 medium shallot, diced
- • 1 teaspoon toasted cumin
- • 1 teaspoon smoked paprika
- • A pinch cayenne pepper
- • 1 cup clam juice or homemade fish stock from shrimp shells and tails
- • 1/2 cup Red Bell Pepper jam
- • 2 tablespoons butter
- • 20 Wild Jumbo Shrimp, peeled and deveined, (if making your own fish stock), shells reserved
- • 4 organic extra-large eggs for serving, fried or poached(optional)

Direction

- For the Red Bell Pepper Jam (makes 1 full cup)
- Preheat your broiler. Place only the bell pepper halves (leave the jalapeno raw), cut-side down on a baking sheet; spray with cooking spray the skins of the peppers; transfer to the upper rack of the oven and broil until the skins are charred and peppers soften, about 25 to 30 minutes.
- Cool slightly and then peel. Place the roasted peppers, jalapeño, garlic and brown sugar in the bowl of a food processor and puree until smooth.
- Transfer the mixture to a saucepan and heat over medium-high; add sherry vinegar, soy sauce and 1/4 cup water; bring to a boil. Cook, stirring often, until the liquid has evaporated and the peppers have a jam-like consistency, 25 to 30 minutes. Cool and refrigerate. Can be made 1 week in advance.
- For the Smoked Sausage and Red Bell Pepper Jam sauce
- To a sauté pan over medium heat, add the olive oil and sweat the sausage until the fat starts to render, about 2 minutes. Then add the garlic and shallots. Cook until fragrant, about 1 minute. Add the cumin, smoked paprika and cayenne pepper and cook stirring for about 1-2 minutes more.
- Deglaze with clam juice or homemade fish stock and add the red bell pepper jam. Allow to reduce by about 3/4. Finish with the butter and keep warm until ready to serve or cool and refrigerate. Can be made 1 day ahead.
- When ready to serve, add the shrimp and cook for about 2 minutes per side. Fry or poach the eggs according to your preference. Serve hot over Polenta or Grits and top with the fried egg. Garnish with some more of the Red Bell Pepper Jam.

270. Shrimp Tacos With Corn Salsa

Serving: Serves 3 | Prep: | Cook: | Ready in:

Ingredients

- Corn Salsa
- 1/2 tablespoon canola oil
- 1/2 red onion, peeled and chopped
- 1 poblano pepper, seeded and chopped
- Kernals from 2 ears of corn
- 2 tablespoons finely chopped cilantro
- Juice of half a lime
- 1/4 teaspoon salt
- Shrimp Tacos
- 1 tablespoon ground cumin
- 1 tablespoon paprika
- 3/4 teaspoon salt
- 1 pound peeled and deveined shrimp with tails removed
- 1 tablespoon canola oil
- 1 large avocado, halved, pitted, peeled, and mashed
- Juice of half a lime
- 1 tablespoon finely chopped cilantro
- 6 corn tortillas, warmed

Direction

- Corn Salsa
- To make the corn salsa, heat canola oil over medium heat in a large nonstick skillet. Add onion and pepper and sauté for 5 to 7 minutes; add corn and sauté 2 additional minutes or until all veggies are tender. Remove from heat and stir in cilantro, lime juice, and salt.
- Shrimp Tacos
- To make the shrimp, mix cumin, paprika, and 1/2 teaspoon salt in a small bowl and evenly rub into shrimp. Heat canola oil over medium heat in a nonstick skillet and sauté shrimp for 2 to 3 minutes or until pink and cooked through.
- To make the avocado spread, mix the mashed avocados, lime juice, cilantro and remaining 1/4 teaspoon salt in a medium bowl until smooth.
- To assemble the tacos, evenly cover the corn tortillas with the avocado spread. Top evenly with shrimp and corn salsa. Makes 3 servings.

271. Shrimp And "grits" With Kahlua Bacon Jam

Serving: Serves 4 | Prep: | Cook: | Ready in:

Ingredients

- For Kahlua Bacon Jam:
- 8 bacon strips
- 1 cup finely diced onion
- 2/3 cup diced tomatoes
- 4 garlic cloves
- 1 tablespoon balsamic vinegar
- 1 tablespoon brown sugar
- 1 teaspoon paprika
- 1 teaspoon chili powder
- 1 cup kahlua
- For shrimp and grits
- 1.5 pounds fresh shrimp (with heads and peel)
- 1 cup creme of wheat
- 2 tablespoons cooking sherry

Direction

- Cook the bacon on a frying pan until brown and crisp. Set aside on paper towel to blot out grease. Cut bacon into small pieces or tear it with your hands.
- Caramelize onion over medium heat (this takes about 8 minutes) until onion is soft and brown and sweet to taste.
- Add garlic and tomatoes. Season with vinegar, brown sugar, paprika and chili powder. Simmer for another 8 minutes for all the flavors to mix. Add kahlua and stir mixture. It will slowly thicken over 3 minutes.

- Add bacon bits and stir around. Simmer for 3 minutes until jam is thick and caramelized.
- Add cooking wine to shrimp in the pan. Pan sear shrimp with canola oil for 2-5 minutes, until shrimp turns pink throughout (that can happen very fast). Salt and pepper to taste.
- Add bacon jam to shrimp and mix thoroughly on low heat, for 1 minute. Turn heat off.
- In a separate pot, boil 3-4 cups of water. When water is boiled, add cream of wheat bit by bit and stir constantly. Keep stirring while water is boiling for 4 minutes until cream of wheat has thickened into almost a paste. Turn heat to low, simmer cream of wheat for another 4 minutes while stirring occasionally. It should thicken some more. Turn off heat when you're happy with the consistency.
- Serve bacon jammed shrimp over cream of wheat. Enjoy every bite!

272. Shrimp And Grits By Way Of Spain

Serving: Serves 4 | Prep: | Cook: | Ready in:

Ingredients

- Polenta
- 1 cup Coarse corn meal
- 2 cups milk (or cream)
- 2 + 1 cups water
- 1 teaspoon kosher salt
- 2 tablespoons butter
- 1/2 cup parmesan (optional)
- Shrimp
- 1 pound shrimp, peeled and deveined
- 3 teaspoons dried oregano
- 1.5 teaspoons smoked paprika
- 1 pinch cayenne
- 1 teaspoon dried roasted garlic (I realize this is an esoteric spice, you can substitute 1/4 teaspoon garlic powder or for a stronger flavor 2 crushed cloves of garlic)
- 1/2 cup fire roasted tomatoes, diced
- 1 tablespoon white wine
- 1 ounce jamon serrano chopped in to 1" bits
- 2 green onions sliced, green and white parts
- 2 tablespoons chopped parsley
- 1 tablespoon olive oil

Direction

- Preheat the oven to 350.
- Combine the milk, water and salt and bring to a boil. Whisk in the cornmeal and let simmer for 30-40 minutes, whisking often. Keep the extra cup or so of water warm on a burner and add as needed to loosen the polenta while cooking.
- Heat a cast iron skillet on the stove over a medium heat, add the jamon and cook until crispy. Remove from pan and set aside.
- Toss the shrimp in a bowl with 1 tablespoon of olive oil and the oregano, paprika, cayenne and garlic. Place the shrimp in the seasoned cast iron skillet and cook in the oven for 4 minutes. Remove. Turn the oven up to 450. Turn the shrimp over in the pan, add in the tomatoes and the wine. Return the pan to the oven for 5 more minutes.
- About 5 minutes prior to serving, whisk the butter into the polenta. If cheese is desired, whisk that in as well.
- Spoon the polenta in to bowls, spoon the shrimp mixture on top and sprinkle with the jamon, parsley and green onions.

273. Shrimp, Avocado & Orange Salad

Serving: Serves 2 | Prep: | Cook: | Ready in:

Ingredients

- Make the Salad
- 1 Ripe avocado, chopped
- 1 Naval (seedless) orange, sectioned and chopped
- 1/4 cup Red onion, minced

- 1/2 cup Grape tomatoes, sliced in half
- 1/3 cup Nicoise olives, pitted and chopped
- 2/3 cup Baby arugula
- Juice of 1/2 a lemon
- 2 tablespoons Sherry vinegar
- 1/4 teaspoon Ground cumin
- 1/4 teaspoon Smoked paprika
- 1/2 teaspoon Salt
- 2 - 4 tablespoons Extra virgin olive oil
- Prepare the shrimp
- 8-12 Medium shrimp, peeled and deveined (quantity depends on appetite)
- 2 tablespoons Extra virgin olive oil
- 2 Cloves garlic, minced
- 1 tablespoon Grated lemon peel
- 1/4 cup Parsley, chopped

Direction

- Make the Salad
- Place the avocado, orange, onion, grape tomatoes, olives, pine nuts and arugula in a large bowl. Add the lemon juice and toss very gently to combine. Set aside and make the vinaigrette
- In a small bowl combine the sherry vinegar, cumin, paprika and salt. Gradually whisk in the olive oil. Set aside.
- Prepare the shrimp
- Heat the olive oil in a heavy bottomed skillet over medium heat
- Add the garlic and sauté for 1 minute
- Add the shrimp and sea salt and sauté until no longer pink (about 3-4 minutes)
- Add the lemon zest and toss. Remove from heat
- Remove from pan and allow the shrimp to cool for 5 minutes
- Once the shrimp has cooled, add to the avocado and orange salad along with the vinaigrette and the parsley. Toss gently to combine. Serve with warm bread and white wine

274. Simple Company Posole

Serving: Serves 8 | Prep: | Cook: | Ready in:

Ingredients

- 3 pounds salt and pepper seasoned browned pork butt cubes, about 2 inch pieces or a leaner cut if you prefer
- 1 onion ¼ inch dice, sautéed in pan after pork
- 10 ounces salsa verde (I've used green enchilada sauce)
- 10 ounces 1/4 inch diced roasted green chiles
- 1 (28 ounce) can of hominy, drained
- 4 garlic cloves minced
- 1 teaspoon cumin, heaping teaspoon
- 1/8 teaspoon smoked paprika
- 1/3 cup New Mexico chile powder
- 32 ounces chicken stock or broth
- salt and pepper to taste

Direction

- Place browned cubed pork, 3 lbs. in a slow cooker with onions, hominy, oregano, garlic, chile powder, cumin, paprika, chicken broth, and roasted chiles. Slow cook for 6-8 hours (until the pork is fork tender), checking the moisture level in case you need to add more stock.
- Serve with Cornbread and garnishes of red sliced radishes, lime wedges, red or white onions, fresh cilantro, crushed chile pequin and chile pequin entero (really hot), and a mix of sliced red and green cabbage
- I forgot to mention that I season the pork with some of the seasonings and marinate overnight. Deglaze the meat and onion pan with 1/4 cup tequila

275. Simple Turkish Eggs

Serving: Serves 1 | Prep: | Cook: | Ready in:

Ingredients

- 2 eggs
- 1/4 cup natural, full fat yoghurt
- 1/2 small garlic glove, crushed
- 1 teaspoon lemon zest (finely grated)
- 1 big pinch of salt (to taste)
- 1/2 teaspoon sweet paprika
- 1 tablespoon butter
- few baby mint leaves (optional)

Direction

- Melt butter over gentle heat until foamy, stir in paprika and turn off heat.
- Make yoghurt sauce by combining yoghurt with salt, garlic and lemon zest.
- Gently fry 2 eggs in a splash of olive oil, until done to your liking. I like my yolks slightly runny.
- Warm your pita briefly in a pan, dollop yoghurt sauce in the center of the pita and smooth with the back of the spoon. Lay the 2 eggs over the sauce and drizzle on paprika butter. Sprinkle on some little mint leaves (if using).

276. Simple, Perfect Poached Eggs

Serving: Serves 1 | Prep: | Cook: | Ready in:

Ingredients

- 1 egg
- 1 teaspoon white vinegar
- Pinch Salt, pepper, and paprika

Direction

- Set a timer for 4 minutes (but do not start it yet) and put your toast in the toaster, ready to start but not yet toasting. Crack an egg into a small bowl and set aside.
- Bring a small pot of water to boil. Once a full boil is achieved, add in the teaspoon of vinegar. Swirl the water into a whirlpool with a spoon.
- Gently, but quickly, slide the egg into the swirling water. Immediately move the pot from the heat and cover. Hit "go" on your 4 minute timer and pop the toast into the toaster.
- After 4 minutes, remove the egg with a slotted spoon. Dab lightly with a paper towel, and transfer to a small serving bowl. Cut the toast into small slices for dipping. Sprinkle the egg with salt, pepper, and paprika. Enjoy!

277. Slightly Exotic Skillet Broccoli And Cauliflower

Serving: Serves 6 to 8 | Prep: | Cook: | Ready in:

Ingredients

- 7 tablespoons extra-virgin olive oil, divided
- 1 large onion, thinly sliced (pole to pole)
- 1 head of cauliflower, trimmed and separated into florets, large florets cut in halves
- 1 head of romanesco or broccoli, trimmed and separated into florets, large florets cut in halves
- 3/4 teaspoon red pepper flakes
- 3 medium cloves garlic, coarsely chopped, and divided
- Freshly ground black pepper
- 1 teaspoon brine from preserved lemons
- 1 preserved lemon, rinsed
- 12 to 15 Castelvetrano olives, pitted and coarsely chopped
- 2 small to medium red peppers, roasted, seeded, peeled, and diced
- 1 tablespoon Sherry vinegar
- 1/2 teaspoon ground cumin
- 1/2 teaspoon smoked paprika
- 2 to 3 tablespoons cilantro leaves (or substitute Italian parsley)

Direction

- Heat 3 tablespoons of olive oil in a 12-inch cast iron or other non-stick skillet over medium-high until shimmering. Add sliced onions and cook, stirring frequently, until softened and starting to brown, about 5 minutes. Add cauliflower and Romanesco/broccoli, and evenly distribute in a single layer. (The pan should be crowded, but if you cannot create a single layer remove a few florets.) Take a minute to wiggle each piece into place to get some surface contact on each floret. Turn the heat down to medium-low. Sprinkle the red pepper flakes and all but 1/2 teaspoon of the chopped garlic over the brassicas. Season with ground black pepper, and sprinkle on the brine from the preserved lemons. Set a timer for 25 minutes.
- While the brassicas are cooking, prep your lemon and make your dressing. Quarter the preserved lemon, and use a spoon to scrape out the pulp. Remove the seeds from the pulp and put the pulp in your blender. Coarsely chop one quarter of the peel, and add it to the blender. Dice the remaining peel and set aside. To the blender add the reserved chopped garlic, all but 1 heaping tablespoon of the diced red pepper, sherry vinegar, cumin, and paprika. Blend until smooth. Scrape down the sides of the blender jar, then while running slowly pour in the remaining olive oil. Taste and add a splash or two more of vinegar if the dressing isn't tangy enough. Set aside. (NOTE: This step could also be done ahead, just re-blend dressing prior to serving if any separation has occurred.)
- After your timer has gone off, check a couple of florets for caramelization. If needed, cook an additional 5 or so minutes. Otherwise scatter the reserved red pepper, diced preserved lemon, and chopped olives over the brassicas. Cover the pan and allow to steam for 5 to 10 minutes as needed to cook the florets through, but still maintain some texture.
- Transfer to a serving platter. Garnish with cilantro just before serving. Drizzle with dressing, and serve the rest on the side. (Note: The brassicas will be under-seasoned without the dressing.)

278. Slow Cooker Stout Beef Stew

Serving: Serves 6 to 8 people | Prep: | Cook: | Ready in:

Ingredients

- 4 pounds ~ 1 inch cubed beef chuck at room temerature
- 3 medium sliced onlions
- 3 large carrots, cut on the bias
- 4 cloves of garlic, diced
- 2 teaspoons beef stock paste
- 2 tablespoons cumin
- 2 tablespoons corriender powder
- 1 tablespoon good smoked paprika
- 3 teaspoons of salt (or to taste)
- pepper to taste
- 0.5 cups currants
- 2 cups good dark stout (I used Stone Imperial Russian Stout)
- 1 cup water

Direction

- Seasoning mix: In a mixing bowl mix together the cumin, coriander, salt, pepper and paprika. Veggie mix: In a mixing bowl mix together the onions, carrots and currants. Add a third of the veggie mix on the bottom of the slow cooker insert. Add a third of the seasoning mix on top of the veggie mix. Add half of the beef on top of that. Add the 2nd third of the seasoning and the veggie mix on top of the beef (you get the idea here). Add the rest of the beef and top the beef with the seasoning and veggie mix. Poor the stout and the water on the sides of the slow cooker insert. Add the beef paste. Cover the slow cooker insert. Turn on the slow cooker on high and set your timer for 8 hours. After that enjoy!!!

279. Slow Roasted Lemon Chicken

Serving: Serves 4 to 6 | Prep: 3hours15mins | Cook: 5hours10mins | Ready in:

Ingredients

- For the rub mixture:
- 2 tablespoons salt
- 1 tablespoon black pepper
- 2 tablespoons granulated garlic
- 2 teaspoons dried basil
- 2 teaspoons dried oregano
- 1/4 teaspoon dried thyme
- For the chicken:
- 1 4- to 5-pound whole chicken
- 1 lemon, halved
- 2 tablespoons olive oil
- 3 tablespoons rub mixture (see above)
- 1 teaspoon sweet paprika
- 8 garlic cloves (up to 10)
- 2 tablespoons flour (optional)
- 2 cups chicken broth (optional)

Direction

- In a small bowl, combine all of the ingredients for the rub mixture until mixed well. Set aside.
- Wash and dry the chicken and rub all over with the juice of both lemon halves, reserving one used half.
- Rub the chicken with the olive oil.
- Sprinkle the rub mixture and the paprika all over the chicken and pat in a bit.
- Place the garlic cloves and reserved half lemon inside the chicken cavity. Cover and refrigerate for 1 to 3 hours.
- Roast the chicken for 5 hours (yep, that's right) at 250º F (that's right, too). After 1 hour, the chicken will start exuding some juice. Tip the chicken to drain juices from the cavity and baste with a brush. Do this every 45 minutes while the chicken is roasting.
- After 5 hours, remove the chicken and serve. Optional: Make a pan sauce in the roasting pan by adding the chicken broth and flour until thickened. Scrape up the fond in the bottom of the pan into the sauce. Sometimes I remove the garlic cloves and mash them into the sauce. Pour the sauce over the chicken to serve. This sauce is purely optional, but is wonderful on the chicken.

280. Smoked Cauliflower Soup

Serving: Serves 4 | Prep: | Cook: | Ready in:

Ingredients

- 4 cups Cauliflower florets, about 1 pound, 2" pieces
- 2 Garlic cloves
- Extra virgin olive oil
- Kosher salt
- Ground black pepper
- 3/4 teaspoon Smoked paprika
- 2 cups White onion, 1 large, 1/2" dice
- 4 cups Vegetable stock, divided
- 1/2 cup Smoked gouda cheese, grated, about 3 oz
- 1 tablespoon Sherry vinegar
- Fresh thyme, garnish

Direction

- Preheat the oven to 450 degrees.
- Toss the cauliflower and garlic with 2 tablespoons of olive oil, ½ teaspoon each of salt and pepper and the smoked paprika. Place on a rimmed sheet tray and roast for 15 minutes.
- In a heavy bottom pot sauté the onions with 1 tablespoon of olive oil and a ¼ teaspoon each of salt and pepper, over medium low heat. Cook until the onions just begin to take on a little color.
- Add the roasted cauliflower, garlic and 3 cups of stock to the onions. Bring to a boil, lower

the heat and cover the pot. Simmer for 10 minutes.
- Remove the lid and allow it to cool for 5 minutes. Using an immersion (stick) or regular blender, puree until smooth. Add the cheese and vinegar and blend until combined.
- If needed use the last cup of stock to thin out your soup as desired.
- Taste for seasoning and ladle in to bowls. Garnish with a little thyme and a drizzle of a good fruity olive oil.

281. Smokin' Chicken Noodle

Serving: Serves 6 to 8 | Prep: | Cook: | Ready in:

Ingredients

- 1 roasted chicken, cut into pieces
- 1 chicken sausage link (sweet Italian)
- 3 large carrots, sliced
- 1 large onion, chopped
- 3 to 4 garlic cloves, whole
- 1/2 fennel bulb, chopped
- 2 tablespoons smoked paprika (sweet)
- 1 to 2 dried chipotle peppers
- 1 teaspoon fennel pollen (optional)
- salt and pepper to taste
- 2 tablespoons fresh cilantro, chopped fine
- 1/2 pound pappardelle noodles
- 1 quart prepared chicken stock (may be added to fresh stock)
- 2 tablespoons olive oil

Direction

- In a stock pot, heat olive oil and sauté (sweat) vegetables, stirring for about 2 minutes. Add sausage link (casing removed), and cook meat until lightly browned.
- Add 3 quarts of water to the stock pot (1 quart of prepared chicken stock may be substituted for a quart of the water.) Add chicken pieces, paprika, garlic, dried peppers. Simmer over low heat for 2 hours or longer.
- With a slotted spoon, remove chicken pieces and bones from the stock. Cut chicken into small pieces and reserve.
- Turn heat up on soup, add noodles and cook until noodles are tender. Add chicken pieces back into pot. Get out a ladle. Get ready to serve. Hot!

282. Smoky Black Bean Burgers On Potato Buns

Serving: Serves 3 | Prep: | Cook: | Ready in:

Ingredients

- For the Burger Patties & Mayonnaise
- 1 tablespoon flaxseed meal
- 2,5 tablespoons water
- 250 grams cooked black beans
- 30 grams almond meal
- 1 tablespoon cilantro
- 1 tablespoon parsley
- 7 grams garlic, minced
- 30 grams red onion, minced
- 0.5 teaspoons paprika powder
- 1 teaspoon cumin powder
- 1/2 teaspoon salt
- 1/2 teaspoon black pepper
- 125 milliliters sunflower oil
- 1 teaspoon cider vinegar
- 1/4 teaspoon salt
- 1 tablespoon dijon mustard
- 8 grams flax seed meal
- 30 milliliters water
- For the Potato Buns & Burger Fillings
- 400 grams mashed potatoes
- 44 grams gluten-free flour
- 1/4 teaspoon salt
- 1 tablespoon mustard
- 1 piece Non-stick cooking spray
- 30 grams romaine lettuce
- 120 grams tomatoes

Direction

- For the Burger Patties & Mayonnaise
- Combine flaxseed meal and water in a bowl. Leave for 5 minutes.
- Combine the flaxseed mix with half of the black beans, cilantro, parsley, garlic, red onion, salt, pepper, cumin, and paprika in a food processor and pulse into a smooth paste.
- Combine this pureed mix with the remaining black beans, cilantro, and parsley.
- Form into patties about 100-110 grams each.
- Pan-fry in a non-stick skillet for 3-5 minutes per side.
- For the Flaxseed Mayonnaise: Combine flaxseed meal and water in a large bowl. Leave for 5 minutes.
- Add the mustard and cider vinegar. Whisk to combine.
- In a thin steady stream, gradually whisk in the sunflower oil.
- Season with salt and pepper.
- For the Potato Buns & Burger Fillings
- Combine mashed potatoes, flour, salt, and mustard in a bowl.
- Form into buns about 75 grams each.
- Pan-fry in a non-stick pan for 3-4 minutes each side.
- Drain on paper towels.
- Assemble the Burgers: Serve the patties on potato buns.
- Add a dollop of flaxseed mayo, some fresh romaine lettuce, and tomato slices.

283. Smoky Chipotle Aioli

Serving: Makes 1 cup | Prep: | Cook: |Ready in:

Ingredients

- 1 large egg yolk, preferably from organic eggs
- 1 tablespoon sherry vinegar
- 1 clove (smoked) garlic, mashed or passed through a garlic press
- 3/4 cup grapeseed oil
- 1/4 cup olive oil
- 1-2 chipotle peppers in adobo sauce, finely chopped plus 1-2 tablespoons of the adobo sauce
- Kosher salt, to taste
- Smoked paprika powder, to garnish

Direction

- Rinse a stainless steel bowl with hot water and then dry with kitchen tissues. Put the egg yolk, sherry vinegar, mashed garlic and a tiny pinch of salt in the clean bowl.
- Using a large balloon whisk, whisk as you gently pour in the grape seed oil in a thin stream. The mixture will thicken and lighten in color as you whisk. Once the grape seed oil is finished, continue with the olive oil till exhausted.
- Fold in the chopped chipotle and add the adobo sauce. Gently combine till color is uniform and peachy pink with smoky red chunks. Check for salt and adjust to taste.
- Refrigerate till ready to use. To serve, sprinkle with a pinch of smoked paprika powder. Enjoy.

284. Smoky Delicata Bites

Serving: Serves 4 as an appetizer | Prep: | Cook: |Ready in:

Ingredients

- 2 Delicata squash
- Salt and pepper to taste
- 1 tablespoon Smoked paprika or more to taste
- 1 tablespoon Olive oil

Direction

- Preheat oven to 400. Cut the squashes in half, scoop out seeds, then cut in 1/2 inch thick slices.
- Toss slices with olive oil, then salt, pepper, and smoked paprika. Arrange on baking sheet

and roast till tender, 10-15 minutes. Serve hot or warm.

285. Smoky Gazpacho

Serving: Serves 4-6 | Prep: | Cook: | Ready in:

Ingredients

- 1 red bell pepper
- 1 Fresno chile
- 2 pounds ripe red tomatoes (roughly chopped, juices retained)
- 1/2 cucumber (peeled and seeded)
- 1/2 small red onion (peeled and roughly chopped)
- 2/3 cup roughly chopped smoked almonds (divided)
- 1 (1-inch thick) slice stale Italian bread (torn into 1-inch pieces)
- 3 tablespoons sherry vinegar
- 2 clove garlic (peeled and chopped)
- 1/2 teaspoon smoked paprika (or more to taste)
- 1/4 teaspoon smoked sea salt (can substitute standard sea salt)
- 1/4 teaspoon freshly cracked black pepper
- 1/2 cup extra-virgin olive oil (plus more for drizzling)
- 18 slices Spanish dry-cured chorizo
- chopped flat leaf parsley (to taste)

Direction

- Roast the peppers: Char the bell pepper and Fresno chile by laying them, one at a time, directly over a gas flame, turning occasionally with tongs until blackened on all sides. Place them in a medium bowl, cover, set aside until cool; rub off the blackened skin, remove stems and seeds, then roughly chop.
- Prepare the gazpacho: Place roasted red bell pepper, roasted fresno chile, tomatoes and their juice, cucumber, onion, half the smoked almonds, bread, sherry vinegar, garlic, smoked paprika, smoked salt and pepper in a blender. Process until as smooth as you like, adding a splash of water if necessary to achieve the proper consistency. It should move freely in the blender, but not be watery (add one ingredient at a time and blend before adding another if all the ingredients don't initially fit).
- Once all the ingredients are smooth, drizzle in the olive oil with the machine running until fully incorporated and emulsified.
- Taste and adjust the seasoning. Refrigerate at least 2 hours to allow the flavors to come together.
- To serve: Just before serving, Heat a large cast iron or non-stick skillet over medium-high heat. Add the chorizo slices and cook until they begin to curl at the edges and brown. Flip them over and cook until browned on the other side.
- Serve the chilled gazpacho in shallow soup bowl, garnished with chorizo slices, remaining chopped smoked almonds, parsley and a drizzle of very good olive oil.

286. Smoky Harvest Tomato Soup With Mozzarella Crostini

Serving: Serves 6 | Prep: | Cook: | Ready in:

Ingredients

- For The Soup
- 2 pounds cherry tomatoes
- 1 small onion, peeled and rough chopped
- 3 large cloves garlice, smashed & rough chopped
- 2-4 tablespoons olive oil
- 1 red bell pepper, seeded & cut in halfe
- 1 small beet, peeled & cut in half
- 1 small turnip, peeled & cut into eighths
- 3 cups chicken stock
- 1 1/2 tablespoons chipotle peppers in adobo, chopped (use less to make less spicy)
- 3 ounces sun-dried tomatoes in oil, chopped

- 1 tablespoon smoked paprika
- 1 ounce tomato paste
- 1 teaspoon salt
- 1 teaspoon pepper
- 1 cup Greek yogurt for garnish
- fresh basil for garnish
- For The Mozzarella Crostini:
- 1 loaf French bread
- 8 ounces fresh mozzarella
- 1 garlic clove
- 3 tablespoons olive oil
- 1 teaspoon finely chopped fresh basil

Direction

- For The Soup
- Place tomatoes, onion and garlic on a baking sheet and toss with 1-2 tablespoons olive oil and ½ teaspoon salt and pepper. Bake on 350 for 30 minutes.
- At the same time place the turnip, beet and red pepper in a tin foil boat, and add 1 tablespoon of olive oil, ½ teaspoon salt and pepper. Roast on 350 for 45 minutes.
- After cooked, remove the skin from the beet, chop the beet and peppers, and add all the veggies to a large pot on the stove. Add chicken stock, chipotle peppers, sun-dried tomatoes, smoked paprika, and tomato paste. Bring to a boil then reduce to a simmer for 15 minutes.
- Use an immersion blender (or food processor) to puree all the ingredients until completely smooth.
- Garnish with fresh basil and Greek yogurt.
- For The Mozzarella Crostini:
- Preheat the oven to 350 degrees.
- Slice the bread into ¼ inch slices...about 20 slices.
- Brush one side with olive oil and bake (oil side up) on a parchment-lined baking sheet for 5 minutes.
- Meanwhile, slice the fresh mozzarella into thin slices (about 10), then cut in half width-wise so they fit nicely on the sliced French bread. Place one piece of cheese on each slice of bread and bake for 6 more minutes.
- Mix together 2 tablespoons of olive oil and 1 minced garlic clove. Heat in the microwave for 20-30 seconds.
- Add the chopped fresh basil to the oil/garlic mixture, and drizzle on the baked Mozzarella crostini. Serve warm with the Smoky Tomato Harvest Soup.

287. Smoky Pickled Asparagus

Serving: Serves a bunch | Prep: | Cook: | Ready in:

Ingredients

- 2 cups white wine vinegar
- 3 cloves garlic, peeled and finely chopped
- 1 tablespoon kosher salt
- 1 tablespoon granulated sugar
- 1 teaspoon smoked paprika
- 1 bunch thin asparagus spears (about 1 1/4 pounds)
- 1 medium shallot, peeled, thinly sliced and separated into rings

Direction

- In small saucepot, whisk together vinegar, garlic, salt, sugar and paprika until sugar and salt have dissolved. Over high heat, bring mixture to a boil; let boil 1 minute.
- Meanwhile, trim bottom inch from asparagus spears. Place spears in a resealable container or baking dish (I use an 8" pan). Top with sliced shallots.
- Pour hot vinegar mixture over asparagus, carefully adjusting asparagus to make sure they're mostly covered (if not completely).
- Let sit uncovered at room temperature 3 hours, stirring occasionally. Store, covered, in pickling liquid in the fridge.

288. Smoky Seafood Fideos

Serving: Serves 4 | Prep: | Cook: | Ready in:

Ingredients

- 7 ounces bag of fideos, or broken angel hair pasta
- 1 medium Spanish onion, chopped
- 3 cloves garlic, smashed
- 1 teaspoon smoked paprika
- 1 teaspoon dried oregano
- 1 pinch cayenne
- one 14-ounce can diced fire-roasted tomatoes
- 1 nutmeg seed, passed over a micro plane 5 times
- 2 1/2 cups seafood stock
- 1 cup dry white wine
- 1/2 cup water or vegetable broth
- 1 bay leaf
- 12 shrimp
- 3 squid tubes, cut in to rings
- 12 clams
- 12 mussels
- 1/16 teaspoon ground saffron or a medium sized pinch of threads
- 3/4 cup frozen peas
- 1 lemon
- 3 tablespoons parsley, chopped

Direction

- Coat a heavy pan in olive oil. Over medium/low heat, add fideos and sauté until they become a warm brown color, about 6 to 7 minutes. Using a slotted spoon, remove them from the pan and set aside.
- Reduce the heat add more olive oil to the pan, if needed. Add onion and sauté for 5 minutes, until almost translucent. Add garlic and sauté for another 3 minutes.
- Add in the smoked paprika, oregano, and cayenne, and sauté for another minute.
- Increase the heat to medium and add tomatoes, shave in nutmeg, and bring to a simmer for 3 minutes.
- Return the fideos to the pan and simmer for 5 minutes.
- Meanwhile, bring stock, wine, water and bay leaf to a boil in another pot, reduce to simmering, adding the seafood one species at a time and removing from the pan and reserving. Cook shrimp 2 to 3 minutes until just pink; squid 1 to 2 minutes until just prior to opaque; clams a maximum of 6 minutes, discarding unopened ones; mussels up to 4 minutes; discard unopened ones. Allow broth to return to a slow boil in between batches. Remove seafood and set aside.
- Add the saffron to broth and let 'bloom' for 2 minutes. Turn the heat off of the broth.
- Slowly add stock into the pot with the fideos, in 3 to 4 batches (like risotto). Let simmer with broth for about 20 minutes. When the pasta has reached desired consistency, add in the peas and seafood. Let steam for 2 minutes, covered.
- Prior to serving squeeze the lemon over the top, and sprinkle with parsley.

289. Smoky Shitake Cranberry Cauliflower Galette With Marmalade Mustard Mascarpone

Serving: Serves 4 | Prep: | Cook: | Ready in:

Ingredients

- 1 frozen pastry sheet (about 9 ounces)
- 1/2 cup water
- 1/2 teaspoon salt
- 1 small cauliflower, cut in 1-inch florets (4-5 cups)
- 8 ounces mascarpone cheese
- 2 tablespoons orange marmalade
- 2 tablespoons honey mustard
- 1 tablespoon extra virgin olive oil
- 1/3 cup chopped shallots

- 1 cup Shitake mushrooms, cut in 1/4-inch slivers
- 2 teaspoons granulated sugar
- 1/2 teaspoon lemon pepper seasoning
- 1/3 cup dried cranberries
- 1/2 teaspoon smoked sweet paprika
- 1 tablespoon balsamic vinegar
- 1/4 cup Riesling or sweet white wine
- 4 slices fully cooked crisp bacon, cut in 1-inch pieces
- 1/2 cup grated Mandhego cheese or a smoky white cheese
- 2 tablespoons chopped fresh basil
- 1-2 tablespoons chopped chives

Direction

- Thaw pastry sheet at room temperature for 30 minutes. Preheat oven to 400 degrees F. Place a sheet of parchment paper on a large cookie sheet, set aside.
- Mix water, salt, and cauliflower florets in a microwave safe bowl; cover and microwave on high for 4 minutes. Leave covered to steam for two minutes or so and drain; set aside.
- Meanwhile, in a small bowl, mix Mascarpone cheese, marmalade, and honey mustard. Cover, and refrigerate until ready to serve.
- In a large frying pan, over medium-high, heat olive oil until warm, add shallots, mushrooms, sugar, and lemon pepper; saute and stir for 2 minutes. Reduce heat to medium, add cranberries, paprika, vinegar, stir and cook for 2 more minutes. Add Riesling and steamed cauliflower; stir and cook for 2 minutes or until wine has absorbed.
- Unfold pastry dough, in a 9" x 10" rectangle, on the center of the lined cookie sheet. Spoon the sauteed mixture on the center of dough, leaving about 1.5-inch outer edge. Sprinkle with bacon and cheese. Bake in oven 22-25 minutes or until puffed pastry is golden brown. Remove from oven; cool 5 minutes. Top with basil and serve with dollops of Marmalade-Mustard Mascarpone sprinkled with chives. This is a lovely dish served warm or at room temperature!

290. Smoky Tempeh & Hummus Sandwiches

Serving: Serves 4 | Prep: 0hours15mins | Cook: 0hours30mins | Ready in:

Ingredients

- Smoky Tempeh and Hummus Sandwiches
- 8 ounces tempeh
- 2 tablespoons low-sodium tamari
- 1 tablespoon apple cider vinegar
- 1 tablespoon maple syrup or agave
- 1 teaspoon olive oil
- 1 teaspoon smoked paprika
- 8 slices of crusty, whole grain bread
- 1 cup pea shoots
- 1/4 cup hummus, or as much as you like
- Hummus with Smoked Paprika
- 1 1/2 to 2 cups cooked chickpeas
- 1/4 cup tahini
- 1/4 cup fresh lemon juice
- 1/2 teaspoon sea salt
- 1 clove garlic, minced
- Water, as needed
- 1 tablespoon olive oil
- 1/2 teaspoon smoked paprika

Direction

- To prepare the tempeh, whisk together the tamari, vinegar, syrup, olive oil, and paprika. Slice the tempeh into thin strips (1/4 inch) and marinate the slices in the mixture for several hours, or even overnight. Preheat an oven to 350° F and roast the strips on a lined baking sheet for 25 to 30 minutes, flipping once through, or heat a few teaspoons of olive oil in a large skillet and pan fry the strips for a few minutes, until each side is golden. Set the tempeh aside.
- To make the hummus, add the chickpeas, tahini, lemon, salt, and garlic to the bowl of a food processor and pulse to combine. Run the

motor and drizzle in some water in a thin stream, stopping often to scrape the bowl down as you work. Stop drizzling when the hummus is taking on a thick, creamy texture; be careful how much you use along the way, or the hummus will be too thin (I start with no more than 1/4 cup water). Once the texture is to your liking, drizzle in the olive oil and add the smoked paprika.

- To prepare the sandwiches, toast the bread. Top four slices with at least 1/4 to 1/3 cup hummus and a quarter of the tempeh slices, and top them with a generous amount of sprouts. Top the sandwich with another slice of bread. Serve.

291. Smoky And Sweet Roasted Pumpkin Soup

Serving: Serves 4-6 | Prep: | Cook: | Ready in:

Ingredients

- 5 cups pumpkin, cut into 1-inch cubes
- 1 onion, diced
- 4 cloves garlic, chopped
- 2 tablespoons brown sugar
- 1.5 teaspoons smoked paprika
- 1.5 teaspoons hot paprika
- 2 teaspoons chili powder
- 2 teaspoons sea salt
- 2.5 cups chicken broth

Direction

- Roast pumpkin at 375 degrees in a baking pan for approximately 15 minutes. Meanwhile, mix together sugar, spices and salt in a small bowl.
- Heat olive oil in a large soup pot over medium heat. Add onion, garlic and 1/2 of the spice mixture. Sauté until fragrant.
- Add cooked pumpkin and chicken broth to pot. Mix well and bring to a boil, then reduce to a simmer. Let simmer ten minutes then blend.

- Taste for spice and add more mixture to taste. I used it all and it was strong, but still good. Use your own judgment though! Top with roasted pumpkin seeds (seen above, with smoked paprika) or a dollop of crème fraiche.

292. Smoky And Sweet Roasted Red Pepper With Tuna

Serving: Serves 2 | Prep: | Cook: | Ready in:

Ingredients

- 2 red bell peppers
- 1 small (2.8 oz) can of olive oil packed light tuna (I use and recommend Flott brand)
- 2 tablespoons finely chopped Italian parsley
- 3 tablespoons Smoky and Sweet dressing (recipe below)
- Favorite local lettuce
- French baguette or Italian bread slices, brushed on one side with olive oil and toasted in a 400 degree oven, oiled sides down, for five minutes
- 3 tablespoons Rosemary-Garlic infused olive oil (see recipe below)
- 1 tablespoon good quality Sherry vinegar
- 1 teaspoon almond butter
- 1/4 teaspoon smoked Spanish paprika
- sea salt to taste

Direction

- Roast bell peppers under a broiler or over the burner of a gas stove. I do not have gas so I broil, placing a piece of tin foil under peppers to catch any juices as they split and blister. Roast until charred and blackened on all sides – my nose usually tells me when it is time to turn them. Once roasted, carefully remove peppers from oven and place in a large shallow bowl. Lately I've been using the foil the peppers were roasted on to cover the bowl and allow pepper to steam for a few minutes. Remove foil, allow peppers to cool, and

- remove stem, skin and seeds. Transfer to a cutting board. With a sharp knife, slice peppers into thin strips lengthwise and then crosswise to end up with 1 inch long pieces. Note: I like using a bowl instead of a paper bag to steam peppers to catch all the smoky sweet juices that are released. If I am careful enough, I can keep the juices relatively seed free and then add it to the peppers before mixing with the tuna.
- Place roasted pepper pieces into a medium sized bowl. Add any juices from original bowl that you used to steam peppers in. Drain most of oil from tuna and add tuna to peppers. Top with finely chopped parsley and 3 T of Smoky and Sweet dressing. Using a fork to break up tuna, toss to combine well. Serve over lettuce and/or with olive oil toasted baguette.
- SMOKY AND SWEET DRESSING: In a small jar with a lid, combine 3T Rosemary-Garlic infused olive oil, sherry vinegar, almond butter and smoked paprika. Close jar and shake vigorously to emulsify. Add sea salt to taste.
- ROSEMARY-GARLIC INFUSED OLIVE OIL: Combine 8 garlic cloves, smashed flat with the side of a large knife, 1 6-8" sprig fresh rosemary and 1 cup extra virgin olive oil in a small saucepan, making sure that garlic is submerged (even if only barely – you can further flatten any pieces that are not submerged). Cook over extremely low heat for 45 minutes. Oil will begin to separate if it boils. Transfer to a clean glass jar with lid and allow oil to cool, then refrigerate. Infused oil is extremely perishable so use within a week. Rosemary infused oil also makes a delicious simple vinaigrette – combine ½ cup rosemary infused oil, ¼ cup balsamic vinegar, 2 t Dijon mustard, salt and pepper to taste.

293. Smoky, Spicy Roasted Corn Soup

Serving: Serves 4 | Prep: | Cook: | Ready in:

Ingredients

- 4 cobs of corn
- 2 pointed sweet red peppers
- 4 cloves of garlic in their skins
- 1 teaspoon sea salt
- 2 tablespoons olive oil
- 800 milliliters water
- 1 medium onion
- splash olive oil
- 150 milliliters creme fraiche
- 1 dried chipotle pepper (or 1 tsp smoked paprika and ½ tsp chilli flakes)
- 1 teaspoon dry roasted cumin seeds, crushed coarsely
- 2 tablespoons chopped fresh coriander leaves or use parsley or chervil instead
- 4 lemon wedges to serve

Direction

- Leave the chipotle pepper to soak in a little hot water. Preheat oven to 190 C/ 375F
- Shuck the corn and slice off the kernels. Set the cobs aside. To make a broth. Slice the red peppers in two and de-seed.
- On a large baking tray, mix the kernels, the peppers, the garlic, the salt and the olive oil – spread out and roast for 25 mins, stirring a couple of times. The corn should be tinged gold in places but don't over-roast – the kernels should still be succulent. When cool enough to handle, chop the sweet red pepper into small pieces.
- While the kernels are roasting, snap the cobs into pieces and place in a saucepan. Cover with 800 ml of water and bring to a simmer. Simmer on a low heat for about 30 minutes.
- Sauté the onion in a large saucepan until floppy and slightly golden.
- Drain the chipotle pepper, cut in half and remove the seeds to reduce the heat. Chop

finely and have a little taste to see how hot it is.
- Squeeze the garlic out of their skins and add to the onions in the saucepan, along with the kernels and the chopped red pepper. Stir in the chipotle pepper to your taste – I used the whole one. Or add the smoky paprika and the chili flakes if not using the chipotle pepper. Add a teaspoon of vegetable bouillon and the crushed cumin seeds
- Remove the corn cobs from the water and discard. Tip the corn broth into the saucepan and bring to a simmer. Do not boil. Stir in the crème fraiche and the herbs.
- Serve with a lemon wedges which really sharpen the flavour and tone down the heat at the same time.

294. Snap Crackle Pop!! Bombay Bhel Puri

Serving: Serves 3-4 | Prep: | Cook: | Ready in:

Ingredients

- 2 cups puffed rice OR unsweetened rice krispies cereal
- 8-10 pieces of puries (Deep fried crisps available from the Indian store)
- 1/4 cup finely chopped heirloom or vine ripened tomatoes
- 1/4 cup finely chopped sweet vidalia onion
- 1/4 cup finely chopped kirby or hothouse cucumber
- 1/4 cup boiled, crumbled potatoes
- 2 tablespoons cilantro/mint chutney
- 2 tablespoons sweet & sour tamarind chutney
- Salt & pepper powder
- A sprinkling of paprika
- 1 cup Sev (for garnishing)
- 1/4 cup finely chopped cilantro leaves

Direction

- Crumble the puries into small pieces and add them to the puffed rice in a large mixing bowl.
- Add the finely chopped tomatoes, cucumber, onion & the potatoes, stir to combine.
- Add the sweet & spicy chutneys & mix lightly till the chutneys coat the puffed rice.
- Quickly (this is of the essence since the puffed rice begins getting soggy), sprinkle with salt, pepper & paprika if desired. Ladle onto a serving plate, garnish with sev and chopped cilantro.
- Serve immediately. The snap crackle & pop indicates the freshness. When that stops, you'll be left with a moist chewy mass of deflated puffed rice. It's still tasty though!

295. Sopa De Ajo (Garlic Soup)

Serving: Serves 6 | Prep: | Cook: | Ready in:

Ingredients

- 2 generous tablespoons olive oil
- 8 large cloves garlic, minced
- 1 cup cubed, stale bread, crusts removed
- 1/2 teaspoon smoked Spanish paprika
- 6 cups water
- 2 teaspoons salt, plus more to taste
- 4 bay leaves
- 3 eggs, beaten well

Direction

- Boil your water with the bay leaves and 2 teaspoons salt. Once it boils, keep it at a simmer.
- Meanwhile, heat oil in a pot over low/medium-low heat. Add garlic and cook until fragrant but not brown, about 5 minutes. Add bread cubes. Cook, stirring frequently so the garlic doesn't burn, 2 to 3 more minutes. Add the paprika and stir to coat everything.

- Add boiling water; do not remove bay leaves. Simmer for 20 minutes. Taste the broth, and add salt as needed. Remove bay leaves.
- Stir the soup pot in wide circles, and slowly stream the beaten eggs into the pot. You want them to turn into wisps and ribbons, not clumps, so keep stirring for a few extra seconds, after everything is added. Serve immediately.

296. Southwest Sweet Potato Salad

Serving: Serves 4 | Prep: 0hours10mins | Cook: 0hours15mins | Ready in:

Ingredients

- 2 pounds Sweet Potatoes
- 1 Red Onion
- 1 Red Pepper
- 3 tablespoons Olive Oil
- 1/4 cup Aioli
- 1 tablespoon Smoked Paprika
- 1 teaspoon Cayenne
- 2 tablespoons Sliced Scallion
- 1/4 cup Cilantro
- 1 Avocado, Sliced
- to taste Salt and Pepper

Direction

- Preheat oven to 425. Cube sweet potatoes, julienne red onion, and small dice red pepper. Toss liberally with olive oil and salt and pepper.
- Roast potatoes and vegetables on parchment lined sheet tray for about 25-30 minutes, until potatoes are soft and roasted.
- Mix potatoes and vegetables with aioli, smoked paprika, cayenne, and scallions.
- Top with sliced avocado and cilantro. Salad can be served warm or chilled.

297. Spaghetti 'in' Meat Balls

Serving: Serves 4 | Prep: | Cook: | Ready in:

Ingredients

- 2 cups bowtie pasta
- 1/4 cup olive oil
- 3/4 cup onion-small dice
- 1 tablespoon garlic-minced
- 1.5 pounds lean ground beef-grass fed
- 2 eggs
- 2 tablespoons paprika
- 1 tablespoon nutmeg
- 2 teaspoons cayenne pepper
- 2 tablespoons dried oregano
- 1/2 cup dried currants (or diced dried cranberries or apricots)
- 1/4 cup pistachios-shelled
- 1/2 cup shredded cheddar cheese
- 1.5 cups tomato sauce (homemade or store bought-organic)-divided
- 2 tablespoons salt
- 1.5 tablespoons black pepper

Direction

- In a saucepan, cook pasta according to directions; if you typically like it al dente, cook it 2 minutes longer this time; remove from heat, drizzle with 1 T olive oil (so it doesn't stick), and reserve.
- Heat 2 T olive oil in a pan and add onions; cook until translucent.
- Add garlic and cook for 1 minute longer; remove contents of the pan and reserve.
- In a large bowl, mix onion/garlic mixture, ground beef, eggs, paprika, nutmeg, cayenne, oregano, currants, pistachios, cheese, half of the tomato sauce, salt, and pepper.
- Working in batches, dice bowties on a cutting board.
- Add to the beef mixture and mix well.
- Roll mixture into 1 to 2 inch balls.

- On medium, heat 1 T olive oil in a pan and add meat balls to the pan; add the remaining 1/2 cup tomato sauce to the pan and cook for ~10-12 minutes, or until cooked through.

298. Spanish Chicken

Serving: Serves 4 | Prep: | Cook: |Ready in:

Ingredients

- 1 1/2 cups chicken stock, lightly salted if using homemade
- a few strands of saffron
- 2 tablespoons lard
- 1 chicken, jointed (see introduction)
- all-purpose flour seasoned with salt, pepper, chili powder and paprika (for dredging)
- 1 onion chopped
- 1 green bell pepper, diced
- 1 red bell pepper, diced
- 2 garlic cloves, minced
- 1 cup rice, uncooked
- 1/4 teaspoon paprika
- 1 dash chili powder
- 1 teaspoon salt
- pepper

Direction

- Preheat oven to 350 degrees Fahrenheit. Put the chicken stock in a small saucepan and add the saffron. Bring up to a boil then turn heat down to low and put on the lid to keep stock warm.
- Melt lard in a large skillet over medium-high heat. Dredge chicken joints in seasoned flour and fry in lard until browned. You don't need to cook them all the way through. Remove to a plate. Sauté the onion and bell peppers in lard until softened. Turn down the heat, if necessary, to keep vegetables from burning. Add minced garlic and sauté one minute.
- Lower heat, stir in rice and cook, stirring, 2 minutes. Pour in warm stock and add paprika, chili powder, salt and pepper. Turn heat to high and bring to a boil. Place chicken pieces on top and move to oven. Bake between 75 and 90 minutes, or until chicken is cooked through and the rice has absorbed all the liquid and browned on top.

299. Spanish Paella

Serving: Serves 12-14 | Prep: | Cook: |Ready in:

Ingredients

- 1 1/2 pounds white firm fish (I use Grouper or monk fish) cut into chunks
- 14 little neck clams
- 14 mussels, scrubbed
- 1 pound squid, cleaned and cut into rings
- 1 pound shrimp, shelled and deveined
- 10 Scallops (if very large cut in halves)
- 1/2 pound langoustines, boiled and cooled
- 3/4 pound chorizo, cut on an angle into 1/4 inch slices
- 1/2 pound ham, cut into cubes about 1/4 inch thick
- 4-5 chicken breasts or chicken parts
- 3-4 Sweet red bell peppers, sliced (preferably roasted)
- 2 bags of frozen peas
- 1 large onion, finely chopped
- 2 chili peppers, finely chopped (optional)
- 2 cloves Garlic, Crushed
- 3 ripe tomatoes, peeled and chopped saving the liquid (I've also used canned diced tomatoes)
- 1/4 cup olive oil
- 1 pinch saffron threads
- 1/2 teaspoon paprika
- Salt and pepper, to taste
- 1/4 cup white wine or brandy (optional)
- 3 cups Valencia Rice
- lemon slices, for Garnish
- chopped fresh parsley, for Garnish

Direction

- For the stock: In a large pot combine fish, shrimp and shellfish in 3/4 quart of water. Boil for 4 minutes and then simmer for 2 minutes. Remove and set aside keeping the water in the pot. Using the same water, boil the chicken for 8 minutes. Again, leaving the water in the pot- remove the chicken and let cool.
- In a large skillet sauté the sausage and the ham in olive oil. Remove from pan leaving the oils from the sausage. Add the onions, chili peppers and sauté till soft. Add tomatoes (including the liquid), garlic, saffron, paprika, salt and pepper. Add the wine or brandy if desired. Simmer until a sauce is made. Taste to adjust seasoning. Place the sausage and ham back into the skillet with the sauce and simmer.
- In a very large Paella pan place the rice on the bottom. Sprinkle the peas on top of the rice. Arrange the fish, shrimps, scallops, and the squid on top. Pour the water that was used to boil the fish and chicken carefully on top. Place the paella pan directly on the stove top and bring to a boil. In a decorative manner place the chicken pieces, langoustines, shellfish, chorizo and ham on the top and place the strips of red pepper between to add color. Allow the liquid to boil for 6 -8 minutes.
- In a 450 degree preheated oven, place the Paella pan for 10 minutes. Remove from oven and garnish with chopped parsley and lemon slices. Serve immediately.

300. Spanish Inspired Ragout With Butternut Squash, Chorizo, And Chickpeas

Serving: Serves 6 | Prep: | Cook: |Ready in:

Ingredients

- For romesco:
- 1/4 cup almonds or hazelnuts
- `1 14.5-ounce can diced or whole tomatoes (including juice)
- 2 roasted piquillo or red bell peppers, jarred or freshly roasted
- 2 large garlic cloves, peeled
- 1/4 teaspoon teaspoon red pepper flakes, or to taste (if your chorizo is spicy, you may want to omit)
- 1 1/2 teaspoons Spanish smoked paprika
- 1 tablespoon + 1 teaspoon sherry vinegar, plus more to taste
- 2 tablespoons olive oil
- kosher salt, to taste
- pinch of sugar (optional)
- For rest of dish:
- 2 tablespoons olive oil
- 1 large onion, finely chopped (yielding about 2 cups)
- kosher salt, to taste
- 1 medium butternut squash (about 2 1/4 pounds), cut into 3/4-inch cubes (yielding about 5 cups)
- 1 15-ounce can of chickpeas (drained and rinsed)
- 8 to 12 ounces ounces fully-cooked Spanish or Spanish-style chorizo (domestic, smoked Spanish-style chorizo works really well here), cut into 1/4-inch slices
- freshly squeezed lemon juice or sherry vinegar, to taste
- Greek yogurt, for serving
- Large handful of chopped cilantro (or parsley) leaves, for serving

Direction

- Heat oven to 400 F.
- To make romesco, in a food processor, pulse the almonds until they're finely ground, about 20 seconds. Add the remaining ingredients, and process until well-integrated. Add more salt, smoked paprika and/or sherry vinegar, to taste, and a pinch of sugar, if needed, to round out the flavors. (Can be prepared, covered, and refrigerated up to 3 days in advance.)

- Heat olive oil in a large, shallow cast-iron casserole or 12-inch ovenproof sauté pan. Add onion and a big pinch of salt, and sauté until softened and translucent but not colored, about 6 minutes. Add the squash and 1 teaspoon of salt, stirring well to coat the squash with the onions and oil. Sauté another 8 minutes, or until the outside of the squash starts to soften, stirring occasionally. Add the chickpeas, chorizo, and romesco – stirring well to coat all of the ingredients with the romesco. It will seem like a lot of romesco, but it will cook down considerably in the oven.
- Transfer the casserole to the oven, and roast uncovered for 30 to 40 minutes (stirring two or three times for even cooking), or until the squash is tender and the romesco has reduced and darkened in color. Remove from oven. Taste, and adjust salt and acidity with a squeeze or two of fresh lemon juice, or more sherry vinegar.
- Serve warm with a big dollop of Greek yogurt and chopped cilantro. I like serving it over a bed of couscous, and a simple green salad on the side wouldn't be out of place.

301. Spiced Potato Cakes

Serving: Serves 4 to 6 | Prep: | Cook: | Ready in:

Ingredients

- 1 1/2 pounds potatoes, left whole and unpeeled (so they don't get waterlogged while cooking)
- 2 large cloves of garlic, smashed to a paste
- 2 teaspoons (heaping) ground cumin
- 1 teaspoon turmeric
- 1 1/2 teaspoons coriander
- 1 teaspoon hot paprika (use less if you're spicy breakfast averse)
- 2 teaspoons salt
- 4 large eggs
- 1 tablespoon butter, plus lots more for frying
- Plain yogurt mixed with your choice of herbs plus lemon juice for serving, or fried eggs, or chutney, or any other sauce you want

Direction

- Put your potatoes in a large pot and add just enough water to cover. Cover the pot, bring to a boil, then turn down to a simmer and simmer until the potatoes are tender enough to be easily pierced through with a blunt knife or a fork (how long this takes depends very much on the size of your potatoes).
- Drain the potatoes and allow them to cool enough to handle. Then, peel off the skins and put the potatoes in a large mixing bowl.
- While the potatoes are cooling, melt one Tbs. butter in a large frying pan until foamy. Add the cumin, turmeric, coriander, and spicy paprika. Cook for one minute, until fragrant, then remove from the heat.
- Add the garlic, the spice mixture, and the salt to the potatoes and smash them up until no lumps remain. Then, stir in the eggs until well blended. You should have what looks and feels like a rather thick batter.
- In the same large frying pan you used to toast the spices heat a couple tablespoons of butter over medium-high heat until very hot and foaming. Drop the potato batter by large spoonfuls into the pan. Cook on the first side until well browned, about 3 minutes, then flip and cook until the other sides are well browned, another couple minutes. Repeat with the remaining batter, adding butter to the pan as needed.
- Serve the potato cakes warm with your choice of topping - yogurt sauce (like raita or tzatziki), fried eggs, chutney...

302. Spicy BBQ Chicken Quesadillas

Serving: Serves 4 | Prep: | Cook: | Ready in:

Ingredients

- For the barbecue sauce:
- ¼ cups white vinegar
- ¼ cups brown sugar
- ¼ cups Worcestershire sauce
- ¼ cups tomato sauce
- 1 tablespoon mustard
- For the chicken and to assemble:
- olive oil for frying
- 1 red onion, finely chopped
- 1½ teaspoons paprika
- 2 teaspoons ground cumin
- 4 chicken thighs, skins removed
- salt and pepper
- 8 x 20cm soft flour tortillas
- 1 cup grated cheddar cheese
- handful coriander, finely chopped
- sour cream to serve

Direction

- Place all of the barbecue sauce ingredients in a bowl and whisk until combined. Set aside.
- Preheat your oven to 180°C. Heat some olive oil in a deep frying pan. Sauté the red onion, paprika and cumin together for a three minutes. Add the chicken thighs and season with salt and pepper. Toss the chicken to coat in the spices.
- Transfer the contents of the saucepan to an ovenproof dish. (Try and use one that allows the chicken to fit snugly in a single layer.) Pour the barbecue sauce over the chicken.
- Cover the oven dish with foil and bake for one hour. Transfer the chicken to a chopping board. Take the chicken off the bone and shred. Place the shredded chicken in a bowl. Add one cup of the barbecue sauce from the oven dish and mix well.
- Spread the barbecue chicken over four flour tortillas. Add a sprinkling of cheddar cheese and chopped coriander. Place another tortilla on top of each one.
- Heat a frying pan over a medium heat. Dry fry each tortilla for a minute on each side. Cut into wedges and serve immediately with some sour cream.

303. Spicy Cannellini Beans

Serving: Serves 4 as a side dish | Prep: | Cook: | Ready in:

Ingredients

- 15 ounces can of cannellini beans
- 2 ounces salt pork, diced
- 1/2 onion, diced
- 2 cloves garlic, minced
- 2 baby bell peppers, diced (or 1/2 regular bell pepper)
- 1 bay leaf
- 1/2 cup chicken stock
- 1/2 teaspoon cayenne pepper
- 1/2 teaspoon paprika
- splash heavy cream

Direction

- Rinse and drain the beans.
- Add salt pork to a cold pan and place over medium heat. Render the fan and allow the pork to crisp up.
- Add in diced onion, garlic, and bell peppers. Sauté until soft and onions start to turn golden brown.
- Add in beans, stock, bay leaf, cayenne pepper, and paprika. Stir and then bring to a simmer. Let the beans simmer for 20 minutes until the stock reduces and thickens.
- Just before serving, stir in a splash of cream for richness.

304. Spicy Corn & Scallop Chowder

Serving: Serves 2 with leftovers | Prep: | Cook: | Ready in:

Ingredients

- 1 poblano pepper
- 1 teaspoon olive oil
- 4 thin slices pancetta, diced
- 1 medium onion, diced
- 1 clove garlic, minced
- Coarse salt and ground black pepper
- 1/2 teaspoon smoked paprika (optional)
- 1/2 cup dry white wine
- 3 cobs fresh corn, kernels removed and cobs reserved
- 1 cup bottled clam juice
- 1 cup chicken stock
- 1 medium Yukon gold potato, diced
- 1/2 pound bay scallops
- 1/2 cup whole milk
- 1 teaspoon cornstarch
- Garnish: chopped fresh cilantro

Direction

- Roast the poblano: situate oven rack to highest position and preheat broiler. Lightly rub poblano with vegetable oil. Line a small baking sheet with foil, place pepper on prepared baking sheet, and place under broiler. Broil pepper until skin is beginning to char, about 5 minutes. Flip pepper, and broil about 5 minutes more, or until it is uniformly soft and skin is mostly brown and black. Remove pepper from oven, place in a paper bag (or in a bowl covered with plastic wrap). Set aside for 8-10 minutes, then remove stem from pepper, and peel away skin (it should come off easily). Cut pepper in half, remove seeds, and roughly chop.
- In a large stockpot, heat olive oil over medium heat. Add pancetta, and cook until meat is crisp and fat has rendered. Remove pancetta with a slotted spoon, and set aside. Pour off all but about 1 tablespoon fat (or leave it alone if there's about that much in the pan).
- Add onions, season with a big pinch of salt and a few grinds of pepper, and stir. Cook until onion is beginning to soften; add garlic, and cook until very fragrant. Add smoked paprika, if using, and stir to combine. Add wine, and using a wooden spoon, scrape any bits from the bottom of the pot. Simmer for 1 minute.
- Add corn, corn cobs, roasted poblano, clam juice, stock, and potatoes, and simmer, covered, about 15 minutes, or until potatoes are tender. Remove cobs and discard, then add scallops.
- Add half-and-half, and simmer (do not boil) until scallops are fully cooked and chowder is lightly thickened. Top each bowl with reserved pancetta or bacon, and garnish with cilantro, if desired.

305. Spicy Egg Curry

Serving: Serves 4 | Prep: | Cook: | Ready in:

Ingredients

- 8 eggs, boiled
- 1 tablespoon avocado oil
- 1 medium onion, finely chopped
- 2 roma tomatoes, finely chopped
- 2 cloves garlic, crushed and finely chopped
- 1 tablespoon fresh ginger, finely grated
- 1 1/2 cups water, or as needed
- 1 1/2 teaspoons paprika
- 1/2 teaspoon red chili powder (optional for heat)
- 1/2 teaspoon turmeric
- 1 teaspoon salt (or to taste)
- 1/2 teaspoon garam masala

Direction

- Boil and peel eggs.
- Cut eggs into halves.
- In a pan, heat avocado oil.
- Saute onions until translucent.
- Add tomatoes and saute until soft.
- Add ginger, garlic, paprika, red chili powder, salt, turmeric, garam masala, water. Mix and

let simmer for approximately 5 minutes, stirring occasionally.
- Gently place the boiled egg halves into the gravy. Spoon some gravy on top of the eggs. Let simmer for another 5 minutes on low heat.
- To serve, garnish with a sprig of cilantro and a sprinkle of garam masala.

306. Spicy Indian Lentil Dal

Serving: Serves 4 | Prep: | Cook: | Ready in:

Ingredients

- 1/2 cup masoor lentils
- 1/2 cup moong lentils
- 1/2 teaspoon turmeric powder
- 1 tablespoon butter
- 1 tablespoon olive oil
- 1/2 teaspoon cumin seeds
- 1/2 teaspoon mustard seeds
- 1/2 onion, finely chopped
- 1 green birds eye chilli (optional)
- 2 cloves garlic, grated
- 1 inch fresh ginger, grated
- 1-2 tsp salt (according to taste)
- 1 tsp garam masala
- 1/2 tsp paprika
- 1/4 can plum tomatoes
- handful fresh cilantro, chopped

Direction

- Wash both dals and place in a pressure cooker. Add water so it is about 1" above the dal. Add salt to taste and turmeric powder. Cook until 1st "whistle" goes off and turn off heat. (If you do not have a pressure cooker, you can also boil the dal in a pan).
- Whilst the dal is cooking heat oil and butter in a pan. Add cumin seeds and mustard seeds. When they begin to sizzle, add the onion and chili.
- Cook until slightly golden and add the garlic and ginger. Let it cook until slightly brown and add the salt, garam masala and paprika.
- Add the plum tomatoes. Mix well and cook for 2-3 minutes or until oil begins to separate from masala.
- Once the dal is ready, remove from heat and carefully release steam from pressure cooker and add it to the masala.
- Mix the masala with the dal. Add the water and stir well. Add the coriander. Check for salt and adjust accordingly.
- If you think the dal is too thick you can add a little water at this point. Bring dal to boil and you're done! Best served with rice :)

307. Spicy Masala Rubbed Tofu Pitas With Mint Cumin Yoghurt Sauce

Serving: Serves 2-4 | Prep: | Cook: | Ready in:

Ingredients

- Tofu Rub:
- 1 tablespoon grated ginger
- 5 cloves of garlic, pressed
- 1 tablespoon garam masala
- 1 tablespoon paprika
- 1 teaspoon chili powder
- 1 teaspoon ground cumin
- 1 teaspoon ground coriander
- 1 teaspoon turmeric
- 1/4 teaspoon fennel seeds
- 1 1/2 teaspoons sugar
- 1 1/2 teaspoons salt
- 1 package tofu drained, pressed and cut into 8 equal slabs
- 2 tablespoons canola oil
- The rest:
- 1 teaspoon tamarind paste
- 1 teaspoon chana masala spice
- 1/2 lime, juiced
- 1/2 cup red onion, diced

- 1 cup finely diced cucumber
- 2 tomatoes, diced
- 1 bunch cilantro, chopped
- 1 cup unsweetened coconut yoghurt
- 1 1/2 teaspoons ground cumin
- 1 1/2 teaspoons fresh mint, chopped finely
- 1 tablespoon canola oil
- 3 pitas, cut in half
- mango chutney
- relish

Direction

- Drain your tofu in a tofu press or by wrapping it in a towel and placing something heavy on top of it for about 20 minutes.
- Using a small bowl mix your fresh ginger, pressed garlic, garam masala, paprika, chili powder, ground cumin, ground coriander, turmeric, fennel seeds, sugar and salt. Add the oil to get a paste like consistency.
- Cut your drained block of tofu in half and then flipping the whole block on its side, cut it into 4 equal slices. You will have 8 equal slices in total.
- Cover the tofu on both sides with the spice rub using a pastry brush or with your hands (easier). Use all of the spice mix and place the rubbed tofu in a covered dish in the fridge to marinate for an hour or two (give or take).
- For the salad: In a small mixing bowl whisk your tamarind paste, chana masala spice and lime juice.
- Chop your tomatoes, cucumber and red onion and add it to the mixing bowl. Stir gently to combine.
- Add your chopped cilantro.
- For the Mint Cumin Yoghurt Sauce: In small bowl mix the coconut yoghurt, cumin and finely chopped fresh mint.
- Heat a cast iron or other skillet over medium heat. Add 1 tbsp. of oil and when hot, cook the tofu for 3-4 minutes per side and flip. Cook the other side for the same amount of time.
- To assemble: Cut the pitas in half.
- Take one half and spread mango chutney on the inside top and bottom of the bread. Add relish to the bottom.
- Add two (or one if you prefer!) slices of tofu and fill the remainder of the pita with the 'salad'. Top with Mint Cumin Yoghurt Sauce. Repeat.

308. Spicy Moroccan Chickpea Soup

Serving: Serves 8 | Prep: 0hours20mins | Cook: 1hours0mins | Ready in:

Ingredients

- 3 stalks of celery, diced
- 2 large white onions, diced
- 6 cloves garlic, more or less depending on personal preference
- 6 splashes olive oil, more for garnish
- 2 teaspoons cumin
- 2 teaspoons coriander
- 3 teaspoons paprika
- 1 pinch cayenne pepper
- 1 dash cinnamon
- 2 serrano chilies
- 2 zucchinis, chopped
- 30 ounces chickpeas (two cans), drained
- 1 can Trader Joe's fire-roasted diced tomatoes
- 32 ounces vegetable or chicken stock
- 1 pinch grated lemon zest
- 1 handful freshly chopped cilantro
- 1 bay leaf
- 1.5 cups baby spinach
- 2 tablespoons yogurt (garnish)
- 1 teaspoon cayenne powder (garnish)
- 1 handful chopped cilantro (garnish)
- 1 handful chopped spring onions (garnish)

Direction

- Add diced celery and onions to a large stock pot, over low to medium heat.

- Next, add the minced garlic cloves. Add the olive oil, turn the heat up to medium-high, and sauté until the veggies are softened; also add plenty of cracked pepper to taste.
- Then spice the mixture, using the cumin, coriander, cayenne pepper, paprika and cinnamon. Finely chop the two serrano chilies (scrape out the seeds if you want less heat) and throw these in as well. Once the spices were added, the mixture will start to boil and achieve a beautiful reddish-orange color. Stir frequently so that the spices don't burn, for a minute or two.
- Add the drained chickpeas, tomatoes and stock- our stock was frozen so we had to let it melt over the course of about eight minutes. The soup will be very watery at this point, but don't worry! It thickens up over the course of cooking. Also add the grated lemon zest at this point, it really brightens up the dish. The soup should remain over medium to high heat, and be allowed to boil.
- After about ten minutes, the soup should start to boil, and the water will evaporate. Continue to stir the soup so that the contents don't stick to the bottom of the pot and burn.
- Five minutes into boiling, we added the handful of freshly chopped cilantro, along with a bay leaf and the zucchini. Don't add the zucchini any earlier than this, otherwise it will break down. At this point, also lower the heat so that the soup is simply simmering.
- Let the soup cook down for another thirty minutes (this is the perfect time to do some dishes and clean up!). Use a flat, hard spatula to flatten some of the chickpeas- they breakdown and thicken up the soup a bit. Continue to stir.
- Three minutes before serving, add the 1.5 cup of baby spinach to the soup and stir. Add it any earlier and the spinach will disintegrate.
- Right before serving, mix together the yogurt and cayenne to make a spicy yogurt drizzle. Spoon the soup into each bowl, top with the yogurt drizzle, as well as a drizzle of EVOO. Garnish with some chopped spring onions and cilantro, and serve immediately!

309. Spicy Pork Ragout With Cannelini And Orange

Serving: Serves 4 generously | Prep: | Cook: | Ready in:

Ingredients

- 2 14 ounce cans cannelini, rinsed and drained
- a couple of good swirls extra virgin olive oil
- 2 pounds boneless pork shoulder, in 2-inch chunks
- 1 medium onion, finely chopped
- 3 fat cloves garlic, minced
- 1 red bell pepper, cored, seeded and finely chopped
- 1-1/2 teaspoons smoked Spanish paprika
- 1 teaspoon ground cloves
- 2 oranges, zested and juiced
- 1-1/2 cups dry red wine
- 3 good sized sprigs fresh rosemary
- coarse salt
- freshly ground black pepper
- good pinch crushed hot red pepper flakes
- chopped fresh Italian parsley for garnish

Direction

- Heat a couple of good swirls extra virgin olive oil in a 4-quart casserole and lightly brown pork without crowding over medium-high heat. Remove.
- Add onion, garlic and bell pepper. Sauté over low heat until soft.
- Stir in paprika, cloves and zest. Stir in orange juice and wine, scraping bottom of pan.
- Return pork to pan.
- Add rosemary, black pepper and red pepper flakes. Bring to a simmer. Let cook for about an hour.
- Add the cannellini beans and let simmer 10 minutes.
- Serve with chopped fresh Italian parsley, a blap of sour cream and a bit of orange zest.

310. Spicy Spanish Garlic Shrimp Gambas Al Pil Pil

Serving: Serves 2 | Prep: | Cook: |Ready in:

Ingredients

- 1/4 cup Extra Virgin Spanish Olive oil
- 3 Cloves of Garlic
- 1 Spanish Red Pepper
- 1/2 teaspoon Smoked Paprika
- 15 Raw Jumbo Shrimp
- Sea Salt
- Freshly Cracked Black Pepper
- Fresh Parsley

Direction

- Thinly slice 3 cloves of garlic, cut off the stem of 1 Spanish pepper (or any other type of pepper that you like), cut it in half and deseed it with a spoon, then cut it into thin slices
- Season 15 raw jumbo shrimp (peeled and deveined) with sea salt and freshly cracked black pepper
- Heat a small non-stick frying pan with a medium-high heat and add a 1/4 cup of extra virgin Spanish olive oil, once the oil gets hot add the sliced garlics and sliced peppers, mix with the oil, after about 1 minute add 1/2 teaspoon of smoked paprika and mix everything together, then add the shrimp in a single layer, after cooking the shrimp for 1 1/2 minutes flip them and cook for another 1 1/2 minutes
- Transfer everything in the pan to a shallow bowl and sprinkle with some freshly chopped parsley

311. Spicy Tomato, Spinach & Egg Galette

Serving: Serves 4 | Prep: | Cook: |Ready in:

Ingredients

- For the dough:
- 1 1/4 cups all purpose flour
- 1/2 teaspoon salt
- 8 tablespoons cold unsalted butter, cut into small cubes
- 1/4 cup sour cream
- 1/4 cup water
- 2 tablespoons lemon juice
- For the filling:
- 2 tablespoons olive oil
- 1 medium yellow onion, chopped
- 3 garlic cloves, chopped
- 1 chili pepper, seeds removed and diced
- 1 1/2 teaspoons Kosher salt
- 1 teaspoon ground black pepper
- 1 teaspoon caraway seeds
- 1 teaspoon ground cumin
- 1/2 teaspoon turmeric
- 1 teaspoon smoked paprika
- 2-3 large tomatoes, about 1 pound, diced
- 2 tablespoons tomato paste
- 2 teaspoons honey
- 1 teaspoon cider vinegar
- 8 ounces spinach, chopped
- 2 ounces feta cheese, crumbled
- 4 small eggs, plus one more to use as egg wash

Direction

- In a food processor, combine flour and salt. Add in butter and pulse until small pebbles form.
- In a small bowl, combine sour cream, lemon juice, and water. Add to food processor and pulse until mixture comes together and forms dough. Wrap dough in plastic wrap and refrigerate for at least one hour, or up to two days.
- To make the filling: In a heavy bottomed skillet, heat olive oil over medium high heat. Add onions and cook until translucent. Add in garlic, chili pepper, salt, pepper, caraway seeds, cumin, turmeric, and paprika. Cook for 1 minute. Stir in tomatoes, tomato paste,

honey, and vinegar. Reduce heat to medium low and simmer for about 10-15 minutes, until it starts to thicken. Add in spinach and mix until slightly wilted. Remove from heat and let cool slightly.
- Preheat oven to 400F.
- While filling cools, divide dough in 4 even pieces. Roll out each piece of dough into about an 8 inch round. Transfer dough to a parchment paper lined baking sheet.
- Place tomato mixture in the center, leaving about a 1½ inch border around the sides. Scatter feta evenly among galettes, then fold the edges of the dough in, overlapping where there is extra.
- In a small bowl, whisk one egg with a few drops of water. Brush the dough with egg wash. Bake for 25 minutes, until dough is slightly golden.
- Remove galettes from oven and using a spoon, gently make a well in the center of each galette. Crack one egg into each galette, taking care to spread the whites out with a knife so that they don't pool on top of the yolks. If you have big eggs, you may consider using only half of each egg white. You can do this by cracking the egg over a bowl and letting some of the white drip out before putting the yolk and remaining whites into the well in the galette. Bake for an additional 5-8 minutes, until whites have set.
- Let cool slightly, then sprinkle with smoked paprika and freshly ground black pepper before serving.

312. Spicy, No Cook Beer Cheese Recipe

Serving: Makes 1 bowl | Prep: 0hours10mins | Cook: 0hours0mins | Ready in:

Ingredients

- 1/4 cup Allagash White beer, plus more to thin out the dip, if needed
- 1 1/2 cups sharp cheddar cheese, shredded
- 1/4 cup pepper jack cheese, shredded
- 1 small clove garlic, minced
- 1/4 teaspoon smoked paprika
- 1 pinch cayenne
- 1 pinch salt
- 2 teaspoons hot sauce, plus more to taste
- 1 teaspoon Dijon mustard
- 1/4 teaspoon Worcestershire sauce
- 1 jalapeño, roughly chopped and with the seeds removed
- 1 small bunch cilantro, roughly torn

Direction

- Pour the beer into a measuring cup or small bowl and let it sit out for at least one hour to come up to room temperature and lose its carbonation. (If it is too cold or bubbly it won't combine properly.)
- Add the cheddar cheese, pepper jack, minced garlic, paprika, cayenne, and salt to a food processor. Pulse the food processor a few times or until roughly combined.
- Scrape down the sides of the food processor and add the hot sauce, mustard, Worcestershire sauce, sliced jalapeño, and cilantro. Pulse the food processor a few times or until loosely combined.
- Scrape down the sides of the food processor and add the beer one or two tablespoons at a time. Pulse until the mixture is smooth, creamy, and fully combined, adding more beer as needed. If the dip is too thick, add 1 tablespoon of beer at a time; if it's too thin, add 1 small handful of cheddar cheese at a time until you've reached the desired consistency.
- Serve immediately with crackers and crudités. (It will also keep in the fridge for up to 1 week.)

313. Split Pea Soup For A Winter's Day

Serving: Serves 6 to 8 | Prep: | Cook: | Ready in:

Ingredients

- 2 tablespoons extra-virgin olive oil
- 1 large onion, chopped
- 3 to 4 large carrots, peeled and diced
- 4 ribs celery, diced
- 3 cloves of garlic, minced
- 3 bay leaves
- 1 sprig each of fresh: rosemary, sage, thyme, marjoram
- 6 whole black peppercorns
- 1 pound dried, green split peas, rinsed and picked over for stones.
- one 2-pound smoked ham hock
- 3 quarts homemade chicken stock
- 2 teaspoons salt, plus more to taste
- Freshly ground pepper and smoked paprika to taste

Direction

- Heat the olive oil in a deep stock pot and add the onions, carrots, and celery. Sauté until soft, about 12 minutes.
- Add the garlic and bay leaves and cook for 2 minutes.
- Make a bouquet garni using the fresh herbs and peppercorns. Tie tightly and place into pot.
- Pour the peas into the pot, and nestle the ham hock on top.
- Pour in the stock, add salt, and bring it to boil.
- Reduce heat to simmer, cover and gently simmer for 2 1/2 hours, skimming foam from the top and stirring occasionally.
- After simmering, remove ham hock from soup and cool. Remove bouquet garni and discard.
- Chop up the ham hock and return to pot.
- Season soup with more salt and plenty of freshly ground pepper and some smoked paprika to taste.
- Serve piping hot with crusty bread or oyster crackers. Garnish with a drizzle of your best olive oil and some crumbled bacon.

314. Spring Vegetable And Red Pesto Tart

Serving: Makes a 24cm tart | Prep: | Cook: | Ready in:

Ingredients

- For the pastry and pesto:
- 200 grams spelt flour
- 100 grams salted butter, cubed and chilled
- 4 tablespoons cold water
- 1 cup dried tomatoes (tightly packed)
- 1.5 cups boiling water
- 1 tablespoon sesame seeds
- 1/3 cup olive oil
- 1 small clove of garlic
- small pinch of paprika
- onion powder
- 1/4 teaspoon pink salt and pepper
- For the filling:
- 1 tablespoon salted butter
- 3 small courgettes, grated
- 1 large leek, chopped
- 150 grams chard, chopped
- small bunch of chives, chopped
- pink salt and pepper
- 3 eggs
- 300 milliliters almond milk
- 1 teaspoon dried Italian herbs

Direction

- To make the pastry: Put the spelt flour and butter in the food processor and whizz for a few seconds until the butter has been incorporated. Add the cold water and whizz for another few seconds.
- Tip the contents onto your work surface and press together into a dough. Add another few drops of water if the dough is too dry. Press

into a disc, wrap in cling film and pop in the fridge while you prepare the pesto and veggie filling.
- To make the pesto: put the dried tomatoes in a small bowl. Cover with the boiling water and leave to stand for 15 minutes. Place the sesame seeds in a small frying pan over a medium heat. Toast the sesame seeds until golden brown.
- Drain the tomatoes. Put them in the food processor with the toasted sesame seeds, olive oil, garlic, paprika and onion powder. Add a grinding of salt and pepper. Whizz for a minute or two until everything is combined and you have a thick pesto. Set aside.
- Melt the butter in a large frying pan. Fry the grated courgettes and chopped leek for a few minutes to soften. Add the chard and stir on the heat for a few minutes to wilt. Take the pan off the heat and stir in the chives and a grinding of salt and pepper.
- Preheat your oven to 180°C and grease a 24cm tart tin. Dust your work surface with a little spelt flour and roll the pastry to a thickness of 3-4mm. Carefully lift the pastry into the dish and press into the edges. Cut the excess pastry away from the edges. Place a piece of crumpled baking paper over the pastry and fill with baking/dried beans. Bake the pastry for 10 minutes. Remove the beans and paper and bake for a further 10 minutes or until the pastry is just cooked.
- Spread the tomato pesto onto the base of the tart. Arrange the vegetable mixture on top in an even layer. Whisk the eggs and almond milk together until combined. Pour over the vegetables, then sprinkle the Italian herbs over the top.
- Carefully transfer the tart to the oven and bake for 35 minutes, or until the filling has set. Allow the tart to cool for a few minutes, then serve with a crunchy, organic herb salad. Make ahead tip - the pastry, pesto and vegetables can be prepared a few hours ahead of time, simply store them in the fridge. Assemble the tart and bake when required.

315. Strawberry Red Pepper Ice Cream

Serving: Serves 4 | Prep: | Cook: | Ready in:

Ingredients

- 1 cup cooked and sugared strawberries, chilled
- 1 cup fire roasted mild red pepper
- 1/2 cup ricotta
- 3/4 cup whole milk
- 3/4 cup heavy cream (it happened to be whipped already)
- 1/3 cup acacia honey
- 1/3 cup organic cane sugar
- 1/4 teaspoon hot paprika (for more heat) or Aleppo pepper flakes (for milder)
- 1/4 teaspoon fennel seed, milled or ground
- 1/2 tablespoon fresh lime juice
- sprinkle of hot paprika or Aleppo chili pepper flakes for garnish

Direction

- Assemble the ingredients in a food processor or blender and puree. Then chill the mix thoroughly. If you do not want heat you could use a sweet paprika instead.
- Pour into an ice cream maker and process according to the maker's directions. Serve right away (or store in the freezer and then let soften for serving).
- Garnish with a daring sprinkle of Hungarian hot paprika or Aleppo chili pepper flakes.

316. Stuffed Chicken

Serving: Serves 2 | Prep: | Cook: | Ready in:

Ingredients

- 2 Chicken Breasts

- small handfuls Spinach
- small handfuls Shredded cheese
- small pinches Garlic Powder
- small teaspoons Olive Oil for each piece of chicken
- small pinches Pepper
- medium pieces One - Two pieces of bacon for each piece
- small handfuls Add a small handful of small, cut tomatoes to each piece, if desired.
- samll pinches Paprika
- Delicious Ingredients!!

Direction

- Cut the pieces of chicken open, like a book.
- Mix everything together except for the bacon.
- Insert everything inside of the chicken except for the bacon.
- When everything is inside, wrap up the chicken with the bacon and place a toothpick inside of the chicken to keep it together.
- Sprinkle each piece with pepper! Bake 35 minutes at 400 degrees in the oven.
- Add tomatoes when you have 5 minutes left, and add a little more olive oil.
- Add paprika, if desired.
- Serve with mashed potatoes and a steamed vegetable!!

317. Stuffed Eight Ball Squash With Roasted Red Pepper Sauce

Serving: Serves 4 | Prep: | Cook: | Ready in:

Ingredients

- Stuffed Summer Squash
- 6 medium zucchini or yellow squash (I used round "eight ball" variety)
- 3 tablespoons extra virgin olive oil
- 1 medium red onion, diced (about 1 cup)
- 1 15-ounce can black beans, rinsed and drained
- 1-1/2 cups cooked brown rice
- 1/2 teaspoon smoked paprika
- 1/2 teaspoon red chili powder (preferably New Mexican)
- 1/4 cup chopped fresh cilantro, plus 2 Tbsp for garnish
- 3/4 cup grated Monterey Jack cheese
- 2 tablespoons chopped scallions
- sea salt
- freshly ground black pepper
- Roasted Red Pepper Sauce
- 2 red bell peppers
- 1/4 cup extra virgin olive oil
- 1 teaspoon freshly squeezed lemon juice
- sea salt (to taste)

Direction

- Stuffed Summer Squash
- Preheat oven to 375 degrees F.
- Trim ends from squash and halve lengthwise. Using a melon baller or small spoon, scoop out seeds from the halved squash. Place halves cut side up in a baking dish, drizzle with 1 tablespoon olive oil, and sprinkle with 1/2 teaspoon salt and 1/4 teaspoon black pepper. Bake until tender when pierced with a knife, about 15 minutes, and remove from oven.
- Heat 2 tablespoons olive oil in a large sauté pan over medium heat. Add red onion and 1/4 teaspoon salt, and cook, stirring occasionally, until onion begins to caramelize, 8 to 10 minutes. Add the black beans, brown rice, smoked paprika, and chili powder, stirring to combine. Remove from heat, stir in 1/4 cup of cilantro, and season with salt and pepper, to taste.
- Fill zucchini halves with the bean and rice mixture, mounding slightly, and top each with 2 tablespoons of grated cheese. Return to oven and bake until cheese is lightly browned and bubbling, 15 to 20 minutes. Garnish with 2 tablespoons chopped cilantro and scallions, and serve with roasted red pepper sauce.
- Roasted Red Pepper Sauce
- Roast peppers on the stovetop over a medium-high flame (or under a broiler), turning occasionally with tongs, until the skin is

- blackened on all sides. Place peppers in a bowl, cover tightly, and let sit for about 15 minutes. Remove skin, stem, and seeds.
- Puree flesh of roasted peppers with olive oil in a blender on high speed until very smooth, about 3 minutes. Stir in lemon juice and season to taste with sea salt.

318. Stuffed Celery With Cream Cheese

Serving: Serves 5 | Prep: | Cook: | Ready in:

Ingredients

- 1 bunch celery
- 8 ounces cream cheese
- 1 cup green olives stuffed with red pimentos
- 2 teaspoons paprika
- salt & pepper to taste

Direction

- In a bowl mix the cream cheese with paprika, salt and pepper
- Chop the olives real small then add to the cream cheese
- Use a potato peeler to softly peel the outsides of the celery sticks (this way you will not feel the strings when biting on it)
- Cut the celery stick to about 2 inches in length
- Fill each stick with the cream cheese mixture and they are ready to serve

319. Stuffing It Up Baby Artichoke

Serving: Makes six baby artichokes | Prep: | Cook: | Ready in:

Ingredients

- 6 Baby Artichokes
- 8 ounces Philadelphia Cream Cheese Onion & Chive
- 8 ounces Philadelphia Cream Cheese Sundried Tomatoes & Basil
- 2 cups Garlic and Herb Bread Crumbs
- 1/2 teaspoon Salt
- 1/4 teaspoon Ground Black Pepper
- 4 Fresh Garlic Cloves (crushed)
- 1 tablespoon Paprika
- 2 Celery Sticks (Chopped)
- 3 Green Onions (Chopped)
- 2 cups Fresh Parsley
- 1 Large Radish (Chopped)
- 1 Large Avocado
- 3 cups 100% Canola Oil
- 4 Large Thick-Cut Sliced Bacon
- 1 Large Lime (squeezed)
- 3 Large Slices of Flat Bread
- 2 cups Butter Milk
- 1 Large Artichoke with Removed Heart
- 0 Drizzle of Extra Virgin Olive Oil

Direction

- Cut bottom off of 6 Baby Artichokes and pull the leaves off until you see light green and/or purple. Pull all leaves out and make the artichokes a flower. Stuff all 6 baby artichokes with 8 oz. of Philadelphia Cream Cheese Onion & Chive (you can over stuff).
- In a medium size mixing bowl pour 2 cups of butter milk and add salt and ground black pepper to taste (at least ½ tea salt 7 ¼ tea ground black pepper). In another medium size mixing bowl mix 2 cups of Garlic and Herb Bread Crumbs, ½ tea paprika, salt and ground black pepper to taste. Set both aside for later use.
- In a large mixing bowl combine 8 oz. of Philadelphia Cream Cheese Sundried Tomatoes & Basil, 2 celery stocks cut into cubes, 3 green onions cut into cubes (use the entire onion), and 2 cups fresh parsley chopped, 1 large radish chopped into cubes, 1 large avocado, 1 large lime juiced and salt & ground black pepper to taste. Add all ingredients in large mixing bowl into a food

processor and mix until smooth. Pour into a large mixing bowl.
- Cut 4 large thick-cut bacon into slices and fry in a large skillet (medium heat). Once bacon is crisp put onto a plate with paper towels to dry. Once all grease is removed from bacon add to large mixing bowl with ingredients from food processor.
- Pre-heat oven to 350 degrees F. cut 3 large slices of flat bread into squares. Spray a baking sheet with non-stick cooking spray, place cut flat bread on baking sheet and drizzle with extra virgin olive oil, heat in oven for 10 mins.
- Take stuffed baby artichokes and drip head first into butter milk then roll in bread crumb mixture and set aside. Heat 3 cups of 100% canola oil in a large skillet (350 degrees F). Put baby artichokes into oil and fry each side for 2-4 mins, remove and let sit for 5 mins to cool.
- Cut heart out of the large artichoke and flower open then add bacon veggie mixture into the middle of the flowered artichoke. Place baked flat bread around large stuffed artichoke on a large serving dish. Take cooled fried baby artichokes and cut in half, place around flat bread and stuffed large artichoke.
- HINT: This dish can be served hot or cold, it will keep very well in the refrigerator for up to 2 days.

320. Sumac Chickpea Salad

Serving: Serves 2 | Prep: | Cook: | Ready in:

Ingredients

- Dressing
- 1 tablespoon Greek Yogurt
- 1/4 crushed garlic clove
- 1 pinch safron dissolved in water (or powder)
- squeeze lime juice
- pepper and salt
- Salade
- 1 cup welled and cooked small chickpeas (or canned)
- 1 tablespoon sumac
- 1 tablespoon paprika
- 3/4 crushed garlic clove
- 1 tomato
- 1 Lebanese cucumber
- 1/2 red capsicum
- Tablespoon chopped parley
- pepper and salt

Direction

- Dressing
- Mix all the ingredients together and set aside
- Salade
- Coat the chickpeas with the sumac, paprika, ¾ garlic clove, pepper and salt. Bake them in olive oil until a little browned.
- Cut the tomato, capsicum and cucumber in chickpea size.
- Mix everything together and garnish with a little parsley.

321. Summer Cooler

Serving: Serves 4 | Prep: | Cook: | Ready in:

Ingredients

- 3 Cucumbers
- 1 Raw Mango
- 1/2 Honey Dew Melon
- 1/4 teaspoon Salt
- 1/4 teaspoon Paprika
- 1/4 teaspoon cumin powder (optional)

Direction

- Peel and grate the cucumbers and strain through a sieve separating the pulp and the juice.
- Peel and grate the raw mango and strain through a sieve separating the pulp and the juice.
- Peel and grate the melon and strain through a sieve separating the pulp and the juice.

- Take 2 tablespoons of the cucumber pulp, 1 tablespoon of the mango pulp and 1 tablespoon of the melon pulp and mix together in a bowl. Add the salt, cumin and paprika to this and keep aside.
- Mix all the juices together in a separate bowl.
- Spoon out 1 tablespoon of the pulp mixture into a small glass and slowly pour the mixed juice over the pulp to top the glass. Chill in refrigerator for half an hour and enjoy.

322. Sun Dried Tomato Chorizo Garlic Shrimp

Serving: Serves 8 | Prep: | Cook: | Ready in:

Ingredients

- 1.5 pounds large fresh wild shrimp, shells removed and de-veined (leave tails on for easier eating!)
- 1 tablespoon olive oil
- 6 ounces dried semi-cured/uncured Spanish chorizo, sliced
- 1 cup finely chopped yellow onion
- 4 garlic cloves, minced
- 1/2 cup sun-dried tomatoes in olive oil, drained and rough-chopped
- 1/2 cup dry sherry
- 1/2 cup white wine
- 1 teaspoon smoked paprika or hot Hungarian paprika if you like it spicy!
- 1/2 teaspoon pepper
- 1 teaspoon salt
- 2 tablespoons butter (optional)
- serve with French or sourdough bread

Direction

- Slice chorizo and sauté over medium-high heat for about 1 minute on each side.
- Remove the meat from the pan and set aside.
- Using the same pan, add chopped onions, and ½ teaspoon salt and pepper. Cook for 3 minutes then add garlic and sun-dried tomatoes, and continue to cook for one more minute.
- Add half of the dry sherry and white wine, all the paprika, and another ½ teaspoon of salt. Allow the liquid to come up to a simmer, then add half the shrimp and cook for 2 minutes on each side (the shrimp should be opaque/pink and curled).
- Remove the shrimp and set aside. Add the rest of the dry sherry and white wine, return the liquid to a simmer, and repeat the steps to cook the remaining shrimp.
- Return the cooked chorizo and all the cooked shrimp to the pan, add 2 tablespoons of butter, and fold together. Let it cook for one more minute, serve warm with French or sourdough bread and garnish with chopped cilantro.

323. Sweet Chili Chicken Wings

Serving: Serves 4 | Prep: | Cook: | Ready in:

Ingredients

- 2 pounds chicken wings and drummettes
- 1/3 cup soy sauce
- 1/3 cup sweet chili sauce
- 2 tablespoons rice wine vinegar
- 1/4 cup honey
- 1 tablespoon sesame oil
- 1 teaspoon chili oil
- 2 teaspoons sriracha
- 2 garlic cloves, sliced
- Kosher salt
- Paprika
- Chinese five spice powder
- Scallions, diced

Direction

- Season the chicken liberally with five spice powder, paprika and salt. Spread on a flat layer on a baking sheet and slide into a

preheated oven at 375 degrees for approximately 20 minutes.
- While chicken bakes, mix the remaining ingredients in a small sauce pan over medium high heat. Once it begins to bubble, reduce to a simmer and cook until it begins to thicken.
- Remove chicken from the oven and drop the pieces into the sauce. Coat in the sauce, cover and simmer another 5-10 minutes until sauce gets thick and dark and coats the chicken. Remove from the sauce pan and sprinkle with scallions.

324. Sweet Corn Tacos

Serving: Serves 4 | Prep: | Cook: |Ready in:

Ingredients

- 3 ears sweet corn
- 3 tablespoons olive oil, divided
- 1/4 cup chopped scallion (green part only)
- 2 ounces Spanish chorizo, chopped
- 1 teaspoon apple cider vinegar
- 1/2 teaspoon smoked paprika
- 1/2 teaspoon salt
- 4 eggs
- 4 flour tortillas, warmed
- 1/4 cup baby arugula
- hot sauce for serving

Direction

- Husk the corn, remove the silk, and cut the corn kernels off the cobs into a bowl.
- Heat 1 Tbsp. olive oil in a large skillet over medium-high heat. Add the scallion and chorizo and cook until scallion is soft and chorizo begins to render, about 2-3 minutes.
- Add the corn and cook, stirring occasionally, until corn is tender and starting to caramelize, about 8-10 minutes. Add the cider vinegar, smoked paprika, and salt and cook 1 minute more. Season to taste with additional salt if needed.
- Transfer corn mixture to a separate bowl and wipe pan clean. Add another 1 Tbsp. olive oil, and once hot, crack in two of the eggs and fry them in the olive oil. Remove eggs to a plate, and repeat with the remaining 1 Tbsp. of oil and other two eggs.
- Place 1 egg atop each of the 4 warmed tortillas. Top each with equal amounts of the corn mixture, thinly sliced manchego cheese, and baby arugula leaves. Serve with hot sauce.

325. Sweet Onion & Corn Quinoa Fritters With Fresh Corn & Basil Salad

Serving: Serves 4 to 6 | Prep: | Cook: |Ready in:

Ingredients

- Fresh Corn and Basil Salad.
- 1 ear of fresh corn, shucked
- 1/2 cup loosely packed torn basil
- 1/4 cup finely minced sweet onion
- 1 teaspoon apple cider vinegar
- 1 teaspoon freshly squeezed lime juice
- 2 teaspoons olive oil
- Salt, black pepper, and crushed red pepper, to taste.
- Quinoa Fritters with Sweet Onion, Fresh Corn and Basil
- 1 ear of fresh corn, shucked
- 1 cup uncooked quinoa, rinsed and well drained
- 1/2 cup all purpose flour
- 1/3 cup minced sweet onion
- 1/2 cup loosely packed minced fresh basil
- 2 tablespoons ground flax seeds
- 6 tablespoons boiling water
- 2 teaspoons sea salt
- 1 teaspoon black pepper
- 1 teaspoon crushed red pepper
- 1 teaspoon paprika
- 2 tablespoons nutritional yeast (optional but strongly encouraged)

- Oil for frying: 2 to 3 tablespoons to start, plus more as needed.

Direction

- Fresh Corn and Basil Salad.
- Carefully shave kernels from the ear of corn with a kitchen knife into a medium mixing bowl.
- Add basil and sweet onion.
- In a small bowl, whisk together apple cider vinegar, lime juice, and olive oil.
- Pour dressing over corn mixture and toss to combine.
- Season with salt, black pepper, and crushed red pepper to taste.
- Quinoa Fritters with Sweet Onion, Fresh Corn and Basil
- In a medium saucepan over medium-high heat, toast rinsed quinoa for 4 to 5 minutes, stirring constantly, until lightly browned and fragrant.
- Add two cups of water and bring to a boil. Reduce to a simmer, cover, and let cook for 12 to 15 minutes until all liquid is absorbed.
- Allow cooked quinoa to cool completely before continuing with the recipe. The quinoa can easily be made a day ahead of time.
- In a small bowl, whisk together ground flax seeds and 6 tablespoons of boiling water. Set aside and allow to cool completely and thicken.
- Place a box grater over a bowl or dish and grate the ear of corn until all kernels are removed. You will wind up with about 1/3 cup of pulpy corn mash.
- In a large mixing bowl combine the cooled quinoa, grated corn, minced onion, basil, flour, nutritional yeast, salt, peppers, and paprika. Stir to combine, being careful not to over-mix.
- Add cooled flax mixture, then stir gently until combined. Season to taste.
- Using a tablespoon, scoop out dough and gently form it into balls using your hands. Roll in a little bit of flour, flatten into a patty and set in a single layer on a plate or baking sheet.
- Heat 2 tablespoons of oil in a heavy skillet over medium-high heat. In batches, add fritters and cook for 3 to 4 minutes on each side, until golden brown and crispy. Add more oil as needed.
- Drain cooked fritters on paper towels. Serve with Corn and Basil Salad.

326. Sweet Potato Gratin With Smoked Paprika And Cayenne

Serving: Serves 6-8 | Prep: | Cook: | Ready in:

Ingredients

- 3 medium sweet potatoes
- 1 1/2 cups heavy cream
- 3 tablespoons butter
- 1-2 teaspoons smoked paprika
- 1/2 teaspoon cayenne pepper
- Salt and Pepper, to taste

Direction

- Preheat oven to 350 degrees.
- Peel the sweet potatoes and slice them thinly. (I usually use my mandolin).
- Set aside enough of the prettiest slices of sweet potatoes to cover the gratin dish you are using. (The sweet potatoes will likely have smaller or half slices in addition to perfect coins).
- In a medium gratin dish, arrange one layer of sweet potatoes. Sprinkle with salt and pepper, a pinch of cayenne and a large pinch of smoked paprika. Dot with butter, and pour over a small portion of the cream.
- Continue with the remainder of the sweet potatoes, sprinkling each layer with the seasonings and dotting with butter. Use the reserved sweet potatoes for the top layer.
- Pour remaining cream over sweet potatoes. Cover the dish with tinfoil.
- Bake, covered for 30 minutes. Remove the foil and bake for an additional 30 minutes, or until cream is absorbed and potatoes have browned.

327. Sweet Potato And Cilantro Quesadilla With Fried Egg And Cumin Oil

Serving: Serves 4 | Prep: | Cook: | Ready in:

Ingredients

- 2 small sweet potatoes, peeled and thinly sliced
- 1/2 teaspoon smoked paprika
- 1 tablespoon lime juice
- 1/2 cup cilantro leaves
- 4 large eggs
- 2 tablespoons olive oil
- 1 teaspoon cumin seeds
- 8 small (about 6-inch) corn tortillas
- Lime wedges, for serving

Direction

- In a medium saucepan fitted with a steamer basket, place sweet potatoes. Cover and steam sweet potatoes until tender, 6 minutes. While potatoes cook, heat 2 tablespoons oil in a large, heavy skillet over medium. Add cumin seeds and cook until toasted, 1 minute. Pour off cumin oil into a small bowl and reserve. (Do not wipe out skillet.) Crack eggs into skillet and cook, without turning, until whites are set and yolks are still runny, 2 to 3 minutes. Transfer eggs to a plate and cover with foil to keep warm. (Reserve skillet.)
- When potatoes are tender, transfer to a bowl with paprika and lime juice; season with salt and pepper and gently toss to coat. Divide sweet potatoes among 4 tortillas; top with cilantro and remaining tortillas. Return reserved skillet to medium-high heat. Cook quesadillas until charred in spots on both sides, about 2 minutes per side, in two batches. Serve each quesadilla topped with a fried egg, drizzled with reserved cumin oil.

328. Sweet And Smoky Beet Burgers

Serving: Makes 8 burgers | Prep: | Cook: | Ready in:

Ingredients

- 1 yellow onion
- 3 tablespoons grapeseed oil, plus extra for searing
- 1 cup peeled and grated raw beets (approximately 1 small beet)
- 3 cloves garlic, crushed
- 1 cup walnuts
- 1/2 cup golden raisins
- 2 teaspoons sweet smoked paprika
- 1/2 cup cooked green lentils, rinsed and drained
- Sea salt and freshly ground pepper
- 2 cups cooked short-grain brown rice or white sushi rice, at room temperature
- 1 egg

Direction

- Slice the onion to a thickness of 1/4 inch. In a medium skillet, sauté the onion in the oil over medium-high heat for 10 to 15 minutes, until it starts to darken and caramelize. Turn down the heat slightly and add the beets along with the garlic, walnuts, raisins, and paprika, and cook for 10 minutes, stirring often.
- Transfer the contents of the skillet to a food processor and pulse several times until chunky. In a large bowl, combine the onion mixture with the lentils, 2 teaspoons salt, and 1 teaspoon pepper. Replace the food processor without washing and add the rice and egg, and pulse to form a coarse puree. Add the rice mixture to the onion-lentil mixture and mix well with your hands.
- Lightly oil your hands and divide the dough into 8 portions. Shape each portion into a patty just under 1 inch thick.
- Heat a heavy-bottomed skillet over medium-high heat and add oil to coat the bottom. Place

the burgers in the skillet and cook undisturbed for 5 minutes. Gently flip the burgers and turn down the heat to low. Cover and cook for 10 minutes, until the burgers have a firm, brown crust. Serve hot with your favorite condiments.

329. Taco Rice Or Takoraisu, Tex Mex Japanese Fusion

Serving: Serves 6-8 | Prep: | Cook: | Ready in:

Ingredients

- 2 lbs ground beef (I use 80% lean)
- 2 medium onions, chopped
- 6 medium garlic cloves, diced or crushed
- 2 tbsp vegetable or olive oil
- 6 tbsp soy sauce, preferably reduced sodium
- 1 tsp table salt
- 2 tsp sweet smoked paprika (some recipes ask for cumin but i don't like it)
- 1 tsp ground black pepper
- 1-2 tsp Sriracha sauce or chili powder
- 4 cups shredded lettuce (I prefer a mix of arugula and spinach)
- 2 cups tomatoes, chopped (I prefer cherry tomatoes)
- 1/2 cup cilantro, chopped (optional)
- 2-4 cups shredded cheese like mozarella or cheddar (or, like me, a combination of shredded cheese and crumbled queso fresco)
- 2 cups salsa (I use storebought, i.e., Pace The Original Piquante Sauce Mild)
- 1 cup sour cream
- Cooked white rice (i prepare 3 cups uncooked rice)
- Optional - Slices of avocado and lime wedges
- Optional - Tortilla chips

Direction

- Heat oil in a sauté pan over medium heat. Add onions and sauté until onions are soft, then add the garlic and stir for 30 to 60 seconds. Add the beef and break it into small chunks if necessary. Once cooked and brown, add the soy sauce, salt, paprika, ground pepper, and sriracha sauce or chili powder. Let it simmer till liquid is reduced. I like to transfer beef to another plate and drain/remove some of the fat (particularly if you use 80% lean like me).
- Spread 1 1/2 to 2 cups rice on each plate/bowl. Top with seasoned beef (maybe 1/3 to 1/2 cup), then the greens (maybe 1/2 cup), tomatoes (maybe 1/4 cup), salsa (maybe 1/4 cup), cheese (maybe 1/4 cup), and a dollop of sour cream (maybe 1-2 tbsp.).
- If desired, top with some cilantro, and place a few tortilla chips next to the rice. You can also serve sliced avocados and lime wedges on a separate plate.

330. Tandoori Chicken Kebabs

Serving: Serves 8 | Prep: | Cook: | Ready in:

Ingredients

- 2 pounds chicken tenderloins
- 1/2 cup chopped sweet onion
- juice from 1/2 of a lemon
- 2 cloves of minced garlic
- 2 tablespoons olive oil
- 1 1/2 teaspoons paprika
- 1 teaspoon turmeric
- 1 teaspoon garam masala
- 1/4 teaspoon coriander
- 1/8 teaspoon cayenne pepper
- 1/2 teaspoon salt
- 1/2 cup plain 2% greek yogurt
- fresh cilantro for garnish
- 8 skewers

Direction

- If you're using wooden skewers, be sure to soak them in cold water for one hour prior to skewering the chicken, so that they don't burn

- on your grill. For metal skewers, lightly grease them with olive oil or cooking spray. Preheat and clean your grill.
- Combine the onions, lemon juice, garlic, olive oil, paprika, turmeric, garam masala, coriander, cayenne, salt, and Greek yogurt in the cup that came with your hand mixer, or in a blender or a food processor. Puree until smooth.
- Trim off the small piece of tendon that may be on some of your chicken tenderloins and then cut into 1" bite-sized pieces.
- Skewer the chicken, and then coat with kebab sauce. Allow them to marinade for 15-30 minutes before grilling.
- Grill over direct high heat (450°-550° F) for 10-12 minutes, turning 2 or 3 times. Be sure to keep the lid closed as much as possible.
- Serve on the skewer, or slide them off with a fork (metal skewers tend to get too hot for serving). Garnish with cilantro before serving.

331. Tandoori Coconut Chicken

Serving: Serves 4 | Prep: | Cook: | Ready in:

Ingredients

- For the marinade and chicken:
- 1/4 cup white vinegar
- two 14-ounce cans unsweetened coconut milk
- one piece 3-inch by 1-inch fresh ginger, peeled and julienned
- 1 clove garlic, crushed
- 4 pounds bone-in, skinless chicken thighs
- For the spice paste:
- 2 tablespoons cumin seeds
- 1/2 teaspoon cardamom seeds (from about 12 to 15 pods)
- 1/2 teaspoon whole cloves
- 3 teaspoons coriander seeds
- 2 bay leaves
- 2 teaspoons kosher salt
- 1/2 teaspoon black peppercorns
- 1 teaspoon sweet paprika
- 2 teaspoons annatto powder
- 3 teaspoons ground turmeric
- 1/2 teaspoon ground cinnamon
- 2 fresh lemons, zest and juice reserved
- 1 cup coconut oil, warm and melted
- 1 red onion, sliced for garnish (optional)
- 2 lemons, washed and thinly sliced for garnish (optional

Direction

- Marinate the chicken: Combine the vinegar, coconut milk, ginger, and garlic in a large mixing bowl and whisk well to combine. Add the chicken, turn to coat, and cover with plastic wrap. Refrigerate for 8 to 12 hours or overnight. Remove the chicken from the refrigerator about 15 to 10 minutes before cooking.
- Make the spice paste: Heat a cast-iron pan or heavy skillet over high heat until hot. Add the whole spices – the cumin, cardamom, cloves, and coriander – to the pan and swirl the spices around for 30 seconds, until they are fragrant. Transfer the warmed spices to a grinder, add the bay leaves, black pepper, and salt, and grind until powdery. Place the spice mixture into a small mixing bowl. Add the paprika, annatto, turmeric, cinnamon, lemon juice and zest, and the melted coconut oil and mix to combine into a paste.
- Preheat oven to 385°F. Spray two broiling pans with nonstick vegetable oil spray. Place the broiling pans in the oven.
- Remove the chicken from the marinade, pat dry with paper towels and place on a rimmed baking sheet and cover with plastic wrap. Discard the marinade and do not reuse in any manner. Allow to the chicken come to room temperature while the pans get very hot, about 5 to 7 minutes. The chill needs to be off the chicken so the paste won't clump, but you don't want it sit out too long, as it's a safety concern. Remove the plastic wrap and rub the

paste liberally all over the chicken. Let stand while the pans get hot.
- Place the chicken on the broiling pans and cook for 25 to 30 minutes, until an instant-read thermometer inserted into the thickest part reads 165°F and the juices run clear when a paring knife is inserted into the thickest part (the roasting time will depend upon the size of the chicken thighs). Garnish with sliced red onion and lemon slices and serve hot with rice.

332. Tangy Creamy Buttermilk Cucumbers

Serving: Serves 6 | Prep: | Cook: |Ready in:

Ingredients

- 3 cucumbers-sliced thinly
- 1 onion-sliced into thin rounds
- 1 cup buttermilk
- 1 cup sour cream
- 3 tablespoons apple cider vinegar
- 3 tablespoons sugar
- 1 teaspoon dried dill
- 2 tablespoons fresh dill
- 1/4 teaspoon salt and pepper
- 1 teaspoon minced garlic
- 1 teaspoon paprika

Direction

- Combine the cucumbers and onions in a deep bowl
- In a separate bowl, whisk together the buttermilk, sour cream, vinegar, sugar, dill, salt, pepper, garlic and paprika.
- Pour the buttermilk over the vegetables and refrigerate for an hour.

333. Thanksgiving Sauerkraut

Serving: Makes about 4 to 6 servings and can easily be doubled | Prep: | Cook: |Ready in:

Ingredients

- 2 tablespoons butter
- 2 tablespoons turkey or chicken drippings or olive oil
- 1 cup rough chopped onion
- 2 tablespoons sweet Hungarian paprika
- 1 to 2 teaspoons salt (depending on the saltiness of your rinsed sauerkraut)
- 1/2 teaspoon black pepper
- 6 cups chopped cabbage
- 2 cups turkey or chicken broth, divided 1/1
- 2 1/2 cups shredded sauerkraut, rinsed and drained

Direction

- In a very large sauté pan, heat the butter and drippings/oil. Add the chopped onion and sauté until softened. Stir in the paprika, salt and pepper.
- Add the cabbage and 1 cup of the broth. Partially cover and continue to cook on medium heat until the cabbage begins to wilt.
- Stir in the sauerkraut and the second cup of broth. Transfer to an appropriate sized baking dish. Cover and bake at 350F for 25 to 30 minutes. Uncover and bake 15 minutes more.
- NOTE: This is also a great side for roast pork or chicken.

334. That Bacon Roast Chicken

Serving: Serves 3-4 | Prep: | Cook: |Ready in:

Ingredients

- 1 (5 to 6-pound) roasting chicken
- Kosher salt

- Freshly ground black pepper
- 3 tablespoons paprika
- 1 large bunch fresh sage
- 3 shallots, cut into wide slices
- 3 tablespoons olive oil
- 4 slices Gluten Free bacon
- 1 cup Gluten Free chicken stock if desired*

Direction

- Preheat the oven to 425 degrees F
- Remove the chicken giblets. Rinse the chicken inside and out. Remove any excess fat and leftover pinfeathers and pat the outside dry. Use about 3/4ths of the shallots and half of the sage to create a bed for the chicken in a large roasting pan, place the chicken on top. Liberally salt and pepper the inside of the chicken. Stuff the cavity with the remaining sage and shallots, reserving one nice looking spring of sage to garnish the chicken. Drizzle the olive oil over the chicken to coat, and sprinkle with paprika, salt and pepper. Tie the legs together with kitchen string or a roasting band and tuck the wing tips under the body of the chicken. Lay the bacon slices over the chicken to cover.
- Roast the chicken for 1 hour. If the bacon looks crispy, remove the bacon slices from the top of the chicken and set aside. (If the bacon isn't crispy, check it again in 5-7 minutes & remove.) Continue roasting the chicken for an additional 1/2 hour, or until the juices run clear when you cut between a leg and thigh. Remove from the oven and tent with foil for 5-10 minutes.
- Place the chicken on a platter for serving, replacing the bacon and adding the fresh sage for garnish.*If you'd like to make a pan gravy, see directions below.
- *For Pan Gravy: Remove the shallots & sage from the bottom of the roasting pan, leaving at least 2 tablespoons of the fat from the bottom of the pan. Place the roasting pan over two burners on medium-high and add the chicken stock and bring it to a boil. Reduce the heat, and simmer for about 5 minutes, or until reduced by half. Serve with the chicken.

335. The Best Buddha Bowl | Chickpea Scramble Breakfast Bowl

Serving: Serves 2 | Prep: | Cook: |Ready in:

Ingredients

- 3 tablespoons aquafaba
- 1 can chickpeas
- 1/4 teaspoon ground turmeric
- 1 teaspoon ground cumin
- 1/2 teaspoon sweet smoked paprika
- 3 tablespoons nutritional yeast
- Salt and pepper, to taste
- 2 spring onions, roughly cut
- 4 garlic cloves, minced
- 1/4 lemon, juiced
- 2 cups baby spinach, roughly sliced
- Seeds from 1 fresh pomegranate
- 1 small sweet potato, roughly chopped and roasted, to serve
- 1/2 avocado sprinkled with black and white sesame seeds, to serve
- 1/4 head leftover cooked cauliflower, to serve

Direction

- Add aquafaba, chickpeas, turmeric, cumin, paprika, nutritional yeast, and salt and pepper to a bowl and mash until only a small amount of chickpeas are still whole.
- Heat some oil in a sauté pan over a medium heat. Add spring onions and garlic cloves and cook until browning and fragrant. Add the chickpea mix and lemon juice, and let cook for 2 minutes.
- Add the spinach and mix through. Cook for a further 5-8 minutes, until spinach has wilted.

- Divide the chickpea mix into two bowls and add the pomegranate seeds. Add the leftover cauliflower, sweet potato and avocado, and serve.

336. Tilapia With Smoked Paprika Butter And Broccoli In Foil Packets

Serving: Serves 4 | Prep: 0hours10mins | Cook: 0hours15mins | Ready in:

Ingredients

- For smoked paprika butter:
- 4 tablespoons unsalted butter, at room temperature
- 1 tablespoon Spanish smoked paprika
- finely grated zest from 1 small lemon (reserving juice for broccoli)
- 1 teaspoon whole-grain or Dijon mustard
- 1/4 teaspoon kosher salt, or to taste
- For rest of dish:
- 4 tilapia fillets, 6 ounces each
- kosher salt + freshly ground black pepper, to taste
- 1 large (or 2 small) heads of broccoli (about 1 pound), cut or thinly sliced into very small florets, about 1/4 to 1/2-inch thick (about 4 heaping cups once chopped)
- 2 teaspoons lemon juice (from lemon you zested)
- 2 teaspoons olive oil
- optional sandwiches ideas:
- 4 large hoagie rolls, toasted or grilled
- good sandwich toppings include: mayo, roasted bell pepper, arugula, Bibb lettuce, pickled red onions, olive salad

Direction

- Heat oven to 400° F. Alternatively, heat your grill to medium-high.
- To make the smoked paprika butter: mix all the ingredients together in small bowl until well incorporated. Set aside.
- Season both sides of tilapia fillets with kosher salt and pepper, to taste. Toss broccoli with lemon juice and olive oil in a medium bowl, and season to taste with salt and pepper.
- On a large sheet pan or baking sheet, lay out four 12-inch sheets of foil. Divide broccoli evenly among the four sheets (about 1 cup on each sheet), then top with a tilapia fillet and a tablespoon of butter, smeared evenly over the top of the fillet. Tightly fold or crimp edges of the foil together several times to create an airtight packet.
- Place sheet pan with the four packets in the oven and bake for about 12 to 15 minutes, or until the thickest part of the tilapia is opaque and cooked through. At about 10 minutes, open one of the packets to check for doneness to be on the safe side. If the tilapia isn't done, reseal and return all the packets to the oven. (Alternatively, the foil packets can be cooked directly on the grates of a covered grill for 12 to 15 minutes.)
- Remove from the oven and carefully open the packets. Transfer the contents to plates, or place the foil packets on plates so each person can open them at the table. Alternatively, tuck the contents into toasted rolls; see ingredient list for sandwich ideas.

337. Tilapia With Black Cherry And Avocado.

Serving: Serves 1 | Prep: | Cook: | Ready in:

Ingredients

- 1 cup Mixed greens (kale, spinach, arangula)
- 1/4 cup Black cherries (chopped)
- 1/4 cup Avocado (chopped)
- 1 tablespoon lemon juice
- 1 tablespoon Coconut oil

- 1 teaspoon kosher salt
- 1 Tilapia fillet
- 1 teaspoon pepper
- 1 teaspoon Smoked paprika
- 1 tablespoon Olive oil (frying)

Direction

- Heat skillet with coconut and olive oil on medium heat.
- Season fish with salt, pepper, paprika and thyme. Fry each side of the fish on the skillet for 4 mins until opaque and fish flakes.
- Meanwhile, prepare salad. Deseed black cherries, dice avocado and add to bowl of mixed greens
- Adjust seasoning to soothe your taste.

338. Tofu Kebabs

Serving: Serves 6-8 | Prep: | Cook: | Ready in:

Ingredients

- 10 Wooden Skewers
- 1 Green Bell Pepper
- 2 Red Onions
- 14 ounces Extra firm block of Tofu
- 1 cup Coriander leaves, chopped
- 1/2 cup Mint Leaves, chopped
- 1 teaspoon Cumin Seeds
- 2 Garlic cloves, peeled
- 1/2 teaspoon inch fresh ginger root, peeled
- 1 tablespoon Lemon Juice
- 1 teaspoon Paprika
- 1 teaspoon Salt
- Oil to grease

Direction

- Cut green pepper and 1 onion into similar sized pieces, preferably into 1 inch cubes. Chop the other onion into coarse pieces; Set aside
- Drain the water in the tofu packet. Cut the Tofu squares into 1 inch cubes.
- In a blender, combine cilantro, mint, onion, garlic, cumin seeds, ginger with a 1/4 cup water. Add water as necessary and blend to a smooth paste. Do not make the mixture runny.
- Add Salt, lemon juice and Paprika. In a bowl, add the onion, green pepper, and tofu pieces to the Coriander and Mint sauce
- Refrigerate for about 2 hours. Soak wooden skewers in water for about 30 min. Preheat the oven to 400F
- Oil/Grease a baking sheet. Alternately thread tofu, onion, and green pepper pieces onto the skewers.
- Bake for 6 minutes and rotating the skewers, bake an additional 6- 8 minutes. I also like to broil on Hi for 3-4 minutes. That is completely optional.
- Serve with the remaining chutney as a dip or drizzle on top

339. Togarashi Grilled Cauliflower With Grilled Spring Onions And Plums.

Serving: Serves 3-4 | Prep: | Cook: | Ready in:

Ingredients

- 1 head Cauliflower
- 3 spring onions
- 3/4 cup extra virgin olive oil, separated
- 1/2 tablespoon togarashi
- 1/2 tablespoon smoked paprika
- 4 black plums
- 1 cup fresh mint
- 1/2 cup fresh cilantro
- 1/4 cup toasted sunflower seeds
- 3 cloves garlic
- 2-3 teaspoons kosher salt, to taste

Direction

- Pour 1/2 C olive oil into a bowl and whisk in salt to taste, togarashi and paprika.
- Slice onions in half, and slice cauliflower into steaks (planks), through the middle of the head. Add to the olive oil/spice marinade.
- Preheat indoor or outdoor grill to high heat, and clean grill grates. When hot, add onions and cauliflower and grill on each side 3-4 minutes until lightly charred. Remove from the grill when done, and set aside.
- Slice plums into wedges or large slices and brush with olive oil. Place on the grill and cook 2 minutes per side, until tender, juicy and you get grill marks
- In a small food processor, combine garlic cloves, cilantro, mint (reserve a few mint leaves for garnish later), sunflower seeds, and salt to taste. Pulse 7-8 times, until ground up and mealy. Add 4-5 T olive oil and pulse again, to get a thick pesto-like consistency.
- To plate the dish: Layer onions and cauliflower on a plate or platter (if serving family style), sprinkle around grilled plums and herb sauce, garnish with fresh mint leaves and drizzle with olive oil. Enjoy!

340. Tomato Cheddar Biscuits

Serving: Makes 6 medium biscuits | Prep: | Cook: | Ready in:

Ingredients

- 2 cups (8 1/2 ounces) all-purpose flour
- 2 teaspoons baking powder
- 1/2 teaspoon baking soda
- 1/2 teaspoon salt
- 1/2 teaspoon ground paprika
- 1/8 teaspoon cayenne pepper (optional, if you like heat!)
- 6 tablespoons cold unsalted butter
- 1/2 cup chopped sun-dried tomatoes (not in oil)
- 1 cup grated cheddar cheese
- 1/2 cup cold milk

Direction

- Preheat the oven to 450° F. Line a baking sheet with parchment paper.
- In a large bowl, whisk together the flour, baking powder, baking soda, salt, paprika, and cayenne (if using).
- Cut the butter into the dry ingredients using a fork or pastry cutter until it's in mostly pea-sized chunks—some chunks can be slightly larger and some smaller, but don't overwork it.
- Add the tomatoes and cheese and stir to combine.
- Add the milk, stir the dough with a fork until it is somewhat evenly moistened, then knead it a few times in the bowl so it mostly comes together in a ball but don't overwork it at all. It should not be cohesive and there should be chunks of drier areas and some wetter areas.
- Turn the dough out onto the parchment-lined sheet, and fold it over onto itself until there aren't any dry spots remaining. Don't think of this as kneading: You want to handle it gently and as you fold, the wet/dry areas will disappear. Fold about 10 times, then gently press the dough down to a rectangle about 2" high.
- Using a sharp knife, cut the dough into 2" squares and separate them slightly on the baking sheet.
- Bake for about 12-15 minutes, or until golden brown. Let cool slightly, then eat!

341. Tomato Soup With Paprika

Serving: Serves 6 | Prep: | Cook: | Ready in:

Ingredients

- 8 tomatoes - medium - very ripe
- 1 onion - medium
- 1 celery stalk - choose a lighter green from the inside

- 1 carrot - medium
- 1 garlic cloves
- 3 tablespoons parsley very finely chopped
- 4 tablespoons Extra Virgin Olive Oil
- 1 teaspoon Paprika
- Salt
- 1 egg, hard boiled for decoration

Direction

- Wash the tomatoes and cut them in pieces. Pass them through the juicer so you have pure tomato juice. If you don't have a juicer, blanch the tomatoes, cut them in quarters, deseed them and pass the tomatoes through a food mill (or purée sieve). The important issue here is that you want the tomatoes to remain red. If you process them in a food blender, this will incorporate air to the tomatoes and they turn pinkish.
- Chop the onion in very small pieces.
- Peel the garlic, cut in half, remove the inside green part and chop very, very finely.
- Wash the celery stalk, trim the base and discard the leaves. Cut the stalk lengthwise in thin strips and then across to obtain very small cubes.
- Peel the carrot and cut it up in very small cubes, the size of the cubes you made with the celery.
- In a large pot over moderate heat warm up the olive oil. Add the onions and let them sweat for a little while, then add the garlic and cook for 1 minute. Add the celery and after 2 minutes add the carrots. This sequence is important so that in the end your carrots still have a crunch to them.
- Add the tomato juice and bring to a boil. If the juice is very watery simmer uncovered for 20 minutes to evaporate some water and thicken the soup. If the juice is nice and thick, simmer covered for 20 minutes. Check the consistency of the soup, it should be thick and you should still see the pieces of vegetables in it. If it's very watery, simmer uncovered until it thickens.
- Season with salt and if acidic add a pinch of sugar. Add the paprika and 2 tablespoons of parsley and let cook for a further 5 minutes.
- Serve hot. As an option for serving, you can hard boil an egg (10 minutes) and after cold, chop it in very small pieces, white and yolk together. Add it on top of the soup, a pinch of paprika over the chopped eggs and sprinkle with some parsley.

342. Uncle Arje's Shakshuka (Eggs Poached In Tomato Sauce)

Serving: Serves 4 | Prep: | Cook: |Ready in:

Ingredients

- 1 14oz Can of Diced Tomatoes
- 1 Red Pepper Chopped
- 1 Sweet Onion Diced
- 1 Garlic Clove Chopped
- 2 teaspoons Paprika
- 1 teaspoon Cumin
- 4-6 Eggs (depending on how hungry everyone is)
- 1 tablespoon Extra Virgin Olive Oil
- Salt to Taste
- 2-3 Chopped Chili Peppers With or Without Seeds Depending on how much Spice You Like (Optional)
- Sprig Fresh Parsley or Mint to Garnish (Optional)
- Drop Greek Yogurt (Optional)

Direction

- Add your olive oil to a heated shallow saucepan that has a tight fitting lid. Once the oil is heated through, add your onions and garlic and salt liberally.
- When your onions are translucent, add your peppers with some more salt. Add about half of your paprika and cumin as well. Fry until the peppers are soft.

- Add the tomato and the rest of your spices. At this point you can add you chili peppers if you like your shakshuka spicy. Taste and adjust your seasoning if necessary. Simmer for about 5 minutes.
- Gently break your eggs one at a time into your simmering tomatoes. Then cover and poach until the eggs are cooked to your liking. Make sure your heat isn't too high!
- Remove from the heat, garnish and serve immediately! I love having shakshuka with some fresh pita or really good crusty bread (unless you are going for gluten free). The best part is using your bread to soak up all of the deliciousness in the bottom of the pan.
- Save any leftover for a fantastic pita sandwich for lunch the next day; or save some to eat over rice, couscous, or quinoa for dinner!

343. Vegan Beetloaf

Serving: Serves 6-8 | Prep: | Cook: | Ready in:

Ingredients

- 3/4 cup raw unsalted sunflower seeds
- 1/2 cup rolled oats
- 1/2 pound mushrooms
- 1 cup cooked adzuki beans
- 1-1/2 cups (packed) grated beets
- 1 small onion, coarsely chopped (about 1/2 c.)
- 2 teaspoons tomato paste
- 2 teaspoons smoked paprika
- 1 teaspoon salt

Direction

- Pre-heat oven to 375 degrees. Lightly oil a 9x5" loaf pan (silicon is best for extracting the loaf later).
- Place sunflower seeds, oats and mushrooms in a food processor and run until a crumbly uniform texture is achieved. Add in beans and pulse a few times to integrate them.
- Place sunflower seed mixture in a large mixing bowl and add beet and onion. Stir well with a heavy wooden spoon. Once vegetables are well-distributed, stir in tomato paste, smoked paprika and salt.
- Transfer beet loaf mixture to the greased loaf pan, using a spatula to smooth the top evenly. Bake for 55-65 minutes, until top is firm and just slightly crisp. Remove beet loaf from oven and let it cool 8-10 minutes before slicing and serving.
- Beet loaf can be made ahead and refrigerated. When ready to serve, reheat at 350 degrees for 15-18 minutes.

344. Vegan Cashew Caesar Salad

Serving: Serves 2 | Prep: | Cook: | Ready in:

Ingredients

- 1/2 cup cashew cream
- 1 lemon, zested
- 2 lemons, juiced
- 2 cloves garlic
- 1 teaspoon mustard
- 2 tablespoons olive oil
- 3 tablespoons nutritional yeast, divided
- 1/8 teaspoon soy sauce
- 1/4 teaspoon salt
- 1/4 teaspoon pepper
- 5 cups kale, stems removed and torn into bite-sized peices
- 1/2 cup salted and toasted sunflower seeds
- 1 pinch smoked paprika
- 1 avocado, diced

Direction

- In a food processor, combine the cashew cream, lemon juice and zest, garlic, mustard, olive oil, 1 tablespoon nutritional yeast, soy sauce, and salt and pepper. Blend until smooth. Taste and adjust seasoning.

- Put the kale in a large bowl, sprinkle it with a pinch of salt, and a squeeze of lemon juice. Massage it until it begins to soften. Combine with the dressing, mixing well.
- Finally, combine the remaining 2 tablespoons nutritional yeast, smoked paprika, and sunflower seeds, and grind to a crumbly texture. Set aside.
- To assemble the salad, mix in the avocado and sprinkle with the sunflower crumble.

345. Vegan Makhani (aka Butter Chicken Without The Butter Or Chicken)

Serving: Serves 4 | Prep: | Cook: | Ready in:

Ingredients

- The Sauce and Rice
- 1 cup basmati rice, rinsed
- 2 cups water
- 1 tablespoon coconut or vegetable oil
- 3 cloves garlic, minced
- 1 square inch ginger, minced
- 1 teaspoon dried turmeric
- 1 teaspoon sweet paprika (I used spanish)
- 2 teaspoons garam masala
- 1 teaspoon ground cumin
- 1/4 - 1/2 teaspoons cayenne (this is optional, I opted for a fully sweet sauce because my kids are wimps)
- 1 (14oz/400ml) can of diced tomatoes
- 3 tablespoons coconut oil
- 1/2 can coconut milk (about 4oz/120mL)
- 1/4 cup raisins
- 1 teaspoon salt
- The Chickpeas (Chana)
- 3 cups cooked chickpeas (canned will work, but rinse them well.)
- the zest of half a lemon
- 1 tablespoon sweet paprika
- 1/2 teaspoon himalayan pink salt
- the juice of half a lemon

Direction

- Using a rice cooker or a lovely bevel-lidded heavy cooking pot, rinse the rice, set in the cooking device with twice the amount of water, and bring it to a boil, then quickly set the heat to low for about 20 minutes. (We all have our rice tricks, use yours!)
- While the rice bubbles away, you can begin your sauce. Start by gathering all the dried spices in a little bowl (minus the salt.) Then chop and prepare your garlic and ginger for cooking. Open your tins of tomatoes and coconut milk, and set up your raisins and coconut oil so that you have everything at the ready.
- In a wide pan, over medium heat, melt the tablespoon of coconut oil until it coats the bottom, then toss in your garlic and ginger and let them simmer until softened and fragrant. This is when you can quickly add the spices and use your senses to tell when it's time to cool the mixture down with your tomatoes. You do not want to burn the garlic and spices, just release the flavours and cook them gently.
- Once you are ready, add the tomatoes and 1/4 cup of raisins, (To be honest, I added the raisins that my son had not eaten from his snack because I felt like the sauce may be more popular if it was a little sweeter.) Add the second teaspoon of Garam Masala and let it simmer together until the raisins are plump and the tomatoes start to bubble (about 5-7 minutes.)
- Use a spatula to scrape the contents of your pan into a blender and blend it all up into a sauce, then let that sit while you cook your chickpeas.
- Using the same pan as your sauce, set a little oil to prevent the chickpeas from sticking, toss the chickpeas in the paprika to coat them lightly, adding more as needed. Then toss the chickpeas in the pan on medium heat and sprinkle with salt and the zest of half a lemon. Let them toast up and darken a little, then squeeze the rest of the lemon juice over them.

Let them cook for a few more minutes while you finish your sauce.
- Fluff the basmati with a fork and serve in flat bowls. (Pasta bowl-styles will do.) Ladle your sauce and chickpeas over the rice and serve with a garnish of chopped coriander (or parsley if you're one of those people who hate coriander.) Smaakelijk!

346. Vegan And Gluten Free Étouffée

Serving: Serves 4 to 6 | Prep: | Cook: | Ready in:

Ingredients

- 1 lb medium-firm tofu
- 1 green pepper, diced, seeds removed
- 1 yellow onion, diced
- 2 small zucchini, sliced in half moons
- 10 ounces portobello mushrooms, chopped
- 3 celery stalks, diced
- 1 cup crushed tomatoes in juice
- 2 cups vegetable broth
- 1/4 cup gluten free flour
- 6 tablespoons olive oil
- 5 garlic cloves, minced
- 10 dashes hot sauce
- 1 teaspoon thyme
- 3/4 teaspoon salt
- 1/2 teaspoon black pepper
- 1/2 teaspoon paprika
- 1/2 teaspoon cayenne * start with 1/4 tsp if sensitive to heat
- 3-5 drops liquid smoke, optional
- 1/4 cup scallions, chopped finely, optional for serving
- 3 cups cooked brown rice, optional for serving

Direction

- Take tofu and slice open the package. Drain liquid and wrap the tofu with paper towels/cheesecloth and set a tray or plate on top of tofu with heavy items on top to press excess water out. Leave tofu for 30 minutes up to several hours. You can apply some manual pressure to speed things up. Remove wet towels. Slice tofu into half-inch pieces. Throw into a large pot that has been coated with about 1 tablespoon of olive oil. Toss to coat. Add a little salt and pepper to taste. Cook on medium low heat, tossing often for 4-5 minutes until tofu is a light golden color. Remove tofu from pot.
- Place additional 5 tablespoons oil into a large pot that the tofu was cooked in and place over medium-low heat. Whisk in gluten-free flour and bring to a gentle simmer, (I reduced the heat down to low to avoid burning the flour.) Whisk frequently. Allow the mixture to cook and simmer until it darkens slightly in color and gives off a nutty aroma, about 10-15 minutes.
- Add celery, onion, and zucchini to the pot. Cook for 4-5 minutes until onion begins to turn translucent. Add bell pepper, mushrooms and garlic to the pot, cook for another 2-3 minutes more until they start to break down, mixing frequently. Then raise heat to medium and toss a few times to mix and coat the veggies. Allow veggies cook just until they soften up a bit, about 5 minutes, watching the pot closely and flipping the mixture frequently.
- Add tofu, broth, tomatoes, hot sauce, paprika, thyme, salt, cayenne and black pepper and optional liquid smoke to the pot. Raise heat and bring to a simmer. Lower heat and allow the dish to cook until vegetables are tender, 15 to 20 minutes, stirring occasionally. Remove from heat, cool for a few minutes and season with salt and additional hot sauce to taste.
- Divide rice among plates and top with étouffée. Sprinkle generously with scallions and additional hot sauce, if desired. Serve.

347. Vegan Butternut Squash Stew With Garbanzo Beans

Serving: Serves 4-5 | Prep: | Cook: |Ready in:

Ingredients

- 2 1/2 pounds butternut squash, peeled and flesh cut into 1 1/2 " cubes
- 1 red onion, thinly sliced
- 16 ounces can of garbanzo beans, drained, rinsed and thoroughly patted dry
- 13.5 ounces full fat coconut milk
- 1 teaspoon freshly grated ginger
- 2 teaspoons Panch phoron/ Bengali five spice (see note #1)
- 1/2 teaspoon ground turmeric
- 1/2 teaspoon ground cayenne (use less if you do not like things spicy)
- 1 teaspoon smoked paprika
- 1/4 cup toasted coconut flakes (see note #2)
- 1/2 lime, juiced (add more if you prefer things tart)
- chopped cilantro, for garnish
- vegetable oil
- kosher salt
- Note #1: You can find panch phoron at any Indian grocery store or online. If you don't have it, use equal parts of mustard seeds, nigella seeds, fenugreek seeds, fennel seeds and cumin seeds.
- Note #2: Since the original dish is on the sweeter side, I used sweetened coconut flakes (roasted at 400F for 3-4 minutes, until they were slightly browned). If you like things less sweet, feel free to use unsweetened coconut flakes.

Direction

- Preheat oven to 400F. Add the cubed butternut squash to a baking sheet. Sprinkle salt and drizzle generously with vegetable oil. Toss to coat evenly and let it bake for about 30 minutes, turning once halfway through to get nice caramelized edges. Set aside.
- On another baking sheet, add the garbanzo beans. Sprinkle with salt and drizzle with vegetable oil and toss to coat well. Bake for about 30 minutes or so until outside is getting to be crunchy. Set aside.
- On medium heat, add vegetable oil to a heavy bottomed pot. Add the Bengali five spice and stir it around for a few seconds until intensely aromatic. Add the onions and a big pinch of salt and saute until softened and translucent.
- Add the ginger, turmeric, cayenne and smoked paprika and saute for a minute. Add the coconut milk and a cup of water and let it simmer for a couple of minutes. Add the roasted butternut squash and lime juice and GENTLY mix everything. Simmer for a couple more minutes. Add a bit more water if you like it to be soupier. Check for seasoning.
- Just before you are ready to serve, scatter the roasted garbanzo beans and toasted coconut flakes on top. Garnish with cilantro and serve with steamed rice. Enjoy!

348. Vegetabel Paella

Serving: Serves 8 | Prep: | Cook: |Ready in:

Ingredients

- 3 cups rice
- 9 cups water or broth
- 2 handfuls green beans
- 1 pound roasted red pepper
- 4 artichoke hearts
- 1/2 pound cooked large white beans
- 1/4 cup toasted pine nuts
- 1 large tomato
- 2 tablespoons pimenton
- 1 pinch paprika
- 4 cloves of garlic
- 1/3 cup olive oil
- 2 cups wild mushroom assortment
- 6 white asparagus

Direction

- In a paella pan sauté garlic in olive oil
- Add chopped mushrooms and sauté till soft,
- Grate the tomato with a coarse grater
- Add pimento and quickly incorporate, add grated tomato post haste as pimento easily burns
- Add water or broth then add rice and paprika
- When it come to a boil add green beans and roasted red pepper sliced in strands as well as the beans
- When the water evaporates and the rice shows add the artichokes sliced and the asparagus
- Continue to cook till all water evaporates and the rice is done

349. Vegetarian Brazilian Bean Stew

Serving: Serves 8 | Prep: | Cook: | Ready in:

Ingredients

- Ingredients for the feijoada
- 500 grams black beans
- 2 carrots – chopped into sticks
- 3 potatoes – chopped into sticks
- 2 onions – chopped finely
- 350 grams green beans – chopped into sticks
- 1 eggplant – chopped into medium chunks
- 3 cloves of garlic – smashed
- 2 tablespoons smoked hot paprika
- 3 bay leaves
- Oil
- Salt to taste
- Side dishes (optional!)
- Cassava (or yuca) flour
- Stir fried kale
- Rice
- Slices of orange

Direction

- Cook the beans in a pressure cooker for 30 minutes with some salt and the bay leaves.
- While the beans cook, wash and chop the vegetables.
- Take the onions and garlic to a big pot and let them brown with a little bit of oil. Mix in the sausages and cook for a bit. Add the paprika and salt. Stir in the vegetables, in stages. I put the potatoes and green beans first, since they have to be well cooked. When they got tender, I added the carrots and the eggplant.
- When the beans are cooked and all the vegetables are getting tender, join everything in the big pot and check the seasoning. As soon as the broth thickens, the feijoada is done! Serve immediately, along with the side dishes of your choice.

350. Vegetarian Chopped "Liver"

Serving: Makes enough for a crowd | Prep: 0hours15mins | Cook: 0hours20mins | Ready in:

Ingredients

- 1 quart Water, plus more to cook eggs
- 1 cup brown lentils
- 2 onions, coarsely chopped
- 3 eggs
- 1 tablespoon olive oil
- 2 onions, thinly sliced
- 1 cup walnuts
- kosher salt
- coarsely ground black pepper
- Paprika, for garnish (optional)

Direction

- In a 2 quart saucepan, combine 1 quart water with the lentils. Set over medium-high heat, boil, then lower heat and simmer for 20 minutes. Drain lentils and rinse with cold water to stop cooking.

- Meanwhile, in a larger pot place the chopped onions and eggs, and cover with water. Heat to boiling over medium-high heat, then reduce heat to low and gently simmer for 10 minutes to hard-cook the eggs. Drain and rinse both with cold water. Peel eggs, then set both aside.
- While all that is going on, heat a medium-sized sauté or frying pan over medium heat. After the pan gets hot, add the olive oil, heat for about 10 seconds, then add thinly sliced onions. Sauté until the onions are browned, about 10-15 minutes.
- Toss lentils, all the onions, eggs and walnuts into a food processor. Process to your preferred consistency. Season to taste with salt and pepper.
- Transfer to serving bowl. Serve with crackers and/or those little cocktail breads that your parents used to buy. To really look fancy-schmancy, dust top of Mock "Liver" with paprika.

351. Vegetarian Festivus

Serving: Serves 8-10 | Prep: | Cook: | Ready in:

Ingredients

- Vegetable Custard
- 1 small butternut squash, peeled and cut into one inch cubes
- 1 large sweet potato, cut into one inch cubes (no need to peel)
- olive oil
- salt and pepper
- 2 rosemary branches
- 1 sage twigs
- seeds from butternut squash
- 2 tablespoons olive oil
- 2 onions, chopped
- 4 garlic cloves, chopped
- 1 jalapeno chile, chopped
- 1 teaspoon oregano
- 1 teaspoon cumin
- 1 teaspoon salt
- half teaspoon pepper
- 1 teaspoon hot smoked paprika
- 1 bunch collards, cleaned and chopped
- 1 tablespoon cider vinegar
- 4 ounces soft goat cheese
- half cup grated Parmesan
- 12 eggs
- three fourths cups heavy cream
- 1 teaspoon salt
- Corn Bread Topping
- 1 1/4 cups buttermilk
- 1 egg
- 1 1/2 cups cornmeal
- 1/2 cup flour
- 1 teaspoon salt
- 1 1/2 teaspoons baking powder
- 2 tablespoons melted butter

Direction

- Toss the squash and sweet potato cubes (3-4 cups before cooking) with olive oil, salt and pepper, rosemary and sage and roast at 400 degrees for about 30-45 minutes. Check from time to time and add a tablespoon or two of water if starting to scorch or stick. The cubes should be soft but not mushy and glazed on the outside. Taste for seasoning.
- At the same time that the sweet potato and squash are baking, toss the butternut squash seeds with oil, a little salt, and a little cayenne and bake until crisp, 10 or 15 minutes. Refrain from eating them all, you need them later.
- Cook the chopped onions in a saute pan over medium high heat with the olive oil until caramelized and almost crisp. Add garlic, Jalapeno pepper, cumin, salt and pepper, paprika and oregano. Simmer over low heat for a few minutes. Stir in collards. Add half a cup of water and bring to a simmer. Cover and cook until the collard is tender, about 15 minutes. The mixture should be moist but not at all wet. Uncover and cook off extra liquid if necessary. Taste for seasoning.
- Beat eggs and cream together with another teaspoon of salt.

- Start to construct your dinner. I used a ten inch deep dish pie pan, brushed with olive oil. Pour in the egg and heavy cream custard. Spoon in a layer of sweet potato and squash. It should be one vegetable cube thick, no more. Sprinkle Parmesan over the custard. Spoon over a layer of collard greens and dot with goat cheese. You may have leftover custard, squash and sweet potato mix and collards depending on the size of your dish, squash and bunch of collards. Worse thigs have happened. You must leave room for the cornbread top. Bake at 350 for 30-40 minutes, until custard is set.
- Mix the dry ingredients for the topping. Beat in the buttermilk and egg and stir in the melted butter. Combine only until blended and pour over the vegetables, spreading with a spoon so that the vegetable layer is completely covered. Sprinkle the squash seeds over the top of the cornbread layer. Bake at 375 for 30 minutes, until cornbread is lightly browned and pulls away from the side.
- Cool at least 10 minutes before cutting. Serve with a relish or pickle on the side. It's quite rich.

352. Veggie Chilli Cottage Pie

Serving: Serves 6 | Prep: | Cook: | Ready in:

Ingredients

- The Mince
- 2 tablespoons olive oil
- 1 Large White Onion, chopped
- 2 Garlic cloves, crushed
- 2 cups white mushrooms, chopped
- 1/2 teaspoon smoked paprika
- 1/2 cup White wine
- 1/2 teaspoon paprika
- 1/2 teaspoon chilli powder
- 1 packet Quorn mince (or 12 ounces any veggie mince)
- 1 x 14 ounces tin of tomatoes
- 1 x 14 ounces tin of kidney beans, drained
- 2 cups vegetable stock
- 1 tablespoon Worcestershire sauce
- The Topping
- 3 pounds potatoes, peeled and diced into large chunks
- 2 tablespoons butter
- 1 tablespoon single cream
- 1 cup grated cheddar

Direction

- In a saucepan sauté the onions, and garlic in olive oil, covered for 10 minutes, or until soft. Add the mushrooms and smoked paprika and cook (uncovered) for 2 minutes.
- Add the white wine and cook for 2 minutes. Add all other mince ingredients and cook for 35 minutes on a medium heat, stirring occasionally.
- Meanwhile, boil the potatoes until soft enough to mash (takes about 20 minutes). Drain and mash the potatoes. Mix in the butter and double cream.
- Adjust seasoning (salt, pepper and sugar to taste) on the mince and mash. Pour the mince into a large baking dish. Spoon and smooth the mash over the mince. Top with grated cheddar.
- Put a grill onto a high heat. Put the pie under the grill until the topping is melted and golden. Serve.

353. Warm Butternut Squash And Chicken Salad

Serving: Serves 2-4 | Prep: 0hours30mins | Cook: 0hours45mins | Ready in:

Ingredients

- For the Salad
- 1 Medium butternut squash
- 3-4 Parsnips
- 3-4 Shallots

- 2 Large skinless chicken breasts
- 3/4 cup Flat leaf parsley
- 3/4 cup Goat cheese or feta cheese
- 3/4 cup Moroccan or Israeli couscous
- Ground coriander
- Sweet Paprika
- Cayenne pepper (optional)
- Salt and pepper
- Olive oil
- Dressing
- 3 tablespoons Olive oil
- 1 tablespoon White wine or sherry vinegar
- 1 tablespoon Dijon mustard
- 1/2 tablespoon Honey
- Salt and pepper

Direction

- Preheat the oven to 350 degrees and start to heat water for your couscous. Put the chicken breasts on a large sheet pan (yes, this is way too big for them). Season both sides of the chicken breasts with salt, pepper, coriander, and paprika. Rather than give exact amounts here, it is better to go by how it looks: you want the chicken breasts to be nicely coated, but not overwhelmed. Add cayenne if you want some heat. Drizzle some olive oil over each chicken breast and put them in the oven. Roast until the internal temperature reaches 165 degrees, roughly 20-25 minutes, flipping them once.
- While the chicken roasts, prepare the vegetables: peel, de-seed, and chop the squash into half-inch cubes; peel the parsnips and cut into inch-long segments; cut any especially wide segments in half the long way. Peel the shallots, and slice each one into three or four rings, depending on their length. Put all of the vegetables in a large bowl, toss with enough olive oil to gently coat them. Season generously with salt and pepper, and add coriander and paprika to taste. Again, if you want some heat, add some cayenne.
- Cook the couscous: if using Moroccan, put the couscous in a bowl and add 3/4 cups boiling water; cover and let set for a few minutes, then fluff with a fork. For Israeli couscous, cook as if you were making pasta. After it is done, add a few drops of olive oil to stop it from clumping.
- When the chicken is done, take it out of oven, turn up the heat to 400 degrees. Let the chicken rest on a plate and add the vegetables to the tray (don't clean it-- that's good flavor on the tray!), and spread them into a single layer. Roast until tender 25-35 minutes.
- While the vegetables roast, make the dressing: add all the ingredients into a small bowl and whisk until everything incorporated. Taste it to make sure it is your liking.
- (Alternatively, you can roast the chicken breasts on a small tray and the veggies on a large tray at the same time at 400. The chicken will cook faster so make sure it doesn't dry out).
- After the chicken has cooled a little, use two forks and shred the chicken. In a large bowl, mix the chicken and the couscous and toss to combine.
- Chop the parsley medium-fine and crumble your cheese of choice. Don't add this to chicken couscous mixture yet.
- After the veggies are tender, add them to the chicken and couscous mixture and toss to combine. Let cool briefly (so that the hot ingredients don't completely melt the cheese). Then add the dressing, parsley, cheese and toss again.

354. Weeknight Enchiladas Verde

Serving: Serves 6-8 | Prep: | Cook: | Ready in:

Ingredients

- 12 8 inch tortillas any kind. I like the flour/corn blended ones
- 1 24 ounce jar salsa verde
- 1 can black beans drained and rinsed

- 1/2 red onion chopped
- 1 each red bell pepper and pasilla chilli, seeded and roughly chopped
- 1 bunch spinach, washed and chopped
- 1 Mexican squash (or 2 zucchini) 1/4 inch dice
- 2 cloves garlic minced
- 10 slices pepper jack cheese (or 1.5 cups mexican blend for a more mellow flavor)
- 1/4 cup Mexican cheese shreads
- 1 tablespoon ground cumin
- 1 teaspoon each ground paprika and ground corriander
- 1/2 teaspoon ground allspice
- to taste salt and pepper

Direction

- Heat the oven to 350
- In a largish pan cook the onion on medium heat until it starts to soften, 3-5 minutes. Add the chili and the bell pepper and cook another 2-3 minutes. Add the squash and cook until it starts to get soft, 3-5 minutes. Add the garlic and cook until fragrant, 1-2 minutes. This part shouldn't take more than about 15 minutes.
- Add the cumin, coriander, paprika, and allspice salt and pepper. Cook for a minute or so to toast the spices.
- Add the beans and spinach and cook about 5-8 minutes until the spinach is cooked down, has released its water and that water is starting to evaporate. The mixture should look slightly saucy at this stage. (Throw in the juice of 1 lime and you have the most delicious vegan taco filling. Nom!)
- pour about 1/2 cup salsa in the bottom of a 9x11 (or 9x9 or 9x13 whatever you have really) baking dish. Now, if you're feeling fancy, you can fill each tortilla with some veggies and 1/2 a slice of cheese. I don't have an abuela to yell at me, so I make mine like lasagne.
- Lay a layer of tortillas down in the sauce. Top with slices of pepper jack cheese, 1/3 the veggie mix and some salsa. Repeat until you use up all the tortillas and veggies. Finish with the remaining salsa and top with the shredded cheese.
- Bake 20-30 minutes, until bubbly and brown on top. If you let it rest for a few minutes the cheese will set back up and it will be easier to dish out. But really, who can wait? It's dinner time!

355. White & Navy Bean Salad With Watermelon Radishes And Lemon Tahini Dressing

Serving: Serves 2 | Prep: | Cook: |Ready in:

Ingredients

- Salad
- 1 cup White Beans
- 1 cup Navy Beans
- 2 Medium-Sized Watermelon Radishes, cut finely into julienne strips
- 1 tablespoon Olive Oil
- Mixed Greens (butter lettuce, mache, frisee)
- Salt & Pepper, to taste
- Lemon-Tahini Dressing
- Juice of 1 Lemon (about 3 tablespoons)
- 1 tablespoon Tahini
- 2 tablespoons Extra-Virgin Olive Oil
- 1 teaspoon Paprika

Direction

- Heat 1 tablespoon of olive oil in a skillet over medium heat.
- Add the beans, and season with salt and pepper.
- Sauté the beans until slightly browned and crispy. (Stir in the pan to ensure even cooking, but gently! It's important to not mix the beans into mush).
- While the beans are cooking, whisk the tahini, lemon juice, paprika, and olive oil in a small bowl.

- Remove the beans from heat and let cool to room temperature.
- Place the beans and radish slices onto a bed of greens (with portion size adjusted to your liking).
- Serve with a drizzle of dressing and a crack of fresh black pepper.

356. White Bean And Barley Turkey Chili

Serving: Serves 4 | Prep: | Cook: | Ready in:

Ingredients

- Chili
- 2 tablespoons olive oil
- 2 pounds ground turkey (I use a mix of white and dark meat, 85/15)
- 1 tablespoon ground cumin
- 1 teaspoon chili powder
- 1 teaspoon smoked sweet paprika
- 2 teaspoons salt
- 1 teaspoon black pepper
- 1 medium onion, finely diced
- 1/2 green bell pepper, finely diced
- 1 jalapeno, minced
- 2 cloves garlic, minced
- 6 cups chicken stock
- 1/2 cup pearled barley
- 5 sprigs of thyme
- 1 14-15 oz can chickpeas, drained and rinsed
- 1 14-15 oz can white beans (cannellini, great northern, or white navy beans), drained and rinsed
- 2 tablespoons oregano paste (recipe follows) - or you can use the store-bought version (found in tubes in the produce section)
- 2 teaspoons apple cider vinegar
- hot sauce of your choosing, to taste
- green onions (white and green parts), thinly sliced, for topping
- sharp aged white cheddar cheese, grated, for topping
- Oregano paste
- 1/2 cup fresh oregano (leaves and soft stems)
- 1/4 cup cilantro (leaves and stems)
- 1/4 cup flat-leaf parsley
- 1 teaspoon sugar
- 1 tablespoon extra virgin olive oil
- pinch of salt and pepper

Direction

- Heat olive oil in a large Dutch oven or heavy bottomed pot with a lid over medium-high heat. Brown the ground turkey, breaking up with a wooden spoon, until no pink remains, about 8 minutes.
- Add the cumin, chili powder, paprika, thyme, onions, green pepper, and jalapeno to the turkey. Add salt and fresh cracked black pepper and continue to cook until vegetables are softened but not browned, about 5 minutes. Add the garlic and cook an additional minute.
- Add chicken stock, bring to a boil and add the barley and thyme. Stir to combine, reduce to a simmer, and cook, covered, for 40 minutes.
- In the last 20 minutes of cooking, add the chickpeas; wait until the last 10 minutes of cooking to add the white beans. In the last 5 minutes of cooking, add the apple cider vinegar, oregano paste, and salt, pepper, and hot sauce to taste. Remove the thyme branches before serving (most of the leaves will have fallen into the soup).
- Serve in bowls topped with sliced green onions and grated sharp white cheddar cheese.
- To make the oregano paste, combine all ingredients in a mini-food processor and process into a paste. Salt and pepper to taste.

357. Whole Roasted Cauliflower

Serving: Serves 6-8 | Prep: | Cook: | Ready in:

Ingredients

- main ingredients
- 1 bunch kale
- 2 tablespoons vegetable oil
- 2 teaspoons kosher or sea salt
- 1 bunch cauliflower
- 1 1/2 cups plain Greek yogurt
- 1 piece lime, zested
- 2 tablespoons chile powder
- 1 tablespoon cumin
- 2 tablespoons paprika
- 1 tablespoon garlic powder
- 1 teaspoon curry powder
- 1 teaspoon black pepper
- none

Direction

- Main ingredients
- Preheat the oven to 400° and lightly grease a small baking sheet with vegetable oil, set aside
- Trim tough ends off kale, place in a large plastic bag with oil and salt, and toss until coated.
- Place leaves side by side on baking sheet and place in oven until dried and crispy
- Pulverize dried kale in food processor or blender to form a powder.
- Trim the base of the cauliflower to remove any green leaves and the woody stem.
- In a medium bowl, combine the powdered kale with yogurt, lime zest and juice, chile powder, cumin, paprika, garlic powder, curry powder, salt and pepper.
- . Dunk the cauliflower into the bowl and use a brush or your hands to smear the marinade evenly over its surface.
- Place the cauliflower back on the prepared baking sheet and roast until the surface is dry and lightly browned, 30 to 40 minutes. The marinade will make a crust on the surface of the cauliflower.
- Let the cauliflower cool for 10 minutes before cutting it into wedges to serve.

358. Yellow Saffron Rice With Feta, Stewed Dates, And Pine Nuts

Serving: Serves 2 | Prep: | Cook: | Ready in:

Ingredients

- 3 tablespoons Olive oil, divided
- 1 cup Long-grained white rice
- 1 heavy pinches Spanish saffron
- 1/2 cup Yellow onion, diced
- 4 Garlic cloves, minced, divided
- 2 1/2 cups Veggie Broth, divided
- 1/4 cup Pine Nuts
- 1/3 cup Pitted dates, chopped
- 5 Small black olives
- 1/2 tablespoon Honey
- 2 Medium tomatoes, chopped
- 1/4 teaspoon Smoked Spanish Paprika
- 1/2 teaspoon Red pepper flakes
- 2 tablespoons Orange or pomegranate juice
- 1 teaspoon Thyme
- 1/3 cup Crumbled Feta
- Salt to taste

Direction

- Before starting the rice, prepare the saffron. Grind to pulpy-powdery consistency using a mortar and pestle or the back of a spoon, as I often do, with a small amount of salt. Add 1/4 cup of hot water. Allow this to steep for 10 minutes or more.
- In a medium pot over medium heat, add one tablespoon of Olive Oil. Add the onions and cook until translucent. Next, add 2 cloves of minced garlic and cook only until fragrant. Mix in the rice and pour the entirety of the steeped saffron and water over the mixture. Next, add two cups of vegetable broth, and bring to a boil. Reduce to simmer and let cook, covered, until the rice is cooked and the liquid has been absorbed.

- Now add the remaining 1 tablespoon of olive oil to the small pot or sauté pan. Add the last 2 cloves of minced garlic over medium-low heat. After they start to become fragrant, stir in the chopped dates and olives. Add the 1/2 cup broth, honey, and red wine vinegar. Add an additional 1/4 cup of water. Bring to a boil over medium-high heat, and then lower to a medium-low heat to reduce, about 10 minutes. Stir occasionally.
- Once the stewed dates mixture has reduced to a thicker consistency, add the tomatoes, thyme, juice, paprika, and red pepper flakes. Continue to cook for another 5-10 minutes on low heat. Salt to taste and add more pepper if desired.
- Stir crumbled feta into the cooked rice. Be careful to just lift rice up and over the feta, almost just spooning it over it. Don't over-stir, or the rice will become mushy.
- Serve rice with stewed dates served on top, and sprinkle with the toasted pine-nuts.

359. ZESTY GUACAMOLE WITH SPICED PITA CHIPS

Serving: Serves 6 | Prep: | Cook: | Ready in:

Ingredients

- Pita Chips
- 2 tablespoons olive oil
- 1/4 teaspoon ground cumin
- 1/4 teaspoon chili powder
- 1/4 teaspoon paprika
- 1/4 teaspoon kosher salt
- 1 pinch cayenne pepper
- 4 6-inch pita breads
- Guacamole
- 3 ripe avocados
- 2 tablespoons chopped red onion
- 2 tablespoons chopped cilantro
- 1 tablespoon fresh lemon juice
- 10 cherry tomatoes, sliced in half
- 1/2 teaspoon kosher salt
- 1/4 teaspoon ground cumin
- 1/8 teaspoon chili powder

Direction

- Pita Chips
- For the pita chips preheat the oven to 400°F. Line a baking sheet with parchment paper. In a small bowl, combine olive oil, cumin, chili powder, paprika, salt and cayenne pepper. Brush both sides of each pita with the olive oil mixture.
- Cut each pita bread into 8 triangles. Place on prepared baking sheet in a single layer. Bake for 8 minutes, flip and bake 5-6 minutes more, until golden and crispy.
- Guacamole
- For the guacamole, mash avocados in a bowl and stir in red onions, cilantro, lemon juice, halved tomatoes, salt, cumin and chili powder.
- Serve with pita chips and garnish with cilantro.

360. Bacon And Egg Potato Salad

Serving: Serves 8 | Prep: | Cook: | Ready in:

Ingredients

- 1 1/2 pounds Yukon Gold potatoes
- 1 teaspoon kosher salt
- 1 1/2 tablespoons red wine vinegar
- 5-6 slices bacon
- 2 stalks celery, finely diced
- 1/2 cup red onion, finely diced
- 2 scallions, thinly sliced
- 3 eggs
- 3/4 cup mayonnaise
- 1 tablespoon + 1 teaspoon dijon mustard
- 1/2 teaspoon kosher salt
- 1/4 teaspoon black pepper
- 2 tablespoons chopped parsley
- 1/2 teaspoon smoked paprika

Direction

- I like to cook bacon in the oven because there's no splatter and it yields a perfect strip of crispy pork. To do it in the oven, preheat to 400 degrees. Cover a rimmed baking sheet with foil. Set a wire rack on top of the cookie sheet. Lay the bacon on the wire rack and cook for about 20-23 minutes until crisped.
- Cut the potatoes into 1" pieces (no need to peel them). Fill a large pot halfway with water. Add the salt and bring to a boil. When the water boils, add the potatoes and cook for 15 minutes. Carefully add the eggs and cook for an additional 5 minutes. Using a spider or slotted spoon remove the potatoes and transfer to a large bowl. Sprinkle the hot potatoes with vinegar and toss to coat. Let the eggs sit in the hot water for another 5 minutes. Then remove them from the water and set aside to cool.
- In a small bowl, combine the mayonnaise, Dijon mustard, kosher salt, black pepper and smoked paprika. Stir to combine.
- Add the celery, onion, scallions and bacon to the potatoes. Peel and chop the eggs and add them to the potatoes. Toss gently. Add the dressing to the potatoes and toss to combine. Sprinkle with a little extra paprika and the parsley. Serve.

361. Beetroot And Oatmeal Baked Vegan Patties

Serving: Makes 14 | Prep: | Cook: | Ready in:

Ingredients

- 450 grams grated beetroot
- 150 grams oatmeal
- 100 grams grated onion
- 1 teaspoon black pepper
- 1 paprika
- 4 tablespoons parsley
- 3 tablespoons basil
- 1 tablespoon lemon zest
- 2 tablespoons olive oil

Direction

- In a large bowl combine together: grated beetroot, onion, olive oil, basil, parsley, lemon zest, salt, pepper, paprika and oatmeal. Mix well until all combined
- From the mixture form patties in the size you like
- Spray with cooking oil a baking sheet/parchment paper.
- Put all the patties on the baking sheet
- Bake 15 min on each side at 200c/400f

362. Fresh Tomato And Summer Squash Soup

Serving: Serves 15 | Prep: | Cook: | Ready in:

Ingredients

- the stock
- Bones leftover from 10 grilled porterhouse steaks
- 2 yellow onions, quartered
- 2 potatoes, quartered
- 2 bay leaves
- handful schezuan (or black) peppercorns
- handful of available fresh herbs
- the soup
- 2 quarts roughly chopped tomatoes
- 2 quarts roughly chopped green squash
- 2 quarts roughly chopped yellow squash
- 5 slices thick bacon, cut into lardons
- salt, pepper, oilve oil, paprika, cayenne
- sour cream
- garlic chives

Direction

- The stock
- Place everything in a pot, fill the pot with cold water until everything is covered

- Bring to a boil
- Reduce to a simmer
- Ignore the beef stock for a couple hours, it needs time for the flavors to develop
- Strain stock, reserve the liquid for the soup.
- The soup
- Find a large pot, 10 quarts or so
- Heat up olive oil in the pot, when hot add the lardons of bacon, dump in a heavy tablespoon of paprika and some cayenne. Season with salt and pepper
- Cook bacon until the fat is well rendered out.
- Add tomatoes, cook down until you get a lot of water out of them
- Add your strained beef stock, bring up to a boil,
- Reduce heat, season with salt and pepper, simmer for an hour or so.
- Add both the green and yellow squash, by doing so you've decided you want to serve this soup in about an hour
- Once you are ready to serve the soup adjust the seasoning to taste, then pour into bowls and top with a dollop of sour cream in the center, then sprinkle with garlic chives.

363. Shrimp Pimentón

Serving: Serves 4 as small plates | Prep: | Cook: | Ready in:

Ingredients

- 3/4 pound shrimp, peeled + deveined
- 1 shallot, minced
- 1 teaspoon hot paprika
- 1 teaspoon smoked paprika
- 1/2 teaspoon cayenne pepper
- 3 cloves of garlic, minced
- salt
- pepper
- lemon juice
- bread, for mopping up sauce
- sugar
- 1 handful chopped cilantro
- 2-4 tablespoons oil, canola/olive

Direction

- Heat up the oil in the pan - medium high to high heat, add the paprika, cayenne, salt, pepper.
- Once the oil is hot, add shallot and garlic.
- Stir frequently, 30 seconds.
- Add shrimp, cook, stirring occasionally, until done.
- Check seasoning, adjust sweetness with sugar, and adjust acidity with lemon juice.
- Garnish with cilantro, serve with bread.

364. Smoky Turkey Empanadas

Serving: Makes 24 | Prep: | Cook: | Ready in:

Ingredients

- for the pastry
- 4 1/2 cups flour
- 2 teaspoons salt
- 2 sticks cold, unsalted butter, cut into chunks
- 2 large eggs
- 2/3 cup water
- 2 tablespoons distilled white vinegar
- for the filling
- 3 tablespoons olive oil
- 1 pound ground turkey (not extra lean)
- 1 medium onion, chopped
- 1 reen bell pepper, chopped
- 3 cloves garlic, minced
- 1 tomato, chopped
- 1/2 cup golden raisins
- 1 tablespoon ground cumin
- 1 teaspoon smoked paprika
- 1 teaspoon Ancho or other chili powder
- 2 tablespoons tomato paste
- 3/4 teaspoon salt
- 1/2 teaspoon ground pepper

- 1 cup crumbled queso fresco
- 1 egg
- 1 tablespoon water

Direction

- Pulse the butter and flour in the work bowl of a food processor until the mixture resembles coarse meal. Note: if you don't have a food processor, work the butter and flour between your fingers until you have the same consistency.
- Beat together the eggs, water and vinegar in a small bowl and add to the flour mixture, stirring until just incorporated. Turn out onto a lightly floured surface and gather the dough together. Knead gently once or twice, just enough to bring the dough together. Shape into a flat rectangle and chill, wrapped in plastic wrap for at least 1 hour.
- Adjust oven racks to the top 1/3 and bottom 1/3 of the oven. Preheat oven to 400 degrees.
- Heat a large skillet over medium high heat. Add the olive oil, onion, bell pepper and garlic and sauté 4-5 minutes until vegetables soften. Add the ground turkey and brown the meat while breaking it apart with the back of a fork or wooden spoon. Add the fresh tomato, raisins cumin, smoked paprika, chili powder, salt and pepper. Stir to combine and cook for an additional 3-5 minutes until mixture is well blended - adjust seasonings if necessary. Remove from heat, stir in queso fresco and place the lid on the pan. Set aside.
- Cut the dough into 4 equal pieces. On a lightly floured work surface, roll out one piece of dough to 1/8" thick. Cut the dough into 5" rounds and transfer to a baking sheet covered with parchment paper. Repeat until all the dough has been rolled and cut.
- (If you're using the store-bought pastry, this is where they come into play.) Mound 2 tablespoons of turkey filling onto the pastry and carefully fold over, pressing along the edge to seal the dough. Use the tines of a fork to press the edge together and make a decorative border.
- Add the egg and water to a small bowl and beat lightly with a fork. Use a pastry brush to paint the empanadas with the egg wash. Bake for 25 minutes, alternating the baking sheets halfway through cooking. Cool on the baking sheet for a few minutes and serve.

365. "Eggs In Pipérade" Pizza With Crispy Prosciutto

Serving: Serves 2 | Prep: | Cook: | Ready in:

Ingredients

- For the Pipérade (adapted from Gourmet)
- 1 large onion, diced
- 2 red bell peppers, finely diced
- olive oil
- 1 teaspoon hot smoked paprika
- pinch cayenne pepper
- 1 garlic clove, minced
- 1 28oz can diced tomatoes with juice
- 1 tablespoon basil, julienned
- For the pizza
- 3-4 large eggs
- 1/4 cup fresh Parmesan shavings
- 1 loaf ciabatta
- 1 clove garlic
- 1/2 pound fontina (or other mild melting cheese like Bel Paese, un-aged Manchego, or Monterey Jack), thinly sliced
- 3 slices prosciutto
- 1 tablespoon basil, julienned

Direction

- For the Pipérade
- In a large skillet over medium heat, sauté the onion and red pepper in enough olive oil to coat the pan. Cook until the vegetables have softened, about 6 minutes. Add the paprika, cayenne, garlic, and cook for another 2 minutes, until the mixture is very fragrant. Season generously with salt, and carefully stir in the tomatoes. Simmer until the sauce has

thickened and the vegetables are very tender, about 5 minutes. Turn off the heat and taste again for seasoning.
- (Optional) In a food processor, puree half of the mixture (this creates a thinner, sauce-like consistency without losing the texture of the veggies completely). Combine with the remaining sauce and the basil and set aside. The pipérade can be made a few days in advance.
- For the pizza
- Preheat the oven to 450 degrees.
- Spread the piperade in a shallow baking or gratin dish. With the back of a spoon, create holes for the eggs (as spaced out as possible). Crack each egg into one of the holes. Place dish in the oven and cook until the whites have almost set, 7-9 minutes. Remove from oven and sprinkle with half of the parmesan shavings. Return to the oven for another minute for the parmesan to melt.
- While the eggs are cooking, cut the ciabatta in half length-wise. Brush the bottom half with olive oil and save the top for another use. Place on a baking sheet and toast in the oven until golden brown. Remove the crusty bread and rub it with the garlic clove. Arrange the fontina slices on the bread and return to the oven. Bake until the cheese has melted, about 2 minutes.
- For the prosciutto, heat a thin layer of olive oil in a large non-stick skillet. When the oil is hot, add the prosciutto slices in one layer. Fry on both sides until each slice has become paper thin and crispy. Set aside to drain on a paper towel. When cool enough to handle, crumble into rustic pieces.
- To serve, spoon the egg and tomato mixture onto the ciabatta so that the eggs are arranged in one neat line. Garnish with the remaining Parmesan shavings, crispy prosciutto, and basil. Cut into two pieces and serve immediately.

Index

A
Ale 21,92,109,110,205

Allspice 67,75

Almond 3,5,6,14,100,160

Apple 5,6,62,122,123,143

Artichoke 3,7,15,207

Asparagus 4,7,77,187

Avocado 3,4,6,7,17,39,50,153,179,193,207,217

B
Bacon 3,4,5,6,7,8,18,19,37,40,41,51,54,62,75,93,140,158,178,207,215,232

Bagel 4,69

Baguette 77

Barley 8,230

Basil 7,122,140,207,210,211

Basmati rice 20,21,72,73

Bay leaf 165

Beans 3,4,5,7,8,22,45,56,60,70,91,114,118,140,147,197,224,229

Beef 3,4,6,7,19,20,25,36,37,52,86,96,152,182

Beer 3,7,15,21,25,44,203

Beetroot 8,233

Biscuits 6,8,136,219

Black pepper 45

Boar 6,142,143

Bread 4,71,77,143,157,207,226

Brie 37,78

Brisket 3,5,43,133

Broccoli 7,37,181,217

Broth 3,32,140,155,231

Brown rice 45

Buns 7,184,185

Burger 3,4,5,7,15,65,102,184,185,212

Butter 3,4,5,6,7,8,30,32,33,34,48,52,53,67,75,85,87,98,113,121,129,139,140,143,147,154,155,157,161,169,174,195,207,215,217,222,224,227

C
Cabbage 4,6,68,143,150

Cake 4,5,6,7,79,111,123,124,168,196

Calvados 122,123

Cannellini beans 147

Caramel 6,86,122,123,156,171,178

Carrot 3,5,6,33,97,116,140,143,156,164,165

Cashew 4,8,84,221

Cassava 225

Cauliflower 3,5,6,7,8,9,13,29,32,33,34,35,36,105,148,153,156,157,158,173,181,183,188,218,230

Cayenne pepper 24,228

Celery 7,140,143,207

Chard 4,12,13,65,138

Cheddar 5,8,45,75,93,107,165,174,219

Cheese 3,4,5,6,7,9,29,44,55,62,75,83,97,108,120,136,141,151,156,165,166,174,203,207

Cherry 3,4,5,7,36,54,102,217

Chicken 3,4,5,6,7,8,26,30,37,38,39,40,41,48,49,64,67,69,72,74,75,78,84,87,92,93,113,121,125,129,130,132,137,140,142,148,150,151,155,173,183,184,194,196,205,209,213,214,215,222,227

Chickpea 3,4,5,7,27,42,43,56,58,71,85,89,98,101,110,111,117,195,20

0,208,216,222

Chilli 8,69,143,227

Chipotle 3,7,45,140,143,185

Chips 3,4,27,67,232

Chives 54,155

Chocolate 3,4,16,43,60

Chorizo 3,4,5,7,38,45,47,59,74,75,133,195,209

Cider 6,139,143

Cinnamon 67,155

Clams 5,107

Cloves 105,129,140,141,143,165,180,202,207

Coconut 3,7,48,49,214,217

Cod 72

Coffee 3,43,48

Cola 3,24

Coriander 6,141,218

Courgette 4,51

Couscous 4,6,78,156

Crab 4,6,52,53,136

Crackers 121

Cranberry 5,7,104,188

Cream 3,4,5,7,13,39,54,55,97,205,207,215

Crostini 3,6,7,27,141,186,187

Crumble 62,73,103,118,192,231

Cucumber 4,7,58,208,215

Cumin 6,7,17,32,74,75,97,98,140,150,199,200,212,218,220

Curry 3,4,6,7,49,69,149,198

Custard 226

D

Dab 181

Dal 7,199

Dandelion 75

Date 6,8,159,231

Dijon mustard 9,19,20,35,37,54,114,120,136,144,160,161,203,217,228,23

3

Duck 3,6,45,166

Dumplings 6,140

E

Egg 3,4,5,6,7,8,15,30,45,54,59,61,62,66,67,68,70,76,77,91,109,110,120,121,135,160,165,180,181,198,202,212,220,232,235

F

Fat 4,71

Fennel 4,6,72,73,158

Feta 4,5,8,50,62,73,102,103,140,231

Fish 3,4,5,24,74,98,123,124

Flank 9

Flatbread 5,117

Flour 67,137,165,174

Focaccia 6,162,173

French bread 26,187

Fruit 6,144,145

G

Game 6,159

Garlic 3,4,5,7,9,27,37,52,54,67,72,75,78,81,88,89,92,97,98,107,121,129,135,140,143,159,183,190,191,192,194,202,206,207,209,218,220,227,231

Ghee 72

Gin 3,33,75

Gorgonzola 3,27,28

Gratin 6,7,164,174,211

Gravy 3,5,20,73,97,216

Green beans 60

Guacamole 4,80,232

H

Ham 5,114

Harissa 3,28
Hazelnut 3,16
Heart 5,91,207
Herbs 5,6,106,139
Hominy 6,150
Honey 3,4,5,6,26,39,40,67,92,143,150,159,208,228,231
Hummus 3,4,5,6,7,17,37,71,94,95,142,162,189

I

Iceberg lettuce 57

J

Jam 3,7,18,177,178
Jus 30,35,56,82,106,146,167,172,175,176,186,197,224

K

Kale 5,6,91,100,101,102,141,161
Ketchup 143

L

Lamb 4,5,88,96,102,103,125
Lemon 3,5,6,7,8,41,72,75,104,105,115,135,142,157,174,183,218,229
Lettuce 3,48
Lime 3,6,9,15,21,24,35,45,48,135,141,150,155,158,207,212
Ling 5,105,106
Lobster 4,63

M

Macaroni 5,115
Madeira 5,108
Manchego 3,5,9,108,131,133,235
Mango 3,21,48,208
Marmalade 7,84,85,188,189
Marrow 3,25
Mascarpone 7,188,189
Mayonnaise 3,15,39,40,107,135,143,184,185

Meat 3,4,5,6,7,38,74,96,97,137,153,193
Melon 208
Mesclun 156
Milk 174,207
Mince 9,37,48,105,141,227
Mint 5,7,114,199,200,218,220
Miso 3,33
Molasses 5,110
Mozzarella 7,186,187
Mushroom 3,4,5,6,12,21,70,99,109,119,140,141,168
Mustard 3,6,7,28,39,40,62,143,147,188,189

N

Noodles 5,109
Nut 4,8,16,67,69,98,231

O

Oatmeal 8,233
Oil 4,7,9,37,39,72,74,81,86,96,140,143,153,155,157,162,163,165,166,191,193,206,207,211,212,218,220,225,229,231
Olive 3,4,5,9,14,21,22,35,37,39,41,45,51,72,74,75,81,85,86,96,100,132,135,140,143,150,153,157,159,160,162,163,165,166,185,193,202,206,207,218,220,228,229,231
Onion 3,4,5,6,7,8,32,37,41,52,61,72,75,84,85,97,117,118,122,123,128,140,143,152,155,156,164,171,193,207,210,211,218,220,227
Orange 4,5,7,84,100,179,201,231
Oregano 37,230
Oxtail 5,108
Oyster 3,21

P

Paella 3,5,6,7,8,13,23,130,131,132,138,166,170,194,195,224
Pancetta 4,57,108

Paprika 1,3,4,5,6,7,8,9,17,19,20,26,34,37,51,52,53,62,64,67,68,72,74,75,81,85,87,91,95,97,102,103,107,108,110,114,121,129,130,132,133,134,135,140,143,147,148,150,151,155,156,159,162,168,174,189,193,202,206,207,208,209,211,217,218,219,220,225,228,229,231

Parmesan 3,5,6,15,35,55,83,128,129,134,147,157,158,161,162,165,168,169,226,227,235,236

Parsley 17,72,176,180,202,207,220

Parsnip 227

Pasta 3,5,14,52,106,128,223

Pastry 110,112

Peach 4,82

Peanut oil 130

Pear 4,78,155

Pecorino 89

Peel 17,30,39,61,62,69,81,82,84,87,107,110,115,128,135,145,153,162,175,208,211,220,226,228,233

Pepper 3,4,5,6,7,9,13,15,17,31,32,37,43,44,52,67,72,73,74,75,78,85,86,89,91,102,121,128,132,135,140,143,151,152,157,162,174,177,190,193,202,205,206,207,211,218,220,229

Pesto 7,204

Pickle 7,187

Pie 3,4,5,8,36,83,85,112,227

Pineapple 24

Pistachio 6,164

Pizza 8,235

Plum 8,218

Polenta 6,140,177,179

Pomegranate 5,6,110,162

Pork 3,4,5,6,7,19,85,89,91,95,99,110,122,126,139,143,144,146,201

Port 3,6,32,140,169

Potato 3,4,5,6,7,8,16,32,48,54,59,61,72,75,78,106,110,111,115,135,137,145,165,171,174,184,185,193,196,211,212,232

Poultry 159

Prawn 6,141

Prosciutto 3,8,35,235

Pulse 29,40,41,89,101,156,203,219,235

Pumpkin 6,7,9,147,162,175,190

Q

Quinoa 3,4,5,6,7,13,30,50,78,96,104,140,155,210,211

R

Radish 4,8,57,207,229

Raisins 5,89

Red onion 179

Rice 4,5,6,7,8,72,78,80,83,97,127,152,155,168,194,213,222,225,231

Ricotta 5,109,128

Roast chicken 133

Roast potatoes 163,193

Rosemary 5,6,113,162,190,191

S

Saffron 6,8,72,168,231

Salad 3,4,5,6,7,8,9,16,50,54,61,100,101,104,106,107,111,115,116,124,125,153,155,158,161,179,180,193,208,210,211,221,227,229,232

Salmon 3,6,35,168

Salsa 3,4,6,7,9,10,12,13,24,48,77,140,144,145,160,178

Salt 9,10,17,21,22,24,28,32,37,41,44,45,47,48,51,52,60,72,73,75,83,85,86,94,97,98,100,104,107,114,118,121,124,129,132,135,139,140,141,143,147,151,153,154,155,157,160,168,173,174,175,179,180,181,185,192,193,194,202,207,208,210,2

11,216,218,220,225,228,229,230,231,232
Sauces 4,52,53
Sausage 6,7,141,168,169,177
Savory 4,6,58,71,169
Scallop 5,7,105,194,197
Sea salt 82,89,135,136,212
Seafood 6,7,75,170,188
Seasoning 32,67,182
Seeds 5,9,85,94,143,157,160,216,218,220
Shallot 73,135,227
Sherry 5,23,66,75,89,100,107,108,135,174,180,181,183,190
Soup 3,4,5,6,7,8,25,32,33,49,52,56,57,76,85,91,147,148,150,165,169,183,186,187,190,191,192,200,204,219,233
Spaghetti 7,37,193
Spinach 3,5,7,12,91,111,115,202,206
Squash 3,5,6,7,8,33,89,139,140,147,154,160,161,169,195,206,224,227,233
Steak 3,9,27,36
Stew 4,5,6,7,8,51,56,85,96,104,125,172,182,224,225,231
Stock 72,75
Strawberry 7,205
Stuffing 7,152,207
Sugar 3,19,67,75,121,143
Sumac 6,7,142,157,208
Sweet potato 154,165,171
Swiss chard 13

T

Tabasco 30,39,42,43,90,91,124,133,134,135
Taco 3,4,5,6,7,21,24,47,59,127,140,153,178,210,213
Tahini 5,8,94,162,229
Tamari 73
Tarragon 5,130
Tea 39

Tequila 44
Thyme 67,141,157,231
Tilapia 7,72,217,218
Tofu 7,8,84,199,218
Tomato 3,4,5,6,7,8,26,36,43,50,52,54,72,76,85,109,115,134,140,143,165,172,186,187,202,207,209,219,220,233
Turkey 3,8,22,37,39,230,234

V

Veal 3,25
Vegan 4,5,6,8,49,97,120,149,221,222,223,224,233
Vegetable oil 39,104,129,141
Vegetable stock 98,183
Vegetables 5,92
Vegetarian 8,225,226
Vermouth 115
Vinegar 4,65,68,75,143,155

W

Waffles 4,67
Watermelon 8,229
White fish 24
White pepper 63
White wine 227,228
Wine 5,7,99,140,176
Worcestershire sauce 36,90,120,124,126,133,134,136,137,144,145,166,169,175,197,203,227
Wraps 3,48

Y

Yoghurt 6,7,153,156,199,200

Z

Zest 9,45,155,160

Conclusion

Thank you again for downloading this book!

I hope you enjoyed reading about my book!

If you enjoyed this book, please take the time to share your thoughts and post a review on Amazon. It'd be greatly appreciated!

Write me an honest review about the book – I truly value your opinion and thoughts and I will incorporate them into my next book, which is already underway.

Thank you!

If you have any questions, **feel free to contact at:** author@slushierecipes.com

Angela Duncan

slushierecipes.com

Printed in Great Britain
by Amazon

61984241R00138